THE BEST OF
ALAN COREN

THE BEST
OF
ALAN COREN

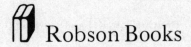 Robson Books

THIS COLLECTION FIRST PUBLISHED IN GREAT
BRITAIN IN 1980 BY ROBSON BOOKS LTD., 28
POLAND STREET, LONDON W1V 3DB. COPYRIGHT
© 1980 ALAN COREN.

Coren, Alan
    The best of Alan Coren.
    I. Title
    828'.9'1408   PN6175
    ISBN 0-86051-121-9

Printed in Great Britain by Redwood Burn Ltd., Trowbridge
and Esher.

Contents

Introduction

If I had my way, this would never have been called *The Best Of*. But it is very hard for hacks to have their way these days, the price of woodpulp being what it is and publishers no longer jocular benefactors in thornproof tweed, beaming at their literary flock through a paternal glaze part-induced by filthy brown sherry, part by the sheer altruistic joy of shelving well-turned tropes in imperishable half-morocco. The modern publisher, for example Computer & Son Limited, is a compact steel cube: when he wants to know if a book merits publication, he digests a marketing programme, and if his whirring bowels give the project the digital nod, the next step is to find a title. The tin synapses then spend a nanosecond or two running through the last five million titles that made money, and come up with a statistically sound contender.

That is how books get to be called The Best Of. People prefer buying a book that comes right out and hustles. You know where you are. Call it *War and Peace*, and right away consumers start asking "Which war? Which peace? What do they mean 'and'?"

Personally, I should have preferred to call it *Some of Alan Coren* or *Not Necessarily the Worst of Alan Coren*; for one thing, I do not know whether it *is* the best of me, no writer is the ideal judge of his stuff, least of all a humorist. If we were to have, you and I, a truly honest title, the book would have to be called *The Stuff That Made Alan Coren Laugh A Bit When He Read It Again*. And *The Best Of* also sounds somewhat terminal to me, as if the computer knows something I don't know, is perhaps linked to a diagnostic alloy colleague at the high-technology clinic where I had my last medical check-up, and reckons that it is a safe bet that I shall snuff it before publication, thus adding a topical piquancy to the event and snap up a few sales on a sympathy-reaction.

For myself – and this is true, or ought to be, of any writer with decent measures of humility and aspiration – I rather hope that the best is yet to be. *The Best of Rabbi Ben Ezra* is a title I should have been more than happy to recommend, had Computer & Son been prepared to run the risk of losing the Saudi-Arabian paperback market.

Even so, I count myself relatively lucky. Between you and me, I think the one the computer was *really* pushing for was *The Best of Someone Almost as Good as Harold Robbins*.

AC

Will Ye No Come Back Again?

Feel like Yeats ("I hear lake water lapping with low sounds by the shore/While I stand on the roadway or on the pavements gray . . ."), standing on pavements gray outside Heathrow, just back from two weeks sailing through Greek islands, still feel deck moving under feet, water sloshing against porthole, wind smacking cheeks; can't get land legs, swaying about looking for taxis, horizon moving through thirty degree arc, people staring at strange bandy figure, seems to have limps in both legs, keeps bracing itself against road, grabbing lamp posts, been knocking back cheap inflight gin no doubt, what matter with his face, looks like parboiled hamburger, some brown, some pink, skin flakes following in small cloud; always happens on return from sun, expensive tan starts cracking at customs, like old wallet, begins peeling at luggage bay, by time cab-rank reached, whole face fallen off.

Exhilaration still there, though, despite fist-sized hole in suitcase (gollywog's head poking out, present for small daughter, will Immigration think midget Pakis being smuggled in?), feel fit, slimmer, relaxed after fifteen days unthink, much sleep, no work, stress, editors, children, traffic, slates falling off roof, phones, bills, pets, ready for hurling self into work, writing off debts, New Life . . . rick neck getting cases into taxi, fingers trapped between case and seat, what matter with face? says cab-driver (thinking: what disease this lurching fool brought back from alien parts? Will own skin start falling off tomorrow, will all contacts start reeling about and grabbing for support, is this what cholera like, swamp fever, beri-beri?)

Chugging along M4, sultry night (England in middle of heat-wave, cab-driver twice as brown as either of us, been

11

eighty degrees in Ilford, ha-ha-ha, never cost me a bob), wife excited at prospect of fetching farmed-out infants, got precise timetable, pick them up just before bedtime, whip home, mutual joy, presents (got son Greek machine-gun; son now got mach-ine-guns from eight different countries, nursery look like IRA bunker, what will prison psychiatrists say when son thirty and ·doing ten years for GBH?), that the trouble with precise time-tables, never take into account Rover 2000 lying sideways across two lanes, fire-engines, police, cars piled up on hard shoulder, hour delay; never mind, ho-ho-ho, these things sent to try us, damn good holiday, see kids tomorrow, put feet up at home tonight, why not open sealed Athens Duty-Free Shop bag, take comforting slug of scotch? Open bag, one bottle cointreau, one bottle something called vεxταp, not our bag, who got whisky, never drink cointreau, as for vεxταp, what is it, could be Greek after-shave, lighter-fuel, anything. Ah well, never mind, make good presents, must know someone who drinks vεxταp, or puts it on dahlias, or something. Nearly had small row, though, who was minding bloody bag, who was looking for bloody taxi, etcetera, what the hell, damn good holiday, great to be home, looking forward to hot bath, clean sheets, yum yum and similar rubbish.

Arrive home; still standing (always expect charred ruin, like *Gone With The Wind*, where Number 26? we ask, old black retainer wiping eyes, Dey done took it fo' a Confed'ate fort, massah, hittin' it wid de cannon all de liverlong night...). Ring doorbell (never take keys on holiday, bound to lose in some flyblown hotel, next thing you know house crawling with Greek burglars), no reply. Funny, should be housekeeper there, big smiles, kettle boiling, where housekeeper, not Bingo night, must be watching box, ring doorbell again, no reply, look at wife, wife look back, wife puts down bags, goes next door, rings bell, neighbours emerge, much bonhomie (such as: What matter with face?), where housekeeper, we say, housekeeper gone, they say, Bingo, we ask, last week, they reply. Rush into neighbour's house, phone mother-in-law, much hemming and hawing, eventually transpires mother-in-law Having Words with housekeeper, housekeeper gave self ten minutes notice, gone forever.

Rush out of neighbour's house (tearing shirt on rose bush, since garden path moving through thirty-degree arc), tell wife, wife shriek, drop bag with bottle of vɛxτɑp, strange smell infiltrate night; how to get in house, keys with housekeeper, rush round back to break window, no need, back door open, last act of revenge, no doubt hoping Greek burglars arriving anyway, on offchance; peer into house, if not Greek burglars, could be muggers, vandals, Provos taping bombs to lavatory seats, maybe squatters (see long court case stretching out, hippies retaining John Mortimer, self got elderly family solicitor, no match for swinging QC, entire family walking streets behind self holding tin cup), but no sound inside. Go in, terrible noise, thing leap at me, it is Percy, world's most affectionate neutered ginger tom, now a mad thing like small cougar, all claws and malevolence; left to forage for self by vindictive housekeeper, Percy now trust no-one, been living off land like Viet Cong cat, also probably brooding on where to lay blame for neutering, I step back, Percy spring past, vanish into night, looking for sheep to savage, or something.

Open front door, let wife in, wife heavy with gloom, housekeepers like gold dust these days, wife due back at work tomorrow, what going to happen to house, kids, etcetera? Unanswerable questions, drag cases upstairs, house thick with old leaves blown through left-open windows, spiders, wasps; open bedroom door, no sheets on bed. Drop cases, sit on bed, stare at floor, get up, run bath, remove clothes, walk into bathroom, put foot in bath, withdraw foot, stare at foot, foot icecold. Put fingers under tap, tap say H, water say C, turn off tap, pass wife in kitchen staring at coagulated blob, remains of pigeon brought in by cat during some atavistic frenzy (or else, urbanely, as calculated insult), pass on to boiler room, boiler cold, phone Gas Board, come off it, says Gas Board, it ten o'clock on a Sunday night, what about Thursday week, no promises of course?

Start boiling saucepans (all full of old food, brazed on by ex-housekeeper with spot-welder), one bath equals forty saucepans, arms feel like yesterday's spaghetti by time bath full, get into bath, bath now cold again, bits of very old steak and so forth floating about, get out of bath, pull plug, dry cold self on dressing-gown (where towels?), bath-water not going away, plug-hole full of meat, get meat out with fingers, drop in loo, flush, meat swirl, swim back gamely to surface, shut lid, leave bathroom, wife sitting on bed holding headless golly, head no doubt ripped off when decabbing case, gutter outside house now got small black head in, no doubt, like voodoo sign. Very appropriate, all things considered.

Go to bed.

Wake up, shave cold, rest of face come off in razor, flush loo, watch meat hurtle about again, shut lid, go to start car to fetch kids, car go yergh-yergh-yergh, battery flat, call cab, wife departs childwards, no room for self plus wife plus children plus cot plus pushchair plus cases plus all other junk due back with offspring. Go out into garden, garden look like Matto Grosso, must be crashed Dakota in it somewhere, expect Ronald Reagan to come hacking across lawn any minute behind machete; come to small clearing, find cat dragging wing across it, cat look at me and look at wing as if working out which meatier, cat growl finally and slope off into undergrowth. Get to fish-pond, three fish floating in it, belly-up and covered in white spores; suddenly, oh my God, remember Doris Maurice! Doris Maurice is tortoise, so-christened by four-year-old son since no-one knew whether it Doris or Maurice, tortoise-sexing not being family talent, go to tortoise-run behind greenhouse, discover matter of sex purely academic now, as Doris Maurice look extremely deceased. Rotten housekeeper, tortoise needs water daily, pick up Doris Maurice, little legs stay outside shell, no panicky withdrawal, look at little face, Doris Maurice dead as doornail. What to tell small son, maybe small son forget Doris Maurice during stay at Grandma's?

Fat chance. Still standing there when small son return, fighting way through jungle, only thing small son forget is father, Where's Doris Maurice? Have had foresight to prop

Doris Maurice against fence, like shot legionnaire in *Beau Geste*, dead tortoise almost indistinguishable from live tortoise, after all, small son rapidly lose interest, we return to house, cat lunges at us, but we get through back door, son grab Greek machine-gun and run upstairs firing, I inform wife of demise, wife very practical girl, instantly goes into pros and cons of burial, suppose mad cat dig it up, drag it in house, that sort of thing.

Decide to put Doris Maurice in polythene bag in dustbin, wife break down, everyone in house very attached to DM, guaranteed (virtually) by Palmer's Pet Stores to last two hundred years (man in shop said one in Regent's Park remembers Captain Cook, bet Captain Cook wouldn't put tortoise in dustbin, says wife, that man had vision . . .). No polythene bag, all we have is Athens Duty-Free Shop bag, put Doris Maurice in, put in dustbin.

Worry. Suppose knock on door next week, policeman there with pitiful cargo, Excuse me, sir, is this your . . . Probably by-laws against such disposal, health risk, RSPCA complaints. Either that or some dustman totting for goodies in for terrible shock, opening Athens Duty-Free Shop bag hoping for cheap fags, gin, maybe even νεκταρ, and what he find? Doris Maurice. Shock could kill; unless he take Doris Maurice for weird souvenir, Greek delicacy, or not even real tortoise, but stone one (not much difference), take home, put on mantelpiece.

Stand at window, looking at dustbin. Feel as though last went on holiday about eight years ago. Always the way, though. Bet if Yeats went back to Innisfree, he'd find all his beans withered, and the clay and wattles fallen off the roof, and the bees all dead, dried up like trout flies, and the linnet's wings being dragged through the gloaming by the cat.

The Sanity Inspector

15

Oedipus Bruce

In Australia a recommendation was made recently that incest between a mother and son should no longer be illegal.

ACT ONE

Enter Chorus. They are citizens of Adelaide. They have corks dangling from their hats. They are all dead drunk.

CHORUS   Our mouths are like the inside of an abbo's trousers. We have all been walking through yesterday's lunch. We are as much use as an earwig's tit. What happened to last Wednesday?

Enter Barry, King of Adelaide, on all fours.

CHORUS   Hallo, Bazza, you look like two ton of old fish-heads.

BARRY   I've just been out in the fly box, saying goodbye to breakfast.

CHORUS   It's not like old Bazza to honk the bacon down the pipes after a night on the frosty tubes. Old Bazza has a gut like a ship's boiler. We have seen old Bazza sink ten gallons of Mrs Foster's Finest without threatening the drainage. Old Bazza must be upset about something.

BARRY   Too right! I was reading my horoscope in *Beer Weekly*, and it says where it's bad dos on the family scene this year, my flaming son is gonna flaming kill me, also beer could go up by as much as ten flaming cents a tube!

CHORUS   Stone the crows, Bazza! Ten cents a *tube*? This could spell the end of flaming civilisation as we flaming know it!

BARRY   Next thing you know, the supermarkets 'll be charging corkage on flaming Parozone! I blame the Japs.

CHORUS   Too right. What's this about your son? We didn't know you had a son. We didn't realise you ever went near your old lady. Isn't she the sheila who looks like a '37 Holden pick-up, sounds like a drag-saw, and smells like a dead dingo?

BARRY   Time was. She's past her best now. Still, when a bloke's tied a few on of a Saturday night, it's no worse than cleaning the chimney in your bare feet. That's how we ended up with young Bruce. He's a bright little bastard, can't be more'n ten months old, and he's already been done twice for being in charge of a push-chair while unfit. I'll be sorry to see him go, straight up.

CHORUS   Go? What are you gonna do with him, Bazza?

BARRY   I'm not risking some flaming kid growing up and doing his daddy with a lead sock. I'm gonna drive him out to Broken Hill and nail him to the floor.

CHORUS   Good on yer, Bazza! Trouble with kids today, they need a firm hand. No flaming authority left. No sense of family. Good luck, Bazza, got to rush now or they'll be picking bits of bladder off the ceiling.

Exeunt.

ACT TWO

The outback, near Broken Hill. Enter King Barry, carrying Bruce, and Wayne, a shepherd. They are all drunk.

BARRY   There you go, Wayne, I've tied his flaming feet together, all you have to do is drop him in the sheep dip. Watch how you handle him, he can go off like a flaming mortar when he's had a few, we had to redecorate the entire bungalow once.

WAYNE   Count on me, Bazza, I'll pop him in the dippo when I go to fill up me bottles. I'm expecting a few blokes over this evening for a bit of a blast.

Exit Bazza. Wayne stands holding the baby for a moment or two, then falls down and begins snoring.

BRUCE   Burp.
Exit Bruce, crawling.

ACT THREE

Twenty years later. During this period, Bruce has been brought up as a sheep by an elderly ram and ewe who found him as a baby. He walks on two legs, but neither he nor his adoptive parents think this in any way odd. This is Australia. Bruce's diet has been grass and sheep dip. He is tall, strong, and permanently drunk, and has picked up a little English from the labels of the beer cans with which the outback is strewn.

It is a hot morning. Bruce is staggering along a dusty track, when he meets another man staggering towards him. The man is Craig, a brewing representative. He is drunk.

CRAIG   Stone the flaming crows, it's Bruce!
BRUCE   You got the wrong bloke, blue. My name's Sixteen
             Fluid Ounces. It was Pull Ring Here for a time, I'll
             give yer that, but it's never been flaming Bruce.
CRAIG   Well take it from me, cobber, it's Bruce now all
             right, they had your picture in *The Daily Beer*, and if
             you want my advice you'll keep away from your
             folks. It says in the paper that as sure as flies lay
             eggs in a wombat's trade-mark, you're gonna fill in
             your old man and marry your old lady!
BRUCE   Yeah, well, the bloke who wrote that never saw my
             old lady. She's got four black hooves and twelve
             nipples, not to mention some bloody peculiar
             personal habits. You'd think twice before jumping
             on a mattress with that.
CRAIG   Don't argue, mate, *The Daily Beer* never lies!
He falls down. Bruce hesitates for a time, then shrugs, sets his shoulders, turns his back resolutely on Broken Hill and takes instead the opposite direction, towards Adelaide.

ACT FOUR

The road near Adelaide. A battered truck is rattling along it, with King Barry at the wheel, lurching in every pot-hole and spilling old beer-cans at every yard. At the top of a little rise stands Bruce, albeit unsteadily. As the truck approaches, he thumbs it down. Barry looks out of the window.

18

BRUCE Afternoon, sport. You wouldn't have a tube of Foster's aboard by any chance? I haven't eaten for six weeks.

BARRY Well, now, blue, that's a very interesting question! A very interesting question indeed. Why not have it engraved on brass and shove it where the moon never shines, har, har, har!

At this, Bruce tears the door off, drags Barry out onto the road, and batters him lifeless with it. He removes eight cans of lager from the body, drains them, belches happily, climbs into the truck, and sets off on a zig-zag course, back towards Adelaide.

ACT FIVE: Scene One

A month later. Adelaide, before the royal palace. It is an attractive wooden bungalow with a pleasing neo-Georgian room-extension in primrose mock-stucco nailed to the front. There are five carriage lamps on the front door, and a gnome holding a sign that reads '38 to 38A Alopecia Avenue'. Enter Bruce, who pushes open the wrought-iron gate and rings a doorbell. The chimes of Viva Espana die away, the door opens.

BRUCE Queen Glenda?

GLENDA That's right. Sorry about the Marigold gloves, sport, I was just worming the cat. What can I do for you?

BRUCE Promise you won't laugh, Glenda, only I met this sphinx up the road.

GLENDA I know how it gets sometimes, blue. I usually get pink spiders running over the flaming sideboard.

BRUCE No, straight up, Glenda, I met this sphinx and it said if I got three riddles right I could come round here and marry you. I didn't have anything else on this morning, so I thought, what the hell, it's better than a poke in the eye with a sharp stick!

Enter Chorus, supporting one another.

CHORUS He'll be flaming sorry he said that!

Exeunt, on hands and knees.

GLENDA So you answered the riddle all right, then?

BRUCE I don't know. The sphinx was legless. It was all he could do to give me your address before he fell over.

GLENDA I swear they put something in it up the factory.

When I was a girl, you could drink thirty-one pints before breakfast.

They marry. The wedding reception goes on for nine weeks. At the end of it, the bungalow has disappeared beneath a pyramid of beer cans. A number of guests are dead.

Scene Two

Some of the cans clatter to the ground. Bruce emerges from the gap, obviously distressed. He has a stick up his nose. Enter Norman, a neighbour. He is drunk.

NORMAN   Stone the flaming crows, Bruce, what's that stick doing up your conk?

BRUCE   I've been trying to poke me flaming eyes out, Norm. I can't seem to get the flaming range. I guess I'll have to wait till I'm flaming sober.

NORMAN   You don't want to go poking yer eyes out, mate. They'll rob you blind up the off-licence. It could cost a flaming bomb! What made you think of it?

BRUCE   I found out Glenda's me mum, Norm. I've only gone and married me flaming mummy!

NORMAN   No cause to pop yer headlights, blue! Mind, I can see it could be a bit awkward. Been a few naughties, have there?

BRUCE   Nothing like that, Norm. Nothing of that order. I haven't been capable, for one thing. Glenda says they put something in up the factory. No, it's giving up the bungalow, Norm. You spend twenty years as a flaming sheep, suddenly you got gas central heating and three flaming low-flush pastel suites, it's not easy to give it all up just like that.

NORMAN   Strikes me you're being a bit previous, cobber. I can't see why you and Glenda can't make a go of it. She's a very nice woman when she's drunk and no beard to speak of.

BRUCE   But it's against the flaming law, Norm!

NORMAN   Then they'll have to flaming change it, mate!

BRUCE   Would they do that, Norm?

NORMAN   Would they . . . ? You just come down the pub with me, cobber, we'll wake up the Home Secretary and put it to him straight!

Exeunt. Enter Chorus, dragging one another.

CHORUS   In Australia, all is flaming possible! In Australia, a new world is flaming born! In Australia, I flaming will! In Australia . . .

They collapse. They lie there. They snore.

CURTAIN

The Rhinestone As Big As The Ritz

The Small Gatsby

'Conservation, thrift, simplicity, self-containment, a withdrawal from conspicuous consumption and profligate competition, a rejection, indeed, of materialism—this seems to be the President's message. It is a considerable revision of the old American Dream.'—U.S. News & World Report

IN MY YOUNGER and more vulnerable years my father gave me some advice that I've been turning over in my mind ever since.

'Whenever you feel like criticising anyone,' he told me, 'just remember that all the people in this world haven't had the disadvantages you've had.'

The reason I have been turning this over in my mind ever since is that it makes no goddammed sense to me at all. This may be because I had to leave school in the fourth grade on account of my parents ate my shoes. They had this thing about not eating animals due to where animals was running out, also not eating anything animals ate so that those animals who hadn't run out yet got to eat regular. In consequence, our family ate anything it could swallow, provided animals wouldn't touch it.

Since my father was one of the most influential paupers in our town, the streets was always full of fat animals and thin people. There was no cars. My father saw anyone driving past in an automobile and wasting precious fossil fuels with no thought to the welfare of his fellow man, he'd drag him right out from behind the wheel and kick him senseless.

When I was eighteen, I was sent East. This was because my father suspected I was developing a taste for potatoes which he calculated the world would run out of around 3150 AD; so that rather than run the risk of losing the family's good name for austerity and self-denial, they took me down to the station and shipped me to New York second-class freight. True, my mother had softened at the last and pushed into my crate through the air-hole a couple of tasty candles she had kept hidden from my father (who believed that world supplies of wax might not last the century), but beyond that and three dollars I had borrowed from the dog (the only one my father would trust not to buy gasoline when his back was turned), I had nothing in the world.

To cut a long story short, which you have to do these days due to where no novel is allowed to be more than four pages long on account of the trees are running out, I fetched up on Long Island Sound and took a nice hole on the beach at West Egg. West Egg is the somewhat less fashionable half of the Sound; you can look across the water to East Egg and see some very famous heads poking out of the sand—leading environmentalists thinking about the possibility of bio-degradable pebbles, leading conservationists working on schemes to harness flatulence, top international paupers with home-made teeth, famous society beachcombers in their seaweed skull-caps—but on the West Egg side there are still people on mains electricity who mix meat with their soya and who, if they don't go so far as actually to own an automobile themselves, certainly know people who own them.

Not that any of this was true of Gatsby.

Gatsby was the most deprived person my side of the Sound, and for all I know anywhere else, too. He had the hole next to mine, and it was just about the worst hole I ever saw. Most nights it fell on him.

Most nights, too, there was a party at Gatsby's hole. Gatsby threw the bleakest parties on the eastern seaboard. There was never anything to eat, and there was even less to drink; there wasn't any music, either, because even if Gatsby could have afforded a needle for a borrowed phonograph, the rigid ethics of the Sound would have prevented him from using it, on account of world supplies of iron was running out.

Everybody came to Gatsby's parties. People would walk from miles away, or if they were coming from East Egg, swim across the Sound: any night, you could see the gleaming lines of home-made flippers drawn up outside Gatsby's hole. But most of the guests never even met their host; they just came because it was a Gatsby party, but they never got around to asking who

Gatsby was or where he was, because they never got around to caring.

I used to wonder why Gatsby threw them. I don't think he liked them. He hardly ever went to them himself. I used to see him standing at the edge of the water in his formal pillow case, just staring out across the Sound towards East Egg.

Nobody ever knew how Gatsby had got to be so immensely poor. Some said he had started from very rich beginnings and managed, by investing ineptly, to ruin himself in less than a year. Some said he had started as a bootlegger on the day they repealed the Volstead Act. But it was generally agreed by the hard-faced bright-eyed brittle people who battened onto his hospitality that he had not been broke for very long: sons and daughters of old families who had been destitute for three generations sneered at their host for a *nouveau pauvre* while he stood motionless in the moonlight, gazing silently east.

The only people who never came to his parties that first summer were the Buchanans. Tom and Daisy Buchanan lived right across the Sound from Gatsby's place, in probably the most fashionable hole in all East Egg. Beautiful, idle, penniless, they were each of them descendants of great families who had been on relief since the early seventeenth century, a provenance unscarred by ownership, or waste, or despoliation, or success. Buchanans had been Nothing In The City for as long as anyone could remember, while Daisy's family had been the only people to travel steerage on the *Mayflower*.

Since Daisy was in fact a second cousin of mine, I had been settled in for less than a month when I paddled across to visit them. Their bright laughter tinkled like cut-glass, or broken old jelly-jars anyhow, when they saw my log, and I remember blushing and hoping against hope that they would put my ostentation down to boyish inexperience. I'm not sure that they ever did, since they lived their life on a plane beyond my understanding.

The very poor are different from you and me.

They were playing stick with a group of glittering young people as I walked up the beach. Stick was that year's elegant game, a form of polo played without horses, mallets, balls, goals, or jodhpurs. You found a stick and threw it about. It was really keen.

24

Daisy looked ravishing. From her earliest youth, she had avoided all soaps, shampoos, cosmetics, ornaments, anything, in short, that had come from animals or the earth and was likely to run out sometime, and it was on account of this that her lovely face selected itself from the company of its merely pretty peers like the beacon of its generation; which indeed it was. She put her grey cheek up for me to kiss, and when she laughed she exposed a row of fashionably neglected teeth lovely as datestones, and when she tossed her head in calculated nonchalance, her uneven ringlets slapped lankly against her pimple-peeping neck like cold tagliatelle.

'Nick!' she cried. 'Where have you been keeping yourself?'

'I'm over on West Egg,' I replied. 'I have a hole right next to Gatsby's.'

At Gatsby's name, I felt a ripple shiver the slim body in my arms, right through the gunny sack.

'Gatsby?' she murmured faintly.

'Surely you know him? He throws those fabulous . . .'

'Oh, she knows Gatsby all right!' cried Tom Buchanan suddenly. 'He used to come by here with his begging bowl after he moved in across the Sound. God knows who he was trying to impress with his poverty! I believe he once told Daisy his parents had starved to death. Do you know, Carroway, I think she actually believed him for a while?'

'That was a long time ago, Tom,' whispered Daisy.

'Yes!' shouted Buchanan, his eyes blazing in his grime-caked handsome face. 'And I made a few enquiries and discovered that far from having starved to death, his people actually owned the New Haven & Hartford Railroad and spent half the year on their diesel yacht in Monte Carlo!'

'Diesel!' I exclaimed. 'Europe! Poor Gatsby!'

'*Poor* Gatsby indeed!' thundered Buchanan. 'Rich, ambitious, greedy, wasteful Gatsby, more like! Rotten little parvenu!'

Daisy pulled away from me, and I could see she had been crying. There were deep grooves in her cheeks. I figured it best that I leave. But before straddling my log again, a thought occurred to me.

'He's throwing a party Saturday night,' I called. 'Why not come?'

Daisy nodded her lovely head, so that the encircling flies spun off in crazy pirouettes.

'We'll be there,' she said.

Gatsby could hardly contain himself. When I shouted the news into his hole, he started so violently that it took me best part of an hour to dig him out. It was then that I realised that Daisy Buchanan represented something to Jay Gatsby that I had not even begun to guess at. He took my arm in a rough grip and led me to the water's edge, and pointed out across the Sound.

'Useta be a green light on the end of her, you know, dock,' he muttered.

'Really?'

'No fooling, I swum over and stuck it there myself. So's I could look at where she was nights. It had this, like, eternacell battery, size of your finger, useta glow.' He turned hollow eyes to me. 'I mean, how much goddamn energy can a thing like that use?'

'I've never seen it,' I said.

'That's on account of where they found it, also kicked it in the goddamn sea right after,' he said. 'She sent me this note about what kind of bum uses up the precious resources of Planet Earth sticking green lights on people's premises. She continued only a parvenoo bum, that's what kind of bum. I never saw her again, old sport.'

'I see,' I said.

'Who'd have figured it?' he said quietly, to himself. 'All that godamn fuss about a green light? What is it with poor people, Nick?'

'I have to go and get dirty for your party,' I said.

I never saw him again.

There was a freak tide Saturday evening, and by the time I'd finished baling out my hole and got over to Gatsby's place, the party was over. There was just Gatsby under a sheet with this red stain on it, and a guy with home-made-spectacles staring at it. Or near it, anyhow. That's one of the troubles with home-made spectacles.

'Rich son-of-a-bitch,' he said.

'What happened?' I asked.

'Middle of the party, guy busts in, says his name is Wilson and when is Gatsby going to settle his garage bill. Everybody stops suddenly and looks at Gatsby. Daisy Buchanan says there has to be some mistake, Gatsby don't have no automobile. Wilson says for her to stop putting him on, if Gatsby don't have no automobile, what is that interesting green foreign job he drives into Wilson's garage every Friday and fills up with super? Gatsby suddenly screams that Wilson is lying, so Wilson pulls out this large iron item and blows Gatsby away.'

I looked down at the sheeted corpse.

'Someone ought to go see Daisy Buchanan,' I said.

'The Buchanans ain't there,' said the owl-eyed man. 'They shut their hole for the summer. Daisy says the wrong class of people is moving in, next thing it'll be TV and barbecued spare ribs. They went to stay with some people they know on the Bowery.'

Owl-eyes shambled off towards the water, and splashed away. I watched his ripples spread out towards Daisy's lightless dock. Gatsby had come a long way to this dark beach, and his dream must have seemed so close that he could hardly fail to grasp it. He did not know that it was already behind him, somewhere back in that vast obscurity beyond the city, where, one by one, the cars were grinding slowly to a halt.

The Rhinestone As Big As The Ritz

Bottle Party

'Boozers are being offered the bender of a lifetime: an alcoholiday in the sun. The special attraction is twelve hours' drinking a day, FREE! Tourists will pay £45 for the trip to the island of Majorca, and for their money they will get unlimited supplies of liquor at a three-star hotel. Tours manager Colin Woolf said: "Our clients will be able to drink until they fall down."'—Daily Mirror

Hotel Borrachera
Playa de Palma
Majorca

38th July 1977

DEAR AUNTIE THING, Alice, tall woman, big yellow teeth,

Well, here we are at the, oops, there's a blotty, hallo Blotty! Who's a pretty Blotty then? at the, you know, and we are all having a wonderful O God Almighty these bloody Spanish pens! THESE BLOODY SPANISH PENS! THESE STINKING BLOODY LONG-HAIRED GREASY SPANISH WOG CHEAP LOUSY ROTTEN

Expen the scusil. Thrown pen over balcony, whee goes pen, hope it sticks in Spanish head, ha-ha, serve them right throwing Norman out of El Wizzo Niteclub just because Norman sick on bongo, no business having bongo where people can be sick on it anyhow, how they expect Norman do Knees Up Mother Thing with six bottles of vino sloshing about in him?

Norman lucky didn't get run over, all mad drivers, also hate dogs, don't realise thing running out of El Wizzo on all fours is man doing brilliant impression of airedale, Norman now got tyre marks all over his nice El Wizzo tablecloth.

28

And what police doing banging on hotel door in small hours, anyone think it crime to borrow tablecloth, no business grabbing Norman either, man got perfect right to be on top of own wardrobe, paid for room didn't he? Only reasonable Norman lash out with Genuine Old Master showing Majorca at sunset. Man was desperate. As I informed magistrate, 'We did not splash three quid on priceless antique work of art just to have rotten fascist pig stick greasy head through it.'

Norman back now, got lice. Also had to share cell overnight with violent criminal, quantity surveyor from Wimbledon staying at posh place in Palma on fourteen-day gin excursion, went mad when barman tried to close bar, bit barman's ear off. Disgusting putting my Norman in with him, Norman never ate anyone in his life.

Glad I brought up food.

Oh God.

Here I am, Auntie, back again! Where was I, oh yes, glad I mentioned food, food quite good, really, except too much paiella, trouble with paiella is you get shrimps in hair when face falls in it after third bottle, steak days are best except when they overcook it and you bruise your cheek.

Went to see fullbight last Monday where is my cigarette and sat in the sun with these gourds Norman bought where you have to squirt the wine into I KNOW I PUT MY BLOODY CIGARETTE DOWN SOMEWHERE where you have to squirt the wine into your mouth, only after the first couple of gourds Norman squirted it into ear of woman sitting next to him, woman scream blue murders, Norman leap up, woman's husband leap up, sock Norman in his O JESUS AUNTIE PILLOW IS ON FIRE PILLOW IS BURNING, AUNTIE, AUNTIE, I MEAN NORMAN, NORMAN, PILLOW IS ON FIRE NORMAN.

O GOD AUNTIE NORMAN IS ASLEEP ON LOO WITH SOMBRERO ON MUST CLOSE NOW BACK LATER.

Back now, Auntie, it nearly dark, whole place smelling of foam. Not my fault, threw burning pillow off balcony, woman on balcony below leaning out drying hair in breeze, pillow land on head, hair flare up like chip-pan, woman shriek, people upstairs smell burning, call fire-brigade, fire-brigade come, no hydrant so attach pump to swimming pool supply, drain swimming-pool dry and find two English couples lying on

29

bottom surrounded by bottles, police doctor say they dead two days. Funny thing, Norman wondered why conger line shorter than usual at El Wizzo last two nights.

Meanwhile man downstairs put wife's head out with fire-extinguisher, woman now not only burned bald but face all wrinkled up from chemicals and suntan fallen off, woman look like old golf ball. Husband ran upstairs, kicked in door, punched Norman in face, Norman fell off loo, now asleep in bath, so everything a bit calmer now.

Poor Norman, got black eye now to go with cauliflower ear received at bullfight after husband of woman with wine in ear sock Norman in his. Terrible blow, after that Norman see four bullfighters sticking four swords into four bulls every time he look.

Everybody know only two bulls and two bullfighters, clear as nose on thing. Two noses.

Anyway, Auntie, after bullfight met very nice English couple lying underneath charabanc, grocer from Birkenhead and lovely wife Arthur. All went out for dinner together, and Arthur danced in soup.

Arranged to meet on beach next day, and great fun burying Norman, falling down in sea, throwing ice cream at boring Swede families, etcetera, until it was time for lunch. Invited couple back to our hotel for five or six bottles. Only when half-way through second course and Arthur asleep on butter dish that Birkenhead grocer suddenly start counting.

'What is it?' I ask him.

'What is two and one?' he reply.

We think for a bit.

'Three,' I say finally.

'Thought so,' he comment. 'We never dug up Norman.'

Rush back to beach, dragging Arthur by foot, Arthur's arms flailing about knocking things off tables as we cross dining-room, bloody lucky most diners asleep under tables, but one or two Germans, French, etcetera start kicking up fuss when chicken legs start falling in laps, screaming, shouting, terrrible thing about foreigners, can't hold their drink.

O GOD AUNTIE I AM SOBERING UP. IF NORMAN COMES ROUND AND FINDS ME HE WILL GO SPARE, HOLIDAY COST-ING HIM FORTUNE HE SAYS, MUST DRINK TWELVE BOTTLES

A DAY JUST TO BREAK EVEN, WHERE TELEPHONE, WHERE ROOM SERVICE?

Hallo Mummie, Auntie, fat old cow, fancy giving us a wooden toast rack for a wedding present NO I DON'T BLEEDING FORGET EVEN IF IT IS TWELVE YEARS YOU FLY-BLOWN OLD RATBAG, feel a lot better now, nice bog bittle inside me, good idea having spiders walking all over the wallpaper, keep the flies off, especially green spiders, hallo green spiders wherever you are, I hope your troubles are few, all my good wishes go with you tonight, I was a spider, too, hee-hee-hee-hee-hee, O TOOTH ALMIGHTY I HAVE BROKEN A GOD ON THE BEDSIDE TABLE

hallo norman

Norman did not want me to wake him up Auntie he has hit me with the bidet HOW DID YOU GET THE BIDET OFF THE WALL AUNTIE, NORMAN, BELOVED, HOW DID YOU MANAGE TO why are my slippers floating past?

I have to close now Auntie, the manager has ordered a car to take us to the airport YES I AM REFERRING TO YOU YOU SWARTHY DAGO PIG I WOULDN'T STAY ANOTHER MINUTE IN YOUR BUG-RIDDEN RAT-HOLE FOR ALL THE TEA IN IN IN I DON'T KNOW WHERE SO STICK THAT UP YOUR CASTANET AND FLAP IT HAR HAR HAR.

You know what it is, Auntie, don't you, you know what it is all right, you know what it is with these bloody people, they're just a load of filthy anti-British bigots, that's what it is!

Hoping this finds you as it as it as it thing,
Your loving niece,
er,

The Lady From Stalingrad Mansions

Bare Essentials

London Edition

London - Paris - Rome - New York - Hollywood

THE
CELEBRITY BULLETIN
10, Dover Street, London, WIX 3PH

CELEBRITY
SERVICE
LTD

499 8511

WEEK OF TUESDAY, 28th SEPTEMBER
- MONDAY 4th OCTOBER, 1976

Established 1952

WHAT THEY ARE DOING THIS WEEK: HERE.

MICHAEL PENNINGTON and   will open on Tuesday in "DESTINY" at The
CHERIE LUNGHI   Other Place, Stratford-upon-Avon.

ALAN COREN and   will open at the Phoenix Theatre on
EUGENE IONESCO   Thursday, in "CARTE BLANCHE".

STAN KENTON and   will appear in concert at the Fairfield

IF YOU RING the number listed above, and if you ask how it comes about that Alan Coren and Eugene Ionesco should be appearing in Mr Tynan's latest flesh-mortifying erotorama, a very nice lady will—as far as it is possible to do so over the telephone—blush, and tell you that it is all a terrible mistake for which they have already apologised to an incensed Mr Coren, whose relatives have been jumping out of high windows rather than face the opprobrium attendant upon the scion of their ancient line running round in public with his clothes off.

Yet despite her fulsomely apologetic denials, may there not still be some unkind souls out there who, when they see smoke, shout 'Fire!'? Is it not possible, I hear some of you say, that literati eke out their paltry livings by leading such devious double lives?

Should I, in short, come clean?

How strange that history is almost invariably made in inauspicious places! To think that the revolution which was to change not just the theatre but the whole tone and temper of modern convention should have undergone its birth pangs at that lowly environ, the Alhambra, Bradford!

We had been engaged to open the second half on that chill February Monday, just a few short years ago: IONESCO & AL, A JOKE, A SONG, A SMILE. We were in our bleak little bedsitter in Mrs Compton-Burnett's Theatrical Boarding House, wiring our revolving bow-ties to the batteries in our hats and polishing the climax of our act (*Ionesco: 'My dog's got no nose.' Me: 'Your dog's got no nose? How does he smell?' Ionesco: 'Awful!'*) when there was the most fearful thumping and barking from the floor above.

'Stone me!' cried Ionesco, snatching off his rubber conk in

32

justifiable irritation. 'How do they expect us to rehearse with all that bleeding racket going on? Are we artistes or are we not?' He hopped to the door on his giant shoes, and wrenched it open. 'IVY!' he roared.

Mrs Compton-Burnett came heavily up the creaking stairs. She pushed a wisp of ginger hair under her mob-cap with a dripping soup-ladle.

'Madame,' said Ionesco, hand on hip, left profile tilted to the bulblight, 'us acolytes of bleeding Thespis are at pains to . . .'

'It's T. S. Eliot,' said Mrs Compton-Burnett, 'he's got that bloody seal upstairs with him again. I don't know how many times I've told him.' She leaned into the stairwell. 'YOU BRING 'IM DOWN OUT OF THERE, MR ELIOT!' she shrieked. 'I GOT ENOUGH TROUBLE WITHOUT CODS' HEADS IN THE S-BEND!'

An upstairs door opened, and T. S. Eliot's top-hatted head appeared over the banister.

'Boris is an artiste,' he shouted. 'You cannot expect him to spend his days juggling jam-jars on his hooter and his nights in a bloody toolshed! A seal has his pride, too.'

'Well, some of us is trying to synchronise revolving bows and funny walks down here,' Ionesco shouted back. 'Don't bloody mind us, mate!'

'TENANTS OF THE HOUSE!' yelled Eliot. 'THOUGHTS OF A DRY BRAIN IN A DRY SEASON!'

He slammed the door again.

'Patter!' snapped Ionesco. 'That's all he is, bloody patter. First house Monday night at Bradford, who gives a toss whether he should have been a pair of ragged claws scuttling across the floors of silent seas? Get the seal on, get your plates up on your sticks, tell 'em the one about the one-legged under-taker, and get off. Never mind your bleeding patter!'

The door across the landing opened, and two fat men in fright wigs emerged. Between them stood a balding midget.

'I don't think you've met Evelyn Waugh's Harmonica Fools,' said Mrs Compton-Burnett. 'Evelyn, Alec, and little Auberon.'

We all shook hands.

'Only trying to rehearse the bloody *Thunder And Lightning Polka*, weren't we?' said Evelyn, testily. 'Got into the middle twelve and going like the bloody clappers, suddenly there's all this shouting, Morris the Musical Dog bites Alec in the leg, little Auberon falls off his shoulders, bang!'

Mrs Compton-Burnett stroked the midget's pate.

'Did he hurt himself, then?' she murmured.

The midget opened its mouth, and a strange discordant wheeze came out.

'Only swallowed his wossname, hasn't he?' snapped Evelyn. 'His organ.'

'What will you do?' I said.

'I'll have a heart attack, that's what I'll do,' said Evelyn. 'I'll bang my head on the wall. Better ideas you got?'

'We should never have left Poland,' said Alec.

They went back inside.

'Come on,' said Ionesco, 'we're on in half an hour, and J. B. Priestley's borrowed my bloody monocycle, we'll have to take the short cut across the allotments.'

A far door opened.

'*Across the allotments?*' cried a voice. 'Why, as you wend your way 'twixt elm and privet, who is this bounding up to you? "Arf, arf!" it goes. "Why, it is Rover the dog!" you cry, "and who is this with him?" "Baa, baa!" "Goodness me!" you exclaim, taken somewhat aback, "what is this little lamb doing so near the pig-sty?" "Oink, oink!" the pigs inform us, their little . . .'

We went back to our own room, and shut the door.

'C. P. Snow,' explained Ionesco. 'A professional to his fingertips. Ever heard his starling?'

I shook my head.

'A masterpiece,' said Ionesco. 'I seen him do it riding bareback at Bertram Mills' one Christmas, I'll never forget it. 'Course, I'm going back a bit now. It was when he was with Compton Mackenzie's Elephant Ensemble.'

'They were great days, I understand,' I said.

'The best, son,' said Ionesco, his eyes moistening. 'Remember Graham Greene & His Krazy Kar? That was one of the Queen Mother's favourites, you know. She used to send Graham a pound of cobnuts from the Sandringham estates every Guy Fawkes' Night. We go back a long way, him and me. I knew him when he was Brian Breene.'

'I didn't know he'd changed his name,' I said.

'Had to,' said Ionesco. 'Started out as a ventriloquist. The

34

dummy used to introduce him, and afterwards people'd come up to him in the street and say "I know you, you're Grian Greene" so he decided to make life easier for himself.'

We packed our props and stage suits in our hold-alls, went downstairs through the reek of cabbage and dove-droppings, and walked briskly through the sleet to the theatre.

Stone-faced matrons thronged the foyer, and bronchitic British Legionnaires, and drunks with Brasso bottles in their hip-pockets, and malevolent small boys a-gleam with bright acne. There was a smell of rainsoaked dandruff.

'Bloody hell!' said Ionesco, the seams lengthening in his sad Rumanian face. 'I'd rather be opening the first half, son, before they've had a chance to get their eye in. It'll be like the bloody Somme after the interval.'

We crept past them, and down the back stairs to the mean little dressing-room we shared with Angus Wilson. He was sitting slumped in the corner, in his horse's head. There was despair written all over the little white legs poking out beneath the dappled torso.

'What's up, then, Angus?' said Ionesco.

The head turned, very slowly, towards us. Its glass eyes rolled.

'Me hindquarters,' it said, 'have gone down with sciatica. I just heard.'

'No!' cried Ionesco, 'old Betjeman not turned up?'

'Crippled,' muttered the horse. 'Lying there like Gregor bleeding Samsa. What am I going to do?'

'*We're* not on till the second half!' I cried, in true showbiz tradition. 'Why don't I do the back legs for you? It's the easy bit, no singing or juggling involved, just the tap-dance at the end.'

'It's very nice of him, Eugene,' said the horse, 'but he doesn't understand, does he?'

'You don't understand,' said Ionesco, to me. 'Angus can't get in a horse with any Tom, Dick or Harry, no offence meant. It's a very intimate relationship. It's got to be built up over the wossname, years.'

'It wouldn't feel right,' said the horse.

'Look,' said Ionesco. 'Suppose we both got in?'

'Don't talk bloody daft,' said the horse. 'Six legs hanging down? We'd look like a giant ant. I'm not billed as ANGUS THE WONDER INSECT, am I?'

'I didn't mean that,' said Ionesco. 'You go off home, me and him'll do your act. The management'll never know.'

'Would you really?' cried the horse.

'Say no more!' replied Ionesco.

We went on fourth, after H. E. BATES, WIZARD OF THE XYLOPHONE, and we managed well enough, despite some personal embarrassment during the somersault, but when we returned to our dressing-room, we found ourselves to be so sweat-wrung that there was nothing for it but to take off the underwear in which we had performed the act and hang it in front of the electric fire to dry. After which we turned to our mirrors in order to make up for our own act. So intent was I upon this, that I did not notice the smell until Ionesco suddenly turned from his dressing-table and said:

'What's burning?'

'Burning?' I said, 'I don't . . .'

'FIRE!' shrieked Ionesco, and I looked round, and our underwear had not only ignited, but had also set fire to the curtains! As the flames licked the pelmets, Ionesco and I rushed, naked, for the door.

The corridor was packed. C. P. Snow was mooing expertly to himself, The Singing Pakenhams were combing one another's coifs, Cyril Connolly and Doris were shoving cards up one another's sleeves—the exit was completely blocked!

'Come on!' cried Ionesco, and we took off in the opposite direction, not knowing, in our panic, where we were going, until, suddenly, we burst through a door and found ourselves in the middle of the spotlit stage, from which the previous act (W. H. AUDEN, HE FILLS THE STAGE WITH FLAGS) had just made his exit.

The audience roared!

The audience shrieked!

The audience cheered!

'Come on!' I hissed, grabbing his bare arm. 'Let's get off!'

'*Get off?*' cried Ionesco. 'GET OFF? Laddie, we'll never get a reception like this again!' He threw an arm around my naked shoulder. 'I say, I say, I say!' he shouted. 'What's got nine legs, three ears, and walks like my Uncle Bert?'

36

It was still not too late for me to run, but the applause of the crowd filled my ears, and the smell of the greasepaint, and the blaze of the lights, and all those wonderful things ravished my senses, and . . .

'I don't know,' I replied, 'what *has* got nine . . .'

And after that, we never looked back.

The Lady From Stalingrad Mansions

On a Wing and a Prayer

'The largest known creature ever to have flown, an extinct reptile with an estimated wingspan of fifty-one feet, has been discovered by fossil hunters in West Texas. The creature had twice the wingspan of the biggest previously known pterodactyl.' – The Times

FROM A HOLE IN A ROCK just outside what was to become Seven-oaks, Homo Britannicus slowly emerged into the grey morning. A single snowflake floated down and settled on his forearm, paused, and dissolved among the thick, matted hair. He watched it disappear, his thin rim of forehead wrinkling.

A second landed on his broad flat nose. He squinted at it until it became a droplet, and until that droplet vanished.

'What's it like out?' called his wife, from the dark recess of the cave. H. Britannicus shivered.

'Bloody freezing,' he said. 'Also, promise you won't laugh, the rain is coming down in bits.'

His wife scuttled out, her lovely knuckles skimming the ground.

'What?' she said.

'Look,' he said. 'Bits.'

She looked at the snow, and she looked at the leaden sky.

'That'll be the Ice Age coming, then,' she said.

'Here,' said H. Britannicus, 'what's that grey coming out of your mouth?'

'It's coming out of yours as well,' she snapped. 'How do I know what it is, I've never been in an Ice Age before, have I?'

H. Britannicus shook his head slowly. Tiny Pleistocene items flew out of his thatch, and hitting the chilly air, immediately became extinct.

'What's it all coming to?' said H. Britannicus. 'Where will it all end? When I was a kid, the summers we had!'

'I blame,' said his wife, 'the tool. All these bone needles, all these flint hammers, it's not natural.'

'Progress,' said her husband. 'You got to have progress.'

He tried to stand a little more erect. It wasn't easy.

'I'm off for a bit of a stroll,' he said. 'I'll catch me death standing here.'

It was just outside what is now the sub-soil of Canterbury that Homo Britannicus glanced up through his rime-hung eyebrows and noticed a figure shambling towards him. It had a pterodactyl on its arm.

'Morning,' said Homo Britannicus, taking a firmer grip on his club, just in case.

'Bonjour,' said the figure.

H. Britannicus raised his club slightly.

'What?' he said.

'Mah nem,' said the figure, 'eez Omo Gallicus. 'Ow eez eet going?'

'Mustn't grumble,' said Homo Britannicus. 'Where are you from?'

Homo Gallicus pointed behind him with his free hand, towards France.

'Ah 'ave walk many days,' said Homo Gallicus, 'wiz a proposition.'

'It looks like an ordinary bloody pterodactyl to me,' said Homo Britanicus. 'And what's that round your neck?'

'Wi call zem onions,' said Homo Gallicus.

Homo Britannicus reached out and felt one, cautiously.

'You'll never kill nothing with that, son,' he said. 'Too soft.'

'Wi eat zem,' said Homo Gallicus.

Homo Britannicus looked at him.

'It takes all sorts,' he said. 'What's the pterodactyl for?'

'Where can wi talk?' replied Homo Gallicus.

They found a small cave, and crept inside, and sat down. Homo Britannicus blew on his fingers.

'I wish we had a couple of sticks,' he said.

'What for?'

Homo Britannicus thought for a while.

'I'm not sure,' he said, at last. He nodded towards the pterodactyl. 'What about him, then?'

'In mah country,' began Homo Gallicus, 'wi 'ave no dinosaurs. Zer dinosaur eez—'ow you say?'

'Extinct.'

'Exactement! 'Owevaire, wi 'ave zer pterodactyl. You, on zer uzzer 'and, 'ave no pterodactyl, but you 'ave zer dinosaur, n'est-ce pas?'

'Just a few,' said Homo Britannicus. 'They're a bit bloody ropey, mind. Past their best, know what I mean? We've let 'em run down, werl, there's no call for 'em these days, is there?'

'Ah beg to diffaire,' said Homo Gallicus. He bent forward, and his black eyes glittered. 'Mah plan eez to mate zer Gallic pterodactyl wiz zer Britannic dinosaur! Wi will produce zer Gallo-Britannic pterosaur, mon vieux! Eet weel be zer biggest flying objeck evaire seen!'

'So what?'

'Zer Ice Age is coming, hein?' said Homo Gallicus. 'In an eon or two, eet weel be 'ere. Wi weel 'ave to find warmaire climate, or . . .' he drew a thick finger across his imperceptible neck. 'Wi cannot walk, eet eez too far; so wi weel climb aboard zer giant pterosaur—*an'wi weel fly there!*'

'Gerroff!' cried Homo Brittannicus.

'Also,' continued Homo Gallicus, unruffled, 'wi weel rule zer worl'! Everyone weel want one. Wi weel clean up zer pterosaur market.'

Homo Britannicus, to be fair, did all he could to fathom this momentous idea: he furrowed his millimetric brow, he scratched his craggy head, he sucked his great green teeth. But it was not until Homo Gallicus began to draw upon the cave-wall with his easy, flowing line, that his partner-to-be was really convinced.

It looked wonderful, in the picture.

Over the next five years, the innumerable, unforeseeable technological problems came forth and multiplied.

For two years alone, the dinosaur and the pterodactyl could not be persuaded to mate at all, and the wretched co-partners were forced to stand by while the two halves of the project shrieked and bit one another. But in the third year, by a process of strategic starving, feeding, and cajoling, the message got gradually through, and the dinosaur fell pregnant.

Ultimately giving birth to an enormous saurian cylinder with six legs and two very small wings. It flapped these latter for a few impotent beats, fell over, and expired.

'Ah well,' said Homo Gallicus, 'back to zer cave-wall!'

Which was all very well, except that the family of Homo Britannicus was finding it more and more difficult to make ends meet: it was not merely that most of their breadwinner's time was spent in husbanding the animals involved, but also that those animals were consuming a vast amount of food. They were being saved from natural extinction only at the expense of the unfortunate hominids who had been forced to cast their lot with them.

'You never told us it would cost this much,' was how Homo Britannicus's wife put it, over and over again.

Whereupon her husband would flatten her with his club, a gesture which over the years was becoming less and less affectionate.

But towards the end of the fifth year (by which time the temperature had dropped to a constant ten below zero, and the emaciated families of the luckless inventors reduced to gnawing for nourishment upon the misshapen bones of past failed experiments), a small pterosaur was produced of rather pleasing proportions. Even more encouraging was the fact that when it flapped its large leathery wings, it actually took off, flew for a few yards, and landed again without breaking anything.

'It works!' shrieked the two Homos, hugging one another and dancing great whorls in the encircling snow. 'A new dawn is breaking!'

'Erk,' went the baby pterosaur. It opened its mouth wide. 'Erk.'

'Eet wants,' said Homo Gallicus, 'to be fed.'

For five more years they fed it, while it grew bigger and bigger. The cold wind that continued to blow through Europe having taken its constant toll, the vegetation was now so sparse that the family of Homo Britannicus spent its every waking hour in scouring the white landscape for pterosaur fodder, they themselves subsisting on grubs and bits of bark and anything else the pterosaur could not use.

'When will it be big enough?' they would plead of the manufacturers, 'when will it be ready? When will it all end? When will the miracle begin?'

And the manufacturers, by now mere hirsute skeletons themselves, would say: 'Soon, soon.'

And then, in the bleak autumn of the tenth year, when its wingspan had reached fifty-one feet, and its sleek giant body was consuming a field a day, and its insistent 'ERK! ERK!' had reached a pitch and volume that would start avalanches rolling a dozen leagues away, they trundled the Gallo-Britannic pterosaur out of its enormous cave, and announced that it was ready.

'Wi weel head West,' cried Homo Gallicus, 'to zer sun and zer fleshpots!'

Homo Britannicus clubbed his wife for the last time, tenderly.

'Back in two shakes,' he said, and gathering the mangy rat-skins about his jutting bones, he and his colleague climbed aboard.

The great wings flapped, and the pterosaur lumbered down the runway in a trail of webby pot-holes, and took off.

The last thing they saw, before the freezing snow-clouds enfolded them, was the pitiful little knot of rags beneath, staring upwards.

They seemed to be praying.

It was warm in the place that was subsequently Dallas.

A group of fat, balding hominids were sitting around a triceratops-shaped pool, examining a roughly circular rock that Homo Texus was rolling up and down.

'I agree,' said Homo Oklahomus, who had made the trip especially to see it, 'it could be very big. It could be, like, very big indeed.'

'With the right packaging,' said Homo Arkansus.

'With the right packaging,' said Homo Oklahomus, nodding.

It was at that point that the sun was blotted out.

'What the—!' cried Homo Texus, letting the wheel roll from his fingers.

They leapt up, as the pterosaur came in to a perfect two-point landing, and ran across. Homos Gallicus and Britannicus jumped down.

'This is private property, buddy!' shouted Homo Texus.

'And this,' cried Homo Britannicus, 'is the Gallo-Britannic pterosaur! It will revolutionise travel, it will open up whole new experiences, it will . . .'

'The hell it will!' shrieked Homo Texus.

'Did you hear the goddam noise?' screamed Homo Oklahomus.

'My God! yelled Homo Arkansus, pointing a trembling finger, 'look at its damn droppings!'

'The environment!' howled the Americans, 'The environment!'

Whereupon, brushing aside the enfeebled European bone-bags, they fell upon the hapless pterosaur, and beat it to death.

Golfing For Cats

Saturday Night Fever

'Saturday Night Fever, *which has so far grossed over sixty million dollars, started life as a magazine article entitled "Tribal Rites of a Saturday Night". It is not just a hip treatment of disco culture: this story of a kid who works and sweats all week, living only for his Saturday night explosion, has a whole life inside it.*'—Time Magazine

HE WALKS DOWN THE STREET. Check out that walk! Do those feet touch the concrete?

He walks so light, just the toes touch, the hips have that roll, he walks like a man wearing plimsolls with one heel off. This is because it is Saturday! And Saturday is the day he was going to pick up his brown brogues from the Lightning Shoe Repairs (Estab. 1958) Co. Ltd., only when he hobbled into their reeking premises he could not find the ticket and was shown the notice: Customers Please Produce Ticket And Oblige No Articles Released Without Ticket Yrs Rspctflly The Mgemnt.

He walks so light, because it's Saturday! People in the street go Wow! Thinking: *That guy has a very lousy wooden leg indeed! Either that or he has a real bad boil somewhere, possibly of carbuncle status! Whichever way you slice it, he is not getting the medical attention he deserves!*

They cannot see his heart. His heart is clattering, rim-shots on a snare drum, because it is Saturday, and Saturday is the day he is going to put the shelf up in the garage. He has worked all week, sweated, ground at the numbing routine of writing, editing, trying to park only the circulation manager is in his place, he has lost a lot of good brain cells all week, waiting for Saturday, waiting to get it all together, put the shelf up.

He limps, that snappy limp, into Galway Hardware, Finchley Road. He pauses at the door, sniffing Finchley Road, it is his street, he owns this street, its dreams, its heartaches, its Sainsbury's, its white dotted line going down the middle! It goes on and on, south to Swiss Cottage, north to Henley's Corner, it is all his, his runway, his arena!

'Hi!' snap, snap, go his fingers. 'I need a packet of one-inch Number Eight screws, I need Rawlplugs, I need all that.'

An old lady looks at him. She is from The Neighbourhood. She is Real People.

'I was first,' she screams.

'Some people can't see a bleeding queue when it's staring them in the wossname!' cries a woman in a hairnet, waving a jeroboam of Sanilav.

He loves them! They are Life!

'I'm sorry,' he says, because he loves them.

'Never mind sorry,' shrieks the old lady, 'sorry won't get my bathplug bought!'

'Was that with or without the chain?' says the ironmonger. Check that style! Check that mongering! This is *uno chi capisce*, this is one who knows.

There is a lot of neighbourhood blah after this, it is a very demotic scene, the people talk about lengths of bath-chain, about plug-diameters, the hairnet with the Sanilav tells about the time she nearly bought the wrong-sized washer for a tap that wouldn't stop dripping, an old guy examining rat-poisons in a corner chips in about how if the plug was too big it wouldn't fit in the hole, but the old lady comes right back at him and snaps that if it's too small then there's no way the water is going to stay in the bath, the ironmonger disappears into the back of the shop, it's a wonderful rich canvas, the guy in the one-and-a-half plimsolls hops from one foot to the other, does he scream, does he bang his head on the wall, does he pick up a hoe and kebab the Neighbourhood People? No! Because it's Saturday, it's the day he's waited the whole week for, it's *his* day!

He just chokes a little, bites through his lower lip, pushes his fist through his trouser pocket. His whole body is *vibrant*.

He limps out of Galway hardware, screwless, into his street. The climate has changed, but it is his rain, he *owns* this rain, it is coming up through the ex-heel of *his* plimsoll! Hell, like who needs garage-shelves anyhow, it's only somewhere to stand the emulsion he was going to paint the ceiling with, and as he kicked over the emulsion that morning as the result of its standing on the floor of the garage instead of on the shelf he hasn't put up yet, what does it matter?

He looks at his partially eau-de-nil trousers. They have a very pleasing effect, in the right light. Even the partially eau-de-nil wing of his car looks pretty good, if you park the car so's you can't see the partially eau-de-nil wing.

He takes out his shopping list, unfolds it, snap, snap, the rain comes down, plop, plop, the list reads: 3 lb flggge, 6 jlllbbb, 4 large schlg, the rest of the list runs off the page as he watches, a week's provisions dissolve on his cuff.

He lopes back ten blocks to his partially eau-de-nil car, a really awesome lope on account of capillary attraction is drawing most of the climate up the sock in the heelless plimsoll, he is drowning from the ground up. Back at his car there is a parking ticket, Saturday is the day he gets parking tickets, his whole body *reacts* to the parking ticket, he drives back to his house, it is easily recognisable due to where none of the other houses in the street have eau-de-nil plimsoll-prints all over the front path.

And still only noon! Still twelve hours of Saturday to go, all his, throbbing!

His woman is there. She looks at him. He looks at her. You can feel the charge. It goes back a long way, this electricity: man, woman, perhaps it goes back as long a way as it is possible to go.

She says: 'Did you get the courgettes?'

He says: 'So that's what they were!'

She says: 'Did you get the four large aubergines?'

He says: 'Ah. Four large aubergines.'

A huskiness creeps into her voice, his lithe shoulders do wild things, shrug, shrug, their conversation rises and falls, they are really communicating, no outsider could guess what is passing between them, only these two know it is about freaky things like why there are eau-de-nil footprints all over the hall carpet or the problems of making aubergine, courgette and mortadella quiche when you do not have any aubergines, courgettes, mortadella or Jus-Rol pastry.

It ends the only way such things can end when man and woman breathe such passion into one another: he takes off his plimsolls and his liquescent socks and slops out of the kitchen.

He is terrifically cool, incredibly laid back: he gets through the whole of lunch with everybody staring at him. The children do not stare at him the whole time; some of the time they stare at their cold lunch. His daughter contrives to stare at both simultaneously, getting down to table level and coming at him over the rim of her untouched plate, like Mister Chad.

He is thinking: *Saturday! It is all worth it for Saturday!*

After lunch, he rolls out to the garden on the balls of his feet, a fascinating gait he has developed as the result of having pieces of Lego dropped into his Wellingtons; he is like some kind of wild animal. Out here, it is *his* garden. That is *his* fence, lying flat on *his* budding peonies; the decapitated buds roll in the windy wet, withered as prunes.

'Yes, that is *your* fence,' confirms another Neighbourhood Person, looking through the gap.

'I thought it was joint-owned,' ripostes the guy, snap, snap, cool as ever.

'No, that's where you're wrong.'

'Oh.'

The neighbour's beagle barrels through the gap and pees on the last intact peony. The neighbour goes back in his house. The dog follows.

Everything in the greenhouse is dead. That frost. Saturday is the day for going to the greenhouse and wondering if the geraniums are still dead.

If anything, they are deader than they were last week.

He looks up at the greenhouse roof, or where it was before the children learned cricket. Through the holes, on a good Saturday, you can see God.

There is nothing he can do in the garden. He could maybe make a shelf for the garage out of the fallen fence, if only he had some screws, some Rawlplugs.

If he had more paint, he could maybe paint the whole car eau-de-nil.

He goes back into the house. It is Saturday, Wales are playing France; except on his television set. This is tuned to a channel where cowboys are playing Indians. He thinks about a sudden dash to the tuning knobs, but a lot of children are staring at him, malevolent from non-lunch, daring him to cross

47

them again.

He goes out of the room with that terrific stylish shuffle, like a man carrying a bathful of rocks on his neck. The light is beginning to fade. *Check out that light!* Saturday is slipping away!

He keeps the *Radio Times* in his lavatory, so the children will not reconstitute it as glove puppets. He leafs through it with Saturday Night eagerness. Soon, zip, zip, it will be time for the fourth repeat of *M*A*S*H*, for *Saturday Night at the Mill,* for a *Lively Arts* interview with William Walton's auntie's butcher, for news of Lebanon, starring cheery Peter Woods. For tomorrow's weather with Michael Fish, or tomorrow's fish with Michael Weather.

He puts a foot on the stair. The foot is numb. Could be pneumonia, pleurisy, gangrene, any one of a hundred really terrific stylish things.

She says: 'Where are you going?'

He says: 'I am going up to the attic to write an article. Sometimes an article can end up grossing over sixty million dollars.'

She says: 'Ha, ha.'

He says: 'I feel like working.'

She says: 'But it's *Saturday!*'

The Rhinestone As Big As The Ritz

The Heathrow Tales

Whan that Aprille with his taxe-formes drere
Comes, draggynge in a new fynancial yeere,
Thenne many folke loke round to see how theye
May kepe the Inlande Revenue atte baye;
And hardly has the litel month begunne
Thanne journalystes start trekkinge to the sunne,
To write of places off the beaten trackes,
And sette expenses off agaynst thir taxe:
A pilgrimage, in shorte, not for their soules,
But (as it is wyth modern mankynde's goales)
To keepe a few bob backe. Thus, did I wende
To Heathrowe, there my further steppes to bende
Towards some sunsoked costa; and I founde
The spotte was thikke wyth pilgrims! All arounde
They milled and chattered, singlie and in groupes;
And everywhere, the bright-emblazon'd troops
Of Travail Agents hopped and chyrped like sparrowes,
Dyspensing labels, poyntinge uppe at arrowes,
Dyscharging these to Lourdes, and those to Rome,
And others who were off to see the home
Inne wich Lorde Byron lived, or John Keates died,
Or Wolfgang Amadeus Mozart cryed
When (being seven) his Daddye would not lette
Him staye uppe to compose a stringe quartette.
And yette, for all the bustle and the cryes,
Not one soule saw I takynge to the skyes,
And eek my own flyte no man came to call;
We merely mobbed the grate departure hall
And gayzed uppe at the indicator-bord,
For such bleeke gleenings as it would afforde
Of flytes not inne, not oute, not onne, not knowne,
Of strykes and goe-slowes; and muche else (not showne)

Like drunken crewes, lost rear doors, and the sounde
Of tickynge baggage, kept us onne the grounde.

Thus was it thatte it came aboute by chance
As we poore pilgrims trodde our loanly dance
Upon the Heathrowe tiles, thatte one of us
(Drop't there two dayes bifor by airporte bus)
Suggested thatte we wile awaye the time
With tales thatte eech wold tell the reste, in ryme!
We clap't, we cheer'd, our weery eyes grew bryte;
We sang the praises of thatte worthie wight!
Then satte we downe, wyth whiskey, beere, and gin,
And wayted for the firste one to biginne.
But lette me, whyle I have the tyme and space,
Ere thatte I ferther in this storie pace,
Sette downe the manere of thatte companye,
And wich they weren, and of what degree;
And eek in what array thatte they were inne!
And at a clericke wol I firste biginne.

A BISHOPPE hadde we wyth us in thatte place,
A slimme yung manne whose bryte and beerdlesse face
Glowed wyth a pinkish-white cherubicke hue,
Broughte on in parte by prayer, but most by Brut.
This worthie manne had turned his mohaired backe
Upon the easeful parishe life: no hacke
For Christ was he, to pat the wrinkled hande
Of borynge windowes, or each weeke to stande
Inne some raine-sodden pulpytte, there to speeke
Some low-paid sermon to the grottie meeke.
Westward he turned his course, towardes those isles
Where heathen soules pursued those living-stiles
Thatte frighte the Christian; where the idle rich
Have found atte laste a litel taxe-free niche
Whereinne to set thir golden calves; to pounce
Whenne golde goes up to ninety-five an ounce,
And where, to ease thir soules, they oft invite
The better class of prieste to spende the nyghte;
Or three months, if the truth were told. So thatte
They ease thir conscience, as we worm a catte.

The prieste in his turn, for the boone thus given,
Makes sure the taxe-evaded soule is shriven,
And coming home all tanned, white teeth a-gleem,
Turns out for cricket wyth his village teeme—
Hee fyndes the countryside the place to dwell;
For theologians writing *What Is Hell?*
(A six-part series for the *Sunday Tymes*)
Need peace and quiet; rural life, too, chimes
Wyth tearynge uppe to towne one day a weeke
So thatte the national presse may heer him speeke
His piece on porno in the House of Lordes,
Or rayle on telly about Christian frauds.

Biside him satte a NOVELISTE, al pale,
Who once, tenne yeeres bifor, had writ a tale
So true, so deepe, so geered to thisse darke age
Thatte, ere the reeder turned the final page,
He knew *Roome Atte The Botom* was the one
To acte on Eng. Lit. lyke the mornynge sunne,
Who sheddes his warmynge beemes on soggie soyle
To maturate the plottes where seedlynges toyle.
Thus, al arounde, we saw the seedlynges bask;
The noveliste, meenwile, clove to his taske,
And lo! ere yet a litel yeere had trip't
He hadde terned out a stunnynge movie scripte
Based onne the boke. It won sixteene awardes
(And, naturally, reeped other fatte rewardes:
The noveliste moved to the South of France).
The nexte yeere saw a wonderful new dance,
The Botom (fromme the musical), by wich
The noveliste now waxed exceedynge rich.
And still the grate creative juices flow'd!
For, after thatte, thisse noveliste now show'd
How righte *Roome Atte The Botom* prov'd to bee
In ninety-seven parts on ITV.
Whereat this prodygal son of his tyme
Turned his unrestynge hande to pantomime:
Roome Atte The Botom Meets Dick Whittington
(Wyth Tomie Steele and Twiggie) was put on
Atte the Palladium. It ranne and ranne!

Was there no stoppynge thisse creative manne?
Alas! His ice showe flop't. His Muse, for once,
Now founde her litel lyre reft of stunts.
And now, with tenne yeeres gone, the noveliste
Muste needes revyve. And his psychiatriste
Together wyth his agente and, of course,
His thirde wife, feel a visyte to the source
Of his firste inspiration mighte wel loose
His writer's block; and—who can tel?—produce
Downe Atte The Botom, or some other sequel
Whose spynne-off possibilities mighte equal
The pickynges of the firste. So here todaye
He goes in serche of Ernest Hemingwaye
(Whose nice short werdes our man always admir'd:
The hand, with polysyllables, growes tired);
He trekkes to Paris, thence to Rome, and soon
Will lie beneeth Pamplona's risynge moon
And fille his dreggy cuppe at thatte fresshe spring
Where Papa roared, biside the bloodstaynd ring.
But things are not quyte alwayes as they seem—
Hee has wyth him an Outsyde Broadcast teeme.

Acrosse the aisle, two HIPPIES sat entwyned,
Hopynge, ere longe, to blowe their tiny minde
Upon the Golden Roade to Samarkand,
Then on across the Kush, through Kashmir, and
At last drop out in distant Khatmandu,
Where grass is not just greene, but cheeper, too.
And there, atte some sleeke Maharishi's foote,
They wil spil oute the necessarye loote
To buy such solace as the saint may proffer
Wythinne the termes of Thysse Month's Special Offer.
I fynde I greeve for thysse unhappie lotte
Whose yung lyves runne increasingly to potte;
Who shal we blayme if, spaced out, zonked, they roame,
Seekynge some mysticke cobblers far from home?
Since we, all shackled in our bourgeois harness,
Can only crie: Yes, we have no Nirvanas!

Behynde these satte another lovynge paire,

52

Thir fingers loste in one another's haire;
A fond GAY COUPLE, bounde for Old Tangier
(A pilgrimage they mayke yeere after yeere).
These worshyppe atte the shryne of Oscar Wilde,
And André Gide, thatte othere faerie's childe,
Whose fin-de-siècle wand'rings inne the soukhs
(So taystefullie recycled inne his bokes)
Soon gayve Moroccan tourism a booste
Stil undiminished; for they have produced
(I feere I rayse uponne the reeder's neck a
Hackle) a kind of homosexual Mecca;
Where all the flockyng hordes of gay devoute
May—in the jargonne of thir faÿthe—come oute.
I wysshe them wel: for *chacun à son goût*,
And who am I, or (wyth respeckte) are you
To say that lit'ry pilgryms shal conforme
To sum olde-fashioned arbitrarie norm?
That onlie those who trek to Brontë doors
Shal be allowed enjoymente on the Moors?

Another wyth us wold not see this waye:
He stoode and stared atte them; he was not gaye
Inne any sense: al pinstryped stoode he there,
And close-cropped, groomed and gleemynge, was his hayre.
His firme grippe held a newe attaché-case,
Sharp-edged, with snaplockes (not unlyke his face).
A BUSINESSMANNE was he, and that an able,
Reared, thoroughbredde, in some goode British stable:
Eton, the Guards, perhaps an LL. B.,
Or else (from Oxenforde) a Greats degree.
At all eventes, a manne wyth Greeke and Latyn,
As polished as the leather chayre he satte in
At Knatchbull, Breene & Smythe (Precision Tools),
His father's firme. He wold not suffer fooles
Gladlie or otherwyse: a chappe who coulde
Not shoote, hunte, fishe or choose the proper woode
Or iron, or thoughte thatte footeball was a gayme
Played with a rounde ball, did not fynde his name
Among the list of clients at KBS.
Wich may explayne the roten bluddy mess

53

The companye was inne; and why this wighte
Was waytinge for a (cheep excursion) flyte
To Boston, and the Harvarde Bisnesse Schoole
In wich this upryte, dapper, sportynge foole
Had been thatte weeke (agaynste his wil) enrolled
By al his borde. For they had herde it tolde
Thatte at this founte of holy bisnesse writ
A sowe's eer mighte be processed and made fit
To be a purse, and thenne investment cashe
Would beate a path and begge the righte to stashe
Itself therein. And kbs wold rise,
A pheenix, to amayze the doubtynge eyes!
It maye be so: myself, I cannot feel
Much hope of succour to the bisnesse weal;
I saw his luggage: rods, a rydinge hatte,
Four tennys racquettes and a cricket batte.

Not far from him, a small, svelte figure satte,
Be-cloked, carnationed, in an opera hatte;
(He wore his opera hatte one day a weeke,
One day his anti-Russian one, and eek
A thirde, reserved for twittynge Wedgwood Benn.)
A MUSIC BUFFE (and Conscience For All Men),
Now bounde for Bayreuth and some Wagnerfest,
That shryne he worship't above al the reste
(Thrilled by the thought that it was Wagner, who
Wold happilie have turned him into glue?)
'Surely you're Bernard Levin, sir!' I cryed;
He turned, he smiled, he hummed awhile, he sighed,
And then began a sentence. But, alas!
Hardlie ten minutes were allowed to pass
Bifor they called Flyte BE 151,
And stil his sentence was not half-waye done.
(Wich onlie shows how German influence
Wil sometymes lead to compromise with sense;
How, with my aircraft throbbynge atte the kerbe,
Could I hang onne for Mister Levin's verb?)

Thus, on a suddenne, was I called awaye,
Torne from my felaweship, the straighte, the gaye,

54

The godlie and the mammonite, the freake,
And al the reste I have no tyme to speke
Of. All those goodlie soules, I feere, remayne,
Stil earthbounde, meeklie waytinge for thir playne.
While you, deere reeder, for thir grippynge tales,
Muste needes hange on, and trimme your eeger sayles
Until such tyme as they returne once more
To shayre the riches of thir blessèd store.
I have no doubte, though, that thir diff'rent tripps
Wil much improve what falls from al thir lipps,
Wen, havynge trod their spiritual paths,
They laye the fruits bifor us: how the baths
In Bethlehem were filthy, how the flies
Were everywhere in Lourdes, and what grate lyes
The brochures tolde! And how the bluddy guides
Robbed Martha blind! We'll heare it all, wyth slides.

Golfing For Cats

Spring Hopes Eternal

IT WAS DARK in No. 6 Shaft of Bolsover Colliery, as it had every right to be. Three thousand feet above my borrowed helmet as the crow burrowed, Spring was bursting in a barrage of sexual pyrotechnics: wheeling birds thwacked in mid-air with the ringing accuracy of those who know their lust to be seasonally momentary; frogs clung to one another with that quiet desperation which renders the sexual comedy poignant; rabbits were shooting from their holes like soft cannonballs, hungry for collision; a billion worms, by nature hermaphrodite, were making their agonising snap decisions; and even the flowers were at it like knives.

But down here, all was dark, mineral, sterile. An eon back, these trees were fecund with hot sap; now, they were mere fused corpses, silently awaiting the ultimate degradation of the Phurnacite mould. Sobering environs for a boy of not yet forty summers: I, too, when geophysics had taken its slow and grisly course, should end up crackling in someone's grate, ten million years hence, kindling clichés in his head as he gazed, dreaming, at my hissing encarboned elbow.

I sighed.

'Oh Gawd,' said a weary voice, 'Mortality weighs heavily on him like unwilling sleep.'

I peered. The gloom yielded nothing.

'I beg your pardon?' I said.

'Keats,' said the voice. 'People come down a mine, first thing you know they're going on about man's brief span etcetera. Wet in the extreme, people.'

My eyes were by this time accustomed to the dark; the shaft was empty. I raised the cage, and looked at the canary.

'It is no good,' said the voice, 'looking at the canary. They are ignorant little bleeders. They go gentle into that good night, as

Dylan put it. Thick as two short planks is how one might sum up your average canary. It is no use expecting them to talk. Cheep, cheep, then it falls off its little perch, stone dead. Your budgerigar, faced with methane, would not pop its clogs without considerable verbal protest, even if it was only *Who's a dead boy, then?* Canaries deserve all they get.'

'I'm sorry,' I said, 'I'm afraid I can't see you.'

'Brace yourself,' said the voice. 'I am up here on the ceiling.'

I glanced up, and my helmet-beam followed the glance.

I dropped the cage.

I grasped a pit-prop for support.

I may have croaked something.

'Yes,' said the voice, 'one does not run into four-foot dragonflies every day of the week. However,' it continued, unplucking itself from the roof and dropping to the floor beside me, 'we do not, contrary to popular myth, sting people. Mind you, we embrace our prey and suck it to death, so it is six of one and half a dozen of the other if you happen to be odontata-fodder, but as human beings are not, I fail to see what all the staggering and gasping is about.'

I licked my lips; slowly, reason papered over the shattered machismo. A sort of reason, anyway.

'You are not,' I said, 'quite what I expected. I saw this story in the *Daily Telegraph*, and being of an inquiring nature, I . . .'

'A good paper,' said the dragonfly, 'excellent foreign coverage.'

'It said you were a fossil.'

'Excellent foreign coverage,' repeated the dragonfly, 'but not the first bloody idea when it comes to natural history.'

'Are you in fact the world's oldest dragonfly?' I enquired, a question which, when I first embarked upon the slippery slopes of Fleet Street, I had never imagined I should someday put.

'Probably,' it replied. 'I look after myself. Careful diet, no nasty habits, plenty of fresh air, all that. Yes, I go back a bit. Coleridge,' it continued, 'couldn't half swat. I nearly didn't make it out of the Regency, you know. He'd have his work cut out now, though, wouldn't he'

It laughed, at a guess. A strange sound, just beyond description, I'm afraid.

'Yes,' I said, 'you are somewhat large, for a dragonfly.'

' 'Course I am, son, 'course I am. I've had the time.'

'And, er, surprisingly articulate.'

'In several languages, though I says it as shouldn't. Were you, for example, a Jap, we'd be nattering away in Nipponese like nobody's business, swopping Jap jokes, all that. Or Swahili, French, Norse, you name it. I've been about, son. I have stood on Thomas Mann's window-sill before now. Ferdinand de Lesseps once pointed me out to his uncle. I also,' and here it nudged me, an experience, given the choice, I should have declined, 'know the identify of Jack the Ripper. But I am not letting on.'

'I see,' I lied.

'It would involve,' said the dragonfly, 'betraying a lady's confidence.'

'Ah.'

'You have to remember,' said the dragonfly, 'I grew up at a time when such considerations were not treated with derision. Call me,' it murmured, 'old-fashioned, if you will.'

'No, no!' I cried, 'I should not dream of it.'

'The world,' said the dragonfly, fixing me with its thousand-faceted eye, 'is going up the spout, in my considered view. Punk rock, soya substitute, nylon carpeting, Kerry Packer, aluminium skis, gay lib, bingo, soft bog-paper, electric toothbrushes. And as for this new Dennis Potter rubbish . . .'

'You have obviously,' I said, 'a thoughtful turn of a mind for an, er . . .'

'Insect, yes. Do not show your appalling ignorance, son. If you turn to volume seven of the *Encyclopaedia Britannica*, page 623 as I recall, you will find the following perceptive remark: "The dragonfly's life is encompassed and guided by vision. It is, however, a mosaic vision." How about *that* for openers?'

'I did indeed read it up before coming down here,' I said. 'I thought the mosaic vision referred to merely concerned the structure of . . .'

The dragonfly turned its bizarre eye upon me again. It glittered like those mirrored orbs that turn slowly above Mecca dance-floors.

'We have already established,' it said, menacingly soft, 'just how much you bloody know about people of the hexapod persuasion.' It turned its huge blue head away from the lamplight. 'Mosaic vision,' it murmured. 'One sees all, one knows all, one is in full possession of the route concerning the Promised Land, one is doomed to stand upon the sidelines and watch the human scrimmage kick itself to ruination. It is,' said the world's oldest dragonfly, 'one of the reasons I am down the bleeding pit.'

'I was going to ask you about that,' I said.

''Course you were, son, 'course you were,' said the dragonfly patiently. 'That is all journalism is, nowadays. Do you hope for a peaceful settlement, despite your enormous tits do you one day hope to become a serious actress, why do you think your book about an underwater vet is top of the best-seller lists, is there any truth in the rumour that you have signed to open the batting for Saudi Arabia, what is your view of the uncertainty regarding the dollar as of this moment in time, just how *much* of a threat is Concorde to the Heavyside Layer? We have come a long way,' muttered the dragonfly, 'from W. T. Stead and Geoffrey Dawson and C. P. Scott and Nat Gubbins. I have had,' it continued, tapping my knee with a fearful foreleg, 'four million sexual couplings of one kind and another. Have you any idea of the disgusting fight there would be in what presently calls itself Fleet Street were I to put my memoirs on the open market?'

'*Four million?*'

'Give or take. I stopped counting after the 1851 Exhibition. The dragonfly has the right attitude to sex, son: the act takes place at a combined velocity of sixty miles per hour. There is consequently no time for unseemly mucking about, no groping behind bus shelters and similar, no post-coital mooning, no doubts concerning impending impotence or multiple orgasm, no discussion of who is treating whom as a sex object, no bogus mysticism elevating simple genetic mechanics beyond their basic significance, no guilt, no fear, no interminable magazine articles or panel discussions—in rather more than three million of my own encounters I did not even have time to catch the name of my beloved.' It sighed, I felt. A sort of melancholy exhalation through the scales. 'That is another reason I am down here. There is no fun in anything any more.'

'When,' I asked, 'did you retire to this pit?'

'Christmas,' replied the dragonfly. 'I had been thinking

about it for some time, mind. What finally persuaded me, I cannot exactly put a name to—no illuminated angels in Regent Street, possibly, the failure of the Rhodesian initiative, perhaps, the fact that bits were falling off Morris Marinas all over the world, the pitiful inadequacy of the Sadat peace plan, the revaluation of the green pound, the rise of Billy Carter, the announcement of ITV's spring schedules, Dutch elm disease, the Horn of Africa, Margaret Thatcher, the Socialist Workers Party, Roddy Llewellyn . . . who can say?'

'Will you never return to the surface?'

It spread four of its legs expressively, balancing brilliantly on the remaining two.

'What point is there?' it cried. 'The world is too much with us, late and soon—a fool, Wordsworth, but nobody to touch him when it came to moaning, I used to watch him stare at mud, it was an education, I don't mind saying. I have had life up to here, son. I shall remain in the pit, with my memories. It is the most sensible course.'

'That may be true,' I said. 'However, today is March 21st.'

'So?'

'It is the first day of Spring,' I said.

The world's oldest dragonfly turned its amazing eye upon me once again. The gleaming facets, if I was not mistaken, had lost a little of their diamantine cynicism.

'Oh, bloody hell, all right!' it said, irritably. 'But I'm only coming up for a bit, mind.'

The Rhinestone As Big As The Ritz

Go Easy, Mr Beethoven,
That Was Your Fifth!

"Shrunk to half its proper size, leathery in consistency and greenish-blue in colour, with bean-sized nodules on its surface." Yes, readers, I am of course describing Ludwig van Beethoven's liver, and I do apologise for going over such familiar ground, but I wanted to put the less musical members of my flock in the picture right from the start. I think they also ought to know that his spleen was more than double its proper size: far too many *soi-disant* music-lovers these days, when they drop the pick-up on *Egmont* or the *Eroica* and retire to their chaise longue for a quick listen, think to themselves *Poor old sod, he was deaf as a brick,* and leave it at that, entirely neglecting the fact that beneath the deaf-aid on his waistcoat Herr van Beethoven sported as misshapen a collection of offal as you could shake a stick at, including a pancreas the size of a pickled walnut and a length of intestine that could have been mistaken for pipe-lagging by all but the most astute German plumber.

I am reminded of all this internal strife by today's *Guardian*, which, in its copy-hungry turn, quotes from the current issue of the *Journal of Alcoholism*, a periodical of which I had not previously heard. Which is odd, since if I'm not on their mailing-list, who is? At all events, this bizarre broadsheet has clearly decided that it is not going to be outdone in Ludwig's bicentenary year by all the other mags, and has hopped aboard the wagon, if they'll pardon the expression, with a succinct length of verbiage by one Doctor Madden, consultant psychiatrist at a Chester hospital addiction unit. He it is whom I quote at the beginning of this *feuilleton*, and if I may say so, Doctor, as one

61

stylist to another, I have rarely encountered so well-turned a memorial to a great man. Why that sentence was not chiselled on Ludwig van Beethoven's gravestone, I shall never know. I gather you've translated it from the report of his autopsy, and it may be that it reads even better in German, but I doubt it: poetry is what "bean-sized nodule" is, and don't let anyone tell you otherwise. Indeed, you may well have altered the listening habits of an entire generation: how shall any of us be able to tune in to *Fidelio* again, without the tears springing to our eyes at the memory of the greenish-blue liver behind it? Will our rapture at the *Emperor* not be intensified beyond measure by the thought of that gigantic spleen, throbbing away like a ship's boiler under the composer's vest?

One flaw, however, mars the sunny scholarship of your piece: not content to commemorate the bicentenary merely by your thrilling evocation of distorted bowel and giblet and leaving it at that, you insist, I'm afraid, on going on to moralise. And it's none of your business, Doc. Having broken the unethical news that Ludwig's organs got this way through a daily consumption of booze that could have floated a Steinway down Kaiserstrasse, you then wind up the scoop with the homiletic clincher: "Beethoven had a brain and mind capable of many years of musical productivity, had his life not been shortened by alcohol." Now, I realise that this oleaginous aside may have been the result of editorial pressure, and that if you hadn't put it in all your readers might have rushed out immediately and begun hitting the sauce in the hope of coming up with a quartet or two, but couldn't you have turned the sentiment a little less harshly? And aren't you being just a teeny bit demanding? Aren't nine symphonies, thirty-two piano sonatas, seven concertos, two masses, sixteen string quartets, and two suit-casefuls of quintets enough for you and the rest of mankind?

And don't you perhaps feel that, after that lot, posterity owes Ludwig a little snort or two?

I suppose not. All human life is divided between those who order by the crate and those who believe that sherry trifle leads to the everlasting bonfire, and never the twain shall meet except on the sodden salient of the *Journal of Alcoholism* for such brief and bitter skirmishes as the one filleted above. You're on one side, Doc, and Ludwig and I are on the other. My own conclusion would be diametrically different from yours, viz, that if Beethoven had *not* been a regular supplier of empties to the trade, he wouldn't have written anything at all, and how does that grab you, abstemious musicologists? If the great man had been confined to Lucozade on the advice of Chester's addiction unit, my bet is that he'd have thrown in the towel at *Chopsticks* and gone down in history as a mediocre hosier.

Because it is no accident that all men of creative genius have toiled in the shadow of the corkscrew—how else is a giant to survive among pygmies, make the mundane tolerable, fence himself off from the encroachments of numbing normalcy? How but through regular intakes of fermented anaesthetic are we—there, I've said it—artists to stave off the canvas jacket and the screaming abdab? How must Beethoven have felt of a morning, his head full of whirling crotchets and jangling semi-breves, to have his housekeeper running off at the gob about the price of vermicelli, or shrieking through his blessed deafness in an attempt to bring home to him the immutable truth that if you send six pillow-cases to the laundry, you only ever get five back? Is it any wonder that he followed up his Special K with a few quick chasers of schnapps? Do you for one moment imagine that the Piano Concerto No. 4 in G Major was written by a teetotaller, given the fact that the decorators were in the haus at the time, Beethoven's shoes hadn't come back from the cobblers, he was four months overdue on his Schedule D payment, his mistress had run off with a door-to-door wurst salesman, and the dog had just trodden on his glasses?

And, worst of all, people like you, Doctor Madden, were constantly nagging him to get on with the bloody music, what about a couple of quick symphonies to follow up the 9th, shouldn't take you more than an hour or so to rattle 'em off, mate, and how would you like to address the Rotarians next Wednesday night, dress formal, and isn't it time you did a personal tour of Silesia, and by the way it's the Prime Minister's birthday coming up, so could you see your way clear to knocking out a little celebratory sextet, no fee naturally, oh yes, I nearly forgot, my wife's brother plays the triangle, not professional of course, but we all think he's rather good, so I've arranged a little dinner-party next Friday to give you the chance of hearing him . . .

I'm amazed his nodules didn't get any bigger than beans, all things considered.

It's a dodgy tightrope along which we creators wobble, Doc: enough booze to close the world off and keep us inventing, but not so much that we allow the golden haze to settle on us permanently, while the piano-strings slacken, and the typewriter rusts, and the brushes dry out and go stiff, and the public yawns and goes off in search of fresh fodder, muttering about what an inconsiderate bleeder that Shakespeare was, snuffing it in his fifties and leaving us with little more than *Lear, Hamlet, Macbeth, Othello, Anthony and Cleopatra*, well I'm not surprised, you know what they say, he couldn't leave the stuff alone, liver like a dried pea, well that's the trouble with artists, isn't it, hoity-toity, too good for the rest of us, they've got to be different, haven't they, bloody bohemians the lot of them, load of boozers, junkies, fairies, layabouts, I mean to say, *only nine symphonies, only thirty plays, only ten novels, only ONE Sistine Chapel* (they say he was so pissed he couldn't get up the ladder), I mean, what do you expect?

Et in El Vino ego, Doc. In a small way, of course. What might *I* not have done, be doing, were it not for the lure of the barmaid's pinny and the brass-handled pump? Ah, the first chapters I have! What prolegomena! What flyleaf notes! A thousand words of the best, then it's off to the local for a self-congratulatory belt, and when I roll home, in a day or two, all is ashes, forgotten, dead. How was it going to go on, this trilogy, before those bottles intervened? Who was this character, and this, and who cares, now? Ah, those publishers' lunches, yes, I'll do a novel, yes, I have this wonderful idea, he meets her, see, and they go off to Ensenada, and her husband, broken by drugs and a lifetime of inferior diplomacy, kills his mistress, let's have another bottle of this excellent Mouton Cadet, but their son returns from the Congo where his mercenary activities have involved him with none other than, my goodness this *is* an amicable cognac, oh yes, you should certainly have the first draft by February, as you say, it's a natural, film rights alone should bring us in . . .

And I wake up in a Turkish bath, some time later, and can only remember that I had my umbrella when I left the house, but was it in the cab, or was it in the restaurant, or am I thinking of my raincoat?

Well, that's it, Doc, another thousand words, another bottle. And that's all you'll get from me today. All I ask is that when my liver and I kick off, and the *Journal of Alcoholism* rings up for a few succinct remarks on posterity's loss, you'll recall all this, and understand a little.

It may surprise you, but I'd hate to be remembered as just another greenish-blue liver, shrunk to half its proper size.

The Sanity Inspector

Your Teeth in Their Hands

*According to a report commissioned by the General Dental Practitioners'
Association, the average dentist is "oppressed by health, ageing, status
ambiguity, social paranoia and social isolation, and has become neurotic
over his inability to achieve the same social recognition as the medical
practitioner". What dentistry requires, clearly, is a new Image, a Folk
Myth, a Kildare or Ben Casey – in short, a Great Romantic Hero.*

The Story So Far: When tall, azure-eyed, blond-haired undergrad
Lord Dunromin flees Oxford two days after stroking his boat to
victory, London's social world is flung into baffled misery. His
unutterably beautiful fiancée, model girl Princess Doreen of Labia,
receives a note from the West London Air Terminal saying that
Dunromin has decided to shoulder the blame for his guardsman
brother's indiscretions in St. James's Park, and leave England forever.
Relinquishing his title, he joins the French Foreign Legion as plain
Garth Genesis, and is immediately posted to the immeasurably disgusting Fort Zinderneuf, deep in the Sahara. The camp dentist has
contracted *le cafard* and pliered himself to death, and the morale of the
men is exceeding low: racked by caries, halitosis, gingivitis and
Bedouin tongue-acne, they are ill-equipped to defend themselves
against the hordes of crazed Touaregs who, fitted out with Oxfam
dentures and Czech machine-guns, are preparing for their final assault
on the garrison. But they have reckoned without Garth Genesis, whose
enormous (yet amazingly witty) brain has applied itself to the task of
learning the dentist's art: within days, aided only by a tawny, half-
naked beauty from Lille (who called at the fort to sell vacuum-
cleaners), Garth completely re-establishes dental hygiene among the
men, working through the night by the dim light of a burning
prisoner to fill holes, extract deficient molars, build sturdy bridgework
until the regiment's teeth are the pride of the Legion. After the
Touaregs are overwhelmingly defeated, Garth Genesis is awarded the
Croix de Guerre, the Legion d'Honneur, and the B.D.S. and bar. By
this time, his brother has confessed his crimes and opened fourteen
male boutiques on the proceeds, whereupon Garth Genesis, after
saving an upper Number Four of a visiting dignitary close to de Gaulle,

is given an honourable discharge. He returns to England and a knighthood for services to Anglo-French relations, and sets up a surgery in Wimpole Street. Soon afterwards, however, a third cousin of the Queen for whom he has been designing a set of evening teeth and matching ear-rings, falls hopelessly in love with him and leaves her husband. *NOW READ ON:*

The Hon. Fenella Strume-Clavering's lovelorn eyes gazed down, intoxicated, as Garth Genesis's lithe fingers probed and caressed the dark, secret places of her mouth. They were the fingers of a dentist: strong, lean, tanned. Virile. Her heart pounded.

"Spit," he said.

She turned her exquisite head, bent over the bowl, unable to spit; a single tear rolled down her nose and splashed against the immaculate porcelain.

"You realise, madame," said Genesis levelly, "that there is absolutely nothing wrong with your teeth?"

She looked away from his unfathomable blue eyes.

"Yes," she whispered. "I know. But I had to come. I had——"

A bell tinkled, and Genesis sprang across to the instrument in one bound with the easy power of a panther trained to answer telephones. He listened, his fine brow furrowing.

"I'll be right over. Do nothing till I arrive."

He replaced the receiver, and turned once more to his ravishing patient.

"That was the Chief Commissioner," he said. "There's a chap at the top of the Millbank Tower threatening to throw himself off. I have to go."

Their eyes met for an enigmatic instant, and she flashed him a brave smile which he had done so much to create. Not for nothing was he known throughout the civilised world as the Benvenuto Cellini of the platinum inlay. He turned on a handshod heel and, in a whiff of lingering halothane, was gone.

*　　*　　*

A gale was shrieking round the roof, as Garth Genesis leapt from the service elevator: only for a second did he allow himself to glance down at the minuscule details of London, four hundred teetering feet below. Then, with a cry of "Let me through, I'm a dentist!" he plunged into the mass of doctors, archbishops, psychiatrists, journalists and back-bench politicians, all of whom instantly fell back reverently to let him pass. Beyond, at the very edge of the overhang, a man instantly recognisable as a TV personality loved by millions hovered between life and pavement. At the sight of Genesis, the matinée idol face broke into a wretched smile: the crowd gasped. Within the famous mouth, the rotted teeth hung like tiny salamis in some toytown delicatessen. "My career is at an end!" moaned the star; but a strong hand flew out to save and comfort. "Nonsense!" cried the great dentist. "Merely a case of arc-light rot. Put yourself in my hands: together we shall save you for posterity!" Weeping, the star stepped slowly back into the land of the living, and, as swiftly as he had come, Garth Genesis left once more. Behind him, the gale plucked the cheers from the mouths of tycoons and clerics and scattered them across a grateful land.

★　★　★

"Gargle, please!"

The Hon. Fenella Strume-Clavering dribbled miserably into the bowl, while her delectable tongue nudged numbly at the gap left by a vanished tooth. It had been a perfectly good canine, and only a fit of wild hysterics on her part had finally persuaded Genesis to extract it for what he had managed to convince himself were psychological reasons. For her, it had not seemed too high a price to pay for one more fleeting visit. She looked up at him with moist eyes.

"I hag leg my hugban!" she cried.

"Please try not to talk," he said gently.

"You doe uggertag!" shrieked the Hon. Fenella. "I hag leg my hugban!"

The great dentist frowned.

"You have left your husband?"

"Yeg!"

He smiled, and his splendid eyebrows rippled deliciously.

"It's merely the effect of the anaesthetic, dear lady," he said. "You'll feel perfectly all right in an hour or so."

Whereupon he bowed, left her in the care of his lovely nurse, and went to keep an appointment with the Prime Minister.

★　★　★

"Frankly and freely," said the Prime Minister, "and I do mean that sincerely, I find myself, as we all of us do, sometimes—I'm sure you yourself do—faced with something of a problem. It's a problem in which we all have a share, it's a problem I know we can lick if we just set aside our little personal differences for a short while, and pull together in this great—and I do mean

great, I mean it most sincerely—this great country of ours. Frankly, fearlessly, honestly——"

"What exactly is the problem, Prime Minister?" said Garth Genesis, from his comfortable fauteuil opposite the throne.

"It's my smile," said the PM.

"Your smile?"

"It's been a good smile, I won't deny that," said the PM. "It's been frank, and fearless, and honest, and sincere for a good three years now, and I don't have to tell you what a strain that puts on the cheeks."

"The burdens of office, Prime Minister."

"Quite. But now, as we move together into the darkening storm, and the shadow of unemployment falls across this great country and my salary, I feel I need something a little special. Something noble. Saintly, almost."

Garth Genesis stood up and handed the PM his hand-tooled pattern book, indicating a couple of possible designs. The Prime Minister's tiny eyes lit up.

"Those!" he cried.

"Impeccable, Prime Minister!" said Garth Genesis. "Joan of Arc upper plate, with a Nelson Eddy lower. And just a suggestion of Attila the Hun, perhaps, at the edges? For integrity?"

"Perfect!" cried the PM, clapping his hands. "Perfect! What can I offer you in return? Ask and it shall be given."

*   *   *

The Hon. Fenella Strume-Clavering spat wretchedly, watched her blood swirl away into the sewage system with lead upon her heart. It was her fourteenth extraction.

"Now you're Goreign Gecretary," she whimpered, "I guppoge you'll gig up gentitry?"

"*Au contraire,*" said Genesis, wiping his wonderful hands on a scented towel, "I shall always be a dentist first, and a Foreign Secretary second." His fine eyes veiled nobly. "Once dentistry gets into a man's blood, once he feels the pulse of the drill in his fingers, the smell of floss in his nostrils, he has given up more than his life, madame. He has given up his soul!"

The Hon. Fenella groped beneath her bloodstained gown and flung out a hand to touch his.

"Gake me wig you!" she cried. "I lug you, Gark!"

He stepped back, hand to his brow.

"I cannot, madame! I fear that destiny has shaped me for other ends. As a statesman, nay, as a dentist, I may not allow the slightest taint to

69

impeach my honour and the honour of my calling! Return to your husband! Return to your little ones!" He paused a moment, and glanced down at his distracted slave. "Besides, madame, have I not this very instant removed your last remaining natural tooth? How could you thus take your place beside me, the first dental Foreign Secretary the world has ever seen, and you with nought but a mouthful of gums?"

With an unearthly, fearful shriek, the Hon. Fenella Strume-Clavering cast off her gown and staggered from the chair that had borne her through so many long years of unrequited passion. The surgery doors swung shut, and her gummy moans faded on the Marylebone air.

But the Rt. Hon. Garth Genesis, B.D.S., heeded them not. Bathed in the roseate glow of an English evening, his handsome form stood silhouetted in the surgery window, gazing out upon the teeth and embassies that awaited him, somewhere beyond the setting sun.

All Except The Bastard

All You Need To Know About Europe

GERMANY

The People
Germans are split into two broad categories: those with tall spikes on their hats, and those with briefcases. Up until 1945, the country's history was made by those with spikes. After 1945, it was made by those with briefcases. In common with the rest of Europe, its history is therefore now known as economics. Ethnically, the Germans are Teutonic, but prefer not to talk about it any more. This ethnos was originally triform, being made up of Vandals, Gepidae, and Goths, all of whom emigrated south from Sweden in about 500 BC; why they emigrated is not exactly clear, but many scholars believe it was because they saw the way Sweden was going, i.e. neutral. Physically, Germans are tall and blond, though not as tall and blond as they sometimes think, especially when they are short, dark Austrians with a sense of destiny. When they sing, the Germans link arms and rock sideways; it is best described as horizontal marching.

The Land
The country, or *Lebensraum*, is extremely beautiful and situated in the very centre of Europe, thus lending itself to expansion in any direction, a temptation first succumbed to in the fifth century AD (the *Volkerwanderung*) when Germany embraced most of Spain, and regularly indulged in since. It is interesting to note that this summer there will be three million Germans in Spain, thus outnumbering the first excursion by almost a hundred to one.

The History
For almost two thousand years, Germany was split into separate states that fought one another. In the nineteenth century, they combined and began fighting everyone else.

71

They are currently split up again and once more fighting one another. If they combine, the result is anybody's guess. Having lost the last war, they are currently enjoying a *Wirtschaftswunder*, which can be briefly translated as "The best way to own a Mercedes is to build one." That is about all there is to German history, since no one has ever known what was going on, and if this is the case, then the Truth cannot be said to exist. Germany has, as you can see, provided many of the world's greatest philosophers.

BELGIUM

The People
Belgium is the most densely populated country in Europe, and is at the same time fiercely divided on the subjects of language and religion. This means that it is impossible to move anywhere in the country, which is packed with mobs standing chin to chin and screaming incomprehensible things at one another in the certain knowledge that God is on their side, whoever He is. That there has not been more bloodshed is entirely due to the fact that there isn't room to swing a fist. Consequently, what the Belgian authorities most fear is contraception: if it ever catches on, and the population thins to the point where rifles may be comfortably unslung from shoulders, the entire nation might disappear overnight.

The Land
The land is entirely invisible, except in the small hours of the morning, being for the rest of the time completely underfoot. It is therefore no surprise to learn that Belgium's largest industries are coal and mineral mining, as underground is the only place where there is room to work. Plans have been suggested for reclaiming land from the sea, on the Dutch pattern, but were always shelved as soon as it was realised that there was neither room for the water that would have to

be removed from the sea, nor, alternatively, any spare land to spread to extend the coastline outwards.

The History

Belgium has always suffered horribly at the hands of occupying forces, which, given the overcrowding, is only to be expected. The bayoneting of babies by Prussians, for example, was never intentional; it was simply that it was impossible to walk about with fixed bayonets in such confined spaces without finding something stuck on the end of them. For the same reason, the sprout was developed by Brussels agronomists, this being the largest cabbage a housewife could possibly carry through the teeming streets.

FRANCE

The People

The French are our closest neighbours, and we are therefore bound to them by bonds of jealousy, suspicion, competition, and envy. They haven't brought the shears back, either. They are short, blue-vested people who carry their own onions when cycling abroad, and have a yard which is 3.37 inches longer than other people's. Their vanity does not stop there: they believe themselves to be great lovers, an easy trap to fall into when you're permanently drunk, and the natural heirs to Europe. It has been explained to them that there is a difference between natural heirs and legitimate heirs, but they cannot appreciate subtle distinctions, probably because French has the smallest vocabulary of any language in Europe.

The Land

France is the largest country in Europe, a great boon for drunks, who need room to fall, and consists of an enormous number of bars linked by an intricate system of serpentine cobbles. Exactly why France is so cobbled has never been fully explained, though most authorities favour the view that the French like to be constantly reminded of the feel of grapes underfoot. The houses are all shuttered to exclude light, as a precaution against hangovers, and filled with large lumpy beds in which the French spend 83.7 per cent of their time recovering from sex or booze or both. The lumpiness is due, of course, to the presence of undeclared income under the mattresses.

The History

French history, or "gloire" starts with Charlemagne, and ends with Charlemagne. Anything subsequent was in the hands of bizarre paranoiacs who thought they were God (Louis XIV) or thought they were Charlemagne (Napoleon) or thought they were God and Louis XIV and Charlemagne and Napoleon (de Gaulle). Like most other European nations, the French have fought everyone, but unlike the rest have always claimed that both victories and defeats came after opposition to overwhelming odds. This is probably because they always saw two of everything.

LUXEMBOURG

The People

There are nine people in Luxembourg, and they are kept pretty busy making stamps. It is not the smallest country in Europe: there are only eight people in Monaco, five in Andorra, and Herr J. F. Klausner in Liechtenstein, so as the fourth non-smallest country in Europe, it enjoys a rather unique position. The people are of middle height, with the small, deft fingers of master-perforators, and all look rather alike, except for their Uncle Maurice who lost an ear on the Somme. They are a rather arrogant people (they refer to World War I as the Battle of Maurice's Ear) but not un-artistic: *My Day At The Zoo*, by the country's infant prodigy, ran into nine copies and won the Prix Maurice for 1969.

The Land

On a clear day, from the terrace of the Salon de Philatelie, you can't see Luxembourg at all. This is because a tree is in the way. Beyond the tree lies Belgium. The centre of the country is, however, very high, mainly because of the chimney on it, and slopes down to a great expanse of water, as they haven't got around to having the bathroom overflow pipe fixed. The climate is temperate (remember that ninety per cent of Luxembourg is indoors) and the local Flora is varied and interesting, especially on her favourite topic, the 1908 five-cent blue triangular.

The History

Old Luxembourg (now the coal-cellar of the modern country), was founded in the twelfth century by King John of Bohemia, who wanted somewhere to keep the lawn-mower. It escaped most of the wars and pestilences that swept Europe in the subsequent eight centuries, often because the people were out when they called, and is therefore one of the most stable political and economic elements in the EEC: its trade-balance is always favourable (imports come in at the back gate and leave by the front door as exports). Luxembourg is also the oldest ally of Stanley Gibbons Ltd., although it is probably most famous as the birthplace of Horace Batchelor.

NETHERLANDS

The People

Like the Germans, the Dutch fall into two quite distinct physical types: the small, corpulent, red-faced Edams, and the thinner, paler, larger Goudas. As one might expect of a race that evolved underwater and subsisted entirely upon cheese, the Dutch are somewhat single-minded, conservative, resilient, and thoughtful. Indeed, the sea informs their entire culture: the bicycle, that ubiquitous Dutch vehicle, was designed to facilitate underwater travel, offering least resistance to waves and weed, the clog was introduced to weigh down the feet and prevent drifting, and the meerschaum pipe, with its characteristic lid, was designed expressly to exclude fish and the larger plankton. And those who would accuse the Dutch of overeating would do well to reflect on the notorious frangibility of dykes: it's no joke being isolated atop a flooded windmill with nothing to eat but passing tulips. You have to get it while you can.

The Land

Strictly speaking, the land does not exist: it is merely dehydrated sea, and concern was originally expressed when the EEC was first mooted that the Six might suddenly turn into the Five after a bad night. Many informed observers believe that this fear is all that lies behind the acceptance of Britain's membership, i.e. we are a sort of First Reserve in case Rain Stops Holland. Nevertheless, it is interesting country, sweeping up from the coastal plain into the central massif, a two-foot high ridge of attractive silt with fabulous views of the sky, and down again to the valleys, inches below. Apart from cheese and tulips, the main product of the country is advocaat, a drink made from lawyers.

The History

Incensed by poor jokes about the Low Countries, the Dutch, having emerged from the sea, became an extremely belligerent people, taking on Spain, France, England, and Austria in quick succession, a characteristic that has almost entirely disappeared from the modern Dutch temperament. It is now found only among expatriate Dutchmen, like Orangemen and Afrikaaners.

ITALY

The People

The median Italian, according to the latest figures of the

Coren Intelligence Unit, is a cowardly baritone who consumes 78.3 kilometres of carbohydrates a month and drives about in a car slightly smaller than he is, looking for a divorce. He is governed by a stable conservative government, called the Mafia, who operate an efficient police force, called the Mafia, which is the official arm of the judiciary, called the Mafia. The Italians are an extremely cultivated folk, and will often walk miles to sell a tourist a copy of the Sistine Chapel ceiling made entirely from sea-shells. They invented the mandoline, a kind of boudoir banjo shaped like a woman's bottom, not surprisingly.

The Land
Italy is boot-shaped, for reasons lost in the mists of geology. The South is essentially agricultural, and administered by local land authorities, called the Mafia; the North is industrial, and run by tightly interlocked corporations, called the Mafia. The largest Italian city is New York, and is linked to the mainland by a highly specialised and efficient communications system, called the Mafia.

The History
Italy was originally called Rome, which came to hold power over Europe by moving into new areas every week or so and threatening to lean on them if they did not fork out tithe (L. *protectio*). It was run by a series of Caesars (Eduardus Gaius Robinsonius, Georgius Raftus, Paulus Munius, etc.) who held sway until the Renaissance, when Leonardo invented the tank and the aeroplane, and thus ushered in modern Italy (in World War II, the Italians, ever brilliant, possessed the only tank with a reverse gear). In the 1920s, the Caesars reasserted themselves in their two main linear branches, the Caponi and the Mussolini, whose symbol was the fasces, which signified "United We Stand," but they didn't.

The Sanity Inspector

77

Half A Pound Of Tuppeny Vice

'When police raided the Love Inn, where the Cambridge rapist had been a customer, the owner was alleged to have said: "There is nothing here. This is just a little family sex shop" '—Daily Telegraph

ON THE KNOTTY rustic lintel beneath the sign of Ye Olde Curiositie Shoppe, the little bell tinkled.

Behind the dusty counter on which lay the dismembered cogs of a cheap Hong Kong dildo into which he was vainly struggling to fit a new mainspring, the proprietor (*Jas. Rumbelow*, ran his copperplate letterheads, *Purveyor of Fyne Thynges to the Gentrie since 1926*) looked up over the gold rims of his bifocals. He laid aside his screwdriver, and beamed.

'Good morning, Mrs Curtoise,' he said.

'Good morning, Mr Rumbelow,' said the customer, a middle-aged lady in a bottle-green swagger coat, lisle stockings, and a hat with three petals missing, 'I was just wondering if you had them gold latex peephole bras and matching suspender belts with the exposé divided-leg panties showing flags of all nations in yet?'

Rumbelow shuffled to the back of the shop, bent over, and shouted down an open trapdoor into the basement.

'Vera, we got any of them Goodnight Las Vegas in a 46?' He turned, on the half crouch, towards the customer. 'It was a 46, wasn't it?'

'Yes. And a 52 hip.'

'And a 52 hip!' shouted Rumbelow, into the darkness.

Scuffling came up through the trap door, counterpointed with spasmodic wheezing and the noise of boxes falling. The stepladder squeaked, and an elderly pink face appeared. A *Penthouse* gatefold was caught in her hairnet by its staple.

'Good morning, Mrs Curtoise.'

'Morning, Mrs Rumbelow. Did you find one?'

Mrs Rumbelow creaked up the last few steps, and into the shop. She shook her head, and the gatefold fluttered to the floor.

'Nearest I come was a 44,' she said, 'but I wouldn't advise it. They give you shocking wind at the best of time, them things. Last thing you want is too small. How about a nice black leather catsuit? I can do that in a 46.'

The customer shook her head.

'Leather doesn't agree with Mr Curtoise,' she said. 'It makes him sneeze in warm weather.'

Rumbelow nodded sympathetically.

'That'll be the tannin,' he said. 'It's like me and rubber, isn't it, Mother?'

'It's like him and rubber,' said his wife. 'We got one of them water-beds off a traveller. A wossname, a sample. Anyway, we filled it off of the upstairs tap, and we got on it, and he was awake all night sneezing, wasn't you? It was like being on the *Titanic*. We was thrown all over the place.'

'I wouldn't have water in the bedroom,' said Mrs Curtoise. 'Call it superstitious, but my old mum used to say "Water in the bedroom, you'll only have girls." '

'I know, I know,' said Mrs Rumbelow. 'I'm the same about lupins.'

'It's a pity about the Goodnight Las Vegas,' said Mrs Curtoise. 'Mr Curtoise'll be ever so disappointed. He put off a Rotary executive meeting specially. I don't know what we'll do tonight, now.'

'There's a new film up the church hall,' said Rumbelow. '*Take Me I'm Scandinavian And My Old Man's On Nights.*'

'We seen it on holiday,' said Mrs Curtoise. 'It's in black and white.'

'What a liberty!' cried Rumbelow. 'There's no pride in workmanship these days.'

'Young people,' sighed Mrs Rumbelow, 'there's no respect.'

'I blame the bomb,' said Mrs Curtoise.

'The Conservatives,' said Rumbelow, 'wouldn't do any better.'

'They're all as bad as one another,' said Mrs Curtoise.

Mrs Rumbelow looked at her.

'I never realised you was political, Mrs Curtoise,' she said.

Mrs Curtoise sighed.

'You got to be,' she said, 'these days. Well, must be off. There's all Mr Curtoise's tights to iron. He likes a nice crease.'

'He wouldn't be an Area Sales Manager,' said Rumbelow, 'if he didn't.'

'Since you haven't got the Goodnight Las Vegas,' said Mrs Curtoise, 'I'll just take a quarter of aphrodisiac toffees.'

Rumbelow shooed the cat away from the confectionery shelf, took down a large jar, unscrewed it, and shook some of its contents into his scale-pan. He watched the needle carefully, added another sweet, filled a paper bag, and flipped it adroitly.

'When you eat them,' he said, handing the bag over, 'don't forget to take your teeth out. They're like bloody Bostik, pardon my French.'

'I know,' said Mrs Curtoise. 'Mr Curtoise thinks they put something in them.'

'Wouldn't surprise me at all,' said Rumbelow. 'Good day.'

The bell tinkled. Rumbelow watched the door swing shut.

'Good job she never took that catsuit,' he said. 'With her varicose veins, she'd have swolled up something shocking. You'd have to soap her to get her out of it. Like boys' heads in railings.'

'Funny you should say that,' said his wife. 'Only yesterday, man came in, wanted a set of railings to stick his head through. You was out in the smallest room at the time, begging your pardon, Father. So I told him we didn't go in for that sort of thing.'

'Only got so much space, haven't we?' Rumbelow indicated the teetering piles of boxes, the stuffed shelves, the heaps of cellophane-covered books that littered the floor. 'Start catering for all tastes, where will it end? Come in for railings one day, next day it'll be railings *and* small boys already conveniently stuck in 'em.'

'Like that fellow last Tuesday,' said his wife, 'coming in here, big as you please, asking for a packet of Welsh letters. Where do you think you are, I said, Marks and Spencers?'

'Quite right, Mother,' said Rumbelow. 'People today, it's incredible! When my old dad started this business up, you could make a nice little living out of nothing more than a slab of prawns and a half gross of Spanish Fly!'

The bell tinkled again, and a thin fifty-ish man came into the shop, dragging what might have been his misshapen shadow.

'Morning, Mr Collinson,' said Rumbelow. 'What's that you've got there?'

Collinson hoiked the thing up off the floor and draped it over the counter.

'That,' he muttered, and his voice was tense, and his pointing finger shook, '*that* is Miss Mary Wonderful, 38-22-36 When Inflated. Or was.'

'Was?' said Rumbelow.

'Woke up this morning,' said Collinson bitterly, 'and there she was, lying beside me, like a burst inner-tube.'

'Well,' said Rumbelow, 'that's what she, er, was, basically, Mr Collinson.'

Collinson glowered at him.

'That's not what you said when I bloody bought her!' he cried. 'Five-feet-two of delectable rubber pulchritude, you said. Just the companion for those lonely winter evenings, you said.'

'I was reading off the box,' said Rumbelow. 'I don't test 'em all personal.'

'She's perished!' shrieked Collinson. He held up the flaccid corpse, and light shone through its perforated bust. 'My beloved is perished! £14.75, excluding pump, and all I got to show is a load of rubber bands!'

Rumbelow pushed his glasses up onto his forehead and peered at the wreck.

'It looks to me like the dog's been at her,' he said. 'That's never fair wear and tear. You haven't left her lying about, have you?'

'Lying about? LYING ABOUT? What do you take me for? I went to a grammar school. Women have always been treated with utmost respect on my premises! The dog's never off his chain.'

Rumbelow cleared his throat, awkwardly.

'Mr Collinson,' he said, 'you haven't, as it were, bitten her yourself, have you?'

'Bitten her *myself*?' screamed Collinson. 'I wouldn't take such liberties! I hardly know her. I've only had her out of the box twice, to watch *Upstairs, Downstairs* with me. You can't rush things. Call me old-fashioned, but that's how I am. *And* I want my money back!'

'You could patch her,' offered Mrs Rumbelow, who had come back in to feed the parrot, 'couldn't you?'

'Ho, yes, I should bleedin cocoa!' shouted Collinson. 'Very erotic, that! For them as likes nipping into bed with a second-hand bike, it'd be just the thing!' He gathered up the tattered rubber, and stuffed it under one arm. 'That does it, Rumbelow! I have shopped here man and boy—and, for a brief period, woman and girl—for thirty-two years! But from now on, it's the new supermarket for me!'

The Rumbelows reeled! The Rumbelows paled!

'THE NEW WHAT?' shrieked Mrs Rumbelow.

Collinson cackled nastily.

'You heard!' he said. 'Four floors of arcane delights, wall-to-wall wossname, free films, seductive music as you browse at your ease, topless experts to help you with your every enquiry, gratis glossy brochures, cheap travel arranged, money back if not at least partially satisfied—*what do you say to that, you old fleabag?*'

With which Collinson spun on his heel, and strode out, the rubber corpse gesticulating beneath his arm like broken bagpipes.

The Rumbelows stared after him.

'A supermarket!' wailed Mrs Rumberlow. 'All chrome and plastic, cold, impersonal! Cheap, vulgar, American! Nobody giving you the time of day, nobody caring, nobody wanting to know! Where is it all going, Father? What will become of us?'

Rumbelow pressed his face against the window, staring out.

'England, what are you doing to yourself?' he murmured.

The Lady From Stalingrad Mansions

The Unacknowledged Legislators of the World

The Poetry Society is falling apart. Rows about personalities, about money, about vanishing booze, fights over control and future plans, mass accusations and resignations have all played their part in what one of the poets has described as the war between poetry and bureaucracy: 'I can't remember when we last talked about poetry at a council meeting' he told the Guardian. *But wasn't it always like that?*

THE MEETING convened at 2.30 pm.

Mr William Wordsworth immediately rose to say, in his own defence, that there was a tree, of many, one, a single field which he had looked upon, both of them spoke of something that was gone; the pansy at his feet did the same tale repeat: whither was fled the visionary gleam? Where was it now, the glory and the dream?

Mr Andrew Marvell said that that was all very well, but it did not justify £28.40 return rail fare to Keswick, plus £14.26 overnight stay at the Come On Inne and £19.70 for a steak dinner for two, plus three bottles of Bulgarian Riesling. There were plenty of trees and fields within walking distance of the Society's premises perfectly capable of raising questions about the disappearance of visionary gleams and similar cod's wallop. Also, he would like to know why the steak dinner was for two people, and did it have anything to do with the pansy at Mr Wordsworth's feet?

Mr Wordsworth replied that he had found love in huts where poor men lie, his daily teachers had been woods and rills, the silence that was in the starry sky, the sleep that was among the lonely hills, and you could not get that kind of thing in Camden

83

Town. As to the steak dinner, he did not see what business it was of anybody else's who had joined him for it.

Mr Marvell said that had they but world enough and time, this coyness, Wordsworth, were no crime, but some of them weren't bloody paperback millionaires and couldn't muck about all day nattering, also this was taxpayers' money and not intended for filling Wordsworth's poofter shepherd oppos with foreign booze. His, Marvell's, mistresses never required more than a bottle of Mackeson's beforehand and a Vesta curry afterwards, never mind a night at the Come On Inne.

Mr Wordsworth said that if he must know, the gentleman referred to was Samuel Taylor Coleridge, exemplar of an imagination, which, in truth, was but another name for absolute power, and clearest insight, amplitude of mind, and Reason in her most exalted mood.

Mr Marvell asked Mr Wordsworth to pull this one, it had bells on. No offence to the Hon Member S. T. Coleridge, but he had recently seen him with an arm round a Chief Petty Officer outside a mission near Albert Dock.

Mr Coleridge replied that it was an ancient mariner and he had stopped one of three. If the other two were here today, he continued, they would corroborate his story. The sailor had an idea for a poem and was looking for someone to go halves with him. Anyway, he had a long grey beard and a glittering eye and was probably old enough to be his, Coleridge's, mother. Father.

Mr John Milton rose to enquire about the sailor's idea: did it have anything to do with Man's first disobedience, and the fruit of that forbidden tree whose mortal taste brought death into the world, and all our woe?

Mr Coleridge said no, he thought it was about a gull or something, why did Mr Milton want to know?

Mr Milton replied that the had paid good money for the idea about Man's first disobedience etc. and was buggered if he was going to see it come out in some tatty down-market form, such as rhyming bloody quatrains, before he had had a go at it. He was envisaging something in about twelve books, it could take weeks.

Mr Alexander Pope asked the Council if they intended subsidising Mr Milton's living expenses while he was knocking out twelve books on fruit. No slur intended, he went on, but he had always considered Mr Milton a bookful blockhead, ignorantly read, with loads of learned lumber in his head. Such laboured nothings, in so strange a style, amazed the unlearned, and made the learned smile. Pardon him, he said, but he spoke as he found.

Mr Milton said Mr Pope was a complicated monster, head and tail, scorpion and asp, and Amphisbaena dire, Cerastes horned, Hydrus and Ellops drear.

Mr Thomas Gray rose to say that this was all very well, but it wasn't getting the cracked pan in the Members' Gents repaired, which was why, so he understood it, the meeting had been convened in the first place. Only yesterday, he said, the caretaker had forbade the wade through water to the throne, and shut the gates of mercy on mankind.

Mr John Greenleaf Whittier enquired as to whether the crack was so wide, so deep, that no man living might this fissure weld?

Mr Milton replied that is was a gulf profound as that Serbonian bog betwixt Damiata and Mount Casius old, where armies whole have sunk.

Mr Pope said my God was he really going to go on like this for twelve bleeding books at public expense? Fixed like a plant on his peculiar spot, to draw nutrition, propagate, and rot?

Mr John Keats said that, as convenor of the Plumbing Sub-Committee, he was looking into the whole question of the refurbishment of the toilet facilities. It would not stop at a new pan and lilac seat; what he had in mind was a bower quiet for them, full of sweet dreams, and health, and quiet breathing.

Mr Pope asked Mr Shelley who his friend was.

Mr Shelley replied that he never was attached to that great sect whose doctrine was that each one should select out of the crowd a mistress or a friend, and all the rest, though fair and wise, commend to cold oblivion.

Mr Pope enquired whether Mr Shelley had met Mr Milton. It was his opinion that if they ever put their heads together, they would be able to come up with thirty-eight books on anything, Still, cold oblivion wasn't a bad phrase to describe the Members' Gents, if that was what he was talking about; better than a quiet bower full of people breathing, mind,

85

though he couldn't, of course, answer for Mr Coleridge.

Mr William Shakespeare enquired of Mr Keats why they did pine within and suffer dearth, painting their outward walls so costly gay? Why so large cost, having so short a lease, did they upon their fading mansion spend?

Mr Keats replied that they required an unimaginable lodge for solitary thinkings; such as dodge conception to the very bourne of heaven, then leave the naked brain.

Mr Shakespeare said that if he understood correctly what Mr Keats had in mind, were the walls of the new khazi not going to end up covered in verse jottings, and would this not be an irritation to those wishing to lock themselves in cubicles the better to read the small print on their contracts so as not to end up with three bloody tragedies running simultaneously on Broadway and not even a percentage of the gross after producer's profits?

Mr Keats said he couldn't help it, the stuff just poured out of him. He informed them that he had been taught in Paradise to ease his breast of melodies.

Sir Edmund Spenser reminded them that at the last meeting, he had sought an undertaking that the new lavatory would be painted in goodly colours gloriously arrayed, but had as yet received no word from the committee as to what these colours might be. Three months had now passed.

Replying, Mr Shelley said he rather fancied azure, black, and streaked with gold, fairer than any wakened eyes behold.

Mr Marvell said what about orange bright, like golden lamps in a green night?

Or, interjected Mr Shakespeare, what about having the majestical roof fretted with golden fire? It might cost a bob or two, he added, but it would not half impress publishers.

Mr Gerard Manley Hopkins said that he personally had always rather gone for dappled thing.

Green, said Mr Walt Whitman, green, green, green, green, green.

The committee looked at him.

Mr Milton expressed the opinion, after a short silence, that they were not getting anywhere. Chaos umpire sat, he continued, and by decision more embroiled the fray by which he reigned.

Mr Pope asked God to help him.

Mr Wordsworth said that as he had opened the proceedings, it was only fitting, not to say nicely constructed, that he should sum up. He then invited the committee to remember that dust as they were, the immortal spirit grew, like harmony in music; there was a dark inscrutable workmanship that reconciled discordant elements, made them cling together in one Society.

Mr Pope said ho ho ho.

The meeting rose at 4.26 pm.

The Lady From Stalingrad Mansions

When You and I were Buddies on the Sidewalks of New York

'*New York police, who pride themselves on being the world's toughest cops, will soon be recruiting homosexuals. New mayor Edward Koch marked his first day in office by drawing up a gay rights charter which makes it illegal to discriminate against them in hiring police and firemen.*'—Daily Mail

AT 7.04 AM, a rim of winter sun touched the leafless trees in Central Park. By 7.12, it had edged the cold stone bridge with orange. By 7.16, it had begun to colour the body that lay on the bridge. The orange came from the sun. The red came from somewhere else.

It was a morning jogger who called the cops. When the black-and-white wailed up at 7.23, the jogger was leaning over the parapet of the bridge, retching. The two cops got out and looked at him.

'Oh my God!' muttered Patrolman Kowalski. 'He's going to *ruin* that tracksuit!'

They minced quickly across. Patrolman Vidal helped the jogger upright, gently.

'It's horrible,' said the jogger. He was middle-aged, paunchy, grey-faced. 'It's the most horrible thing I ever saw.'

'It's not so bad,' said Kowalski. 'I know this really terrific hand-laundry on the corner of Lexington and 44th, they can do miracles. All the guys go there. Cottons, man-mades, even silks, they can bring them right up like new. Am I right, Jerome?'

'Ask for Cheryl,' said Vidal to the jogger. 'He's very tall, kind of willowy, but with these big capable hands. I got muscatel on this kimono I had one time, I thought it would kill me, but Cheryl got right to work . . .'

'I mean the corpse,' croaked the jogger. He pointed, waveringly.

'I know what you mean,' said Kowalski. 'A canary coat with damson pants, he looks like some kinda cheap dessert.'

'The back of his head,' said the jogger, 'it's shot away.'

'You haven't touched anything?' said Patrolman Vidal.

'Of course not.'

'Don't be offended,' said Kowalski. 'Some guys are very freaky for cadavers. We had a lieutenant in our precinct one time, he always came to station stag nights in white pancake and a shroud. I couldn't relate to him at all. Nor could Jerome.'

'He could tango like there was no tomorrow,' said Vidal, 'but his neck always smelled of formaldehyde. It was really, you know, weird. Like it was some kinda deliberate turn-off.'

'I think he was a closet straight,' said Kowalski, picking a strand of thread that had caught in Vidal's badge and was blowing in the keen morning wind. 'I heard he got married after he transferred to Yonkers.'

'Look, I don't want to put my, you know, where it's not wanted, but don't you think you ought to report this?' said the jogger.

'Oh my God,' sighed Vidal, 'it's rush-rush-day, everyone! Next thing you're gonna be telling us you're a taxpayer, right?'

He trotted delicately back to the patrol car, snatched up the dash-mike.

'Car 64, Patrolman Vidal here, we have a 286 in the park, possible . . . oh, hi, Bruce! I didn't recognise your voice, you're so *throaty* sometimes, did you manage to get bean sprouts? Oh, hey, that's really terrific, Maurice and I can pick up the lychees on the way back. What? Yeah, a dead one, took it in the head. Oh, come *on*, Bruce, lousy old jokes is the last thing I need this time in the morning! What? I don't know, I haven't turned him over, I'll ask Maurice.' He leaned back out of the car window. 'Hey, Maurice, what does he look like?'

'It's not too easy to say, with half a head and all,' called Kowalski, who was kneeling by the body, 'but he's kind of the Burt Reynolds type.'

'Jesus!' muttered Vidal. 'Maurice says he reminds him of Burt Reynolds, Bruce. Bruce? Oh my God, Brucie, don't do one of your weepie numbers on me, listen, the guy was wearing a canary jacket with purple pants, you'd have *hated* him. Also, he was wearing sneakers, a real schlock, even this straight jogger threw up. You wanna send Homicide over now? Great! What? Oh, come *on*, Brucie, not over the line, there could be people listening, anyway the park is filling up, there's folks all around. Sure I do, Bruce. No, really, I mean it. Ten four.'

At 7.58, a lilac convertible purred up to the bridge. Two detectives got out. Their cheeks were crimson with cold. Their ears glowed.

'You took your time,' said Kowalski, consulting the wafer-thin Patek Philippe fob-watch that hung, its tiny baguettes twinkling, just below his badge.

The lieutenant took a step forward, so that his jutted jaw was a millimetre from the patrolman's nose. He was half a head taller, and twice as wide in the shoulder. From these shoulders, his oblong head rose neckless, like a bristled rock.

'Where do you get off criticising *me*, you bitch!' he shrieked.

'Easy, Lewis,' murmured his sergeant, 'everyone's looking.'

The lieutenant glanced quickly around, flashed his gold bridgework, shot his jade cufflinks, tossed his bullet-head.

'We came via Harlem,' explained the sergeant to Kowalski. 'We had the top down, we thought we'd cruise a little, Lewis is very into blacks right now.'

'I like the new paint job,' said Kowalski.

The lieutenant, who had walked a little way off and, arms furiously folded, been tapping his crocodile-shod foot, now turned, mollified.

'Thank you, Maurice,' he said. He smiled. 'You don't think the leopardskin is maybe a little *outré*?'

'I think *you* can get away with it, sir,' said Kowalski. 'I mean, very, very few people could get away with it, but *you*, no problem.'

'Well, thank you, Maurice. Don't call me sir. You have really terrific taste, I've noticed that before. Hasn't Maurice got really terrific taste, Bernard?'

The sergeant stared smoulderingly at the lieutenant.

'I don't see where it's so goddam terrific,' he muttered. 'You wouldn't catch me dead in black barathea. I think you're getting to be a uniform freak in your old age, Lewis.'

'I didn't *choose* this lousy outfit, Bernard!' snapped Kowalski.

'It's my dream to go plain clothes. I have this marvellous imported cashmere poncho from Saks Fifth Avenue, I've been just dying to wear it to work, it has the terrific added advantage of where you can draw and fire from under it, not to mention where the holster doesn't ruin the line of your suit in the first place, it could be *very* big.'

'I think that's a wonderful idea, Maurice!' cried the lieutenant. 'We could *all* have them, it could sweep the entire NYPD, don't *you* think that's a wonderful idea, Bernard?'

'What *I* think,' said the sergeant, 'is that some of us might be just a *teeny* bit, well, bulky for it, mightn't we, Lewis?'

'I don't think Lewis is bulky at all,' cried Kowalski. 'He's big, yes, but he can carry it. He has the walk. I am reminded of Broderick Crawford.'

The lieutenant looked at him.

'I had no idea you wanted to go into the plain clothes squad, Maurice,' he said. 'You should have said.'

'I flunked my orals,' said Kowalski.

They looked at him for a while. A lark rose, busily, across the bridge.

The lieutenant cleared his throat.

'Anytime you want to become a detective, Maurice,' he said, 'you give me a call, okay?'

They were still smiling into one another's eyes when the jogger came up to them.

'Look,' he shouted, 'what are you gonna do about this goddam corpse, I am waiting to give a statement, I am freezing my butt off here, I ought to be taking a shower, your muscles can lock solid, I ought to be at Schlumkiss, Schlumkiss, Terwillikin & Schlumkiss, I am a taxpayer in this lousy . . .'

'Who,' murmured the lieutenant, 'is the little creep in the drecky ready-to-wear?'

'He found the body sir, I mean Lewis,' said Kowalski. 'I told him to take the tracksuit to Cheryl.'

'You did good, Maurice,' said the lieutenant. 'Personally, I would take it to the garbage chute, but *chacun à son moutons, n'est-ce pas?*'

'My God, you speak French!' cried Kowalski.

'*Un petit peu,*' said the lieutenant.

'That's wonderful,' said Kowalski, 'you wouldn't believe how embarrassed I get when Jerome tries to order sometimes. Do you know that truly marvellous new little Basque restaurant on 54th Street, they have a way of folding the escargots in a . . .'

'ARE YOU GOING TO TAKE A STATEMENT FROM ME OR ARE YOU NOT?' screamed the jogger.

'Oh, for goodness sake!' exclaimed the lieutenant, rolling his piggy eyes upwards. 'What is this life, if full of care etcetera, baby?'

'I guess you ought to take a look at the body, Lewis,' murmured Kowalski.

'Okay, Maurice, but just for you, I want to make that absolutely clear.' He glanced over the jogger's agitated head, towards the bridge. 'Oh, yeah, why looky here, it's a stiff!'

'Aren't you gonna go any closer?' shouted the jogger.

'What are you, crazy or something?' snapped the lieutenant. 'I have enough trouble sleeping nights without going right up to people, they have their lousy head shot away!'

'*You* have trouble sleeping?' enquired Kowalski. 'You look so, I don't know, *secure*. I'd never have guessed.'

'I had a bad week, Maurice,' said the lieutenant. 'We had this kid holed up in a liquor store, we had to rush him, I broke my heel.'

Kowalski was still commiserating when Patrolman Vidal came up. He glared at his colleague.

'Just in case you hadn't noticed, Maurice,' he muttered, 'this is one of my Looks!'

'I'm sorry to have left it all to you, Jerome,' said Kowalski, 'I was talking to the lieutenant.'

'I noticed.'

'Don't be that way, Jerome. It isn't like you. Did you find anything on the body?'

Vidal sniggered.

'I thought you'd never ask,' he said.

'I don't like you when you simper, Jerome,' said Kowalski. 'Did you identify the victim?'

Vidal shook his head.

'Nothing on him,' he said, 'except this locket.'

Kowalski took the little golden heart.

'Open it,' said Vidal.

'Oh my God!' cried Kowalski, staring.

'What is it, Maurice?' asked the lieutenant.

Kowalski caught his breath, held out the dangling locket.

'It's—it's a picture of you, Lewis,' he stammered.

The lieutenant gasped. He staggered. He clutched the lilac convertible for support. But he was a cop, and a good one. He bit his lip. He recovered. He removed his grey fedora.

'Take your hats off, boys,' he muttered. 'They shot the Commissioner.'

The Rhinestone As Big As The Ritz

Red Sky At Night, The Refinery's Alight

Being some extracts from A. Coren's
ENCYCLOPAEDIA OF NEW ENGLISH FOLKLORE

Singing Home the Muck

"Ere she cum, the bubblin scum,
Down from Foskett's Alloys!
Ere cum a dollop o' sunnink brown,
Off of Gribling's Mills!

"There float a poisoned cat,
There go a chokin fish!
Ho hum, tiddle-I-wee,
Here be a sterile newt!

"My ole wife be covered in boils,
My little kid be bald!
Sing Fa-gargle-dong,
All the ducks is dead!"

Just three of the charming verses of *Singing Home The Muck*, a traditional part-song sung by English villagers as, withered arms bare and trousers rolled up to their radioactive knees, they stand at evening in their local water-supply and fish for effluent. Many a night you may come upon them, their heads just visible above the detergent foam, groping for extruded tubes, asbestos waste, rotten fish, crude oil, packing cases, rusty wire, and all the other denizens of stream and rill so highly prized by Englishmen.

Woodworm Tuesday

On Woodworm Tuesday (2nd after Insolvency Sunday, and the first Tuesday of Spring), the traditional Estate Agents' Race is held in villages and hamlets throughout England. Although the origins of this colourful rural event are lost in the mists of chicanery, many anthropologists believe it commemorates the sale in AD 834, after much haggling, of Aelfthrith Cottage, derelict home of the Idiot of Picester, to a merchant of London. As soon as the Idiot took possession of the money and the merchant occupation of the house, the roof, so the story goes, fell in, the doors dropped off, the cesspool overflowed, the foundations sank, and the woodworm, belching the last of the genuine oak beams, immediately "felle upon ye marchaunte and devowred hym hole" (*Chronicle of Mercia*, cap. XVII).

Whatever its folk heritage, the Race itself is a delightfully engaging spectacle: local Estate Agents are required to run the traditional Stonesthrow to the Station, tossing as they run a colour print of a fully modernised thatched cottage standing in two acres of unspoilt woodland, and crying "FIVE HUNDRED POUNDS OR NEAR OFFER! FIVE HUNDRED POUNDS OR NEAR OFFER!" The winner is given as his prize the first media executive of the season to arrive from Knightsbridge, who is directed to the winner's offices by the village Reeve and attendant Virgins of the Parish.

Old Man's Austin

Along England's remoter byways and hedgerows, as the older plants shrivel and disappear, they are rapidly being replaced by colourful clumps of Old Man's Austin, Lady's Mini, Rusty Ford, My Son's Honda, and similar sturdy and enduring growths which, botanists think, may be a natural evolution from such earlier strains as The Common Bedstead, Potty, Grandpa's Mattress, and Sink. Naturally enough, much folk legend has sprung up around the new flora: local people believe, for example, that Broken Windscreen can cause holes in children and that Seeping Oilsump has some

95

weird effect on grass. The Folk Society, in company with the Society for Psychic Research, is also collating a number of reports that, at the time of the full moon, the ghost of Old Pete, the mythical Minister for the Environment, can be seen flitting among the new vegetation, cackling hysterically.

Cublington Fair

A regular event, held in Buckinghamshire, and traditionally associated with Airport Bill, the local name for the Devil. (There are analogues at Stansted and Foulness.)

The Fair begins with a march of Freeholders, usually middle-aged, who parade with quaint hand-lettered signs nailed to long staves which they wave above their heads, shrieking imprecations the while in the hope of averting the curse of Airport Bill, who, they traditionally believe, will appear to them in the form of terrible noises in the sky, and break their greenhouses. After the procession, they gather in a convenient public place and imbibe large quantities of *gin*, traditionally held to be a restorative/aphrodisiac, a clear, aromatic liquid made with money. They then begin to laugh and grope, and vie with one another in creating new oaths directed at their leaders; the evening usually ends when one of these, The Grinning Man, is hanged in effigy.

Fine Afore Seven, Buggies Arter Eleven!

A prophetic shriek, commonest among Southern villagers, though also to be heard in the West Country, Bucks, Berks, and anywhere close to the remains of one of the old Motor Ways, that pattern of dilapidated stone tracks that was laid down by casual primitives in earlier times. The meaning of the phrase is that, if the day's weather has been good, then midnight will see the arrival of the South Kensington Young Boutiquiers' Rally and Bar-B-Q, or similar: these are bands of Little People who come out to play only when England's more beautiful villages are asleep. In their highly coloured vehicles, Mokes and Buggies and Dragsters and the like, decorated with dozens of quartz lights, wind-horns, multi-barrel exhausts, dangle-dollies, borzois, and drunks, they roar through the dark lanes, honking horns, hurling bottles, over-revving, screaming, backfiring, and generally plaguing human beings in a hundred mischievous little ways. Often they kill cats, chickens, dogs, as they go, and, in the morning, their tracks may often be seen on the grass, frequently across gardens, new crops, and village greens. It does not do, so they say, to meddle with them, and most villagers, when the first notes of *Colonel Bogie* trumpet across the moonlit hills, pull the sheets over their heads and try to think of something else.

Up Jack's Pylon

An old game, played by village children, who delight to climb those strange iron constructions which are to be found wherever the countryside is, or was, prettiest, and may be a result of some aberration on the part of Druids. The children scramble to the top of these, and the winner is fused permanently to the National Grid.

Blind Ned of Westminster

A persistent figure in English folklore, so much so that there must have been more than one original, as his name crops up throughout the length and breadth of the country. The legend is that at certain times of the year, Blind Ned leaves Westminster and, led by his mad cur, Profit, stalks the land in a bizarre, haphazard fashion, the pattern of which not even the most brilliant students of the arcane have so far been able to divine. And wherever Blind Ned's foot falls, so the legend goes, factories spring up of a loathsome ugliness, and great swathes of mean little boxlike houses, and concrete shopping precincts, and great glass towers; and, hypnotised by the seductive fluting of Blind Ned and the mesmerising dance of Profit, human beings fall in behind them and are borne off to their wretched doom.

Key in The Hat

A time-honoured rite, strongly sexual in undertone, mostly

found in semi-rural areas such as Wates Number 456/32a, Span 447, Happihomes Twelvegrand Plus, and similar instant villages. Lacking more ancient rites to occupy their time, the villagers gather in groups, first at one home, then another, on a strict rota system; and, having absorbed much *gin* (see above) and gone through the ritual Talking—starting with the subject of au pairs, then on to the new Rover, the Permissive Society, louvre doors, Majorca, pot-training, Sainsbury's value, *Elizabeth R*, and the insignificance of pornography (this pattern rarely changes)—they start giggling, and the Host gets his ritual bowler, and all the men throw their car keys into it, and, the partners having been duly selected, everyone goes to bed, where, so the story goes (although there has been little concrete evidence), they talk about au pairs, the new Rover, the Permissive Society, louvre doors, Majorca, pot-training, Sainsbury's value, *Elizabeth R*, and the insignificance of pornography.

The Sanity Inspector

The Short Happy Life of Margaux Hemingway

'*Meet Margaux Hemingway, the biggest girl to hit the fashion scene since Twiggy. She's blonde, six feet tall, and a grand-daughter of the famous Ernest. "Modelling is a tough business," she says.*' – Daily Mail

YOU KNOW HOW IT is there early in the morning in Granada with the bums still asleep against the walls of the buildings; before even the ice wagons come by with ice for the bars? Well, we came across the square from the truck to the Pearl of San Francisco Cafe to get coffee and there was only one beggar awake in the square and he was getting a drink out of the fountain.

We sat down at an outside table, in the sun, and we looked at him.

'There is only one beggar,' I said.

Harry looked away. He unslung the big Pentax ESII with the 250mm Takumar and squinted up at the sun.

'There is a hard white light bouncing back off the stucco,' he said.

'It is going to be one of those days,' I said.

'Yes,' he said, 'it is going to be one of those days.'

Charlie came up and sat down.

'I would not use the big Pentax, old one,' he said. 'It will make the big clatter. It will frighten the beggar.'

Harry swung the ESII around and put his eye down it, straight at the fountain.

'I like to hear the clatter,' he said. 'I like this thing with the shutter. It is a man's noise.'

'Cojones,' said Charlie. He spat in the grey dust.

'I guess it is time for the girl to go,' said Harry.

'Yes,' I said. I got up.

The beggar looked up at me when I got to him, and for a moment I thought he was going to give me a fight. But I had the Schiaperelli voile on with the big black Gucci boots and the solid brass Akko buckle at the belt, and it held his eye for just long enough. I put my arm around his shoulders before he could move.

'Que cosa?' he said.

'Nada,' I said. 'Nada e nada e pues nada.'

Harry let go with the Pentax. Clack, went the shutter. Clack. Clack.

The beggar wriggled a bit, but I held him. We got a lot of good shots that day. They came out in *Vogue* and *Harper's* after that, and I looked very good, with all these brokendown houses in the background, and my dress flowing over the beggar, and the beggar looking damned Spanish, and all.

The extras came over the wall, and we could not miss them. Jimmy just sat behind the heavy Arriflex and the extras came over the wall, out of the old Mission, and Jimmy just pressed the button and kept on pressing it, and the extras went down and when they went down they stayed there in rather sad little heaps, like broken dolls, their skirts up over their legs.

I had to step across them, after that. They were all looking up at me, and their eyes were open, and they had these fixed smiles on their faces.

'For chrissake,' said Jimmy, 'hold up the goddam toothpaste!'

I held up the toothpaste.

'This is the one,' I said. 'For healthy gums and bright, bright teeth, this is the one.'

The American was early for the appointment. He came into the bar and he mopped his forehead with a spotted silk handkerchief and he walked across to a table and he picked up more nuts than he could manage and some of the nuts spilled out of his hand and he looked at the carpet for a long time, but he did not stoop to pick up the nuts.

He licked his lips after that, and he mopped his face again, and he walked across to the counter and on the way he knocked over a chair and he apologised even though there was nobody sitting in the chair and nobody to apologise to.

He asked the barman something, and the barman nodded, and pointed to me with a glass he was wiping, and the

American buttoned his jacket and unbuttoned it again and walked over to me. He was about fifty and he was going to fat and there was one bead of sweat in the cleft of his chin.

'I am Edward Mankiewicz of Mankiewicz Associates,' he said.

'I know,' I said.

'May I sit down?' he said.

'Yes,' I said.

'I did not intend to sit down at first,' he said.

'That's all right,' I said.

'At first I thought we might stand at the bar,' he said.

'Sometimes it is better not to stand at the bar;' I said.

'Yes,' he said. 'Sometimes it is better to sit at the table.'

'That is the way it is, sometimes,' I said.

'I will get straight to the point,' he said. 'I would like you to model the new range of Miss Mankiewicz Modes for spring.'

'I thought it would be something like that,' I said. 'I am sorry, but I have all the work that I can handle, right now.'

He took his hat off and fanned his face with it.

'I can offer you ten thousand dollars,' he said.

'That is a lot of money for a modelling job,' I said.

He put his hand on my knee. I could feel the moisture seeping through my Thai silk. You know the way it is with Thai silk.

'We want you very much,' he said.

I looked at his hand.

'So it is that way?' I said.

'What way is the way it is?' he said.

I looked at the hand again, hard.

'That way is the way it is,' I said.

He took the hand away, quickly.

'No,' he said, 'that is not the way it is. I was just being friendly. This is a modelling job.'

'You say that,' I said, 'but how do I know that it is the truth?'

He looked away.

'Because I have a wound,' he said.

'Oh,' I said.

'It is from the war,' he said.

'It is in the place of which we do not speak?' I said.

'That is the place it is in,' he said.

I looked out of the window. There were many strong young

101

men in bathing costumes lying by the hotel pool.

'I am sorry,' I said, 'I did not know.'

'Why should you know?' he said. 'The war is a long time ago.'

'There are times when I feel I cannot go on with the modelling,' I said.

'You must go on with the modelling,' he said. 'There is nothing any of us can do about the war.'

'Yes,' I said, 'I suppose so.'

The helicopter came and took Jimmy away soon after three p.m. It just came and took him away, and I saw him going up into the white sky. I could see the big Konikoflex 35mm poking out of the gunport for a long time. I knew Jimmy was on the end of it, but I could not see him any more, I could just see the sun winking on the big Konikoflex 35mm.

I started the climb up the big rock. There was one roped to me above, and one roped above him, and for a time I thought we would not be able to do it, and when the hole appeared in my tights and my hairpiece caught on the overhang, I felt that thing in me which we do not say but which is always there.

And then we came over the ridge, and the wind was blowing across the peak, and I could hear the helicopter hovering above us, and I looked up and I waved the bottle, and I shouted out:

'It's the right one, it's the bright one, it's Martini!'

And it was all right, after that.

You know the way it is in Pamplona. Suddenly everybody is running in the streets and there are flags and children and the big women in the mantillas and you get caught up in it and you drink a lot of the red wine and you forget what it is that you have to do in the afternoon.

We went into the bodega after the thing in the streets was finished because we had to talk about what it was that we had to do in the afternoon, and a lot of people came up to me to shake my hand and to have their photographs taken with me because there are always people who want to have their photographs taken with you when you are one of the big ones and they show these photographs to their families and they point to themselves in the picture and they say:

'That is me with the big one, it was taken on that day when

she did six straight cover pictures in the afternoon, Dios! but they do not make those any more who can do six straight cover pictures in an afternoon!'

So I was sitting there at the table and there were all the reporteros and all the fotografos and all the aficionados, and then there was another who came up to the table and stood there. It was an old one.

And I looked at the old one, who was not just an old one, but who had also been a big one, some say a great one, some say perhaps the greatest one of all.

'Welcome, old one,' I said.

'Go with God, young one,' said the old one.

'A glass of wine, old one?' I said.

'Perhaps you should not take a glass of wine with the old one, young one,' said the one who was my manager. 'They say it brings the bad luck.'

'I obscenity in your bad luck,' I said.

'Gracias, young one,' said the old one.

We drank a glass.

'Is it possible for me to assist you this afternoon?' said the old one. 'I could stand in the corner and be a fuzzy one. I do not expect to be a big one, any more.'

'It is not good for a big one to appear as a fuzzy one,' I said.

'It is true I was a big one,' said the old one. 'I was known as the thin one. But they do not want the thin ones any more.'

'Better that you go now,' I said, 'than that they see you as the old thin fuzzy one.'

'It is not easy, the modelling,' she said. 'Go with God.'

'No, it is not easy,' I said. 'Go with God, El Twiggy.'

Golfing For Cats

Value for Money

"The Royal Philatelic Society is to sell part of the unique collection of early Italian stamps bequeathed to it in 1914 by Prince Alphonse Doria Pamphilj, then one of the best-known philatelists in the world. The most valuable item is a Sicilian half-grano printed in error in blue instead of in yellow. It is one of two recorded examples and is expected to fetch over £5,000. Both copies were originally on one letter found by a boy in Syracuse, Sicily, about 1890. One stamp was removed and the one left on the envelope went into the Ferrari collection which was sold in the 1920's by the French Government as part of German war reparations. The present owner is unknown." – The Daily Telegraph.

I OUGHT TO make it quite clear that I'm not one of those men who nudges you in the Tube to point out that the price paid to keep a Leonardo in the country is equivalent to 743 council houses. Nor have I ever dared assess the value of a book to anyone but myself; is fifteen bob (=1 set of cellular underwear) too low a price for a Collected Shakespeare? Would £65 (=1 telly) be nearer the mark? What's it worth to hear the Eroica? Similarly, if a bloke runs up to pluck my sleeve and tell me he's just bumped into a woman who's price is above rubies, I won't offer him an argument. Without, perhaps, fully appreciating the worth such things represent, I'm capable of recognising the reasons for it.

Not with stamps, though. Their value is never established in terms I understand. Those enormous pre-Raphaelite jobs that flow in-

cessantly from Central European presses, depicting in minute Tech-
nicolor detail the siege of Stalingrad or the Hungarian football team,
turn up in job-lots in the *Boy's Own Paper* at two bob a thousand,
while a misprinted scrap picked out of the gutter by a Sicilian beggar
on a dog-end hunt gets knocked down in Bond Street for £5,000.
Oh, I know about rarity value; it's the basis of that very propensity
that bothers me. I can think of nothing else that comes under the
gavel simply because it happens to be an inferior specimen of its
breed. A diamond doesn't soar in value because it's chipped and
turns grey in the rain. An inferior Rembrandt fetches less than a
masterpiece. Bidders don't engage in punch-ups in the aisles because
a Sévres milkmaid with three ears has finally come up for auction.
Stamps, however, depend for their worth on the pure accident of
somebody's ineptitude. A chap stops his serrating machine to put the
kettle on, and the result is a row of stamps with holes in the middle
to render them priceless. Sometimes the rarity is caused by a miserable
disaster; perhaps it involved the brave lads working after hours to
turn out the first day's issue of the Borneo 2c green when a party of
locals surrounded the tent, ate the printer and his mates, and burned
everything in sight except for a block of 2c green, picked out of the
rubble years later by a Stanley Gibbons safari.

One wonders whether these gems are really worth saving. On that
day when the curators of our culture are glancing in terror at the skies
and stuffing a hurried selection of treasures into bomb-proof hampers
for the benefit of posterity, will they make room for a blue half-grano
from Sicily with a note to the effect that because it wasn't yellow it
was worth two reasonable Picassos? How will our heirs react when
they dig up the Mona Lisa to discover she has one eye on either side
of her nose and no moustache, yet still seemed to retain some value
for their peculiar ancestors?

Perhaps I ought to have met a philatelist or two, or strolled among
the revellers at some Stampmen's Annual Funfeast, joking about
swops and tweezers. As it is, I imagine them as a race of desperate
unshaven men with bi-focals and nervous hands, living in great brown
Victorian houses in Streatham and Penge cluttered up with yellowing
loose-leaf folders and dusty glass cases; men who sleep on camp-beds
in the hall, who wake two minutes before the postman comes and

leap horribly upon the mail with steaming kettles and magnifying-glasses, rabid for an odd shade of magenta or an inverted head. Or perhaps they're all like Prince Alphonse Doria Pamphilj, relics of the Golden Age of Philately, fat, tired moguls surrounded by their tatty treasures, propped up in a tasselled bed with a telephone in each hand, in hourly contact with their stampbrokers, shouting: 'BUY!' 'SELL!' 'HOLD!' and sending parties of asthmatic clerks through the stamp collections of the dead, searching, searching, searching. Really, one can't but think of such characters as a pretty distasteful bunch; what other joys but those of greed and exclusive possession are to be won from sitting in Harmer's salerooms, bidding in thousands, and carting off the exorbitant prize for a long winter's gloat?

Nevertheless, I'd been prepared to allow each man his own eccentricity until I saw that bit about the *other* Sicilian half-grano having been sold by the French as part of German war reparations. There's an element of black farce about the involvement of this Sicilian misprint in the wretched machinery of war, and death-compensation, a sense of out-of-jointedness. What did the half-grano fetch in 1920? Four dead officers? Sixteen enlisted men? We may never find out now; the present owner is unknown. One hopes he's happy with his possession, that's all.

Still, I have to admit that a fair part of my own bitterness is concerned with the agglomeration of misshapen junk I have accumulated at enormous irretrievable expense over the years. These *objets grotesques* have never quite made the saleroom grade, and I fail to see why. After all, they're unique, with the exact credentials that qualify the half-grano as a prestigious collector's item. I have, for instance, a navy-blue jacket (originally part of a set, the blue trousers having been snapped up in a jumble sale, present owner unknown) which was supposed to have been made in grey, but due to oversight and incompetence, wasn't. In addition to this priceless blunder, the item also has one sleeve longer than the other, and is shy of a breast pocket. There's no other like it in existence, I swear. I have, too, a clock which runs backwards and chimes every twelve minutes, a treasure that has deceived horologists throughout the civilised world. And, in unwrapping it just the other day, I spotted that the 1951 *Manchester Guardian* in which it was swaddled contains the word 'skinch', a palpable misprint that to my knowledge has not reappeared. Now, there can't be more than — what? — fifty copies of this particular paper still in mint condition, and most of those will be in sacrosanct files. And this is no mere shrivelled-up square inch of mouldy paper; the lucky buyer would have a full square yard of densely packed misprints for his money, which, at half-grano rate, ought to put it in the million-pound bracket.

But I don't intend to let it stop there. It so happens that the Albanian government, adjudged guilty by the International Court at the Hague in 1949 of sinking two British warships, still hasn't forked out the requisite £843,947. Let's not be too harsh on them; maybe it's not easy for the Albanians to lay their hands on ready money. But for the sake of easing Anglo-Albanian relations, I am prepared to offer my entire collection to them to be sold at whatever auctioneer's they choose. It can't be worth less than two million, but I'm no philatelic shark; I'm prepared to let the lot go for a hundred thousand. Honest.

The Dog It Was That Died

Me Aristocrat, You Jane!

A report from America that anthropoid apes were not just more intelligent than was formerly supposed but might actually be taught to speak a few simple phrases, opened up vast areas of speculation. Since Edgar Rice Burroughs was no longer around, I took it upon myself to ...

A great stillness lay upon the shire. In the lush green thickets, not a bird sang, not an insect rustled. In the dense copses, no mammal moved, no reptile crawled. In the silver streams, the trout lay leapless; and in the wild ponds, as in the ornamental lakes, exotic mallards and alabaster swans alike tucked their heads among their feathers, and drowsed. The very gnats hung in the heavy air, motionless.

"Bloody good day, Sunday," murmured the Earl of Grey-stoke, turning in mid-snooze, and settling. The *Business Observer* slid from his lap, softly, and lay, unread as ever, on the velvet lawn. The other house-guests flexed slightly at his grunt, and the faint creak of old basketwork echoed across the clearing: a few acres of greensward held by enormous effort against the hungry foliage of Bucks., in the centre of which stood the great peeling pile of Spiffins, the Greystoke seat.

They might, perhaps, have slumbered thus forever in that close atmosphere, had not, at that very moment, a strange and unsettling cry rung across the still countryside, an ear-shattering "AAAAH-AAAAAH-AAAAAAH!" accompanied by the crash of breaking branches and the odd counterpoint of rhythmic thumping. The house-guests stirred, and sat up, and blinked at the suddenly waving trees, as through them, a split-second later, burst a short figure in black jacket, striped trousers, and Eton collar, swinging from limb to limb. Lithely, he dropped to the ground, and stared at them, suspicious as all small boys at the sight of visitors.

"My son, Lord Greystoke," said the Earl, and his heir hurtled up to shake the proffered hands. If any of the guests found it somewhat odd that Lord Greystoke's knuckles should be brushing the ground, or that the young Etonian should be sporting a thick black beard, they were, of course, far too well-bred to comment upon it; but one or two of the ladies with young but ultimately marriageable daughters could not entirely suppress a look of disappointment at his Lordship's extravagant bandiness. Too many gymkhanas, too early, they reflected, sighing; always a problem with country families.

They brightened, however, when Lord Greystoke snatched a sandwich from the waiting tea-trolley with his foot and popped it into his mouth.

"I say, that's jolly good!" cried a baronet.

"*Jolly* good!" exclaimed another. "Chap's an athlete!"

"Bags of spirit!" echoed a third. "How's his bowling?"

Lord Greystoke declined to comment. Instead, he was staring hard at the coiffure of the Dowager Duchess of Speenhamland, and baring his lips in a terrible grin.

"And what can I do for you, my little man?" she asked.

"I think he wants to examine your scalp," said the Earl.

His heir began jumping up and down enthusiastically.

"What fun!" cried the Dowager Duchess. She bent her head obligingly. Greystoke began to poke around on it.

"Enquiring mind," observed the Bishop of Bicester, nodding.

"Probably end up one of these scientist chappies," said a Viscount, "there's a lot of it about, I understand."

"Too deep for me, I'm afraid," said the Earl.

Everyone chuckled agreement. Satisfied, Lord Greystoke shot up an elm and began shaking its topmost branches.

"He's adopted, of course," said the Earl, as they watched his heir. "Parents worked in a circus, I believe. Good family, though. Truck overturned, killed 'em both, mile or so from here. Found the little lad wandering about in a daze. Took him in, brought him up as one of the family. Only thing to do."

"Bloody good show," said a baronet.

The ladies dabbed their eyes.

Lord Greystoke had a splendidly successful career at Eton. During his six years, he accumulated a dozen or so useful phrases (he was somewhat brighter than the average boy), and commended himself socially wherever he went, since he was anti-intellectual, enormously athletic, and had a way of looking at unpopular masters while bending a school railing between his bare hands that ensured an untroubled life for an understandably large number of close friends. He had also thrown the house bully through the library roof, and led his side to victory in the Wall Game for the first time in history, filling Slough General Hospital in the process.

Sexually, he remained something of a mystery. Once a month, he would go off to Whipsnade for the weekend and return looking happier and calmer; but, naturally, no-one ever pressed him on the subject. They were all, it must be remembered, members of the English upper classes, and stranger things had happened, even in the best-regulated houses.

It came as a surprise to none that, in his final year, Lord Greystoke became Head of Pop.

He failed to get into Oxford, despite the most benevolent-sounding Closed Scholarships, which was a source of tremendous relief to his father.

"Bloody good show!" said the Earl, when his son showed him the letter. "Thought for one ghastly minute you were turning into some kind of swot!"

"Rather not!" said Lord Greystoke, taking a banana from his monogrammed case and slipping it into his mouth, sideways.

"Bloody good!" said the Earl.

"Bloody good!" said Lord Greystoke. "Toppin'! Rippin'!"

"That's the kind of talk I like to hear!" cried his father. And got him into a good Guards' regiment.

Which was no mean feat, since Greystoke, though broad and muscular, was some two feet shorter than the requisite length of officer, and one or two voices could be heard muttering in the mess to the effect that they didn't know what England was coming to when the Ghurkas towered over a Coldstream; but money and influence prevailed, and, once in, Lord Greystoke again commended himself utterly to his peers, both professionally and socially, as well as, of course, intellectually. Within a fortnight, he had broken the collarbone of the Sergeant-Instructor, who looked on unarmed combat lessons as battles in the class-war, had placed a potty atop the Albert Memorial in the fantastic record time of fourteen seconds, and had beaten the Honourable Artillery Company's team at the Royal Tournament in the race to swing a twelve-pounder over a wall by tucking it, single-handed, under his left arm and grasping the rope in his right.

Furthermore, he turned out to be wonderful with animals. Every morning, as the dawn mists were melting in Hyde Park, he could be seen leading not only the Regiment's horses but also their dogs and the neighbourhood squirrels through the most complex and stirring manoeuvres. He seemed, uncannily, to speak their language.

The regimental goat loved him like a brother.

Evenfurthermore, his success at regimental dances, hunt balls, coming-out parties, and the like, was unparalleled! The life and soul of every party, he was wont not only to swing from the chandeliers of the Dorchester or the Grosvenor and lay out the waiters with magnums of Bollinger hurled as easily as if they had been coconuts, he had also been responsible for incinerating Annabel's and throwing The Who into the Serpentine.

He tended, inevitably, to smell a bit when hot.

In short, Lord Greystoke was everything that an officer and gentleman should be.

"What about the Stock Exchange?" said the Earl, when his son returned to civilian life.

"Bloody good," said Lord Greystoke.

"Or Lloyd's?"

"Or Lloyd's," said Lord Greystoke. "Bloody good."

So he deposited his hundred thousand; and had a job. His title also qualified him for three dozen assorted director-ships—he was, of course, required to turn up at board meetings once a year to say "Bloody good!" and collect his salary—and as he had also lent his cachet to a new discotheque, a chain of boutiques for the shorter man, and a trendy treetop restaurant in Cheyne Walk, he was not only one of the richest young men about town, he was also one of the most eligible. True, he had an unfortunate habit of ramming bollards with a succession of Lamborghinis (his feet being unable to reach the brake), but this only served further to consolidate his growing reputation as wag, wit and playboy.

It was at a party at Antonia Fraser's to celebrate the opening of his first photographic exhibition that Lord Greystoke, as he was bound to do, fell in love.

It was a perfect match; everyone said so. The most eligible peer in England and the daughter of a world-wide grocery chain that had never turned in an annual dividend of less than twenty per cent.

" 'Andsome he ain't," said the world-wide grocery chain as he watched the couple descend the steps of Brompton Oratory, "but he ain't 'alf got tone."

"Right," said his wife. "And you can't buy that, can you?"

The world-wide grocery chain smiled. "I just 'ave," he said.

But when the happy couple returned from their Acapulco honeymoon, it could be discerned that the broad smile on the face of Lord Greystoke was not mirrored in the pale and haggard countenance of his lovely bride. Indeed, hardly had they touched down and Lord Greystoke gone off for a quiet scratch, than Lady Greystoke ran sobbing to her mother.

Who listened, for a long time, to a tale too bizarre even to be as exciting as it had promised; and said, when the final stillness came:

"Well?"

112

Which wasn't the sort of advice Lady Greystoke was after at all.

"What shall I *do*, Mumsy?" she said.

"Do?" said her mother. "You'll 'ave to get used to it, won't you? Think of your dad and me. They're asking us everywhere."

"But—"

"But bleeding nothing! What you don't understand, my girl, is 'e's an aristocrat. They're diff'rent, 'n'they?"

"Not 'alf."

"So you'll just 'ave to grin and bear it, won't you?"

So she did.

The Sanity Inspector

Partridge in Pear Tree for Sale, makes Wonderful Chips

McGraw-Edison Company,
Parkade Plaza,
Columbia,
Missouri 65201.   29 December 1974

DEAR SIR:
I enclose, in case you have forgotten it, your recent advertisement in the *New Yorker* in which you offered an item for, and I quote, 'those who appreciate the finest in art and toasters'.

As a person of this kind, I was delighted to receive this opportunity of a lifetime on Christmas Day from my dear wife, Alice, formerly Miss Alice Terwilliken of Gazebo, Maryland, where her family have earned the respect of all for nearly three generations. I say this only to point out that my wife is also a person of the type you specify, having helped organise the Gazebo Museum of Maryland Art, with its many fine jugs and samplers, and also visited, with me, the Louvre of Paris and seen the Mona Venus in all its very old splendour during the recent Europe convention of top chromium executives of which I am one of, and proud to represent not only my company but also these United States, at Rome, Italy.

As you say in your ad, your Springbok Toaster came with its own serial number and certificate of authenticity, for which I was very grateful, as there is nothing worse than owning a fake pop-up toaster and work of art combined; we have a wonderful home full of valuable Louis XIX furniture purchased on our trip, including the chair Marie Antoinette was sitting on when they cut her head off, and it would be tragic to louse it up with a toaster where people came in and said 'That's a phony, don't you people know a bum artwork when you see one?'

114

**TOASTMASTER OFFERS YOU FINE ART THAT ALSO MAKES BREAKFAST.
THE LIMITED-EDITION SPRINGBOK TOASTER.**

The Springbok is for those who appreciate the finest in art and toasters.
It's a one-of-a-kind interpretation of an original painting by a well known American
wildlife artist. This work of art captures the elegant beauty of the Springbok Gazelle
in all its natural warm earthtones. In turn, Toastmaster was able to faithfully
reproduce the subtle coloration on long-lasting porcelain enamel panels that have
a matte finish to give the look and feel of the original canvas.
Certainly, it's the only fine art piece in the world that can prepare all kinds
of toaster foods. And prepare them well.

Also, we were both very impressed with the quality, and my wife joins me in saying where it beats her how you can do it for only $29.95. You say that 'Toastmaster was able to faithfully reproduce the subtle coloration on long-lasting porcelain enamel panels that have a matte finish to give the look and feel of the original canvas', and you are absolutely right! Many of our friends who we asked over to feel our toaster expressed amazement that, if you shut your eyes, you would think you were feeling an old master. One close friend, and he really knows about these things being a member of the Print Of The Month Club and someone who regularly goes out of his way to see a black-and-white movie, said that the last time he felt anything that good, it was a Rembrandt.

You say 'It may be a collector's item someday', and my wife and myself readily concur in this, since we already have a collection of pop-up toasters of which this will certainly be the

115

showpiece. We did not collect these with an artistic view in mind, since none of them contains a genuine signed picture on it, let alone has the look and feel of canvas; no, we collected them because in most cases they only popped up for around a week or so, then they started to burn the toast black and crumble it and throw it around the room and all that kind of stuff which, as you know, is what toasters do after a while.

It is that which brings me to the, like, nub of my enquiry today. In your advertisement, as you can see, you say 'Certainly, it's the only fine art piece in the world that can prepare all kinds of toaster foods', and this is that to which I am taking exception to, on account of it doesn't, and this gives me something of a problem.

I am very partial to Welsh rabbit. This is not, of course, an animal of any kind, being a toasted item, and speaking as one who is fond of all of God's creatures (which is another reason for my delight at having a genuine Springbok Gazelle on the side of my toaster), I am not the kind of a man who would stick a rabbit in a toaster, even if you could force it into the slot, which I personally doubt, without bending or otherwise damaging the valuable work of art. No, Welsh rabbit is toasted cheese-on-toast, and as such comes under the heading, I would have thought, of 'all kinds of toaster foods'. At least, I would have thought it until quite recently, i.e. last evening, when my dear wife had to go out, as usual, to her evening course on The Negro Past And Present which is helping her to, you know, understand things besides just art etcetera. Anyway, she asked should she fix me something, and I said: 'No, dear, I will fix myself something on my wonderful Christmas gift, that way I can eat and improve my mind at the same time'.

So I put a nice thick slice of Swiss cheese on a slice of bread and butter, and I put it in my new toaster, and I pushed down the slide, and it came on perfectly, and I sat back to gaze at my limited edition, marvelling at the look of original canvas and thanking the Lord that I lived in a country where, despite panics over world inflation and oil and so forth, a connoisseur could still pick up a masterpiece at only $29.95. It was while I was pondering these things that I became aware of an extremely unsavoury smell which seemed to be issuing from my work of art. Even as I wondered about this, there was a big flash, and a plume of smoke came out of the slot, right about where the Springbok Gazelle's head is located.

I turned off the switch and examined my gift.

116

It transpires that I now have a work of art with cheese in its mechanism. I am afraid, too, that in the panic that followed this untoward downturn in my, or rather, my wife's investment, I hid the damaged item and opened the windows to clear the smoke etcetera. Luckily, my wife came in late—she had stayed behind to ask a question about sweat glands—and did not enter the kitchen before retiring. And this morning, I made a point of coming downstairs early to prepare breakfast so that I could make the family's toast in one of our old toasters, which was not the spiritual and educational experience I have become used to since Christmas Day, but at least it turned the goddam bread brown.

So my wife still does not know of the incident, and here I am at my office seeking your expert guidance. I guess I could have this toaster repaired, but I know that the restoration of a work of art is a delicate and expert technique, and I do not want some ordinary electrician lousing up my limited edition. Even if I send it back to you and the original artist, I have my doubts: will it still count as an original work of art even if it has new works? It seems to me it will be a reproduction, and that the accompanying certificate of authenticity will therefore be worthless. Should I forget about it as a working toaster altogether, and hang it on the wall as just a work of art? I have thought of this, but it occurs to me that part of its value comes from the fantastic way it combines art and toast, and if it can only do one thing, i.e. be art, then it is not much good, added to which a toaster is damned difficult to hang, being much wider than a painting, and people will bang their heads walking past. This will give rise to embarrassing situations, such as your guest dabbing his forehead and saying 'What the hell *is* that and why is it hanging there?' and you explain that it is a work of art and toaster combined, and he says 'Then why isn't it standing on a table where it can toast?' and you explain that it has cheese in it and does not work, and he says 'Then what do you mean it is a work of art and toaster combined, if it doesn't damn well toast?'

Personally, I like a good conversation about aesthetics, but I do not want one every time a friend opens his head up on my Springbok Gazelle.

Do you think I ought to buy another? My worry about this is that the more original art works of this kind there are in circulation, the less each one will be worth, and, anyway, what do I do with the busted one?

I mean, people like me, it goes against every principle we

117

have to throw a work of art in the trashcan, also if word gets around or someone sees it in my garbage, it could knock the bottom out of the whole market.

Please advise me soonest. I know you have a deep appreciation of artistic things, and I look to you for help in my hour of need.

Yours truly,
Edgar J. Milbro

Golfing For Cats

Doctor No will see You Now

'CIA agents who lose the qualities that make good spies are retired at fifty under special pensions, according to testimony yesterday before a House Intelligence Sub-Committee. "A 70-year-old James Bond is kind of hard to imagine," said Republican Senator Sam Stratton.'—Herald Tribune

BOND TENSED IN THE DARKNESS, and reached for his teeth.

There was something in the room.

You did not train for fifty-three years without developing that imponderable acuity that lay beyond mere observation. Indeed, you found that as the years went by, this sixth sense came, perforce, to replace the others: these days, he could hear dog-whistles, with or without his batteries in.

At least, he assumed they were dog-whistles. Nobody else seemed to hear them.

The teeth fell exactly to hand, there between the senna and the Algipan on his bedside table. He waited a calculated split-second for the cement to cleave snugly to his palate. It felt good. It should have: it was made for him by Chas. Fillibee of Albemarle Street, the world's premier fixative man. Senior British agents had been going to Fillibee since before the War; he knew their special requirements. When Witherspoon 004 had gone into the London Clinic to have his prostate done and the KGB had taken the opportunity to lob an Ostachnikov nuclear mortar into his grape-box, the only thing left intact between Baker Street Station and the Euston underpass had been Witherspoon's upper plate.

Very carefully, Bond slid his hand beneath his pillow and closed it around the ribbed butt of his Walther PPK 9mm Kurz with the custom-enlarged trigger guard by Rinz of Stuttgart which allowed the arthritic knuckle of Bond's forefinger to slide smoothly around the trigger. His other hand took the light switch.

In one smooth, practised move, Bond snapped on the light switch and simultaneously peered around the room.

There was a shadowy, half-familiar figure by the dressing table. Bond fired, twice, the fearful reports cracking back and forth between the walls, and the figure reeled.

'So much,' murmured Bond coolly, 'for Comrade Nevachevski!'

Miss Moneypenny sat up in bed, her grizzled bun unravelling, her elegant muffler in fetching disarray.

'You silly old sod,' she said.

Bond beamed, deafly.

'Yes, wasn't it?' he said. 'Inch or so wide, mind, should've been straight between the eyes, but, my God, he didn't even have time to draw!'

'YOU'VE SHOT YOUR WIG-STAND!' shouted Miss Moneypenny. She stuck an ephedrine inhaler in her left nostril, and sucked noisily.

Bond put on his bi-focals.

'Ah,' he said. He brightened. 'Still a bloody good shot, though, eh?'

'I should cocoa,' said Moneypenny. 'It ricocheted off the hot-water bottle. God alone knows what it's done to your rubber sheet.'

'Bloody hell,' said Bond.

He switched the light out again, and lay back. As always, after untoward events, his wheeze was bad, crackling round the room like crumpling cellophane.

'Shall I rub you in?' murmured Moneypenny softly, from her distant cot.

'Don't start,' said Bond.

Moneypenny sighed. At sixty-eight, it seemed, her virginity was moving slowly but surely beyond threat.

Bond shuffled nonchalantly into M's office and tossed his hat in a neat arc towards the polished antler. The hat fell in the waste-bin. 007 stared at it for a time, and finally decided against picking it up. On the last occasion upon which he had attempted a major stoop, it had taken four osteopaths to unwind him.

'Good morning,' said M, 'if you're from Maintenance, I'd like you to know that the roller towel is getting harder and harder to tug. I don't know what they're doing with them these days. I think they put something in them at the factory. When I was a lad, you could pull them down between thumb and forefinger. Possibly the KGB has a hand in it. Also, I have great difficulty in pulling the soap off that magnetic thingy.'

'It's me, sir,' said Bond, '00—'

He frowned.

M stared at him glaucously from nonagenarian eyes.

Bond took off his James Lobb galosh, and removed a slip of paper.

'7,' he said. '007.'

M trembled suddenly. He tugged at a drawer, but it did not budge.

'I've got a gun in here somewhere,' he said. 'By God, you'll know it when I find it! You're not 007, you swine, I've known 007 fifty years, he's bright ginger!'

'I shot my wig,' said Bond, gloomily.

M relaxed.

'No good getting angry with a wig,' he said. 'It's only doing its job.'

'You sent for me,' said Bond.

'In the CIA,' murmured M, 'I'd have been retired forty years ago. I would have one of those thermal pools with a thing that makes waves in it. I would have my own genito-urinary man coming in on a weekly basis. A TV hanging from the ceiling, mink linings for the cold snap, a hollow cane with Remy Martin in it, a rare dog.'

'About this job,' said Bond.

M blew his nose, ineptly.

'Usual thing,' he said. 'MIRV-launching Russian satellite has been brought down by a defecting Albanian inter-galactic tail-gunner in the pay of the Irgun Zwei Leomi. As you would expect, it has fallen down inside Vesuvius: crack KGB, CIA, Mafia, Triad, and IRA teams are already racing to the spot. I promised the PM we'd send our best man.'

'Oh, good,' muttered Bond. 'You don't think Snuggley might fit the bill better?'

'003?' said M. 'His leg's gone in for its annual service. No, James, it's you—bags of parachuting, ski-ing, scuba-diving, unarmed combat, all that, right up your street.'

'Quite,' said Bond.

'Pop along and see Charlie in Special Equipment,' said M.

'This,' said Charlie, 'is probably the most advanced truss in the world.'

'It's snug,' said Bond. 'What are all these pockets for?'

'Spare surgical stockings,' said Charlie, ticking off his fingers, 'international pensions book, collapsible alloy crutches, Sanatogen capsules, arch supports, emergency pee bottle, mittens, underwater deaf-aid, thermal liberty bodice, and a handbell in case you fall over somewhere and can't get up.'

'Super,' said Bond.

'Also,' said Charlie, 'we've been over your Morris Traveller and, ha-ha, tarted it up a bit. Apart from the fact that you'll now be able to get it up to fifty-five—'

'Christ!'

'—there's an emergency inertia brake that brings it to a dead stop in the event of the driver having a heart attack, plus two big orange lights on stalks in both wings enabling you to drive it through narrow spaces, a foot-button that throws your window out instantly in the event of nausea, an inflatable anti-haemorrhoid ring set in the driver's seat that activates at the first scream, and a 3× magnifying windshield that enables you to read road signs without getting out of the car.'

'Fantastic,' muttered Bond.

'Good luck, 007,' said Charlie, 'and good hunting!'

He shook Bond's hand, but gently.

Bond nosed forward out of the roundabout, onto the Dover road.

People hooted.

The Traveller lurched forward, stalled, lurched on again.

007 ground into third gear. He glanced in his mirror, for the tenth time. Somebody was following him. They had been following him since Blackheath, almost two hours ago.

At the next traffic light, Bond got out, and walked back.

'I don't sell off the float, grandpa,' said the milkman.

'Why have you been following me?' said Bond levelly.

'I got no option, have I?' said the milkman. 'First off, we're the only two vehicles doing fifteen miles a wossname, second off, every time I bleeding pull out to overtake, you start wandering all over the road.'

'Evasive action,' snapped 007. 'Don't tell me you weren't trying to force me into the ditch. You're with SMERSH, right?'

The milkman took his cap off.

'It says Unigate on here,' he said.

'Ha!' cried Bond, and sprang into a Nakusai karate crouch, his left hand a club, his right fingers a dagger.

The milkman got out and helped him up.

'It's this knee I've got,' said Bond.

'Shouldn't be out, old geezer like you,' said the milkman. 'It's freezing.'

Bond laughed one of his short dry laughs. Once, men had gone white at the very sound.

'Be warm enough, soon, eh? I trust you're bound for Vesuvius?'

The milkman looked at him.

'I got Mafeking Crescent to do, and a bulk yoghurt up the telephone exchange,' he said, 'then I'm off home for *Pebble Mill*.'

'A likely story!' cried Bond. 'What's under that moustache, you Chinese bastard?'

007 made a lightning grab at the milkman's upper lip, misjudged the distance, and caught his forefinger in his opponent's mouth. The milkman closed his teeth on Bond's frail knuckle, and the agent fell back into the road. As he lay there, a bus-driver walked up, stood on him absently, and said to the milkman.

'These bleeding lights have gone green twice, sunshine.'

'Don't blame me,' said the milkman, 'this old bugger stuck his hand in my gob.'

The bus-driver glanced down.

'It's this ten pounds Christmas bonus they're getting,' he said. 'It's driving 'em all barmy. They've been smoking on the downstairs deck all morning.' He bent down, and hauled Bond upright. 'Come on, uncle, I'll see you across to the Whelk & Banjo.'

He took Bond into the public bar, and sat him on a stool, and went out again.

Bond took five pills. His hand was shaking, his heart was pounding, there was a tic in his right eye, and his bronchitis was coming back. He ought to get on, it was four clear days to Naples, given that he refused to drive at night and wanted to pop into the clinic at Vitry-le-François for his monthly check-up.

But, then again, was it worth it? The KGB might hit him, the CIA might shout at him if he couldn't keep up, his surgical skis were as yet untested, and as for swimming the Bay of Naples, he had noticed in himself of late an unsettling tendency to sink. Added to all of which, his SMERSH counterpart was a big Balinese stripper fifty years his junior, and he doubted that his current sexual techniques would persuade her to defect, given that he preferred doing it in his herringbone overcoat these days, apart from the fact that he had last performed a mere eight months before and seriously doubted whether his forces were yet in a position to be remustered.

It wasn't a bad pub, all in all, thought Bond. He could write out a report from here, elaborating a bit. After all, what could they expect for fifty quid a week after stoppages?

The barman looked up at Bond's cough.

'What'll it be?' he said.

'I'll have a small Wincarnis,' said Bond. He took off his balaclava. 'Shaken, not stirred.'

The Rhinestone As Big As The Ritz

Let Us Now Phone Famous Men

A child's game, at root, like all good things. After all, could any-thing match that first fine discovery of the telephone and all it stood for? That first realisation that, contained within ten simple digits, lay the infinitely possible? Out there—the infor-mation seeped into the infant brain in all its diabolical clarity —lay six billion ears, all the people in the world, available for contact and mystery and insult, unable to resist the beckoning of one small and villainous forefinger. We used, my tiny evil friends and I, to congregate at the nearest parentless house, and dial into the void, and innocent mouths would answer, and gullible ears would wait. Ah, to be only eight and wield such limitless power over adults! To fell a vicar with a practised oath, to turn bass breathing on a solitary spinster, to order fourteen tons of coal from Rickett Cockerell and have it de-livered to the schoolmaster of one's choice—what could match this for delirious joy? Only the pièce de résistance of scouring the phone-book for a citizen called Dumm or Barmie and phoning him to enquire if he was. What nights we spent in illicit spinnings of the dial, tottering helplessly about our living-rooms, gasping at our own wit and ingenuity and smash-ing our milk-teeth on the fender in the thrashing throes brought on by such hilarity!

I wonder, sometimes, if the men who were boys when I was a boy still do it. It's not a question you can ask of bald, august solicitors, of doctors nursing kids and mortgages, of paunched executives: but do they, a quarter of a century on, creep down, perhaps, at 4 a.m. and ring their enemies to offer six free foxtrot lessons, or scream indecencies at subscribers doomed to names like Bott and Hoare?

I thought of them last week, those tiny swine who helped mis-spend my youth. Because it suddenly occurred to me to crank the whole game up to a more sophisticated notch: perhaps it was the opening of direct dialling to New York, perhaps it was the acreage of puerile posters by which the Post Office whips us on to take advantage of their miracle offers, but, whatever the spur, I decided to spend the day trying to telephone the leaders of the world. Why not? After all, they had ears like anyone else, they had desks with phones on, they were put in power, more or less, by insignificant souls like me: surely they could set aside a few seconds for a chat, an exchange of gossip, an acknowledge-ment that the silent majority had a right, occasionally, to speak?

So I phoned Mao Tse-Tung.

"Who?" said the girl on 108 (International Directory En-quiries).

"He's the Chairman of the Chinese People's Republic," I said. "It's probably a Peking number."

There was a long silence. I could see her there, repolishing an immaculate nail, shoving a wayward curl back beneath her head-set, sucking a Polo, wondering whether she should go on the pill.

"I'll get the Supervisor," she said, finally.

"Nobody ever phones China," said the Supervisor.

"Why not?"

"I don't know," she said. Her voice was diamantine. "I only know why people phone places, I don't know why they don't, do I?"

Ruined by syntax, I pled help.

"You could phone the Chinese Chargé d'Affaires in London," she said. "The number is 580 7509."

580 7509 yielded a high-pitched moan. My Chinese may be less than flawless, but even I could tell that no human larynx was involved.

I phoned the Operator.

Who phoned the Engineer.

Whose Supervisor phoned me.

"It's NU," he said. For a moment, I felt excitingly privy to some piece of inside dope about Post Office/Chinese Legation affairs: clearly, from the man's weary voice, it was old Enn-Yu up to his tricks again, Enn-Yu the phone-bugger (I don't mean that the way it looks), the tamperer, the Red Guard saboteur; Enn-Yu, the man who had plagued the GPO for years with his intercepted calls and weird Oriental devices fitted out in the Legation basement.

"Who's Enn-Yu?" I said.

"Not In Use," he said, and a small world crashed. "They're always switching their lines down there. Every six weeks, they want a new phone number. Hang on," he said, and voices muttered in the background, and far bells rang. He came back. "It's 636 9756 this week," he said.

"Harro!" shouted a voice at 636 9756.

"Hallo," I said. "I want to know how I can telephone China."

"Why?"

"I want to speak to Chairman Mao."

"Why?"

"I have a personal message to deliver."

Breathing. Whispering. A new, more senior voice.

"Not possible terrephone China!" it shrieked. "Not possible terrephone Chairman! What you want?"

I explained again. It turned out that there were no lines between England and China. Nobody ever telephoned China. Nobody *would* ever telephone China.

"How do *you* speak to China?" I asked.

A third voice came on.

"GET OFF RINE!" it screamed. "GET OFF RINE QUICK NOW!"

And rang off. The whole thing had taken forty-seven minutes. More than enough time for thermonuclear gee-gaws to have wiped both Asia and Europe off the map. I knew the PM didn't have a hot line to Mao, and it bothered me.

I dialled again.

"Yes?" said 108.

"I'd like," I said, "to speak to Mr. Kosygin."

She muffled the phone inadequately.

"I think it's him again," I heard, distant and woolly. There was giggling. I waited. The Supervisor came on.

"Are you," she said, and the syllables fell like needles, "the gentleman who just wanted to speak to Mao Tse-Tung?"

"Yes," I said.

I sympathised. She had, I knew, a vision of this solitary loonie who had let himself loose on the telephonic world, prior, no doubt, to rape or suicide. I wondered if they were playing for time with their long, reflective pauses, trying to trace the call, trying to dispatch a van-load of GPO male nurses to my gate. But all she said was:

"Russian Inquiries are on 104."

"Have you got his address and phone number?" said 104.

"No," I said, "I thought you'd have it."

"They never send us directories," she said. "It's only them and the Rumanians that don't. Everyone else sends us their directories."

"Then how do you phone Russians?"

"You have to have their number. We keep," she grew confidential, "a list of hotels and factories, a few things like that. We're not supposed to, but we do. I've got the Kremlin number. Do you think that would do?"

"Yes, that sounds very good."

"There's an hour's delay to Moscow. I'll get them to ring you back, and he might come to the phone. That'd be nice, wouldn't it?"

"That would be very nice," I said. "In the meantime, as you're European Directory, could you get the Pope for me?"

"Oooh, you are *awful*!" she shrieked. Her voice faded, and I could just catch it explaining the situation to the other girls. Time passed. She came back.

"You're not going to say nothing dirty to them, are you?" she said. "Excuse me for asking, but we have to."

I reassured her.

"I'll have to keep your number by me," she said, "in case there's complaints, you know, afterwards, like. No offence meant, but you'd be surprised how many people ring up foreigners and swear at them."

I agreed, wondering who. Insights were bursting in on every hand. It clearly wasn't all beer and skittles, being a world leader, trying to keep up the balance of payments and build new schools and hold back the opposition, with Englishmen phoning you up all hours of the day and night, shouting "Eff off!"

She gave me the Pope's residential number. I dialled direct, 01039 6 6982. It was engaged. Odd. Was he, perhaps, on The Other Line? Or just on the balcony, waving? I tried again, trembling slightly at his proximity—five hundred million subjects under his thumb, and that thumb about to curl over the receiver in response to a far, agnostic call.

"Allo."

"Your Holiness?"

Pause.

"Wod?"

"Am I speaking to the Pope? *Il Papa?*"

Scuffling.

"Allo, allo. Can I 'elp you?"

"May I speak to the Pope?"

A long, soft sigh, one of those very Italian sighs that express so much, that say *Ah, signor, if only this world were an ideal world, what would I not give to be able to do as you ask, we should sit together in the Tuscan sunshine, you and I, just two men together, and we should drink a bottle of the good red wine, and we should sing, ah, how we should sing, but God in His infinite wisdom has, alas, not seen fit to . .*

"Can the Pope," I said, determined, "come to the phone?"

"The Bobe never gum to the delephone, signor. Nod for you, nod for me, nod for Italians, nod for nobody. Is not bozzible, many regrets, 'Is 'Oliness never spig on delephone. You give me your name, I give mezzage to 'Is 'Oliness, 'e give you blezzing, okay?"

"Okay," I said. A blessing, albeit proxied, was something.

"Don menshnit," he said, kindly, and clicked off.

By great good fortune (or even the grace of God: who knows how quickly a Pope's blessing might work?), there was a different operator on 108 when I tried to reach Richard Nixon. He put me on to 107, who got me the White House in three minutes flat, which gave tricky Dicky a thick edge over Mao, Kosygin and Il Papa when it came to accessibility. I thought you'd like to know that, Dick, since I didn't get the chance to tell you myself. Accessibility, as Harry Truman might have said, stops here. Or almost here. The lady secretary at the White House was extremely kind, incredibly helpful and understanding; doubtless because, given America's readiness to empty magazines at those in power, you can't be too careful with nuts who phone up to speak to the President. Fob them off with a "Get lost!" one minute, and the next they're crouched on a nearby roof and pumping away with a mail-order Winchester. The President, she said, was down in Florida, at Key Biscayne, where his number was 305 358 2380; someone there would speak to me. They did, and they were just as syrupy and sympathetic, and who knows but that I mightn't have got into the Great Ear if I hadn't played one card utterly wrong? What happened was, the call from the Kremlin, booked, you'll remember, an hour before, suddenly came through on my other phone, and I was mug enough, drunk with bogus eminence, to say to the American voice:

"Sorry, can you hold on a sec, I've got Kosygin on the other line?"

It was a nice moment, of course, but that's as long as it lasted. America hung up. Tread carefully when you step among the great, friends, their corns are sensitive.

I rather liked the Kremlin.

"Is that Mister Coren?" they said.

It's no small thrill to think one's name has echoed down the corridors of Soviet power, from room to room, while nervous men, fearful of the punishment that follows bureaucratic cockups, have tried to find out who one is, and what one wants with the Prime Minister. After all, so much is secret, so much unknown. I might have been anybody, even the sort of Anybody whose whisper in a top ear could send whole switchboardsful of comrades to the stake. Who was this Coren, this cool, curt international voice who seemed to be on such good terms with Alexi N. Kosygin that he thought nothing of phoning him person-to-person? For men who remembered Lavrenti Beria, no kindness to strangers was too much. Which is no doubt why I actually got to Kosygin's private secretary, who was himself extremely civil.

"I merely want to present the Prime Minister with my good wishes," I told him.

He was heartbroken that the Prime Minister was inextricably involved at present, but swore to me that my message would be passed on immediately. And I have not the slightest doubt that it was. It's a long way to Siberia, after all, and the cattle-trains leave every hour, on the hour.

Which left me with just two numbers in my little black book: Havana 305 031 and Cairo 768944. It took me a day to get through to one, and three days to reach the other (all calls to Egypt are subject to censorship), and when I finally did make contact, Fidel and Anwar were, needless to say, busy elsewhere. Both, however, promised faithfully to ring me back, which is why I leave them till last. Courtesy I like. Not, though, that they actually *have* rung back, but who knows? Even now, the dark, dependable forefingers may be poised over their respective dials, groping along the cables for a chance to chew the fat and swop a joke or two. If not, and if they read this first, don't worry about it, lads. It's nothing urgent.

I just wanted to say hello.

The Sanity Inspector

A Small Thing but Minoan

'We can be quite precise about the date. 4,000 years ago in Crete, during the Middle Minoan Period, linear writing in pen and ink was born.'—Fodor Guide to Crete

AGOROPHON SQUINTED UP at the noonday sun. It gonged down out of a brass sky; the arid rock baked; insects gasped, crept slowly for the shade of crevices.

'Beats me why you dragged me all the way out here,' he said irritably. 'Day like this, what you want is your feet in a basin and a bird standing behind you with a large frond.'

'I've got something to show you,' said Memnos. 'It's private.'

Agorophon looked at him.

'It's not that rash again, is it?' he said.

Memnos shook his head. He groped down inside the neckline of his smock, while his friend watched uneasily.

'There you are,' said Memnos, handing him a fragment of dried leaf, 'have a butcher's at that.'

'If it's a scab,' said Agorophon, 'I'm not going near it.'

'It's a leaf,' said Memnos, 'it's got something written on it.'

'*Written* on it?' cried Agorophon. 'How can you chisel a leaf?'

But he looked at it.

'You're right,' he said, at last. 'Squiggles. What a miraculous thing Nature is!'

'It's not natural,' replied Memnos. '*I* did it. I did it with ink.'

'Ink?'

'It's something I made from roots.'

'I thought that was gin,' said Agorophon.

'Different roots,' said Memnos. 'You don't drink this one.'

'Pity,' said Memnos. 'You can have enough of gin, this weather.'

132

'You write with it,' said Memnos. 'You dip a twig in it, and write.'

'Get off!' cried Agorophon. He looked at the leaf again. 'All right, what does it say?'

'It says X. P. Memnos, Number 9a, High Street.'

'What's it for?'

Memnos shrugged.

'It's all I could think of. You could give it to people. It's better than carrying a bagful of them stone visiting cards. Also, you can just dash 'em off. Instead of sitting there all day with a mallet.'

'Easier on the thumbs,' said Agorphon, 'I'll give you that.'

Memnos looked away from his friend, out over the broiling landscape, feeling faintly hollow. Disappointed wasn't quite the word. But, then, what was? The Cretan vocabulary was small, detailed, a lot of synonyms for food, weapons, internal organs, not much more. Perhaps it would expand, now, with the tedium of chiselling gone.

'Mind you,' said Agorophon, breaking into his reverie, 'I'll be glad to see the back of cuneiform, I don't mind saying. I could never make head nor tail out of it, it was just triangles. If we'd stuck with hieroglyphs, I could have got somewhere. I could have made something of myself. I used to enjoy reading hieroglyphs, all them little parrots, frogs, titchy houses, all that. I don't know why they gave it up.'

'Progress,' said Memnos.

'Yes, well,' said Agorophon.

Memnos frowned down at his leaf.

'I wonder what I ought to write first?' he murmured.

'Make marvellous betting slips,' said Agorophon.

'Very interesting,' said Old Memnos, looking disparagingly at the leaf. 'When are you going to go out and earn a living?'

'I want to be a writer,' said his son.

'What kind of work is that for a man?' said his mother. She dropped a rabbit's head into the pot, stirred it absently. 'I see them sitting in the square every day, hammering tablets, covered in dust. Labourers is what they are.'

'But this is a very fast system,' protested her son. He dipped his twig in a vial of murky liquid, and dashed off his address, ten times over, on a large piece of goatskin.

'Hang on!' shouted Old Memnos. 'She was making me a vest out of that!'

'It's got our address on it now,' said his son. 'That's another valuable asset.'

'I doubt whether you could market *that*,' said his mother. 'I don't see where there's much call for addressed underwear.'

'If you got run over,' said her son, 'they'd know where to bring you.'

His mother sniffed.

'About the only thing *I* can think of,' she said, 'is shopping lists. With stone shopping lists, time you've chiselled *Two kilograms brussels sprouts*, they've gone out of season.'

'I was planning on something bigger,' said Memnos, as the old hollowness moved through him once more. 'A personal statement, perhaps. Possibly rhyming. About love, or death, or going barmy. Something major.'

'Here!' cried his father. 'What about posters for tourists? They're always coming here from the mainland; we could do posters advertising dancing folklorique up the town hall, souvenir shops where they could get them little minotaurs for holding toothpicks, guided tours of the labyrinth. We could go down to the boats and hand 'em round, we'd get ten per cent off the retailers, we could clean up!'

'It's not exactly what I had in mind,' said his son.

His father glared at him.

'Advertising,' he said, 'that's where the money is!'

'Kids!' said his wife. 'Do they listen?'

He sat under a tree. Flies buzzed around his ink. He chewed his twig for the hundredth time. Around him, the parched ground was strewn with crumpled leaves.

He took a fresh one from his bag, smoothed it out, laid it on the board across his knees. Slowly, tongue curling over his upper lip, he wrote:

'It was a dark and stormy night.'

He stopped.

His mind teemed with shapes, people, mountains, ships,

jokes, accidents, names, dreams. They floated about, they interleaved, they fragmented.

He tore up the leaf, and plucked another.

'It was the best of times,' he wrote, 'it was the worst of . . .'

'OY!'

Memnos looked up.

Agorophon was galloping down the hill, scattering goats. He fetched up, breathless.

'Journalism!' he gasped.

'What?'

'Nice big leaf, rhubarb, palm, something like that, bring it out every day, nail it up in the town square, stand a couple of big blokes in front of it with clubs, people want to read it, they have to pay! Main news, discus results, drawings of birds with their skirts up, spot-the-javelin contest, seer forecast, classified ads—how about it?'

Memnos shook his head.

'It would be selling out,' he said.

Agorophon clenched his fists.

'At least,' he muttered, 'it'd be selling.'

'That is not,' murmured Memnos, 'what it's all about.'

'It's what some of it's about, mate,' snapped Agorophon.

It took Memnos several years to sail to the mainland, and hardly a night passed on that terrible voyage when he did not regret his decision to leave Crete, nor long for the old companionship of the simple Cretans who had wanted him to abuse his gift.

And when, at last, he arrived, and sat on the pebbled beach, what, he asked himself, had it all been for?

And then he knew.

He had something to write about now.

When the sack of scribbled leaves was full, he strapped it to a mule, and he trekked into Athens, and—

What did one do with a great poem?

He pushed through the hanging beads.

'Is this,' enquired Memnos timidly, 'the registered office of

Homer, Homer, Homer, Homer, Homer, Homer & Homer?'

'Yes,' they said.

'I understand,' said Memnos, putting his sack down, 'that you recite great poetry?'

'Sometimes it's great,' said all the Homers, 'sometimes it's not so great. You win a few, you lose a few. Also, it depends how much you can remember. We take it you know about the oral tradition?'

'It's over,' said Memnos, not without a hint of triumph. 'Mine's written down.'

The Homers looked at one another, sharply.

'*Written down?*'

'It's in two parts. One I called *The Odyssey*. The other I called *The Iliad*.'

'Catchy,' said the Homers. 'Could be very big.'

'Also,' said Memnos, 'I can teach you to read it. Then you could read it aloud everywhere, and I would get rich and famous.'

'So teach,' said the Homers.

And he did.

And when he had gone, the seven Homers split the manuscript up into seven parts, and each Homer learned his seventh by heart.

Then they burned the manuscript.

'Tough on the kid,' said the Homers, 'but business is business.'

The Rhinestone As Big As The Ritz

Learn Omniscience the Easy Way Today!

Purnell's New English Encyclopaedia comes to you every week as an absorbing and lavishly illustrated magazine. But this is a magazine of permanent *value. Week by week it grows into a valuable library of learning.* From A to Z week by week. *In just 18 weeks you will have in a permanent binding Volume I of the complete 12-volume set. The next 18 weeks will see the completion of Volume II . . . and so on, until you have all 12 volumes.* – Advertisement.

YOU MAY NOT have known me in the old days before Sir Mortimer Wheeler and Sir Bernard Lovell and the rest of the editorial gang at Purnell's got their hands on me, because I didn't get around very much. How could I? A shy, diffident lad with less General Knowledge at his fingertips than you could shake a stick at, I spent most of my time listening to lectures at Caxton Hall trying to cure my stammer, my unsightly blushes, and a curious, self-effacing, pigeon-toed walk that is the legacy of something now lost forever in the pre-natal mists. I was, you see, the victim of a specialist education (O, where were the Snows of yesteryear?), the War, and a highly individual brand of galloping acne, all of which left me in post-adolescence as one of those flowers born to stammer unseen, and rightly so. I became the sort of chap who turns up at beer- and-cheese parties carrying a bottle of Veuve-Clicquot to apologise for the pointlessness of his presence, and spends the rest of the evening standing in the corridor with a sickly grin on his face hanging up the coats of new

137

arrivals, and occasionally slipping off to the bathroom to twist alone. (Thinks: *Imagine what a twit I must have seemed before receiving the first instalment of Purnell's New English Encyclopaedia! I can laugh now, but it wasn't funny at the time, I can tell you! Then, one day, when I was trying to think of why the chicken crossed the road, to the embarrassment of all, my best friend leaned across and whispered: 'Stupidity!' in my ear. And then I knew what I had to do.*)

It's all so different now. It seems like only yesterday that the first instalment of Purnell's arrived through my letter box. It *was* only yesterday, actually (Thinks: *Time was, I wouldn't dare make a joke like that! What confidence knowledge gives you! Just wait until I get the 'Wetnurse—Wit' instalment in October 1968, packed with new jokes for all the family!*) There it lay, No. 1, 'A — Aconite', and today I'm a changed man. I spent all day reading it up and committing it to memory and in the evening my wife gave a small dinner party, as a sort of, well, launching ceremony. Nobody special, just a few of her friends who have come, over the years, to regard me as a blot on the history of the human race.

It wasn't without a certain trepidation that I awaited the first arrivals. After all, general knowledge may give you that extra something, but I wasn't sure I could confine the conversation within the — let's face it, Sir Mortimer — rather narrow limits of A — Aconite. At 8.30, the Plunketts arrived, and I leapt to greet them with such eagerness that something which I can only describe as fear flashed across George's eyes as he drew my arms from his neck.

'Hallo, old man', he said. 'My, but you're lucky to see us! Nearly had a nasty accident coming off the old A3, didn't we, Phoebe?'

'Accident?' I cried. 'Not one of the 350,000 that occur each year in Britain?'

'Probably one of those,' said his wife, a curiously wry lady.

'It has been estimated', I said, leaning nonchalantly against the door-jamb and folding my arms, 'that if traffic continues to increase at the present rate, and accidents commensurately, 10,000 people will be killed annually in Britain by 1980'.

The Plunketts looked at me with new interest.

'What about a drink?' said George, and I smiled at him confidently.

'Experts', I said, examining a fingernail, 'believe the greatest amount of alcohol a driver should have in his blood is 0·1 per cent. In practical terms, this means a limit of $1\frac{1}{2}$ pints of beer, or three small tots of spirits'.

"I'll have three small tots of spirits, then', said Phoebe, and we all laughed uproariously, though I couldn't see why. Roll on May 1966 when the 'Jerboa — Jutland' instalment will tell me all I need to know about Jokes.

Soon after this, the Hubbards and the Folletts arrived together, and before long we were all sitting round talking about Abidjan, the capital of the Ivory Coast which has a population of nearly 200,000, many of whom live in Treichville, an industrial suburb. Later, pleasantly exhausted by our chatter (would you believe it, *nobody* had heard of Abbas the Great, the most important sovereign of the Persian dynasty of the Safawids (1557—1628)? Harry Hubbard had heard of somebody called Baldwin, but I think he was just making the name up to show off. Anyway, I pretty soon changed the subject to acanthocephala — a class of parasitic worms, not unlike tapeworms — and that shut him up, I can tell you!).

At dinner, I was a little chastened to discover that my wife had been unable to obtain aardvark steaks at Sainsbury's, but I got over the lull in conversation by describing, in what must have been fascinating detail, the running of an abattoir, and how infected carcases and entrails are rendered down for fertilizer and soap. At the end of the main course, I turned to my wife, a smile playing somewhat mischievously about my lips, and said:

'Would you like me to accumulate the plates, dearest?'

She was oddly silent, but nodded briefly.

'Yes', I continued, standing up, 'let me be the accumulator, ha-ha-ha. Not, of course, the apparatus able to absorb energy and give it back when required . . . . '

'No?' asked Alfred Follett, his face rapt.

'No', I replied. I laughed. 'I shouldn't like to be coated with lead dioxide (or PbO_2) which is then transformed into lead sulphate (or $PbSO_4$), you know. It would undoubtedly kill me.'

I caught a wistful look in Alfred Follett's eyes, and I realised that he would probably have given anything to know as much as I do about accumulators. But it isn't given to all men, that kind of knowledge;

one has to know how to use it wisely.

After dinner, the talk ranged over every conceivable subject, from abyssal deposits to abu-Nuwas (an eighth century Arab poet who ridiculed the life of the desert), from William Aberhart (the famous Canadian politician) to the accordian. I cannot remember ever having had so sophisticated an evening. The time seemed to fly by on Achilles heels, I think is the expression. It felt like no more than an hour after dinner when everyone got up to leave; it was in fact one hour and eleven minutes, although my wife said that the time was so packed with interest and information and so on, that it felt like four, which cheered me up enormously, since I had been afraid that the guests might have felt cheated by my not being able to tell them any more about Aconcagua than the fact that its chief industry is rearing sheep and goats.

The Plunkets and Folletts had already run down the path by the time I'd helped Winnie Hubbard into her coat, so she and Harry were the only ones I could ask to come again.

'Sorry, old chap', said Harry, 'but we're off to Greece for a month tomorrow'.

'Really?' I said. 'Not to Achaea, by any chance, that district in the north of the Pelopennese which is 1,160 square miles in area, with a population of 236,000?'

'No', he said. 'To Athens'.

Athens! By heavens, so near and yet so far! Next week's instalment, in fact.

'You *must* come and see us when you get back', I said.

I hope they do. I can't wait to hear what I have to say about it.

The Dog It Was That Died

It's A Long Way To Cannelloni

"The British soldier is becoming a gourmet. To wartime soldiers brought up on bully beef stew, the Catering Corps cookery book would seem unbelievable. It contains 1,076 recipes. But their resources will be tested to the full next week, with the arrival in Aldershot of shooting teams from all over the world for the Central Treaty Organisation Small Arms Shooting Competition." – Sunday Telegraph.

In the dank dug-out, one candle flickered. The heavy air reeked of fatigue and soaked serge and garlic and saltimbocca alla romana. Above, along the old duckboards, old ducks went up the line to death, to be stuffed, spitted, sauced, and then forgotten. There had been some talk at Base of raising a memorial to the Unknown Duck, when it was all over, but it would be a long time before that day came. In the no-man's-land between the clattering mobile canteens and the rat-tat-tat of the Kenwood .303 foodmixers, young pigs squealed horribly, and died. The awful stink of burning flesh was everywhere.

At a makeshift chopping-table, Captain Stanhope sat over his cookery book, ball-point poised. It wasn't easy to find the right words. Taramasalata, had the brigadier said? Or was it tarragon? Or tagliatelle? They had all been out here too long. Stanhope's eyes were ringed with dark shadows from too much stuffing; his fingers were scored from dicing with carrots; his hair was falling out.

Sergeant Trotter, who had been there and back, and there again, and seen it all, who had done the porridge at Alamein

141

and smoked the haddocks for the Imjin River brunches, came down the rickety stairs, slopping an enamel mug. He put it on Stanhope's table.

"Go on, sir," he said. "Get that inside you."

Stanhope sipped the fragrant skate-liver-and-jasmine broth.

"He should have been back by now, Trotter."

"You can't never tell, sir. It's no good thinking the worst. Every cloud has a silver lining."

"Good old Trotter!" Stanhope, despite the heaviness breeding about his heart, laughed the brave young laugh that had carried him through so much, through a hundred collapsed soufflés and a thousand curdled bortschs. Stanhope had seen many flies in many soups. "Good old Trotter, you always know the right thing to say!"

"An apple a day keeps the doctor away, sir."

"God knows that's true, Trotter."

"Persil washes whiter, sir."

Stanhope sighed and nodded.

"Young Raleigh's a child, Trotter. He's only been with us two weeks. He doesn't have the experience. He doesn't have the nerves. They're sending them to us straight from domestic science school, Trotter."

"He'll make out, sir. He's got an old head on young shoulders, has Mr. Raleigh. A stitch in time saves nine, sir."

"I suppose you're right, Trotter. But he's never tackled more than a bread-and-butter pudding, or an apple crumble—and now he's out there facing the Turks with nothing more than a teenage sauce corporal and a few green private can-openers to help him. The Turks'll make mincemeat of them!"

"I had a recipe for human mincemeat once, sir," murmured Trotter, "it's not so bad. Don't you fret, sir. Many a mickle makes a muckle."

Erratic bootsteps thundered overhead, amid weak, sporadic cheering. Stanhope leapt up. As he did so, a fresh-faced youth burst through the doorway, his chef's hat awry and ketchup-stained, and flung himself into the dug-out.

"Raleigh!" cried Stanhope. "Thank God you're safe!"

142

The young lieutenant wiped his gravied hands on his apron. He looked hard into Stanhope's addled grey eyes.

"It's sheer bloody hell out there, sir!" he cried. "The Turks have broken through our fish pie and it's only a matter of minutes before they begin mopping up."

"God, they're filthy eaters!" muttered Stanhope.

"Give 'em a taste of cold veal!" cried Trotter. "He can't face cold veal, can't Johnny Turk!"

"What about our left flank, old chap?"

"Dreadful, sir," said Raleigh. "Complete bloody shambles. The French are chucking everything they can think of at us— seventy-three orders of tête de veau vinaigrette, forty-eight entrecôtes de quatre saisons, including seventeen saignants, twenty-two bleu, nineteen without parsley, six with rosemary but no thyme, twelve with thyme but no basil, and nobody wants chips. My men are beginning to crack, sir. And I'm afraid the German assault on the knackwurst is beginning to tell—if the sauerkraut gives out, it's going to be impossible to hold them!"

"Dear God!" shouted Stanhope, "It's started earlier than anyone anticipated!"

"You mean—?"

Stanhope hurled his ladle aside.

"Yes, Raleigh, it's the Big Push! And only this morning I had a dispatch rider up from Base saying that Intelligence reckoned we could hold 'em off with two-eggs-chips-sausage-and-beans for at least a week."

"What do they know at Base?" shrieked Raleigh, his slim frame trembling, "sitting around in their shiny kitchens, surrounded by clean Formica and remote-control cookers and waste-disposal units, making one another zabaglione and matelote de brochet au vin rosé? How long is it since any of them was out here, trying to prise the eye out of a sheep for a tableful of Iranian brass who'd have your leg for an hors d'oeuvres as soon as look at you?"

"Steady, old chap!" Stanhope's firm hand came down on Raleigh's lonely pip. Suddenly, an inhuman shriek rocked the dug-out, and a wild-eyed figure sprang through the Habitat beads, waving a Webley. He was dressed in a black tailcoat and a long white apron.

"It's Frobisher!" hissed Stanhope. "He's blown his top!"

"It's the waiting!" screamed Frobisher. "I can't stand it any more!"

"The waiting's always the worst, sir," said Trotter soothingly.

"Seven tables!" howled Frobisher, searching desperately for the trigger, "Two Spanish, two Greek, two Italian, and some madman sitting under the stairs who says he's from the IRA and if I don't bring him a plate of potatoes on the double he'll pull the pin and blow the entire canteen to bits."

"You've just been out here too long, old man," said Stanhope. "We all have."

"None of you has been what I've been through!" sobbed Frobisher. "You forget I'm only seconded to the 17th/21st Entrées. I came from the Queen's Own Yorkshire Light Sommeliers. We were a class mob, we could sniff a '47 Margaux from fifty paces, we could tell a Krug from a Bollinger with our gasmasks on, and there was always a half-bottle or two left over to slip up your pinny after they blew Last Post." His voice broke. "I'll teach those bastards at Command! What's a bloody bullet look like, for God's sake?" He poked frenziedly in the chamber with his corkscrew, sobbing and shaking. "I can't take any more!"

Stanhope drew Raleigh aside.

"I think it's an old omelette wound he sustained at the Royal Tournament," he muttered, "when we were trying to do a fines herbes against the clock. Never been the same since. I'd better get that thing away from him." He set his splendid jaw, reached quickly inside his battledress, and took out a small blue envelope. "Look, I wrote this to Molly when the first hors d'oeuvres started. It's my own recipe for gefilte fish au poivre. If anything happens to me, Raleigh, I'd like you to—"

Suddenly, with a frightful culinary oath, Frobisher hurled the gun aside.

144

"Useless bloody thing!" he shrieked. He wheeled, and sprang for the stairs. "It's quicker this way!"

"After him, Trotter!" cried Stanhope. "He's making straight for the Dutch front tables, and you know what their appetite's like—they'll have an apple in his gob and a litre of sauce béarnaise running over his back before you can say Regulo Four!"

But it was not to be! An instant later, before even Trotter could unsheathe his trusty carvers, a weird and terrible multi-lingual din shook the dug-out and filled the gloom with un-answerable questions. Together, unhesitating, Stanhope and Raleigh leapt through the curtain, sprinted for the nearest dessert trench, and hurled themselves in. The air was full of flying onion rings and gnocchi, and prunes were everywhere. Gingerly, they pulled themselves up, and peered over the top. In time to see the khaki backsides of a dozen foreign regiments hurtling for the far horizon, the scattered victuals congealing in their wake.

"Dear Heavens!" cried Raleigh. "It's a bloody rout!"

"What happened?" shouted Stanhope. "What happened?"

A flying figure leapt the rim, and crashed beside them.

"Potter, sir, Sergeant I/C Soups and Cold Appetizers, it was Frobisher, sir, come on like a thing possessed, we couldn't stop him, sir. Before we knew what was happening, he was serving the French up hamburger waffles with jello, he was dishing out squid cous-cous to the Americans, he was hitting the Israelis with ham salads, he was serving haggis to the Dutch and raw roast beef to the Indians—I never seen nothing like it, sir, I never seen hard men break and run. I never seen commandos vomit."

A tear welled up and flashed in Stanhope's eye.

"Gentlemen in England now a-bed," he murmured, "shall think themselves accursed they were not here, Raleigh."

"Will he get a gong, sir?"

"Two, I shouldn't wonder," said Stanhope. "Lunch and dinner. He's saved the Catering Corps, Raleigh. Look at that!"

The broken foreigners had stopped, had turned, were shuffling humbly back. In the silence, bellies rumbled, like far guns.

"Raleigh lad," said Stanhope, "order up two hundred cheese omelettes, and never mind about the rinds. I think our guests are just about ready for their lunch."

The Sanity Inspector

Father's Lib

"The City University of New York has offered its male staff paternity leave on the same terms as female staff get maternity leave. It is believed to be the first time such a provision has been offered in an American labour contract." – The Times.

There are a number of things that are going to be wrong with this piece.

Some of them will be noticeable—a certain sogginess here and there; a tendency, uncharacteristic in the author, to use one word where two would normally do; arguments, if you can call them that, which start, falter, then peter emptily out; odd bits of disconnected filler, such as laundry lists, a reader's letter or two, notes from the inside cover of my driving licence, a transcript of my tailor's label; that sort of thing.

There will be phrases like "that sort of thing".

Some of the things that are going to be wrong will not be noticeable—the fact that the writer has a tendency to fall off his chair between paragraphs; to knock his coffee into his desk drawer; to rip the trapped ribbon from his typewriter and tear it to shreds, moaning and oathing; to wake up with a start to find the impression 1QA"ZWS/XED @ CRF£V on his forehead where it has fallen into the keys; to light a cigarette while one is still ticking over in the ashtray; to stop dead, wondering where his next syllable is coming from.

Nor will you notice, since the typographer, sturdy lad, will be backing up the young author like a seasoned RSM shoring a pubescent subaltern before Mons, that a good half of the words are misspelled, if there are two "s's" in "misspelled," that is; and if it shouldn't be "mis(s)pelt," anyway.

I'm glad that sentence is over; if it was a sentence. Was there a verb there?

But, for once, ineptitude will be its own defence; inadequacy its own argument. The very fact that readers this week are about to receive (have, indeed, already in part received) a substandard article with the tacks showing and the sawdust trickling out the back only proves the writer's thesis: which is that the concept of paternity leave has been a long time a-coming. That it has come to the United States, pioneer of the ring-pull can, automatic transmission, monosodium glutamate, the Sidewinder missile, and sundry other humanitarian break-throughs should be no surprise to anyone; what is grievous is that there is little sign that the blessed concession is to be adopted on this side of the Atlantic.

Not in time for me, anyhow. And—hang on, that little light on the bottle-warmer that goes out when the teated goody reaches the required temperature has just done so. All I have to do now is unscrew the cap on the bottle, reverse the teat, replace the cap, shake the air out, nip upstairs, prise apart the kipping gums before she's had a chance to wake up and scream the plaster off the wall, whang in the teat, sit back, and,

Dropped it on the bloody floor.

That's what I like about the three a.m. feed—that deftness in the fingers that only comes after two hours deep untroubled sleep, the clarity of the eyes rasping around behind the resinous lash-crust, the milk underfoot due to inability to find slipper and fear of turning on light in bedroom to search for same in case wife wakes up, thereby destroying entire point of self groping around in first place.

I'll come back to the argument in a minute. Now have to boil teat, mix new feed, screw, light goes on, light goes off, unscrew, reteat, rescrew, shake, nip upstairs, prise apart kipping gums, correction, prise apart screaming gums, that's my daughter, five weeks old and more accurate than a Rolex Oyster, it must be 3.01, must get feed done by 3.05, it takes

148

exactly four minutes from first scream for three-year-old son to wake up, where's my panda, where's my fire-engine, I'm thirsty, I'm going to be sick, news that he's going to be sick delivered on high C, thereby waking up wife at 3.09 exactly, wife shouts What's going on? whereupon son shouts Mummy, father shouts Shut up, lights start going on in neighbouring houses . . .

3.04 and fifty seconds, breath coming short and croaky from stairs, got feed mixed, teat boiled, all screwed down, whip out miniature daughter with .001 to spare, pop in teat, falls on it like Peter Cushing on an unguarded throat. I lean back in nursery chair, feet tacky from old milk, left fag burning beside typewriter on kitchen table, know fag will burn down on ash-tray rim, like Chinese torture in *Boy's Own Paper*—"When frame leaches thong, Blitish dog, thong tighten on tligger, burret brow blains out, heh, heh, heh!"—fag will fall off ash-tray, burn hole in table, possibly burn down house, Family Flee In Nightclothes.

I am actually writing this an hour later, madness recollected in tranquillity, if you can call tranquillity thing involving cat which has woken up in filthy mood to find milk on floor, there-fore licking up milk off floor, therefore in middle of floor when I come back to kitchen, therefore trodden on.

Anyhow, back to an hour ago, still feeding daughter, she beginning to drop off halfway through feed, terrible sign meaning can't go on with feed since daughter asleep, can't not go on, because if she goes down half-full, she'll be up again at 4.38, screaming, son up at 4.42, where's my panda, where's my fire-engine, wife up at 4.46, saying If you're incapable of doing a simple thing like a feed etcetera to sleeping form, thereby transforming it into waking form, fall out of bed in netherworld confusion, thinking fag burning house down, look around for something to Flee In, since don't wear Nightclothes, sub-editors all change headlines for 5 a.m. edition, Nude Phantom Terrorises Hampstead Third Night Running.

Wake daughter up, she cries, must be colic, hoist on shoulder, legs all colicky-kicking (I'd like to see James Joyce change a nappy), pat on back, crying goes up umpteen decibels, bring down again, mad gums grab teat, bottle empties like a Behan pint, relief.

Change daughter, all dry, smooth, cooing, give final burp with little rub, daughter hiccups, sick drenches dressing-gown sleeve, daughter's nightdress, change daughter again, can't find new nightdress, walk around numb and sicky, daughter shrieking now, since, having displaced part of feed, requires topping up, else valves will grind or crankshaft seize up, or something, back downstairs with daughter on shoulder wailing, feel like mad bagpiper, mix new feed one-handed, screw, light goes on, light goes off, unscrew, reteat, rescrew, shake, carry out with daughter, slam kitchen door with foot. Wake up cat.

Get upstairs, son wandering about on landing with dismembered bunny, I want a pee, can't explain holding daughter and feeding same is priority, since Spock says AVOID SUCH CLASHES THIS WAY TO JEALOUSY ETCETERA, lead son to lavatory with spare hand, holding bottle against daughter, daughter can now see bottle like vulture over Gobi, windows rattle with renewed shrieking, leave son peeing in sleepy inaccuracy on seat, back to nursery, finish feeding daughter, son roars I CAN'T GET MY PYJAMA TROUSERS UP, try to rise with daughter, bottle falls, teat gets hairy, hammers start in skull, but thanks, dear God, daughter now full, asleep, plonk in crib, turn out light, hurtle sonwards, son not there.

Son in bedroom, shaking wife, I CAN'T GET MY PYJAMA TROUSERS UP.

I creep, broken, downstairs. You know about treading on the cat. I look at the garbling in the typewriter. It stops at "hang on, that little light on the bottle-warmer that goes out." Sit down, smelling of regurgitation and panic, stare at keyboard, listen to dawn chorus going mad, man next door coughing his lung into the receptacle provided, far loos flushing, new day creaking in on its benders.

What I was going to write about before I was so rudely interrupted was, I see from the first tatty gropings, an article about how enlightened America was to introduce paternity leave for new fathers so that they wouldn't have to work for the first few weeks and could help cope with the latest novelty item, instead of going off to the office, the shop, the surgery, the factory.

Or the typewriter.

I had all these great arguments in favour of introducing the system over here, I had all the points worked out, it was all so lucid, so right, so uncounterable: I should bring about an instant revolution.

What arguments they were!

And if I only had the strength left to get them down on paper.

The Sanity Inspector

Long Ago and Far Away

Much talk is talked of the need for the Dunkirk spirit today. But suppose instead that we had had today's spirit at Dunkirk?

UP TO HIS WAIST in the filthy sea, oil lapping his sodden webbing, bomb-blasted flotsam bobbing about him, he sucked his teeth, and shook his head.

'I'm not bleeding going in that,' he said, 'I'm not bleeding going home in no rowing boat.'

'Right,' said his mate.

'Eighteen blokes in it already,' he said. 'Conditions like that, they're not fit for a pig.'

'Not fit for a pig, conditions like that,' said his mate.

'Got brought here in a troopship, din't we?' he said. He cupped his hands towards the rowing boat, and the man leaning towards them over its stern, arm outstretched. 'GOT BROUGHT HERE IN A BLEEDING TROOPSHIP!' he shouted, 'Ten square feet of space per man!'

'Regulations,' said his mate, nodding. 'All laid down. Nothing about going back in no bloody rowing-boat. Get away with murder if you let 'em, some people.'

A Stuka shrieked suddenly overhead, levelled, veered up out of its dive, back into the flakky sky. Its bomb exploded, drenching the two men.

'Not even got a roof on,' he said. 'What happens if it starts coming down cats and dogs halfway across? You could catch pneumonia.'

'Get a chill on the liver,' said his mate.

'*And* there's seasickness. It's not as if I'm a sailor. I'm not saying it isn't all right for *sailors*, am I? All right for them, open bloody boat. I mean, it's their line, know what I mean? But I'm a gunner. That's what I got took on as, that's what I am. If I'd wanted to be a sailor, I'd have got took on as a sailor.'

'I'm a cook,' said his mate. 'Cook, I said when they asked me up the recruiting. I didn't say bleeding admiral. I didn't say, I want to be a cook on account of I'm interested in the standing up to me waist in water, did I?'

'Course you didn't.'

An Me109 came low over the surface, strafing the scummy sea. A machine-gun bullet took his hat away.

'You'd have got more as an admiral, too,' he said. 'You get compensation, working in filthy conditions. I reckon they owe us special benefits. Nothing about all this in basic training, was there? Prone shooting and a bit of the old bayonet, dry conditions, two bob a day, all meals.'

'When was the last time you had a square meal?' asked his mate.

'I never thought of that!' He took a notepad from his saturated battle-blouse, licked his pencil, scribbled. 'I never thought of that at all. Three days ago, as a matter of fact. Bleeding Cambrai, if you can call two spoons of warm bully a square meal.'

'FOR GOD'S SAKE GET A MOVE ON!' cried the man in the stern.

The two privates waded awkwardly forward.

'Not so bloody fast, mate,' said the first. 'I require a few moments with the brothers here.'

The eighteen stared at him over the gunwales. Red fatigue rimmed their eyes, their bandages were thick with oil, their helmets were gone, leaving their hair to whiten with the salt.

'It has been brought to my attention by Brother Wisley here,' he said, 'that we are being expected to work in conditions unfit for a pig. Not only are we not being allowed to pursue our chosen trade, we have been dumped here in what can only be described as the sea, we have been required to leave our tools behind on the beach, we have not had a square meal for three days, and as for the statutory tea-break, I can't remember when. I won't even go into the overtime question.'

'We won't even go into the overtime question,' said his mate. 'But may I draw the meeting's attention to the fact that members of the Kings Own Yorkshire Light Infantry can be seen on our left climbing into a cabin cruiser?'

153

The eighteen turned, and looked.

'Bloody hell,' said a corporal.

'Well might you say bloody hell, brother!' said the first private. 'Course, I'm not saying our brothers in the KOYLI are not entitled to what they can get, and good luck, but the anomaly of the heretofore mentioned situation currently under review before the meeting by which we of the Royal Artillery. . . .'

'And the Catering Corps.'

'. . . and the Catering Corps, Brother Wisley, thank you, by which we of the Royal Artillery and the Catering Corps do not enjoy parity is one which threatens all we hold most dear.'

'RIGHT!' cried the man in the stern, 'Get in, or shut up, we haven't got all damned day, Jerry's throwing. . . .'

The private held up his hand.

'Just a minute, squire,' he said, 'just a minute. After frank and free discussions with my ad hoc executive here, we regret to inform you that deadlock has been reached in the negotiations, and unless you are prepared to furnish us with such basic requirements. . . .'

'I'm getting out anyway, brother,' said the corporal. He eased himself over the side. 'Come on, you lot, I have no intention of allowing my brothers on the floor to be manipulated by a cynical management and subjected to actual distress to serve the whim of the bosses.'

'Well said, brother!' cried the private.

The eighteen slid into the icy water.

The rowing boat came about, and sploshed off towards another queue. But a bomb, exploding between it and them, gave the private time to wade up to the head of the line, and the man on crutches leading it.

'I know these are difficult times, brothers,' announced the private, 'but let us not use that as an excuse to allow ourselves to be led like lambs to the slaughter. Solidarity is our watchword, brothers.'

The line hesitated.

'We could be, er, needed back home,' said the man at the front, 'couldn't we?'

The private stared at him bitterly.

'Oh, got a troublemaker, have we?' he said loudly. 'It's amazing, there's always one, isn't there?'

154

'Always bloody one,' said a voice down the line.

'Thank you, brother.' He poked a finger into the leader's chest. 'You'll get that crutch across your bonce in a minute, son,' he said. He spread his hands to take in the gradually assembling crowd of waterlogged soldiers. 'Got a man here believes all he reads in the newspapers! Got one of your *thinkers*! Doesn't know all this scaremongering is just put about by the gumment to screw the working man, doesn't realise that your *real* situation is all very nice, thank you, doesn't . . .' The private broke off as a couple of Heinkels came howling in from the dunes, their tracer slicing a red swathe through the crowd, drowning his words '. . . doesn't appreciate that gumment propaganda is being cunningly directed to militate public opinion on the side of nationalistic interests contrary to the welfare of the entire work force, does he?'

'I think we ought to vote on it,' said a fusilier who had been standing next to a man dismembered in the last strafe.

'Oh, yes, and I don't think!' snorted the private. 'You won't catch me out with no snap show of hands, brother, contrary to the democratic secret ballot as we know it. I should cocoa!'

The men shifted their feet uneasily. The private had articulated it all so clearly, and, after all, the men who had brought the little boats were, for the most part, men of a class they had long learned to mistrust. Nor did they wish to betray their mates, with whom they had come through no small adversity; and it could not be denied that it was at just such fraught moments as this that advantage could be taken of them, with their defences down, and the odds in favour of those who sought to control them.

And, after all, were things so bad that they should forget all else but short-term salvation? They were not yet dead, were they, which was rather more relevant than the emotionally-loaded evidence that others could be seen to be dying. They had, had they not, stuck it out on the beach up until then, why should they not continue to stick it out now?

Slowly, but with what certainly appeared to be determination, the entire waiting army turned, and began to wade back towards the littered dunes, and the devil they knew.

There were, of course, one or two who glanced over their shoulders in the direction of England; but, naturally, it was too far away for them to be able to discern anything, even had the darkness not, by then, been falling.

Golfing For Cats

The Hounds Of Spring Are On Winter's Traces, So That's Thirty-Eight-Pounds-Forty, Plus Making Good, Say Fifty Quid

This is the week, according to my much-thumbed copy of *Milly-Molly-Mandy Slips A Disc*, when Winter officially knocks off for a few days, the swallows return from Africa to foul the greenhouse roof, and you and I be a-diggin' and a-stretchin' and a-sweatin' as we work away with that most indispensable of gardening tools, the wallet.

And, as no newspaper or magazine is currently worth its salt without a few inches of pithy advice to the dehibernating gardener, it has fallen to my lot to deliver this year's handy hints. And if you think a sentence containing both salt and lot has been cobbled together as a subtle augury of the doom lying just beyond the french windows, then you might as well stop reading immediately: anyone who has time to work out textual cruces of that convoluted order clearly has nothing more effortful to bother about than a window box with a plastic begonia cemented to it. This piece is for committed gardeners only; although those who have not yet been committed may, of course, read it while waiting for the ambulance.

Fences

This is the time of year to get together with your neighbour over the question of repairs to fences, trellises, and so on, that have deteriorated or even collapsed during the winter. I have always found that the best implement for dealing with this problem is a small hammer. If you have a large neighbour, then take a large hammer.

157

Blackwood

Similar to the above, and particularly satisfying for bridge-players. You creosote your fencing somewhat enthusiastically, with the result that your neighbour's herbaceous border drops dead. He then digs a large trench on his side, until light shows between the soil and your new fencing. This is known as the Small Spade Opening. The conventional reply is Two Clubs.

Corm, Bulb, Tuber and Rhizome

Not, of course, the long-established firm of country solicitors they might appear to the uninitiated, but the business end of those perennial plants which we gardeners carefully took up at the first sign of winter. At the first sign of spring, take them carefully out of their boxes and throw them away.

Exactly why all perennial roots die during the winter is an issue on which botanical opinion has long been divided: many experts argue that those stored in garages have an adverse reaction to being run over, and that this, coupled with the frost coming through the window the sack fell off in October and that nobody's wife got around to putting back up, explains why so many bulbs go flat and black during the weeks immediately prior to replanting.

Many other things, however, can carry off the apparently healthy corm, e.g. dogs, children, dailies with empty tubs at home, but since the plants will be dead anyway, these do not call for the hammer treatment.

Things like Geraniums

Now is the time to go and look at the things like geraniums which you left in the ground all winter, knowing that if you lifted them, potted them, and stored them the way the books recommend, they would all die of mould. Left in the ground, they die anyway but at least you don't break your nails. If they haven't died in the ground, they are not geraniums but merely things and your best bet is to burn them off with a blow-lamp (see below under BLOW-LAMP) because otherwise they will take over the entire garden by March 23.

Blow-lamp

Now is the time to take down your blow-lamp and run. Because of an extremely complicated chemical process it would take far too long to elaborate upon, much gets up blow-lamp spouts between Michaelmas and yesterday morning. When you attempt to prime and light the blow-lamp, it ignites your suit. The way to avoid this happening is called £3.95.

Motor Mower

The motor mower is exactly similar to the blow-lamp in principle, but rather more sophisticated, which means that after it ignites your suit, it takes your fingers off at the knuckle as well. The best thing to do is call in an expert, but make sure you phone before April 3, 1948, as they get pretty booked up at this time of year. You can always use a HAND MOWER if you want to lose the entire hand. This comes about through trying to remove last year's long grass which has become wound round the axle and, by an extremely complicated chemical process it would take far too long to elaborate upon, turned to iron. Again, there is a traditional country remedy for both these problems and your bank manager would be pleased to advise you.

Lawns

Now you have your new lawn-mower, you will want to get something to cut, since all lawns are annual. A few tufts here and there may have survived the winter, but upon closer inspection these will turn out to be clumps of clover, saw-grass, couch-grass, and the cat. What your lawn needs now is feeding and planting. Many people ask me how I achieve a lawn like a billiard-table, i.e. no grass anywhere and full of holes, and I usually recommend any one of a dozen products now on the market in which various chemicals have been carefully blended to ensure that you will be back next year

159

to try again. If you read the labels on these products, you will see that they may not be used either after it has rained or before it is due to rain, thus protecting the manufacturers from complaints lodged by anyone other than an astrologer with his eye in. Sprinkle these on the grass, watch them blow onto the roses, dig up and burn the roses, wait two days for the grass to be eaten away, dig over, pave, and sell the mower back. You can, of course, avoid this costly process by using lawn sand, a preparation used by experts wishing to turn lawn into sand, and there is much to be said for having a nice stretch of beach between your fences: put up an umbrella, a couple of deckchairs, and an electric fire on a long lead, and you could be in Baffin Land.

Manure

Now is the time of year when you will want to think about top-dressing your rose-beds, and why not? There's no harm in thinking. Many people, it seems to me, worry far too much about finding true horse manure, when the commercial preparations available are just as good, bearing in mind that by the time you get them off the shovel, the roses have already begun to succumb to rust, leaf-mould, white-spot, black-spot, and greenfly. There is little point, surely, in chasing up and down the country with a spade and bucket merely in order to give a few dead twigs a nice send-off.

Seeds

Children, I find, are always amazed that everything in the garden was once a little seed; particularly so when the packet of Sweet William they have nurtured so painstakingly is soon burgeoning as an assortment of diseased hollyhocks, misshapen sunflowers, chickweed, and an evil-smelling groundcover that spreads like lava and is almost certainly carnivorous.

In the garden, seeds fall into two categories (a) the cracks in the path, and (b) where starlings have breakfast. To avoid wastage, therefore, grow all seeds in a greenhouse where, if it is properly heated, they will die before they can do any damage.

Water

No garden can possibly flourish without adequate supplies of water. Now is the time of year to cut off the split ends of hoses so that they fit snugly onto the tap, or would if the jubilee clip hadn't rusted solid during the winter with the drip that was coming out of the tap before the pipe burst during the cold snap. Having replaced the upstand pipe, tap, and jubilee clip, bandage the fingers and secure the neatly cut hose; which, as a result of having been neatly cut, will now be some nine inches too short to reach the one bed which requires permanent watering. Never mind, any nurseryman or ironmongers will be able to supply you with an extra length of hose and a connecting-link with which you can easily fail to connect the new bit with the old, since the old is too thick to go into the end of the connecting-link. The best course is to buy an entirely new hose of the required length; there is no other method of finding out that the tap you have just soldered onto the upstand pipe (since you had no means to hand of threading the pipe to take a nut) is itself .05 of a millimetre wider than the hose.

While you're at the nursery/ironmongers, be sure to buy a sprinkler: there are two main varieties, the one that fails to spin round, and the one that fails to sweep from left to right and back again. Personally, I prefer the latter: at least you get half the garden sodden and know which side the shrubs are going to rot. The other variety sets up little oases at random, and it is all too easy, when strolling across a recently watered stretch, to find oneself sinking up to the shin in a tiny local quicksand.

Gardening advice articles

Now is the time of year to stop writing gardening advice articles and move into a tower block. *The Sanity Inspector*

The Ford Papers

As the 38½th President of the United States disappeared into the political sunset, his thoughts turned naturally towards the composition of that mandatory ex-Presidential volume, his Memoirs. *This is the first draft of the complete book. I did the spelling.*

CHAPTER ONE: A DATE WITH DESTINY

It was, I think, my great predecessor Warren Harding who kept saying 'Here's another fine mess you've got us into, Stanley,' and there have been times when I knew exactly what he meant.

This doesn't seem to be one of those times.

I can't remember who Stanley was, either; it was probably Harding's Vice-President, I guess. One thing I do know, their car kept falling apart.

Well, it has been said that few are called but only many are chosen, and when they came to tell me I was President of the United States, I was looking for my blue cap out back in this yard we had at the time. It never did turn up; so much intervened, South East Asia, Hirohito's state visit and having to eat fried seaweed, going to Helsinki and forgetting my brown brogues, still, I guess it'll be where I left it, and now there's time on my hands, I'll ask around, you never know with caps.

It was in August 1974 they came to me and said that President Nixon had decided to resign; I was amazed, he was at the height of his popularity, and he had always been very civil to my wife and myself, all I could think of was he had been offered a better job. After all, he was no chicken, you have to think about your future these days, I am always trying to get this across to people. Anyway, I told them I was very happy for the Nixons and hoped a house went with it, and I gave them five dollars towards the barometer which I guessed was why they had come by, and I told them I would serve the new President to the best of my ability. They all laughed at that, I guess they were feeling tense, or something; then it hit me. It was I they was talking about! I remember running into my wife Carol, Betty, and shouting 'I'm the new President, let's go to a movie and eat Chinese after!'

CHAPTER TWO: THE GUYS ON THE TEAM

I swam a lot that Fall. One of my clearest memories of those first weeks in office is the backstroke. You do it with your face looking up, as opposed to down, and not everyone can do it on account of you crack your skull against the side all the time, and unless you're pretty damned careful, it can cost you a whole lot of money in tiling. I'm lucky, due to I know this decorator from the old days in Grand Rapids, he gets twenty per cent off all sundries of that nature.

Anyhow, I put together a really hot cabinet, Ted Levi had been the President of the University of Chicago, John Dunlop was an economics professor at Harvard, F. David Matthews had been President of the University of Alabama, and Hank Kissinger and Jim Schlesinger also had a lot up here, as everyone knows. It was terrific just listening to them talk, like going to one of them black-and-white movies.

I guess I have to admit that I got off to a pretty shaky start in foreign affairs, partly owing to where I had ripped the map pages out of my Captain Marvel Diary For 1974 to clean my pipe. This happened before I was President, of course, I would not do such a dumb thing now; this explains why I had such a tough time with Congress over military aid to Cambodia in 1974, I think they lost a little confidence in my strategy after I told them I planned to drive down that afternoon and see the place for myself. I waved the sandwiches to show I didn't intend to blow money in expensive restaurants while I was there, and some of the old guys fainted.

Right after that, the Cambodians retaliated by seizing the *Mayaguez,* and I sent in the Marines. This was hailed, as you know, as a masterstroke of positive strategy and sent my popularity way up at home; I didn't understand this, on account of sending in the Marines was all I could think of, I had always thought that was what you did if you were the President, I had

163

seen *Sands of Iwo Jima* fourteen times, and the Marines won *every single time*! Why mess around with a winning formula, is my motto.

CHAPTER ONE AGAIN: I REMEMBER ABOUT THE BLUE CAP
I remember about the blue cap. I used it to plug the gas-filler in that old Studebaker I used to run. Boy, that's a relief, I'm pretty attached to that cap, I wore it the night I walked into a tree on Elm Street, Spokane!

All I have to do now is remember what I did with the Studebaker.

CHAPTER THREE, OR MAYBE FOUR: ANOTHER DATE WITH DESTINY
In September, 1974, I pardoned Richard Nixon. It was a controversial decision, I understand, but I don't see why. Anybody can take a better job, it's just they get so damned offended in Washington, I'll just bet nobody else shelled out a whole five bucks.

That winter, I studied hard on foreign affairs, which everyone said was my weak spot, personally I reckon it's a hell of a lot better than my breaststroke, but there you go, people are funny. It was good I boned up on foreign affairs, though, because Hirohito came on a state visit that November and when I saw that little Nip coming up the White House steps, my first instinct was to plug him before he could pull one of them long swords they all carry, only I remembered Henry's briefing and it all went off okay, except I naturally never let him get behind me or between me and the door.

CHAPTER SIX: I GET CAMBODIA STRAIGHTENED OUT
I just got Cambodia straightened out (*see Chapter Two*). They released the *Mayaguez* in May 1975, not the Fall of 1974.

The Studebaker was a black '69 sedan. You can't just *lose* a thing like that, in my opinion.

CHAPTER SEVEN: MOSCOW, TEL-AVIV, CAIRO
It was during the winter of 1974-5 that I engaged in my round of talks with the leaders of the Soviet Union, Israel and Egypt. This was, I think, the first time in the history of the world that a

US President had got so much in in so short a time, it was very like the week Myra and me, Betty and me, spent in Yellowstone National Park when we saw bears, the Mirror Lake, Old Faithful the geyser, climbed nearly three mountains and also got to see *Sands of Iwo Jima* at a drive-in outside Pitchfork, Wyoming. Or it might have been Yosemite National Park.

Boy, could that Studebaker travel! Of course, in them days, it still had its own filler-cap.

Anyhow, these talks I had were of terrific importance to the future of democracy and world peace and the oil and all, so it's only right I should spend a little time here in recording what passed; though, naturally, a hell of a lot of stuff is secret, and I wouldn't put it in a book, you know how people talk about what they read, sometimes it ruins a movie, people sitting behind you going on and on about the damned book it was based on.

Still, some things I am at liberty to divulge. Anwar Sadat, I recall, was very keen to continue the détente, and I go along with that: he and I are currently the two most powerful men in the world, and there are special responsibilities. I did my best to make Leonid Brezhnev see that, but you know Jewish people, I love them very much but they can be damned excitable, look at the way they paint New York green every March 17, and I don't think he was listening too well, and as he has no interest in swimming, it all kind of petered out. Yitzhak Rabin is a great guy, he swims in the Nile every morning, and he gave me his autograph, he is in no way high-hat. All in all, the whole thing was a terrific success, a lot of foreigners in the White House and not even a teaspoon missing when we counted up.

CHAPTER PROBABLY EIGHT: AUSTRIA AND THE MOON
In June 1975, I fell down three times, most notably at Austria Airport in Austria. There has been a lot of comment about this, and I guess I should set the record straight. Well, people forget that a President is a man with a lot on his mind all the time. Other people walk around, they can concentrate on making sure the left leg comes after the right leg, and the relevant arms are getting swung in the proper order etcetera, but it's not so easy for a President. All the time I was doing that walking, I was thinking: *I know I put that goddam blue cap down somewhere*.

In July, I talked to the Apollo-Soyuz link-up. It was a very symbolic occasion, showing how co-operation between two great nations can lead to wonderful understanding. It is my firm belief that relations between us and the Soyans have never, in consequence, been better.

CHAPTER TEN?: THE SPIRIT OF '76
Between the summer of 1975 and now, much has happened. I won't go into all the details, because it makes the headaches start, but it now looks like I'm going to have to stop being President. I don't feel too sore about that, I have a lot to do, such as looking for the Studebaker and so on, and if the people of America feel that it is time for a change, that is what this great democracy stands for. However, I would just say this: in six months time, it looks as though the United States is going to have to choose between, My God! an old movie star and a guy who builds peanuts. Is this, I ask myself, the sort of destiny the Foundling Fathers had in mind four-score-years-and-ten ago when they fought for independence from the Indians?

I have never tasted Mr Reagan's peanuts or seen any of Mr Carter's movies, but one thing I know for sure: whoever wins, the United States Presidency will not quickly recover its credibility.

The Lady From Stalingrad Mansions

A Little Leaning

'The pub should become a major centre of further education, TUC chief Len Murray told an Open University conference yesterday. Education should begin where people gathered together.'—Daily Mail

THE MAN IN THE HERRINGBONE overcoat raised his Guinness.

'Drink deep,' he cried, 'or taste not the Peruvian spring!'

He drank. They all did.

'Alexandra Pipe,' said the man in the herringbone overcoat.

'Who?' enquired the man in the Orient scarf.

'Only one of our greatest poets,' snapped the man in the herringbone overcoat. He fixed the man in the Orient scarf with a ballbearing eye. 'Or poetess,' he said, 'if you want to be pedantous.'

The man in the Orient scarf said nothing.

'What does it mean?' asked the man in the Wimpey jacket.

The herringbone overcoat looked at him, pityingly.

'It is one of the most famous couplings in the language, you ignorant nurd,' he said. 'A little leaning is a dangerous thing/Drink deep, or taste not the Peruvian spring!'

They thought about this for a while, nodding respectfully.

'That Tower of Pizza,' said the Orient scarf, finally. 'There's a thing.'

'You're right there,' said the Wimpey jacket. 'I wouldn't like to have been on that job. There was people dropping cannonballs off.'

'Garibaldi,' said the herringbone overcoat firmly. 'And it was apples. They was testing for gravity. Garibaldi had this tower built so's he could drop apples off and see if there was any gravity about. It's where we get *eureka* from.'

'What is?' said the Orient scarf.

167

'Stone me, don't you know bleeding nothing?' cried the herringbone overcoat. '*Eureka* is Italian for gravity. Every time one of his apples hit the ground, they all shouted out.'

'I thought he invented the biscuit,' said the Orient scarf.

The herringbone overcoat banged down his empty glass on the marble table-top. A number of customers looked round. A man at the next table leaned across.

'Do you mind?' he said sharply. 'There's people over here trying to discuss the Second Law of Wossname.'

'Oh, pardonnez-moi!' replied the herringbone overcoat, heavily. 'I assumed all the scientists was in the public.'

In the blotched temple of the man at the next table, a small vein began to writhe like a lugworm.

'One of these days,' he said, 'your whole bleeding faculty is going to find itself looking for teeth all over the car-park.'

He turned back to his seminar, who were painstakingly constructing a molecular chain out of crisps.

'Physicists!' snorted the herringbone overcoat to his class. 'I wouldn't send 'em out to post a letter. Where was I?'

'Garibaldi,' said the Orient scarf obstinately, 'and his biscuits.'

'Yes,' said the herringbone overcoat. 'Answer me one thing: did I *say* he never invented the biscuit? He didn't spend all his time dropping apples off things, you know. In them days there was no such thing as specialisation; people used to do everything. It was called the Resemblance.'

'Why was it called that?' said the Wimpey jacket.

'Werl, because everything resembled everything else, I shouldn't wonder. No job too large or small, as it were. Take Leonardo D. Finchley, he'd run you up a bicycle in the morning, you'd come in dinner-time to collect it and he'd knock off your portrait while you was stood at the till. Afternoons, he used to go out sculpting. Amazing, for a Wop.'

The Wimpey jacket, whose forehead had been growing more and more furrowed, suddenly brightened.

'I don't fancy their chances in Argentina, mind,' he said. 'If it was up to me, I'd drop Bettega back to midfield and put——'

The herringbone overcoat withered him silent.

''Course,' he said, 'the English was no slouches when it come to the Resemblance. Take Sir Sidney Phillips, poet, soldier, critic——'

'Clarinettist,' said the Orient scarf.

'What?' snapped the herringbone overcoat.

'And bandleader,' said the Orient scarf. 'We got his *Canadian Capers* up home. With *Sweet Georgia Brown* on the flip side.'

The herringbone overcoat chewed his lip for a moment.

'Yes, werl,' he muttered, 'that just bears it out. Anything they cared to turn their hands to. He had his head chopped off by Queen Elizabeth of course, so it wasn't all beer and skittles.'

'No!' cried the Wimpey jacket. 'Recently?'

'Queen Elizabeth the *First*,' sighed the herringbone overcoat.

'Ah. Werl, he was no Acker Bilk,' said the Orient scarf. 'Even so, killing him's coming it a bit strong. Wonder why she bothered knighting him in the first place, if she didn't like clarinets?'

'Because,' cried the herringbone overcoat, leaning forward and poking the Orient scarf in the chest with a thick forefinger, 'he only come back from America with fags and chips, didn't he?'

'Gerroff!'

'Straight up. Yes, he was probably the best friend the working man ever had. Which reminds me, who's getting them in?'

The Orient scarf rose reluctantly, and went off to the bar. The herringbone overcoat scowled after him.

'Always chipping in,' he muttered, 'always got sunnink to say for himself, hasn't he? And he's pig-ignorant. There's none so dumb as them who won't be taught. I'm seriously thinking of washing my hands of him. Far as I'm concerned, he can go and do bloody geology with them poufs in the snug.'

The Orient scarf returned with the glasses.

'Flora Robson,' he said.

'What?'

'She was doing Queen Elizabeth a couple of Sundays back. On the box. And I'll tell you one thing, there was no mention of Sid Phillips. *And* it was someone else brought the fags back.'

'Sid Phillips was probably dead by then,' murmured the Wimpey jacket tactfully.

The herringbone overcoat ignored him.

'*Flora Robson?*' he shouted. 'Stone me, I don't think I've ever come across anyone as dumb in all my years of teaching! Flora Robson, sonny boy, was as black as the ace of wossname! Flora Robson, may I remind you, was the one who sang *Old Man River* in *Gone With the Wind*! And whatever else Queen Elizabeth may have been, she wasn't a nig-nog!'

The Orient scarf glowered at him sullenly.

'Next thing,' ranted the herringbone overcoat, purpling, 'next thing, you'll tell me I don't know nothing about people of the coon persuasion! Ten years working with 'em up the depot. I prob'ly know more about the Indian Mutiny than Buffalo bloody Bill himself!'

'Indian Mutiny?' enquired the Wimpey jacket, desperate to change the subject, partly because the thermodynamicists at the next table were now, as the result of the noise, beginning to wrap their belts around their fists.

The herringbone overcoat softened at his prize student's question.

'Captain Blight,' he explained. 'He cast all these blackies adrift in an open boat and they went off to the Pitcairn Islands and gave everybody VD.'

'No!' exclaimed the Wimpey jacket.

'It's in all the books,' confirmed the herringbone overcoat. 'Hardly surprising there's a swing to the Conservatives, is there? You wouldn't catch me dead in one of them Tandoori restaurants, I can tell you!'

'Bloody hell,' said the Wimpey jacket, paling. 'We had one of them Vesta curries Tuesday.'

'Yes, werl, that's what history's all about, isn't it?' The herringbone overcoat tapped the table with his matchbox. 'Those who refuse to learn from their mistakes are doomed to repeat them.'

'That's good,' said the Orient scarf, 'who said it?'

The herringbone overcoat looked at him, hard.

'I did,' he said. 'Don't you ever listen to nothing?'

The Orient scarf did not reply.

'It's a wonderful thing, education,' said the Wimpey jacket.

Un Cottage De Weekend

'. . . so when Gilbert had such a *succès fou* with his *Trotsky And Hancock: Parameters Of Caring*, twelve impressions and the Prix Chomsky, we thought, well *I* thought—you know Gilbert, give him a few weeks on a narrow boat each year and his Sunday soccer on Primrose Hill and he's perfectly happy with Highgate—I thought it would be rather nice to splash the Canadian rights on a little place in France, *un chaumière*, or is it *une*, a small farmhouse, perhaps, a *pied-à-terre*.

For weekends, short trips, half-terms, all that kind of thing.

Somewhere in the centre, somewhere *tout rural*, away from, well, English cyclists in Halford anoraks, if you know what I mean, and those terrible people in white Rovers who always leave the *Guide* on the table, even in the most fearful hamburger places. Did you see *Une Partie de Campagne*, by the way, all those wonderful vests, those forearms, you could smell the earth. That's what we were after. Not the Dordogne, of course, it's become so common, you see louvred doors being delivered to even the tiniest villages, we passed through one once and Gilbert spotted five different faces from telly commercials, and they were all wearing new berets and waving *baguettes* terribly ostentatiously, I'm sure none of them ever opened a book in his life.

Their children had tee-shirts with pictures of Wagner on them.

Lot-et-Garonne is really the only place to be, you know. The naturalness of it. *Le sans-souci*, as we say down there. Our little *ferme* used to be the village pesthouse, you know; you can still see where sufferers from scrofula banged holes in the foundations with their heads, because Gilbert chipped away all the plaster and exposed the original cell walls, he's truly wonderful with rough tools, once he's out of an academic environment.

171

Man is naturally a maker, after all, and none more so than Gilbert; he treats reason as a livelihood, no more than that.

He is both Rousseau *et rousseauisme*, if you follow me.

I'm the same. I make a rough *terrine* when I'm down there exactly as it has been made for eleven centuries, you steam the live rabbits then jump on them in clogs just before they're completely asphyxiated, and then dice them with a *sauve-pichet*, it's a kind of single-headed axe. I bake my own bread, too, and Gilbert has an arrangement with a local vineyard, he pays five francs a cask for a wonderful black wine, the locals use it for shrivelling head-lice, I believe it may have something to do with their religion, their observances are quite medieval at times.

We encourage it, where we can. There's a terrible danger of their wonderful primitive spirit being overtaken by *le supermarketisme*, I have seen young women carrying frozen *haricots*; many of the houses have central heating, although Gilbert is doing something about it, he got together with a few close friends in the village and they tarred and feathered the heating engineer, I don't think he'll come back. It was quite a victory. Gilbert can be very dominant, you know, he's very different down there from the way he is in lectures, he wears studded wristbands. We never take deodorants down there. I let my armpits flourish, too; it puts us in touch. *C'est très engagé.*

April is our favourite time of year, the children can help with the slaughtering. Little Cordelia has been butchering lambs ever since she was old enough to wield; it's one of the things missing in progressive boarding schools, I sometimes feel one can have too much Idries Shah and Jerome Robbins, don't you? The twins have neck-wringing races with the chickens, they're such enthusiastic boys! They dance the *pisanne* nude, well we all do, it's a wonderfully stimulating local dance celebrating the sexual energies of the hog. Pig-farming is so important down there, sow-fertility is never far from one's thoughts. We introduced the *pisanne*, as a matter of fact, we thought it was about time the region had its own dance, the locals took it very well, they don't all join in, of course, at least not yet, but they all come along and clap and hoot when we dance it for them.

It may be the rhythm of the *pisanne* that's behind the awaken-

172

ing of sexual experiment down there. That and the fact that we've been distributing the pill, and holding seminars on Oriental concepts; well, Gilbert felt that the Roman Catholic church was repressing natural peasant instinct, strangling it, even. I think they're happier, now.

We are, certainly. It's marvellous to have this completely alternative world to escape to, away from professorial responsibilities, and agents, and accountants, and TV interviews, and dinner parties, all the well-dressed chatty dreariness of the whole London bit . . .

France is so civilised, I find.'

The Lady From Stalingrad Mansions

And is there Magpie still for Tea?

Lord Blake, Provost of Queen's College, Oxford, has blamed television for the decline in literacy and taste standards among undergraduates. – Daily Telegraph

THE MELLOW CLOCK bonged four across the grassless mud of Judas College quad, and the flakes of Jacobean masonry dislodged by its dying stroke had not yet floated to the ground before the square was filled with the throng of undergraduates hurtling towards the JCR television set for *Jackanory*.

The Senior English Tutor watched them from his first floor mullion, and sighed. Once, the quad had been a flawless stretch of emerald; but that had been many years ago, when even a freshman could read *Keep Off The Grass* without moving his lips.

A knuckle tapped upon his door.

'Come!' said the Senior Tutor.

The door opened, and a red-eyed face peered round it.

'Good afternoon, Cobbett,' said the Senior Tutor, 'sit down.'

'Sorry I'm a bit, you know, late,' said the undergraduate, easing himself into a creased fauteuil. 'I didn't want to miss the last bit of *General Hospital*, did I?'

'Did you what?'

'What?'

'Never mind,' said the Senior Tutor.

'It's where Doctor Armstrong is worried about what Staff Nurse Holland is going to say about Doctor Chitapo's wossname with that Student Nurse Stevens on account of him being a coon and her brother Jeremy that's hanging about with the one from the chip shop with the big knockers not exactly going a bleeding bundle on it all. I don't know what Student Nurse Stevens sees in Chitapo, I reckon she ought to have listened to Mr.

174

Parker Brown's advice, all these people coming over here, where's it all leading, right?'

'I'm sure I don't know,' said the Senior Tutor.

'There you are then,' said Cobbett.

'I thought we might return this session,' said the Senior Tutor, 'to *Hamlet*. You will recall that. . . .'

'I think we got a condenser going,' said Cobbett. 'All through *Emmerdale Farm*, they was dwarfs.'

The Senior Tutor looked at him.

'The revenge tradition,' he said, 'was a framework which. . . .'

'Werl, not *exactly* dwarfs,' said Cobbett. 'Normal bodies, know what I mean, but little legs. And in close-up, all their noses stretched out. And when they all went out to look at that cow with the rash on its thing, it was about nine feet long and its thing was practically on the ground, like a bleeding great dachshund. It could be,' said Cobbett gloomily, 'the tube.'

'You did read *Hamlet* this week?' asked the Senior Tutor.

'What? Oh. Oh, yes, I read it, all right. I mean, not every word, as you might say, but I know what it's about, don't I? I know the, like, gist. What a load of rubbish!'

'Ah,' said the Senior Tutor.

'But,' said Cobbett, inclining his head, 'a good title. I'll give you that. Crisp. Derivative, mind—*Kojak, McCloud, Colombo, Callan, Barlow*—but crisp. What's he a Dane for, though?'

'I'm afraid,' said the Senior Tutor, 'I don't quite follow.'

'That makes two of us,' said Cobbett. 'I can see where you couldn't put him in a wheelchair, I can see why you wouldn't want him to suck lollipops or have a glass eye or anything, I can see where you'd want him to have some sort of original gimmick, but a *Dane?*'

'He was a Prince,' said the Senior Tutor, lamely, not certain why he was saying it, 'he was a Prince of Denmark.'

'There's that,' agreed Cobbett. 'There's never been a royal cop series, I grant you. *A British* royal cop, werl, you might have got away with that. I'm not saying you wouldn't have got away with that. *Charles*, possibly. Not much of a title, but good locales, know what I mean? Good twists. You could have him tracking down a different royal murder every week, who threw Prince Philip off the royal yacht, who strung Angus Ogilvie up in the Sandringham laundry-room, what was the head of the Archbishop of Canterbury doing in the Queen Mother's hand-bag, all that kind of thing, yes, I take your point there.'

'Oh good,' said the Senior Tutor, faintly.

'But a Dane,' said Cobbett firmly, 'no way. Unless he was nude: people expect Scandinavians to be nude, he could be the first nude cop. Not necessarily the first *royal* nude cop, I'm not saying that. Could be a very big puller, that. You could shoot the rooftop chases from below, where he jumps the twenty-foot gap, a lot of possibilities there. You remember in *Danish Dentist On The Job*, where the hygienist with the curly. . . .'

'No,' said the Senior Tutor.

'Oh, well,' said Cobbett, not without derision, 'all that read-ing, I don't s'pose it leaves you time for much. Anyway, all right, it's supposed to be the start of a Danish royal cop series, I accept that, it's a reasonable novelty—but what a plot! What a load of old cobblers, right? The murder gets done with this bloke getting poison poured in his ear, and then he comes back as a ghost. What are we watching, *Tom and Jerry*?'

'There has been much speculation,' said the Senior Tutor, 'on the wisdom of employing a supernatural device in a situ-ation which is so much more sophisticated than the retribution tradition from which it springs. In Thomas Kyd, of course. . . .'

'I'll just bloody bet there has!' exclaimed Cobbett. 'You wouldn't catch Kojak buying information off a walking sheet. Mind you,'—and here Cobbett wrinkled his pale face in painful thought, and began, slowly, to nod—'mind you, there's nothing to stop the victim coming back from the dead, if you do it right. They find him in this orchard with an earful of woss-name, and his heart's stopped and everything, but there's still this faint pulse in his brain, so they scoop it out and weld it to a lot of bionic arms and legs they've got, and next thing you know he's come back as the Six Million Dollar Dane, running through the castle at sixty miles an hour and squashing Claude's head like a ping-pong ball!'

'Claudius,' murmured the Senior Tutor.

'And him,' said Cobbett. ' 'Course, there wouldn't be much room in it for young Hamlet. You'd have to cut his part out.'

The Senior Tutor walked carefully to the window, opened it, and breathed deeply.

'If we might leave the mainstream of the plot for a moment,' he said, 'I should like to hear what you made of Act V, Scene 1. The gravediggers, the comic relief and parallel, the return to a. . . .'

'It's not what *I'd* call comic!' cried Cobbett. 'Two men in a hole, it's a dead pinch from *Steptoe*, you might get a spin-off sitcom series out of it, but I very much doubt it, all that two-men-together routine, it's old hat, it's Hancock and Sid, it's Bootsie and Snudge, it's not very 1975, is it? Personally, I'd have 'em sharing a flat, the two gravediggers living downstairs, say, and the wife of one of 'em living on the floor above, and they put this advert in for a third, and it's this girl, see, and—here, I just remembered, you know when we were discussing that one with the coon who does his old lady in, and I said it had a lot of comic possibilities? Well, how would it be if you had the gravediggers and the bird and their first wives upstairs in the one house, and you had the Othellos moving in next door? A sort of *Whatever Happened To Love Thy Wife Next Door The Second Time Around*, know what I'm driving at, you could clean up with a show like that. You've got the problem of what to do with Hamlet again, though, haven't you, unless you make him this comic nude Danish cop who's always rushing in starkers and arresting the wrong people.'

The clock chimed again, once. Cobbett sprang to his feet.

'Whoops, 4.30, *Yogi Bear*!' he cried. 'That's all we have time for this week, I'm afraid, it's been wonderful talking to you, thank you for having me on the tutorial, next time I shall have with me *Macbeth*, and. . . .'

'I look forward to that,' said the Senior Tutor.

'Yes, a cop in a kilt, it could spell the end of bald detectives altogether, and we keep his old woman in, *Macbeth and Wife*, don't you just see Rock Hudson and—oh my God, 4.35!'

His footsteps clattered on the ancient stairs, and he was gone. The Senior Tutor looked down from his window for the last time, watching his protégé disappear across the quad, into the gloaming, doing his silly walk.

Golfing For Cats

177

John Bull's Other England: The Far West

IT'S NO ACCIDENT that little is done to encourage foreign visitors to approach this island from the south-west; it is an aspect singularly lacking in prestige. Shepherd them in under the cliffs of Dover, yes; usher them up the great green carriage-drive of the Solent, certainly; and, if possible, leave them bobbing on the tide for a bit, squinting at the land-mass and thanking God that the race behind the beetling crags is slow to anger. But never let them in at Land's End, where the impression they will get from the bow-rails is of an extremely thin country, no more than a couple of kilometres across at its widest, and undeniably low. Legend, in fact, has it (it has almost everything in the West Country) that an excursion was mounted as early as the third century BC by bored Roman mariners on a forty-eight hour pass in Brest; who, having negotiated some two hundred miles of Channel in filthy weather, suddenly saw this narrow, liver-coloured atoll off the port bow and immediately put about with a pang of bitter disillusionment it took two centuries to overcome.

By one of those coincidences with which geography is rife, Land's End is the westernmost point of the English mainland, and since earliest times it has been as a magnet to Englishmen fascinated at the prospect of their being intelligent life somewhere out there beyond the mists. Indeed, five miles inland is a geegaw called Lanyon's Quoit, knocked up some four thousand years ago by men eager to balance a seventeen foot stone slab on three six-foot uprights. It has long been fashionable to regard this as a barrow, but a likelier explanation is that it was erected so that New Stone Age citizens could get a better view out to sea, in the hope that there was something edible there. The Cornish have always been a practical race.

They are also a distinct race. One of the six Celtic nations, they share with their siblings (the Scots, the Irish, the Welsh, the Manx, and the Bretons) a deep-seated scorn for Anglo-Saxons, and are constantly rooting around for an excuse to dissociate themselves from ties imposed on them by that fickle mistress, geology. They feel their closest affiliation with the Bretons, and consider the English Channel to be a purely temporary measure; Cornishmen subscribe unanimously to the belief that Atlantis is buried beneath the Waters which separate Cherbourg from the Lizard, and only live for the day when the Channel will be dredged by the UN and the area in question roped off and fortified against English intruders. This belief embraces the certain knowledge that the inhabitants of Atlantis, Cornishmen all, have made the requisite adjustments to the new weather conditions, and lead an idyllic existence pottering about the sea-bed in their gills and making effigies of Joan the Wad, awaiting the Day of Liberation. There is also talk of oil-rights.

The Cornish language is the only one of the Celtic tongues which has gone to join its ancestors (Sanskrit and Latin, to mourn but two), but serious efforts are being made by secessionists to resurrect it. R. Morton Nance, a pre-war Grand Bard of Cornwall, was responsible for the remarkable play, *An Balores* (The Chough), a toothsome dramatic gobbet which compares the Cornish language to a chough which has been shot dead and has come to life again. Experts on choughs say this is a fair comparison, but lay opinions differ. Suffice it to remark that the similarities between Cornish and Welsh, and the ties of ancient blood, have been enough to cause the sandwiched inhabitants of Devon grave concern; many of them feel that the slogan "CHOOSE OR PERISH!" which has been daubed by infiltrators on walls from Plymouth to Ilfracombe constitutes a grave threat to the Devon tourist industry, and can only be expunged in blood. Large numbers of Cornishmen feel, in their turn, that if that's the way it has to be, then it's all right with them; rancour still smoulders at the memory of Cornwall's defeat in 838 at the hands of King Egbert, who invaded the country from Devon with a mob of Viking tearaways and opened it up to English settlers. The huge Cornish sales of *The Carpetbaggers* were entirely due to the belief that the book dealt sympathetically with the desecration wrought by Egbert's followers; the discovery that this wasn't the case only served to exacerbate the situation, confirming the eternal Cornish suspicion that Englishmen live only for the chance to put one over on them.

Urban Cornwall, however, has come to grudging terms with its proximity to England. Penzance, after all, is best-known as the terminus of the old Great Western Railway. It also contains an antiquarian bookshop specialising in the literature of Cornwall and the Scilly Isles (a charming outcrop, famous chiefly for flowers and Harold Wilson, a combination which fortunately defies description). Penzance, whose rateable value of £637,099 levied at 10/2 in the £ compares favourably with any in the land, is a centre of the gnome industry. From the thriving kilns of thousands of Cornish potters, gnomes, pelicans, tortoises, sun-dials, and lumps of rock cunningly worked and shaped to look like lumps of rock are brought to the railhead at Penzance for shipment to all parts of the country. Suburbia owes a great debt to these craftsmen; it is too often forgotten that, without them, children in Guildford and Hendon might never have seen a penguin at all. Art, in fact, is Cornwall's primary industry: to date, the bay of St. Ives has earned almost three million dollars in pictorial dish-cloths alone, and if all the paintings of St. Michael's Mount at sunrise were placed end to end along the M1, the world would be a better place. Villages like Polperro expanded up hillsides solely in order that their inhabitants could take better photographs of the bays below for sale to postcard concessionaires; through sheer good fortune, these hills have themselves become profitably graphic by-products. Non-fishing is also an important source of revenue to these little ports; at the drop of an American Express traveller's cheque, non-fishermen can be persuaded to pose alongside children, wives, mothers-in-law, to crouch Cornishly beside lobster pots and permanently unmended nets, or simply to stand in their non-fishing boats with one oar over their shoulder gazing movingly out towards the eternal sea on which they do not rely for their very existence.

Truro's fame, of course, rests largely on its Anthony Trollope pillar-box in Quay Street, against which the novelist was wont to lean while composing novels before breakfast, and the town has justly become the administrative centre of Cornwall. Fowey, on the other hand, is the export centre for china clay, indispensable to the manufacture of stomach powders and lipstick; the stuff itself is dug out of the ground near St. Austell, and unfair criticism is levelled at the city authorities on account of the filthy white slag-heaps that now fill the landscape; critics forget that some day, somehow, someone in St. Austell is going to find a market for slag, and strong men will fight to kiss the hem of his garment as he is carried through the streets.

Apart from these teeming conurbations, Cornwall is fraught with scenery, most of it round the edges; these are separated by granite moors, notably Bodmin, which reaches its zenith in Brown Willy, a tor rewarding climbers with unparalleled views of the sky. Further away lies Perranporth, the shrine of St. Piran, patron saint of the tin trade, who currently seems to be undergoing a low point in his professional career, to judge from the derelict workings with which the environs are dotted; and beyond that, Tintagel, traditional home of King Arthur table-mats, Merlin tea-spoons, and genuine Tristan and Iseult book-ends.

But the main thinking- and talking-point in Cornwall today is, predictably enough, its ruler. Due to one of those genealogical quirks to which all of us are prey, he is both Duke of Cornwall and Prince of Wales, thereby happily uniting the two areas in a great pan-Celtic union. Unfortunately, he is also marked down as the next King of England. How Cornishmen will face the coming nightmare of divided loyalties, only the years can tell.

To cross the border into Devon is to enter a different county. The grim, almost alien, landscape of Bódmin gives way to the grim, almost alien, landscape of Dartmoor; but these are superficial differences. Basically, Devon is much more a part of England itself; the distinction can best be summed up by saying that Devon dreams of the day when it will be able to send a team to compete in the County Cricket Championship, whereas Cornwall dreams only of sending in a Test team. Devon has no separatist aspirations, no indigenous language, no tin, no gnomes, and even its colonial ambitions towards Lundy Island have grown more mellow with the passage of time and the realisation that there's no money in puffins.

Historically, Devon appears to have spent much of its time as a sort of transit camp: recent centuries have seethed with native Devonians going somewhere else, and outsiders passing through. The sixteenth century all but depopulated the area of anyone capable of putting one oar after the other. It was almost as if Devonians had been waiting for an excuse like a Virgin Queen hungry for territory (all other appetites being subject to unwholesome gossip) in order to get away from home base. Hawkins, Drake, Grenville, Raleigh, eagerly accompanied by local crews, were off and going like the clappers as soon as the wind was right; why, who knows? (Except, perhaps, the women of Devon.) And a few years later, an even more disgruntled bunch, the Pilgrim Fathers, chose Plymouth as their launching-pad, as if to emphasize that it summed up the worst of what they were dissatisfied with. Even William of Orange, Dutch and therefore abnormally equable, landed at Brixham, presumably on the advice of equerries who believed in a baptism of fire; he stayed less than a week. Dryden, being a satirist, naturally loved Devon; whereas Coleridge, a more sober lad alto-gether, was born in Ottery St. Mary and never mentioned the fact for the rest of his life. (The Man from Porlock, traditionally held responsible for the collapse of *Kubla Khan* by bursting in for a quick natter while the poet was dreaming, never actually existed; he was merely a symbol created by Coleridge to point out how great a poet he might have been if only he could have exorcised his traumatic memories of the West Country.)

Devon, then, has had to depend on a transient population for its existence. Understandably enough, when plans for a maximum security prison were mooted in 1801, Devon leapt at this chance of maintaining a stable population and offered Dartmoor at a ridiculously nominal rent, completely undercutting every other tender; yet, despite the most rigorous precautions, Dartmoor still has the highest break-out rate of any prison in the country (these statistics were painstakingly unconfirmed at the time of going to press, however, and the author is willing to haggle). Realising, therefore, its peculiar situation, Devon decided early on to cut its losses and consider itself merely as a place to visit, since which time tourism has become its major industry and life force. Stop any citizen in the streets of Dawlish, or Lynmouth, or Ilfracombe, make a noise like negotiable tender, and from under his Dacron smock he will produce hot scones, first editions of *Westward Ho!*, stone jars of cider, registered packets of mailable clotted cream, fragments of Exeter Cathedral crypt, fresh mackerel, and sepia postcards of weird quasi-athletic rites as yet unpractised east of the Exe. He will probably be leading a wild pony that has been in his family for generations, and can always be prevailed upon to sing a chorus or two of the fortunes of Uncle Tom Cobbleigh (his great-grandfather) in local dialect.

Architecturally, the most fascinating single feature of the county is that there are no private houses. Drop in by chance at any of the eighteen thousand winsome thatched cottages that infest the landscape, and you will find a man from Birkenhead or Lewisham coming down the stairs with a shrimp-net, or a Sussex child talking to its crabs in the bath. Most of the other architecture in the country has fallen to pieces, notably the Norman Castle at Totnes and some forty pre-dissolution monasteries; serious efforts were, of course, made to install h & c, priv.ʼ baths, TV lnges, writ. rms. etc., but when the conversions were found to be prohibitively expensive, the speculators cut their losses and sold the lots off in little bags to visiting Americans; Exeter, for example, possesses a fine Norman gatehouse, kept as a tourist come-on, but the rest of the old Norman town is now owned by a coach-party of

Dupont Nylon executives who came by one April day and took it back to Redwing, Minnesota. Still, Wortham Manor, a fine eleventh-century granite pile can be visited for 4/– including tea. And a child can see Buckland Abbey for sixpence.

All of which explains far more satisfactorily than a dozen volumes of English history why Devon and Spain have always been at daggers, not to say grappling-hooks, drawn. Philip II's megalomaniac dream, after his annexing of Portugal in 1580, of a vast Hispanic holiday resort stretching from the Costa Brava all the way to the Algarve constituted the threat of a death-blow to the Devon tourist industry which could only be answered with steel and grape-shot. There can now, in view of the subsequent realisation of these ambitions, be little doubt that the lemming-like rush of Devonians to the sea in the sixteenth century sprang from a widespread fear for the safety of their guest-rooms and tea-shoppes. Certainly, they chose their moment of time, and grasped it; the defeat of the Armada marked the beginning of the end for Spanish dreams. It has taken them four hundred years to regain the tourist initiative, and, naturally, things are again about to come to an international head, cloaked in a political guise. And Spain should tread with care; for, when Gibraltar, as it must sends out a plea for mercenaries with guts and honour, the men of Devon will once more rally to the call.

All Except The Bastard

The Still Centre

IF THERE IS one thing more than any other which does not sum up life in the Midlands, it is the endless processions of Greeks making their way to Hucknall Torkard. You may come upon them any day, usually towards evening, walking slowly down the middle of the road from Nottingham, carrying the traditional Ordnance Survey Map, the bottles of rezina, the volumes of Thucydides, and singing the poignant sunset dirges designed to welcome the squid boats home to Koypolis, twelve hundred miles away. From time to time, they stop, and the men, clad in their picturesque, ambiguous kilts, dance together in long melancholy lines. On a clear night, you can hear their thumbs clicking forty miles away.

They are, of course, making for the grave of Lord Byron, just as English tourists tread the tearworn path to Missolonghi. The friendly Midlanders treat these strangers with the legendary hospitality shown to all immigrants who have return tickets, and much has been done to strengthen the ties between the two nations by these colourful visitors and their drachmae.

But if this tells us little, or even nothing, about what life is like in the still centre of England, it does bring up the whole question of why a man should have chosen to die in a foreign swamp rather than look for a job in Nottingham. The Midlands is constantly throwing up such paradoxes; and as it is the nub and locus of all things English, to understand it is to understand the whole. Treatises on that nebulous property, the English character, lamely attempt to explain our eccentricities in terms of class, or behavioural codes, or climate; there seems to be a deliberate, perhaps polite, refusal to see them as diluted tributaries of that weird undercurrent of madness which rises from some Nottinghamshire source, and has run at full tide through so many Nottinghamshire men. Men like Sir Thomas Parkyns, of Bunny, a village five miles south of Nottingham itself; known as the Wrestling Baronet, he dedicated a treatise on wrestling, *The Cornish Hugg*, to George I, and when no-one had the decency to translate it into German, Sir Thomas quietly went mad, and spent the rest of his life putting up small statues to himself. Men like the 5th Duke of Portland, who did nothing but build gatehouses on vacant lots around the county. Or Lambert Simnel, who got himself crowned King of England in Dublin, came to East Stoke in 1487 to claim his inheritance, and was pounced on by that humourless monarch, Henry VII. And it is surely unnecessary to remind anyone that Notts contains Gotham, whose inhabitants are remembered mainly for such rational contributions to progress as clocks without works (so that their owners may live forever) and a plan to catch the moon in a bucket.

Whatever the dark reasons for this galloping madness, they were enough to drive out Nottinghamshire's five creative talents—Byron (to Greece), D. H. Lawrence (to Mexico), Richard Parkes Bonington (to France), Alan Sillitoe (to Majorca), and Samuel Butler (to New Zealand). Even today, despite the National Health Service and *New Society*, Nottingham Station teems with young, bearded men with knobbly staves and old typewriters, all waiting for the train that will save their sanity and carry them directly to paperback rights and a bijou villa in taxfree Corfu. Why Notts is central to things English is, unquestionably, its power to drive its sons beyond its borders; foreigners, fed by the BHTA on an image of Britons as stolid, mono-syllabic men sitting under oak trees holding a cricket-ball and a thatch-ing-hook, never seem to realise that rebellion *against* these leaden elements is exactly what made Britain great. And Nottinghamshire, lying like a great placid lily on its pupating sons, had the effect, not of aborting them, but of incubating them until their stings were honed, and the calm surface of the pond shook with their rippling exodus. It is immaterial whether or not Robin Hood existed; it is sufficient that legend saw fit to set this two-fisted ur-Marxist in a Nottinghamshire context. It was inevitable that the fiercest battleground of the war between Monarchy and Commonwealth should have been here, along with the bloodsodden religious debate given as its official excuse. Inevitable, too, that Linby should have been the point where Watt's spinning machines revolutionised an industry and a society, and where the Luddite counter-revolution reached its most wretched intensity. England has suffered four great revolutions: industrial, religious, social, and sexual. Nottingham had them all first. Oliver Mellors, be it remembered, was a Nottinghamshire lad—by turns bucolic and urbane, tender and randy, devout and profane, archaic and anarchic. Notting-hamshire straddles England and makes itself felt with a force and direction of which the gamekeeper would have been justifiably proud.

If Notts is a hotbed of rebellion and change, or just a hotbed, Leicestershire, to the south, is its exact antithesis: a cool, pastoral county, which makes boots. Its most famous son, Robert Burton, devoted his life to the composition of *The Anatomy of Melancholy*, and no-one that knows the area has ever asked why. Originally that part of Mercia given over in the ninth century to the Danes, Leics remains under their pervasive influence, its inhabitants pursuing their lives with the diligence and attention to minutiae which characterises southern Scandinavia. The people walk the soft green lanes in their new creaky boots, eating the world-famous pork pies and matchless cheeses, thinking about irrigation, and pigs, and sleep, and God, and wondering how it happened that fox-hunting became a political issue. Life moves at a peaceful lope, a long, gentle undulation, free from intensities of joy or despair. If *The Anatomy* is Leicestershire's magnum opus, Tennyson's *In Memoriam* is its most typical statement, and one understands the poet's motives in seeking out Shawell Rectory as a place to reflect:

> And gazing on thee, sullen tree,
> Sick for they stubborn hardihood,
> I seem to fail from out my blood
> And grow incorporate into thee.

A sensation, I am certain, that all Leicestershire natives will instantly recognise.

Given, then, that Leicestershire is a melancholic place, an area of flat, pale green landscapes veined with sluggish grey canals and warted with ugly redbrick villages, and that it is populated with slow, reflective Danish emigrés full of cheese and sober thoughts, it is hardly surprising that a mad phenomenon like fox-hunting should have found here its fountainhead. Anyone who has spent any time in the chilling October mists of this flat land will recall how the languid pace of life, the dullness of the terrain, and the proliferation of gloomy philosophers can press against the temples and curdle the marrow. Against this background, the only creature which seems to have successfully overcome the weight of Leicestershire sobriety is the fox. Attractive, hedonistic, clever, parasitical, colourful, unproductive, irresponsible, he is a symbol of all that Leicestermen are not. And, as such, he is an infuriating irritant, like the chap you knew before you were married who is now a bachelor supported by beautiful women and constantly drops in to see you on the way to the airport. The fox, to all appearances, drinks life to the lees, and the only way around the perpetual insult which his

186

existence provokes is to go out on a nice morning with forty dogs and a hundred chaps and tear him to shreds. If the climax of a hunt is not a pretty sight, it is only because the spectacle of the middle-class wreaking vengeance on a non-conformist can turn the strongest bowel. It is even possible to find hunters who conceive their sport as a divine mission; the fact that a layabout like the fox ultimately gets it in the neck proving that life can be made to conform to moral principles, if only the hounds get the scent of the malefactor. The fox, too, can be made to stand for any upstart daring to threaten the security of what is left of the Squirarchy; and it's more fun to get up on a horse than to stay at home sticking pins in plasticine models of Harold Wilson.

Since we are in the vicinity, it would be crass not to mention Rutland.

"One has no great hopes from Birmingham. I always say there is something direful in the sound"—thus Mrs. Elton, in a slander scripted with characteristic clumsiness by Jane Austen. Birmingham has long had to bear such taunts, and it has borne them with the staunch apathy which befits the home of Cadbury's Drinking Chocolate. Bournvita is the opiate of its people, and it must have gone a long way towards fostering that bland imperviousness to criticism with which Birmingham sits in the middle of Warwickshire on its great, fat, spreading rump. Warwickshire, the third component of the central Midlands, constantly lays claim to recognition as "the county closest to England's heart", and students who ponder on our current arteriosclerosis would do well to examine this great gobbet of social cholesterol lying so close to our vital source. Not that its Town Hall does not possess the finest organ in the country; not that the Harborne Botanical Gardens do not smell sweet and blossom in the dust; and—what else was there? Oh, yes—not that St. Philip's Cathedral doesn't have four Burne-Jones windows; but it is difficult not to sympathise with the fears of men from Worcs and Staffs across whose borders the Brummagen suburbs had spread like semi-detached lava that will not be denied its diet of grass and trees and flowers. And yet, physical beauty is less important than the essential loveliness of soul which lies below skin-depth; if Notts is the quintessence of English *élan vital*, if Leics typefies our curious bucolic streak, Warwicks (or Birmingham, since the two are fast becoming geographically synonymous) contains much of that greatness of heart which the world is beginning to notice beating beneath our impassive British masks.

Earlier, I mentioned the four major revolutions which effected fundamental change in the social structure of this island, and the part played by Nottinghamshire in their development. But we are about to enter on a fifth, and equally significant one, and this time it is to Birmingham we have to look as a touchstone and example. And as a guide. *The Times*, with its customary foresight, circumspection, hindsight, and eye for a good subtle slogan, has called them "The Dark Million". They are, as it were, the maquisards of our racial revolution, that unnervingly rapid process by which Fuzzy-Wuzzy and Gunga Din, those big dusky children who used to ask for nothing more than a good scrap and the memorial of a few rousing pentameters, have suddenly turned up on the factory floors of their Mother Country. Understandably enough, it's all come as a bit of a shock to find that they wear ties, raise children, speak English, believe in God, seek love, work hard, use assegais sparingly, and think that the Commonwealth constitution guarantees free movement to all the members of that great big happy family regularly referred to at 3 p.m. every Christmas Day.

Naturally, the county closest to England's heart has shown the stuff that made this nation great, and taken them to its benevolent bosom. Despite surprise that the new citizens don't seem to have learnt much about our ways from all those years of hobnobbing with the British Raj, the Kenya Police, the mining bosses, the Rhodesian farmers, and the friendly Nassau tourists, Birmingham has been quick to initiate them in our customs, and to integrate them into our society. Unions, employers, shopkeepers, landlords, churches, school-teachers, parents, and many privately-founded citizens' organisations, have all got together to explain to their coloured friends the difficulties of settling in England and to warn them of problems they may find themselves facing. At the last General Election, Birmingham and its suburbs took the opportunity of proving to the world that England considers the new conditions to be a serious subject, deserving wholehearted attention, and the rest of the country has felt the pulse of its geographical heart, and responded with a speed and concentration of which we can all be proud. It is as if Birmingham, Warwicks, had said to itself: "No, we are not Birmingham, Alabama. Nor will we ever be." And those who know the tenacity, the compassion, and the feeling for England which the people of Birmingham possess, will readily acknowledge that any problems will be ruthlessly exterminated before they reach proportions likely to disturb the sweet sleep of the Bournvita belt.

All Except The Bastard

North by North-West

IN THE YEAR 573 BC, so the story goes, the poet Liun-Tsu was approached by one of the literary disciples with which the suburbs of Mukden were then overrun. Catching the old man by his sleeve, the boy asked a question of the sort which the world has since come to expect from the average Oriental lip: "Master," he said, "what is to sustain us in our sadness?" Whereupon the seer turned his kindly saffron face towards the lad, and replied: "We walk towards a golden land, into the sound of divine laughter."

Liun-Tsu might, in his wisdom, have been talking about Lancashire; it takes more than mere geography to invalidate a dream. If there is one thing which sets this teeming sub-continent apart from the sobriety of Yorkshire, to the east, and the apathy of the Atlantic, to the west, it is its permanent atmosphere of comic riot. The history of Lancashire is written in hysterics a foot high; like Falstaff, it is not only witty in itself, but the cause that wit is in other men; it is the hilarious knock-about act on the end of the English cultural pier. And it never closes.

There is, naturally enough, considerable speculation as to when the joke actually started; some scholars become nervous if research is not pursued at least as far as the (probably obscene) joke about what the three Manx legs were all running away from; others agree that the whole business stems from a handful of extant Mercian graffiti describing conditions on the other side of Offa's Dike, built in the eighth century AD to separate Lancashire from civilisation. But whatever the primary sources of the Lancashire farce, no responsible academic would deny that its Modern Period began with the foundation of Wigan in 1246. Wigan was the first English city to be conceived as a basis for jokes; and it served bravely as the sole butt until the rise of the Victorian music-hall created an insatiable demand, to satisfy which Manchester (1838), Bolton (1838), Oldham (1849), Bootle (1868), and Accrington (1878) were all founded in double-quick time; since when the mention of their very names has been enough to send the coldest audience into uncontrollable fits and soften them up for the first real joke of the evening, which invariably involves a character with a similarly local name. Records show that on the first occasion when the name Ramsbottom was mentioned on stage, six men choked to death.

Not surprisingly, eight centuries as a comic prop has left its mark on the people; not just on their minds, or their attitudes, although these, too, have been moulded by the constant tides of laughter, but on their actual physiques and physiognomies. This effect has been intensified by social selection; while other counties have created folk-heroes with knotty arms (Somerset), barrel-chests (Suffolk), strapping thighs (Lincs), ruddy complexions (Kent), and so on, Lancastrians have taken a rather different course. Perhaps in no other area in the world could Wee Georgie Wood, Jimmy Clitheroe, Arthur Askey, or Davy Kaye have achieved greatness. Lancashire is a county where fathers pace the corridors of labour wards, waiting for news of a red nose, or ears like jug-handles, or a novel squint. Parents watch eagerly, prayerfully, for the first signs of projecting teeth, of a funny walk, of ginger hair, of anything that hints at the possibility of their offspring turning into another Ken Dodd. (Even when such ambitions are frustrated, the prodigy can sometimes get by on trust: the Wise half of Morecambe and Wise relies for much of his popularity on a phrase to the effect that he is "the one with the short hairy legs". The audience accepts this without evidence and laughs itself sick on the assumption that this is exactly what you'd expect to find if you looked up a typical Lancashire trouser leg.) If all else fails, the child is sent off to learn to play the violin execrably, to sing off-key, or to develop its natural accent to the point of unintelligibility. And considerable reliance is placed on clothes and other effects chosen carefully for hysteria-potential. A walk down the main concourse of a town like Blackburn at, say, 5.35 in the afternoon makes *A Night At The Opera* look like a state funeral: pavements and gutters teem with tiny agitated Lancastrians in oversized clogs, cloth caps, rosettes like dinner-plates, long mufflers, gorblimey trousers and collarless shirts. The incredible din, the manic hilarity, is not simply the result of an excess of luminous noses, squirting buttonholes, collapsible trousers, detachable plastic ears, and farting handshakes; it goes far deeper than that, into that essential substratum of Lancashire life where something funny is constantly happening to people on their way to somewhere else. And the fact that, at knocking-off time, some forty thousand Blackburners are at that moment embarking on another eventful journey between loom and fireside means that forty thousand farcical situations are all germinating at once.

Of course, as with all complex and sophisticated societies, the working-out of these situations follows prescribed patterns and codes. The cries of "Ey-oop, then!" or "I say, I say, I say," the pratfalls, the swift exchanges of hats, the removal of dentures (stays, braces, glass eyes, toupees etc.), the wet roar of communal raspberries, the collisions with lamp-posts and busty girls, are all part of a ritual as rigid as a quadrille or a *suttee*; it is only *within* these predetermined touchpoints that improvisations can be practised. This element of automatism, of social conformity, on which all such of comedy depends, runs throughout Lancastrian life. A pub, say, which does not have a resident Englishman, Irishman, Scotsman and Jew standing at the bar for the use of customers might as well close down; similarly, if the landlord doesn't make his daughter available to commerical travellers in the Snug, his licence is never renewed. And props like long woolly underwear, chamber-pots, parrots, bloomers, false bosoms, and spittoons are as essential to a successful landlord as dartboards and pickled onions.

Not surprisingly, all Lancashire relationships are constructed along lines designed to elicit the maximum comedy from any given human situation. All mothers-in-law are fat, warty, puritan and flatulent, and live in the best bedroom (the one, in more opulent establishments, next door to the lavatory); all wives are belligerent, teetotal, avaricious and sexually neutral; all children either scream, or throw up in charabancs, or, more usually, do both simultaneously; all friends are permanently sozzled; all enemies talk with a suspect, simulated-southern accent; and all dogs are old, loyal, brave and emotional, asking nothing more of life than the chance to be epitaphised in a song, a little song, a little song entitled *Just An Old Mongrel But Now He's Gone There's An Ache Where My Heart Used To Be.*

Work, being a major part of waking life, has naturally become the major joke. The Industrial Revolution, driven on by such sons of Lancashire as James Hargreaves, Richard Arkwright and Samuel Crompton, threw up as its richest by-product the greatest stock of factory jokes the world has ever seen. The whole complex labour-management relationship was reduced to a ridiculous farce from which it has little chance of recovering, since the organisation set up to effect a balance between the two forces itself became a laughing-stock within hours of its inception. Perhaps the most important piece of joke-material in the whole history of Lancashire was the founding of the TUC in Manchester in 1868. It presented Lancastrian workers with a virgin field of comic situation and character, and gave the world those imperishable heroes, Trades Union leaders, Committee Organisers,

191

and Shop Stewards. The highpoint of any of the old *Workers' Playtime* programmes was always the moment when the star comedian mentioned the most officious, serious-minded and hardworking (i.e. the most hilarious) shop steward by name; to anyone who heard these programmes, the sound of five thousand howling mill-hands falling to the canteen floor and rolling among the tables will go with them to the grave. And it is almost entirely due to the ravages wrought by Lancashire comedians on their own leaders that employers refuse to take Trades Unions seriously. Unfortunately, employers are, without exception, humourless men, the iron having been driven into their souls by the fact that, since the Industrial Revolution, there has never been anything but trouble up at the mill. The Lancastrian upper-middle classes are born into the pall of gloom that hangs over this knowledge, and into the atmosphere of angry fear caused by the millworkers' refusal to treat the situation as anything but an uproarious hoot. The failure to break down industrial and class barriers in the North-West is a direct result of a three-way tension: labour is always straining to make new jokes about management, management lives in permanent apprehension of the jokes about to be made, and union negotiators exist in a state of neurosis from being unable to explain either the jokes or the gloom to the respective antagonists. There is little chance of the gulfs narrowing: about ten years ago, when England discovered sociology, whole busloads of field-survey teams took off for Lancashire; the net result of even the best of the assorted outcomes, *The Uses Of Literacy*, was to explain the North, rather inadequately, to the South, who promptly forgot; in Lancashire itself, of course, the Hoggart bit became just one more joke (the recurrent one about comic intellectuals with college scarves and moss behind their ears).

The apotheosis of the Lancashire joke is Wakes Week, which is a sustained shriek from start to finish, the noise centring primarily on Blackpool, Southport, and Morecambe. During this period, the cloth cap gives way to the cardboard copper's helmet, the headscarf to the celluloid stetson; black pudding is thrown over in favour of candy-floss, and the quart replaces the pint as the standard unit of measurement. It is a time of dodgems and lust, of hangovers and winkles, of hokey-cokey in the Tower Ballroom and hankey-pankey on the sands. A Wakes Saturday night along the Golden Mile looks like an evangelist threat made flesh; Imperial Rome on the skids must have been very like this, the annual Big Dipper ride up to the edge of the everlasting bonfire, with Reginald Dixon playing Nero to the life.

None of which brings us to Liverpool.

For Liverpool stands apart, a city state, separated from its Lancashire hinterland by race, by language, by industry, and by mood. They do not spin in Liverpool, and consequently they do not joke; they lack the uniformity necessary for a background of sharable laugh-material. They unload ships, mill flour, crush oilseed, make bobbins, tan leather, refine sugar, pack tobacco, strain paint, bottle barley-sugar; this disparity, matched by the social disparity between the Welsh, the Chinese, the Indians, the Jamaicans, the West Africans, and the two brands of Irish, gives them nothing in common with the cotton belt; it doesn't even give them much in common with one another. And this is the real reason behind the Mersey Beat.

How anyone can mistake the teenagers' music, long hair, exotic clothes, habits, behaviour patterns, attitudes and morals as defiant non-conformism is beyond the comprehension of Merseysiders. It may look this way set against the fixed generation-hierarchies of the rest of England; but seen in the context of complete social disorder on the part of Liverpudlian adults, the whole thing becomes instantly explicable. The older generation of Liverpool is black, white, yellow, brown, Hindu, Catholic, Buddhist, Protestant, turbanned, cheong-sammed, dungareed, shawled; and it speaks twenty different languages and dialects. For youth, the only course of rebellion lay towards conformity, and if their standard is primitive, that's only because their society is in its infancy. Jeans are its fig-leaves, beat music is its ritual chant, and long hair, inarticulate grunts, solo dancing are its predictable characteristics. Banding together in groups of four and five for mutual protection and competition are its first faltering steps in community living. It is all, somehow, rather pure and beautiful. It is a civilisation in its infancy.

And it is the one thing in Lancashire we must all take very seriously.

All Except The Bastard

The Mysterious East

WHAT, EXACTLY, IS Orientalism? Is this word, coined by the West, used to describe a *genuine* property, a queer, ancient compound exhaled by centuries of *moo goo gai pan* and paper flowers and atonal songs and ritual suicide? Something tangible which comes only with vertical language and exploding populations and paddy-fields and gnomic poetry? Or do we use the word to label, instead, some artificial quality imposed out of fear, ignorance and superciliousness by timid Occidentals on a rather simple agricultural civilisation about whose human fertility the West has recurrent saffron-coloured nightmares? After all, Christianity is far more complex and mysterious than Zen; Wittgenstein more labyrinthine than Confucius; Joyce more weird than Ts'ao Chan; and quails in aspic more abstruse than prawn chop suey. Whence, then, the mystery? Whence inscrutability?

Anyone maddened by the apparent irrelevance of such questions to the subject of Ipswich and Beccles should take a large map of the world and hold it up to a bright light. It will not be long before he is thunderbolted to the quick by the physical similarities between East Anglia and China. No other country in the world is shaped like these two huge eastern buttocks of land; and, if the sheer weight of geophysical evidence still hasn't convinced the sceptic of the analogy, let him examine the way in which the rest of England considers its Orient. It is virtually identical with the world's attitude to South-East Asia.

Both countries have suffered from the Western assumption that physical isolation automatically means temperamental isolationism; the isolationism is, in fact, entirely Western in origin. And from this initial misrepresentation springs the familiar bifurcated attitude that what you do not understand must be either (a) mysteriously sinister or (b) hysterically funny. So into the joke-books of a billion Occidental Joe Millers goes the hilarious paraphernalia of, in the one case, yellow faces, sing-song voices, chop-sticks, rice-cultivation, pig-tails, comic peasants, and funny names (e.g. Hangchow, Nanking), and, in the other, red faces, rural burrs, clay pipes, turnip-cultivation, tweed caps, comic farm-labourers, and funny names (e.g. Hockwold cum Wilton,

194

Newton Flotman). As for the sinister aspect, this is also compounded of a thimbleful of half-digested facts, most of them topographical: East Anglia is seen as a great, flat, soggy wilderness where bearded tits and bustards, not elsewhere found, croak and carol in the shrouding mists, where wild geese woo the moon, and where the sea laps hungrily at the reclaimed land it sees as its stolen property, held at bay only by the actions of witches, warlocks and tiny hunchbacks with sprigs of mildewed bindweed.

The saddest feature of all this irresponsible myth-making is that the inhabitants of these countries ultimately begin to approximate to the myth-image; if the outside world seeks to impose exclusiveness and oddity on you, then you may choose, out of bitterness, to manufacture your own brand of separatism. And, just as China, for so long mocked and rejected, has responded by widening the rift from its own side of the line, so, too, East Anglia has come to separate itself from Mother England. The process there, however, started much further back in time.

In 400,000 BC, to judge from excavations at such thriving knapping-sites as Whitlingham, there was little to separate East Anglian Man from his siblings throughout the uncivilised world: a stooping, hirsute, knotty character, with scant frontal projection and a limited vocabulary, he was slow to anger; to almost anything, in fact, except perhaps to the manufacture of flint axe-handles, with which the area is rife. He also perfected the Small Round Stone, used for braining anything that wandered past the front of his hole. He was, in short, no different from the run-of-the-mill prehistoric biped. However, one singularly important fact must not be overlooked: at this period, England was still joined to Scandinavia, and the bulk of the population inhabited its eastern side; but there were extensive squatter settlements dotted around the rest of prehistoric Britain. These Western people remained a rather aimless, negative race for several eons; they left very few axe-handles or even Small Round Stones and consequently cannot be considered anywhere near as sophisticated as the East Anglians. During the Mesolithic Period, between 10,000 and 50,000 BC, the East Anglians were knocking up harpoons, hammers, tiny jugs, and rude sleds by the gross; and still nothing was going on in the West, except the production of throwing sticks, and a few square rocks probably used for smashing anything these small, moronic communities could lay their fumbling hands on.

By 10,000 BC, however, Britain was beginning to separate from the mainland of Europe; the lowlands between started to fill up, first with salt marshes, later with lagoons, and finally, at one horrifying bound, the North Sea. This transitional period was a time of great stress for Meso-Neolithic East Anglian Man; some threw in their lot with the Continent, and, as the water rushed over their stricken lake-dwellings, they began splashing towards Denmark, Holland, and so on. Many, not quite trained to make even the simplest decisions, simply sat there while the stuff slopped up to their eyebrows, pondering the futility of Neolithic life, and quietly perished. The rest plumped for England. East Anglia was born; but now it was a minority area—suddenly, the cretinous, brutish oafs in the Western sector were top men on the totem. Prejudice was born. It was 9,086 BC.

During the next few thousand years, the West was filled with a slowly evolving race of power-maniacs, elementary arms manufacturers, and, naturally, fighters. Woad-covered gangs of Bronze and Stone Age tearaways roamed the countryside hacking one another to pieces with crude swords, spears and choppers, and generally despising the mild men in the East who were preoccupied with stopping the sea from dining off their families, and with developing primitive agricultural systems and fishing boats. In the West, the pattern of the modern world was being created in all its bloody malevolence; in the East, man was meekly cultivating himself into obscurity. The Anglo-Saxon takeover in the East was a peaceful enough affair; and the subsequent pre-Norman punch-ups between Mercians and Northumbrians and West Saxons left the East virtually unmarked. They accepted Christianity quietly, happily; it seemed, in all its fine impossible idealism, to be just what they were looking for; of the extant one hundred and eighty Saxon church-towers in England, one hundred and nineteen are in Norfolk alone. It might have been our Paradise; we lost it, and perhaps that lies behind much of our scornful separatism.

Gradually, during the Norman Period and the Early Middle Ages, the gulf widened. The Norman temperament was totally alien to the East Anglian; London, which by now had become the controlling centre of the country, paid no attention to East Anglia, except to blow the occasional Middle English raspberry towards the rural Orient. Little by little, the men of Suffolk and Norfolk let the iron corkscrew into their souls; the practical, optimistic ones decided to cut their cultural losses and conformed to the picture the West was forming of them: sullen men with knotty fingers and a predilection for simple, basic things. They went away, usually alone, to cross-breed pigs and cows and sheep; many succeeded, producing the Large Black pig, the Dun cow, the Black-faced sheep, the Suffolk Punch horse; but many failed, and for years the country was infested with curious three-legged hybrids, miniature bulls, barking horses and hens that gave milk and went mad in the dark. Abortive animal husbandry created an even deeper sullenness and resentment in those sections of the population involved in the biological misery; it also gave rise to great waves of witchcraft, black and white, which, instead of clearing up the mess, worsened it. A village of some eight hundred souls in northern Norfolk became the disciples of a cow with two heads; when it died, the village broke up in disorder and its inhabitants scattered the madness in tiny dangerous fragments throughout East Anglia.

There was also, of course, serious revolt against the ridicule from the West. In 1549, Robert Kett raised 16,000 men outside Norwich in order to force the King's hand in giving a square deal to the peasants, whom the King, a lad of twelve, had no doubt only seen in primitive panto-mimes and therefore considered to be an even bigger laugh than his elders did. After four thousand of the rebels were slaughtered, the rebellion folded. During the Civil War, Cromwell, a Huntingdon man whom many maleducated but socially eminent Londoners therefore thought of as a comic East Anglian, put Norfolk to the sword and the flame, merely in order to prove this particular point groundless. East Anglia has since been singularly unrebellious, restricting its open resentment to small pockets of resistance like that of William Dowsing, the Laxfield Puritan iconoclast, who spent much of the seventeenth century in desecrating Suffolk churches for the glory of the Lord, George Crabbe, who employed the bulk of his poetry as a stick to beat Goldsmith's rural ignorance with, and the unknown madman who hung the bells in East Bergholt church upside down for reasons best known to himself, and then vanished.

East Anglia is, even more depressingly, an area deeply involved with death, dying and interrment, a taste observable in so many Far Oriental societies for whom living is a wretched process the end of which is the only cause for celebration most of them ever have. The reason probably holds for Suffolk and Norfolk too. These counties are curiously proud of their ancient barrows, cairns and pits, which, seen close to, can be bitterly disappointing for the tourist, looking as they do either like unsuccessful bomb-shelters or like amateur elephant traps. Worse, from the beginning of the Great Social Rift, most of the East Anglian upper classes spent their time in commissioning horizontal statues of themselves to be placed on huge stone sarcophagi, in which they could be laid to rest, safe at last from the sarcasm of the West. The one great literary genius of Norfolk was Sir Thomas Browne, who made a career from the incessant contemplation of death (or Death, as they like to think of it locally); he at least came to terms with the gloominess of East Anglian life; but, inevitably, the oppressive mood comes through in such characteristically sour statements as "Charity begins at home" (*Religio Medici*) "For the world, I count it not an inn, but an hospital, and a place, not to live, but to die in" (*Ibid*) and "Hercules is not only known by his foot" (*Urn Burial*). And, despite his desire for translation to a better place than Norwich, he was nevertheless clearly disturbed at the possibility of "that unextinguishable laugh in heaven" (*The Garden of Cyrus*).

There really is no need to analyse what for want of a better word can be called modern East Anglia; everything is just as it was, a little gloomier, perhaps, a little more sullen, a little more fatalistic. The few optimists still pursue agricultural development, the ringing cadences of Turnip Townshend, Coke of Holkham and other sod-turning pioneers committed to faithful memory; the rest survive, and, each year, the really sour gather in small malicious groups on the Norfolk Broads to jeer at the aquatic inadequacy of the only West Anglians they ever get the chance to see.

It is not easy to predict how this slow, corrosive process will end; but it is just possible. Already East Anglia has put out a tentative feeler towards the twentieth century by building a fertiliser plant on advanced lines; but it has done this experimentally, half-heartedly. If the area is finally to be accepted as an unqualified (and, hence, uncomic, un-mysterious and unalien) part of the country which for nigh on half a million years has looked on it as an embarrassment to England's dream of an industrial/militarist/progressive society, it must continue the conforming process begun, so recently and so very late, with the construction of the nuclear-powered eyesore at the pretty seaside hamlet of Sizewell. It must build in the image west of its frontier. It must bulldoze unlandscaped concrete motorways across its churchyards and village greens; it must envelop its quiet country towns in open-plan developments, tinfoil supermarkets, haphazard skyscrapers, bingoleums, bowling alleys, Hotscoff beefburger bars, drive-in laundromats, black concrete bus-garages; it must fill its unprofitable, wildfowl sanctuaries with billboards, neons, gas-stations, dog-tracks, industrial waste, jerry-built council estates, half-planned factory areas

198

shoddy apartment-blocks, and death-heaps of rusting abandoned cars.

It must, in short, Wake Up To The Facts Of Life Today And March Shoulder To Shoulder With The Rest Of Britain Into The Glorious Future.

All Except The Bastard

Border Territory

FACED WITH A situation which threatens to loom beyond its comprehension, the State of Texas possesses one cast-iron last resort in its
locker: it stands up, as one man, waves the Lone Star flag, and cries:
"REMEMBER THE ALAMO!" As last resorts go, the world has
seen better; but Texas has yet to find anything as universally applicable
or successful. It regularly carried the day from the Halls of Montezuma
to the shores of Tripoli; it sent men seventeen feet above the earth on
the end of vaulting-poles, while all the world wondered; when
President Kennedy was shot down in a Dallas street, it sprang to the
self-defenseive Texan lip like Pavlovian drool; and, no doubt, should
Richard Milhous Nixon find it necessary to push a few buttons to keep
the world safe for democracy, those three words will pass into the
waiting universe with all the rest of the gaseous waste. It is the cry of
strong men returning to the womb to read the writing on the wall; it
is the cry of Border Territory.

Well, so much for Zane Grey, and good luck to him; no finer man
ever drew ten per cent of the gross. He would have understood the
badlands of Durham and Northumberland the way no Englishman
beyond their frontiers can. He knew that bordermen are not like other
mortals. Border country breeds them that way; it is Alamo country,
conceived in fire and gore, and its natal memories are of battlefields,
and enmity, and courage, and suspicion, and a brand of fine, brave
stupidity you only get when two strangers meet and one of them has
a better gun. Border country spends much of its working life as either
a battleground or No-Man's-Land and demonstrating such nice
philosophical brain-teasers as the bullets that whistle through Jerusalem,
or the wall which separates the good Germans from the bad, or the
bad from the good, depending on your geographical and political
position relative to Checkpoint Charlie.

The image of the Geordie as a hard-grained suspicious man living in
a society where the closed mind is a social prerequisite as traditional as
the closed fist is not a figment knocked up by strangers in the manner
of the East Anglian myth discussed at the last sitting. Northumberland

has been border territory for two thousand years; Durham, too, has shared the environmental lot of these hundred generations. It was no accident that England's first practical railroad ran from Stockton to Darlington, and no further, when another half-mile of track would have carried it into Yorkshire; George Stephenson was a Newcastle lad, and would not betray his birthright so lightly. Who knew to what vile ends the facilities for thus crossing the border territory might not be used? After all, it was less than a century since the 1745 rebellion, and many an octogenarian standing on Darlington Station platform in 1822 must have waited for the 8.15 with sombre misgivings stirring in his head. Nor might the gleaming metals have been appropriated by the defensive English alone—in Warkworth, in 1173, William the Lion of Scotland herded the villagers into the parish church and burned it to the ground. Bordermen could hardly expect to fare better at the hands of nineteenth-century Methodism.

But the toughness, the suspiciousness, the xenophobia of border natives goes back beyond Anglo-Scottish animosity to the period of Hadrian's Wall. Before the Romans decided that Britain had a definite Northern limit, what is now border country was just so much car-boniferous limestone topped off with heather, from clumps of which various groups of comparatively primitive locals would emerge and bash one another as a way of life necessitated by the shortage of food and goatskins. These were apolitical skirmishes, largely non-racial, and looked on by all involved as part of the ineluctable 9 to 5 warp and woof. The Romans then arrived and dug a ditch called the Vallum. This, they claimed (being political sophisticates), was not intended as a military fortification, but merely as a line of demarcation. It shared, however, with the later Berlin wall and the ageless children's game, the quality of canny provocation: That line we have just drawn between you and us is now *our* line—step over it and we'll bash your rotten face in. The onus is thereby put on the side not quick-witted enough to have drawn the line first. The Picts, unaware of what made the Roman mind tick, promptly stepped over the Vallum and got the big stick, after which they retreated, reformed ranks, and created the situation by which the Romans could claim as necessary the erection of a coast-to-coast wall, forts, barracks, deterrents and all the other accoutrements of civilised society. Scotland was born in spite of itself; and Roman Britain (i.e. England) came, naturally enough, to regard the Durham-Northumberland area as its front line, a scorched-earth region inhabited by cannon-fodder. Clearly, no self-respecting southerner would wander into the area; and the only way a Scot could do it was by chancing his arm with the legionaries. Gradually, the trifurcated hate and resentment built up: hate came south from Scotland, fear came north from England, and within Northumbria, an occupied territory, hated and feared by its neighbours, the seeds were sown. It has been a sturdy growth.

The Border Ballads trace the development of border separatism. If you will turn to page 314 of your *Oxford Book of Ballads*, you will fall upon a nugget of ur-racialism which, in its social, sexual and political implications might have wept from the pen of J. Baldwin. It concerns a "faire flower of Northumberland" who fell for a Scots prisoner her father had taken in some battle or other; sold on the idea that this Celtic stud was going to carry her back home and marry her, she steals gold, horses, *und so weiter*, and as soon as the Scot is over the border, he delivers the unsettling line: "For I have a wyf and childern five" and rides off cackling into the mists. The faire flower subsequently shuffles back home to her father, who immediately comes up with the fatalistic punch-lines:

> "You arena the first the false Scots have beguiled,
> And ye're aye welcome back to Northumberland."

It was a sentiment that fathers in Wessex were rarely called upon to express, and fully encapsulates the predominant belief in border families as to which end of England has the stick and which the lollipop. Northumberland still has the lowest rate of intermarriage between its sons and daughters and those of other counties (Durham excepted); and the general southern drift which has affected so many parts of the North has drained these two counties proportionately far less than, say, Yorkshire or Lancashire, despite the relatively greater difficulties of life in the North-East. Nor has there ever been much cultural infiltration from the border; its language is more exclusive than that of any other English region, its idiom is self-contained, self-nourishing; it has produced no major writers, no artists, no musicians; and yet it has a flourishing internal culture, a strong oral tradition of poetry and legend, and an army of oil-painting miners. The trombone is ubiquitous. What did come south from Northumbria, however, was Christianity; or, at least, the reconversion of England, initiated at Lindisfarne in the seventh century by St. Aidan. Nowhere on this island was more qualified to disseminate a doctrine of love and peace and spiritual commonwealth, which bordermen obviously saw very early on as a fair alternative to the broadsword and the pike as a means of getting together with neighbours; it was rapidly adopted by the rest of the country, just as rapidly adapted, and within four hundred years England was ready to march eastwards and spread the gospel by means of the broadsword and the pike. This may not have been what St. Aidan had in mind; it may also have been directly responsible for the border's washing its hands of any further cultural responsibility to the rest of the country.

Certainly, the rest of the country has never been too eager to recognise any responsibility to the border; Lindisfarne may have been St. Aidan's stamping ground, but the true cradle of English Christianity is more likely to be found in the home of the Venerable Bede, a place whose name will be remembered for as long as men accept that betrayal was a fundamental element of Christ's career. Jarrow is the North-East's Alamo, if the parallel is to be not glorious victory, but heroism and disaster and an ineradicable memory. There were other names in 1931, names like Sunnybrow and Tudhoe Colliery and West Auckland and Witton Park, one- or two-pit towns, one- or two-factory dormitories, which, to quote the conventional euphemisms we use to protect ourselves from reality, "fell into an everlasting sleep" from which the North-East has been given little encouragement to recover. Between the callousness and selfishness with which England treated its border territory in the third century AD and the callousness and selfishness with which it treated that same territory in the twentieth century AD, there is little qualitative difference. There is only seventeen hundred years. And one could hardly hope for progress towards sympathy in so brief a time.

After the Jarrow rebellion and its inevitable (given the Southern attitude outlined above) abortion, the border returned once more to its pattern of withdrawal, stoicism, and tight, internal life. It is unlikely that the bordermen expected much in the way of results, anyhow; they remained characteristically unvociferous during the later thirteen marvellous years of Tory affluence when nobody had ever had anything so good before, largely because it would have been foolish to expect long shrift from either Harold Macmillan or Alec Douglas-Home; the border had had long experience of the habits of gun-toting Scottish rulers, and no doubt counted it a blessing that they weren't actually herded into crypts and ignited. To be fair to the Conservatives, they did give the North-East a Minister all to itself. It was Quintin Hogg, (Eton and Christ Church), M.P. for St. Marylebone. He had every sympathy for the plight of the North-East, and once went there to tell them so.

October 16th 1964 was a day of rejoicing from the Tweed to the Tees; trombones honked and sparkled in the streets, women danced, and strong men wept for joy. Not that the borderpeople, even then, expected the miracles which had not been forthcoming for two thousand years; but they believed that, somewhere in the bright morning of Wilsonian Democracy, there would be ten minutes for them. Schools would burgeon, houses mushroom, industry boom, and Browns rush in where Quintins feared to tread. The corridors of power had begun to echo with accents which were, if not exactly Tyneside, at least a damned sight closer to comprehensibility than the tinny ring of Etonian Scots, and from these fine new lips, the promises fell like monsoon rains to wash away the thirteen years of drought. The rainy season was short that year; the land absorbed the water, and when it had finished, the structural alteration in the dust turned out to be minimal. Belts would be worn tighter, and the bright morning would have to be postponed; there would be a curb to public spending. In Birmingham and Dorking and Hampstead, the people groaned and bitched and threatened, wondered where their next expense-account meal was coming from, and tried to envisage life as a one-car family. North of the Tees, the bordermen recognised that they had no right to ask for preferential treatment to bring them into line with the traditional standards of the south, set their jaws, and put the Northumbrian bagpipes back on the shelf.

Three hundred miles to the south, a Mr. James Callaghan said, with his charming smile: "We must at all costs avoid a repetition of the 1931 situation." All around him, the people furrowed their brows and tried to think what he was talking about. And, with that bitter irony which bordermen have learned to accept as one of life's basic premises, it was only in that part of England where his words had most meaning that they were least needed.

All Except The Bastard

Semitopia

AS THE SPARKS fly upward, Middlesex was born to doom. It came into the world like the bastard son in some second-rate Elizabethan melodrama, fumblingly conceived and born with horrid congenital diseases; and, having done the appropriate amount of strutting and fretting, destined to quit the stage coughing, misshapen, maladjusted and unloved. After years of the sort of Anglo-Saxon bickering typical of the era which invented the Civil Service, Middlesex was hacked from Mercia twelve centuries ago or thereabouts. It spent a mere two hundred uneasy years in its original form; in AD 1000, Hertfordshire was torn from its hapless vitals, taking with it most of what was noble and of good report. For the next eight hundred years, Middlesex limped along as best it could, before being disembowelled in the creation of the County of London in 1888. Less than eighty years later, the broken, disillusioned remains of Middlesex disappeared forever, gulped into the Greater London maw. Had it, at the time, been able to speak, Middlesex might justifiably have croacked: "I have done the State some service, and they know it" and expired with a certain feeble dignity. As it was, it just went, leaving nothing but a sad flotsam of old signposts, cricketers, and enamel motor-car plaques bobbing on the metropolitan tide.

The question, of course, that immediately springs to mind and lip is: "Why should a dog, a horse, a rat, have life / And thou no breath at all?" It could be argued that what this country needs is more questions like that; it goes right to the heart of county patriotism and country purpose, and if for no other reason than that Middlesex should not have died in vain, it demands an answer. Will the next generation of the two-and-a-half million Middlesex natives feel a cultural deprivation, a loss of roots, and identity, and ethnic meaning? Indeed, will the present population grow into an embittered race, fraught with dispossession, and end up sitting around the simulated embers in their new amorphous Plastihome Developments, murmuring in low sour tones of the glorious days before the City came to Hayes or out to Edgware strode? Already, the protests have been lodged, the preservation societies founded, the petitions circulated; all across the lost county, from Staines to Enfield, historians, naturalists, sociologists and native sentimentalists are storing away the pitiful acorns of this society about to disappear into eternal hibernation—the quaint speech inflections, the porcelain ducks, the fragments of uncut moquette and formica, the low-flush lavatory suites, the chiming doorbells, the plastic roses, the wrought-iron gates, the stone herons, the luminous name-plates in which the imaginative effort of the people is concentrated—"Frede-liza", "Dunwanderin", "Casa Mia", "Welivere". But these are merely the outward and visible signs of that inward and spiritual *élan* which reached its apotheosis in Middlesex: Middlesex was the quintessence of Suburbia, the capital of Subtopia, and with its demise, the Subtopian dream comes to an end. When Greater London standardisation has finished its spread, when Middlesex is nothing but labour-saving ticky-tacky self-contained communities founded by Span and Wates and their neutralising confreres, what, exactly, will this island have lost?

To begin with, semi-detachment. The semi-detached house, of which there are more in Middlesex than any other county in Britain, was not just a habitation and an art-form, it expressed a unique (and uniquely English) attitude of mind. It stood for half-committal, half-friendliness, half-isolation, half-a-mindedness; it stood for wary circumspection, partial ambition, social compromise. It stood, in short, for the New Britain of the post-Victorian era; at the end of sixty glorious years, an Englishman's home had turned into his half-castle. (The very name *Middlesex* might have been designed for our new brand image.) This coincided with the rise of our newest class, a half-breed class, which might be called the working-middle, or lower-middle, which came to its semi-detached homes with a heritage of terraced tradition, with social mores and instincts learned over the centuries in row upon row of Mafeking Villas and Paradise Crescents; to these people, the essential class-lines had been drawn between the solid rows and the detached residences in which the upper classes lived. They aspired towards the ethos of The Larches and The Laburnums, and suddenly there was a half-way stage between the two, a Mini-larches, not one thing nor the other. And that was when status was born, in the semi-detached limbo between two fixed social situations; because status operates not between diametrical opposites, between social blacks and whites, but in nebulous intermediary positions. It thrives on gradations, on shades of subtle greys, on the differences between front doors, and cars, and the size of telly-screens, and school uniforms, and grocery bills, and Continental holidays.

With the rise to eminence of Middlesex in the 'twenties and 'thirties, all the pent-up urges and needs of the bulk of the British population were given their heads. So much that was fine and beautiful in the English character was suddenly released; the shared suppression by Them (the Upper Classes) bred and fostered in the terraces went; people were no longer held down in resigned contentment, unambitious neighbourliness, common bonds that never got anybody anywhere; they were suddenly translated into semi-detachment, into the marvellous stone and steel-windowed Siamese twins that throve in Wembley and Stanmore and Edgware and Shepperton and Osterley and Isleworth; families were locked together with their new ambitions and desire for self-improvement, in groups of two. It was you and The People Next Door, and the cry was Compete Or Perish! It was a great and stirring era; for once, as in our finest and happiest wars, everyone was working to one end, striving to achieve a single purpose and that purpose was victory: everything from the clothes one wore and the food one ate to the education one's children received and the funeral one's parents enjoyed was channelled into the great and insatiable furnace of status-seeking. Men worked with a will in their offices and gardens, on their waste-disposal units and their car accessories, on their wives' appearance and their sons' achievements. And, always, there was the face on the other side of the communal garden-fence, the spectre with the new power-hedgetrimmer or the iridescent concrete gnome, the alloy-framed greenhouse or the two-channel TV. Men rose to the new antagonisms; suddenly, nobly, they were ready to shed blood over who the communal fence actually belonged to, whose tree it was that threatened one's hollyhocks, who had the right to wash his car in the shared driveway, whether one half of a semi was entitled to a rich-grained, chromium-knockered front door when the other had just fitted a wrought-iron and frosted glass masterpiece at enormous expense. Should one's Grammar Schooled daughter play with the Secondary Modern twins next door? How much ought one tip the postman, the dustman, the milkman, given the unknown fiscal quantity across the privet hedge? People at last began to think and feel —needing allies, they went further afield than their neighbouring enemies, sought support from the people down the road who were detached from this particular quarrel but who had a green front gate like yours and had had similar trouble over it with *their* semi-neighbours.

This will die now, with Middlesex. Already the multiplanners are at work, and whole tracts of the county are being razed and new dwellings are going up to suit the Greater London standard of the universal midclass home. The aim, now, is a return to terrace anonymity, to non-antagonising sameness, to, above all, the profits attendant upon mass-development along predetermined and pre-costed lines. The New Ideal Homes developments, the Span- and Wates-type man-made communities have suddenly deprived people of the opportunities for competition and advancement that they learned and tested in the semis. However, these urges do not die; the semi-spirit lives on. Already, in most of these new artificial communities a social distinction is being drawn between the twenty three-bedroomed houses at £7,250, and the twenty four-bedroomed ones at £7,950, based not on the practical distinction of the extra room, but on the social distinction of the extra coinage. The developers may landscape all the front lawns, say, to a given size and formula; but in the back gardens, the recherché shrubbery, the expensive flora are pushing their heads up through the sifted and standardised sod in the eternal battle for social advancement. We are not a country to tolerate the standard car, despite its practical advantages, nor the standard house, nor the standard school; we shall fight them not for any wishy-washy aesthetic ideas, but out of the sort of individualism and enterprise and self-improvement that only money can buy. To walk through a modern development of the sort which will soon replace the semis of old, dead Middlesex is a moving and elevating experience; suddenly, from behind a bush will appear a little lad in an Eton kit, a living challenge to the Comprehensive children in the eggbox next door; we may see basketwork Minis, and Rovers in privately-commissioned twin-tone regalia; through the ubiquitous picture windows we shall see all the rich Liberty and Heal's trappings, each empty bookcase more Scandinavian than the rest. Suppressed, harried, sidetracked, blanketed by contemporary terracing and universalised plastic tiling, the spirit of Middlesex lives on. London may attempt to foist its standardisation and even its dream of a foolishly uncompetitive society on the Homest of the Home Counties; but beneath the double-glazing, and the undersealing, and the deodorisation, the Subtopian, midclass, Middlesex personality survives, red in tooth and claw.

Where, then, does Hertfordshire stand in this battle for survival? Hertfordshire was, after all, cut from the sirloin of Middlesex, like Eve from Adam; surely it must feel some sympathy and understanding and regret, even if only from the view of Middlesex's death as a cautionary tale for Hertfordshire? No. The execution of her mother county came as an enormous relief to Herts. As with most parental relationships, that between the two counties has always been one of mutual mistrust and misunderstanding and enmity. Added to which, the semi-detached ethos has snowballed to encompass the way in which the two counties see one another; they are semi-detached counties, fraught with the competitive instinct, staring over the common border with a mixed expression of fear and scorn.

Hertfordshire has always held the upper hand. In the midclass status-scale, enormous prestige is attached to the quality of the neighbourhood *in toto*; there can be little denying that Herts is a better neighbourhood; more prosperous, more imposing residences, more successful business-men. It has tone. It also has that prerequisite qualification for social pinnaclism, a more rural atmosphere; it has more Green Belt, more open spaces; it has, in short, a bigger and better garden than that of its semi-partner, Middlesex. It has a piece of the Chilterns, for which Middlesex throughout the short bitter relationship between the two counties never forgave it, and it has rivers which actually look like rivers. Herts people are constantly claiming that they are country people, really, that they use London as a convenient shopping area, but remain sophisticatedly detached from its urban grubbiness and mean-ness of spirit. London is all right for Middlesex, and vice-versa; when the vice-versa was proved by the action of the Greater London Council, Herts was ecstatic. London's appetite would now be satisfied, and Herts would go free; more, the choice showed that Middlesex was considered more suitable for a continuation of urban sprawl than pretty green Hertfordshire. This was the ultimate semi-detached victory—Hertford-shire had been separated forever from the stigma of its birth. Detach-ment had been conferred upon it.

It was a great and wonderful day.

All Except The Bastard

209

Bohemia

ENGLISH BOHEMIANISM IS a curiously unluscious fruit. It does not belong in the great, mad, steamy glasshouse in which so much of the art of the rest of the world seems to have flourished—or, at least, so much of the pseudo-art. Inside this hothouse, huge lascivious orchids slide sensually up the sweating windows, passion-flowers cross-pollinate in wild heliotrope abandon, lotuses writhe with poppies in the rich warm beds, kumquats ripen, tremble. and plop fatly to the floor—and outside, in a neat, trimly-hoed kitchen garden, English Bohemians sit in cold orderly rows, like carrots.

In our Bohemia, there are no beautifully crazy one-eared artists, no *sans culottes*, no castrated epistolarians, no genuine revolutionaries, no hopheads, no lunatics, not even any alcoholics of note; our seed-beds have never teemed with Rimbauds and Gauguins and Kafkas and d'Annunzios and Dostoievskys; we don't even have a Mailer or a Ginsberg to call our own. Our Bohemia is populated by Civil Servants like Chaucer and Spenser and Milton; by tough-nut professional pen-mongers like Shakespeare and Dryden and Johnson, who worried as much about underwear and rent as about oxymorons; by corpulent suburban family men like Thackeray and Dickens and Trollope. And whenever an English oddball raises, tentatively, his head, he's a pitifully pale imitation of the real thing—Thom. Gray, sad, thin Cambridge queer, Cowper, mad among his rabbits, Swinburne, a tiny fetishistic gnome as far from Leopold von Sacher-Masoch as water is from blood. The private lives of our great powerhouses of passion, Pope and Swift, were dreary and colourless in the extreme, and Emily Brontë divided her time between *Wuthering Heights* and the Haworth laundry-list. And history, though it may offer our only revolutionary poet the passing tribute of a literary footnote, will probably think of William Morris mainly as the Father of Modern Wallpaper.

There was, however, one brief moment in this socially unostentatious culture of ours when we were touched, albeit gingerly, by the spirit of Bohemia. I am not (how could you *think* a thing like that?) referring, of course, to the Wildean shenannigans at the *fin* of the last *siècle*, which were the product not of an authentic Bohemianism but of the need to dig up a literature and a *modus vivendi* you could wear with spats and a green carnation: that Café Royal crowd was the first Switched-On, With-It Generation England ever had, and the whole megillah should be taken with a pinch of pastis. No, the gang I have in mind are the Lake Poets, who had, for once, all the genuine constituents of real adjustment problems, social malaise, illegitimate offspring, numerous tracts, a hang-out, a vast literature, and, most important of all, a date: 1798. And since at first sight, and for several thereafter, the Lake District, a sopping place of sedge and goat, seems as unlikely a Bohemian ambience as you could shake a quill at, much can be gained by examining the area itself; one can do no better than take the career of its most eminent son, a William Wordsworth, and relate it (as all the local tourist offices do) to every cranny, sheep and sod between Windermere and the Scottish border.

I realise, naturally, that the aforementioned bard left a meticulous record of all that made him what he was, but since all writers are extraordinary liars, poseurs, distorters, and self-deceivers, I have chosen to ignore most of his farragos and interpretations; and for the background to this chapter, I am not indebted to *The Poetical Works Of William Wordsworth* (5 vols, Oxford 1940–49), *Wordsworth: A Re-interpretation* by F. W. Bateson (London 1954), *The Egotistical Sublime* by J. Jones (London 1954), or *Wordsworth and Coleridge* by H. G. Margoliouth (London 1953). In particular, I am not indebted to *Strange Seas of Thought: Studies in Wordsworth's Philosophy of Man and Nature* by N. P. Stallknecht (North Carolina 1945). However, I gather from friends in the trade that no work of serious scholarship is complete without a list of references and sources three times the size of the thing itself, so for devotees of this sort of *narrischkeit*, a fuller bibliography will be found sewn inside the lining of my old green hacking-jacket.

Cockermouth, Cumberland, was the spot where, on April 7, 1770, William Wordsworth first drew breath, and the location goes a long way towards explaining his characteristic lugubriousness. In the Old Hall, now derelict and seeping, Mary Queen of Scots was received after her defeat at Langside in 1568; her gloom was plumbless, and her host, Henry Fletcher, gave her thirteen ells of crimson velvet for a new dress. This could hardly have compensated for having her army trodden into the mud, but it ranks as one of history's nicer gestures to Mary.

Nearby stands Harry Hotspur's house, contracts for which had just been exchanged when the new proprietor was butchered at Shrewsbury, in 1403, and within spitting distance can be found a few lumps of twelfth-century castle: this was captured in 1313 by Robert the Bruce, and spent the rest of the century under constant attack and bombardment by any Scots infantrymen who happened to be in the neighbourhood. During the Wars of the Roses, it was first Yorkist, then Lancastrian, and the catalogue of woe was finally brought to an end during the Civil War, when it was demolished by the Roundheads. A mile or so away, at Moorland Close, is the 1764 birthplace of Fletcher Christian, leader of the *Bounty* mutineers, and the 1766 birthplace of John Dalton, the physicist whose nefarious theories led ultimately to the destruction of Hiroshima.

Given this agglomerated misery, it isn't difficult to see how young Wordsworth could become aware, very early, of the general rottenness of intelligent bipeds, by comparison with whom the local trees, thorns, and general flora assume a commendable innocence. One imagines John Wordsworth taking his little offshoot on trots through the topography, pointing out the various scenes of butchery and nastiness, totting up the huge casualty list, and pondering aloud on the question of how long it would take that diabolical infant prodigy John Dalton to come up with a hydrogen bomb. It's little wonder that William decided early on who his friends were, and began associating with daffodils. Not that the idea of Nature possessing a mean streak escaped him, either; the news that Fletcher Christian got his comeuppance for interfering with the rights of breadfruit was undeniably traumatic for young Wm.—thereafter, as the *Prelude* indicates, he couldn't break a twig or step on a toadstool without feeling that the crime would be expunged in blood.

He went on to Hawkshead Grammar School, where little seems to have happened to him, except that he befriended a lad called John Tyson, who immediately died, aged twelve, to be later commemorated in "There was a boy, / Ye knew him well, ye cliffs and islands of Winander..." This drove Wordsworth even further towards the mountains and shrubbery, who were obviously bound to enjoy a longer life-span and weren't going to peg out just when William was getting to know them. This was now his period of greatest involvement with Nature, a time spent sculling about the lakes with which the area is infested and grubbing about in the undergrowth, one ear cocked for the song of earwig and slug, the other for That Still Sprit Shed From

212

Evening Air. It rained most of the time. And, as the years rolled by and William grew to pubescence, talking the whiles to roots and knolls, he became more and more aware of humanity in general as a collection of blots and errors. One could rely on the crocus; every year it re-emerged from the turf, developed into its tiny, private perfection, and then quietly pegged out. And other mates of the poet, like Skiddaw and Scafell and Easedale Tarn, changed very little from year to year. But as the maturing bard pottered around Cumbria, he bumped inevitably into some of the area's human population, later immortalised and now available in paperback, who served only to convince him that after the fifth day, the Almighty's unerring talent for creating perfection deserted him: the life of Wordsworth the Teenager teemed with mad old women, decayed sailormen, idiot children, dispossessed cottars, impoverished leech-gatherers, bereaved lovers, unscrupulous potters, orphans, mutes, destitutes, and chronic bronchitics. Why the Lake District should have seethed with such sad misfits and sufferers to the point where Wordsworth never met anyone else is a question I gladly leave to medical historians or any similar forager with the necessary time on his hands. But I would just like to point out to all those scholars who have wondered why Wordsworth should have been a believer in metampsychosis, (that dubiously scientific process whereby souls pass on from one corporeal form to another as the sub-sequent mortal coils get shuffled off) that he quite clearly needed the hope it offered: souls inhabiting the forms of Lake District inhabitants were so unfortunately lumbered, that only the belief in their ultimate transmogrification into a hollyhock or woodlouse sustained Words-worth's faith in God's pervading goodness. There is, indeed, much evidence to show that the poet would have given his eye-teeth to have been a clump of heather.

In 1787, he went up to Cambridge. Everyone drank port and spoke Latin, and the nearest Cumberland beggar was three hundred miles to the NW. Wordsworth was desolate, left the university, utterly unnoticed, and took ship for the Continent. It was here that he bur-geoned and ripened under the cucumber-glass of Italian culture and Gallic revolution, suddenly exposed to all that the Lake District was not: Bohemianism took root in the Cumbrian corpuscles, and in the general uproar following the coup of 1789, Wordsworth sang in the streets, went about with his shirt unbuttoned, and seduced the daughter of a French surgeon. Again, scholars have been baffled by the whole Annette Vallon business: why the mystery, the concealment of Wordsworth's bastard son, the failure to return with its father to England? What the scholars have in textual fidelity, they lack in imagination; even without dwelling on the unwholesome possibility that Wordsworth's boudoir techniques, picked up at secondhand from observations of Esthwaite sheep, must have left much to be desired, we can make a fair guess at Annette's response to the poet's suggestion that she accompany him back to the fells to meet Mad Margaret, Peter Bell, Old Matthew, and the rest of the gang. At all events, Wordsworth came home alone, and unable to face the quiet of the Lakes, took Dorothy down to Somerset, which by now had got a reputation for having Coleridge on the premises. The two met up. Coleridge had already collected a Lake Poet, Robert Southey, and together they had concocted a form of early communism which they called Pantisocracy, so that by the time Wordsworth fixed his wagon to their star, the nub of Bohemianism had been unmistakeably shaped: of these two ur-Marxists, Southey had already distinguished himself for his opposition to flogging, Coleridge was smoking pot and seeing visions, and the pair of them had been writing like things possessed. With Wordsworth in tow, the poetic output stepped up enormously, and in 1798, he and Coleridge hit the market with their *Lyrical Ballads*, and everyone took off for the Lake District. The years that followed were ambrosial for Wordsworth: at last he could stop mooning about and involving himself with the problems of the educationally sub-normal citizens of Westmorland and Cumberland, and throw himself into the serious business of Bohemianism. Night after night the fells echoed to revelry and pentameters as the wild poets of Cumbria entertained thinkers and versifiers from all over the civilised world. Scott came, and Lamb, and Hazlitt, and de Quincey, until the nights of riot and boozing and composition surpassed anything the literary world had seen since William Shagsper, Kit Marlowe, Francis Bacon, the Earl of Oxford and Robert Greene had all stabbed one another in the Mermaid Tavern, leaving the responsibility for Elizabethan drama entirely in the hands of a Mr. W. H. Grobeley, the inn's landlord, who subsequently wrote it to avoid suspicion falling on his hostelry. No visit to Dove Cottage, Grasmere, is complete without examining the outhouse where Hazlitt's father, a Unitarian minister of strong liberal views, attempted to put his hand up Dorothy Wordsworth's skirt, and at Greta Hall, Keswick, can be seen the faded, bloody marks following a fight over the rent-book by its two most illustrious tenants, Coleridge and Southey.

But ultimately, as it will, Bohemianism died. Coleridge left in 1809,

214

went south, and died of opium poisoning. Southey became Poet Laureate in 1813, and took to wearing hats and drinking lukewarm herb tea. In the same year, Wordsworth became the Distributor of Stamps for the County of Westmorland at £400 per annum, and as befitted a civil servant, moved to Rydal Mount, turned his back on liberalism, and finally petered out in 1850, leaving his cottage to de Quincey, who hadn't touched a drop for the past thirty years.

Today, there are few reminders of those high and far-off times: the occasional grocer with the ineradicable Hazlitt family nose, or the Coleridge lip; fading graffiti on some derelict farmhouse wall, retailing bizarre local legends in the language and forms set down in the famous *Preface* of 1798; the empty gin-bottles that have bobbed on Ullswater and Bassenthwaite for the past century and a half; a crumbling gazebo on the outskirts of Keswick, built by Southey and from which he would pounce on passing milkmaids. Naturally, there are far more memorials to the more respectable aspects of the Bohemians' life and work, and during the summer, the roads of the two counties are filled with coachloads of people from Bromley and Philadelphia being driven to Gowbarrow Park to look at the descendants of the original daffodils.

The traditions, too, are dead. Not only is the local population conspicuously sane, sober, ungrieving, unstarving and totally unlike the *dramatis personae* of Wordsworth's records, the visitors are similarly unpoetic and unBohemian. They throng the Lake District between April and October in great tweed crowds; they wear sensible shoes, and corduroy knee-breeches, headscarves and duffle-coats, balaclavas and plastic macs; they carry stolid-looking walking-sticks, and rucksacks, and notebooks for pressing bog asphodel and saxifrage in, and Aer Lingus bags containing tomato sandwiches and flasks of Bovril; they have rosy cheeks, and hearty, uncomplicated laughs, and sturdy calf-muscles; they eat ham teas, and hold sing-songs in Youth Hostels, and go to bed at nine o'clock to listen to the wind in the eaves. Or else they come in Ford Cortinas and Bedford Dormobiles, with primus stoves and Calor Gas and tents from Gamages, to take their children boating on Windermere. And every year, they pay homage at the verdant shrine of someone whom they vaguely remember as being a poet, or something, simply because the guide book has led them to his grave, and because all tombs demand equal reverence. So they stand, heads bowed briefly, in St. Oswald's churchyard, Grasmere.

Never for one moment realising that Wordsworth himself would have thrown up at the sight of them. *All Except The Bastard*

215

I'm Gonna Sit Right Down And Write The Times *A Letter*

THE FIRST CUCKOO, a selection of letters to *The Times* edited by Kenneth Gregory, has just been published at £4.50. Why anyone should, in these dark fiscal days, fork out this sum for a book which does not include my own famous correspondence to that paper and the ensuing hoo-ha, is beyond me. I may write to *The Times* about it. On second thoughts, I may wait until night falls upon the great metropolis and follow Mr Gregory with a sockful of gravel.

On third thoughts, I shall reproduce the entire correspondence in full.

Intentions of Miss Doreen Nugent
From Mr Alan Coren
Sir, I was interested to read (March 8, 15, 20, April 3, 6, May 14) that Mr Bernard Levin is passionately in love with Miss Kiri Te Kanawa, a singer. While I do not know, nor greatly care, what 'Vitae summa brevis spem nos vetat incohare longam' means, may I beg the favour of your illustrious columns to seek the advice of wiser heads than mine in the matter of Miss Doreen Nugent, spinster, of Finsbury Park?

I have been escorting Miss Nugent since August 9, 1970, when I met her at a Czech Wine 'n' Cheese Nite at the Rat and Cockle, Brondesbury. I do not mean, of course, that the wine 'n' cheese was Czech, but the nite was, i.e., it was for Czech people to get together and reminisce. I must add that I am not Czech, nor is Miss Nugent, but entrance was not restricted, and we went upstairs in the first instance to see what the banging on the ceiling was, which turned out to be a hokey-cokey, and we were invited to stay.

Since then, our friendship has blossomed into love; or at least, mine has, but Miss Nugent has taken to sticking her hat pin in my hand when I put it on her knee in the cinema and similar. As five years have passed, I feel I have the right to know what my prospects are: I am 36 years old, with my own 1963 Hillman, and earning a good wage, and I do not suffer from any real diseases to speak of. We both like Austrian food, Ruby Murray records, dogs, and hill-walking, and are opposed to insecticides and slavery. But she tells me that she wants to wait for a better linguist. Should I put my foot down, or start studying odd languages like Tamil, or give her up, or what?

Yours faithfully,
ALAN COREN
23 Tudor Street, EC4.
June 3, 1975.

Intentions of Miss Doreen Nugent
From His Excellency the Czech Ambassador
Sir, May I presume upon your good offices to correct any possible misinterpretation that your esteemed readers might be encouraged to put upon the observations of your correspondent (June 3)?

The so-called meetings that take place at the Rat and Cockle, Brondesbury, do so without any sanction from the Government of the People's Republic of Czechoslovakia. Indeed, the group responsible, which calls itself the Friends of Free Czechoslovakia, is in actuality a neo-Nazi band of fugitive traitors dedicated to the undermining of democracy in Central Europe. It comes as no surprise to me, nor to any freedom-loving person, I am sure, to hear that these fascists think nothing of doing the hokey-cokey with no thought for the comfort or the wishes of others, at the same time masquerading as people who themselves have been subject to unwarranted impositions upon their so-called rights.

Nor can I understand your correspondent's assumption, implicit in the 'of course' of his second paragraph, that there is no Czech wine or cheese. I need only mention the toothsome Slovodny, made from pear pips, and the rich lingering flavour of Osczny Dom, produced from pig's milk, to give the lie to that! To my mind, and to the mind of democratic

217

people everywhere, there is no finer meal than a slice of Slovodny washed down with a sparkling goblet of Osczny Dom.

Yours faithfully,
JANOS BILAK,
25 Kensington Palace Gardens, London, W8.
June 5, 1975.

Intentions of Miss Doreen Nugent
From the Bishop of Angmering
Sir, Am I alone in wondering about the etymology of hokey-cokey?

Yours faithfully,
ERIC ANGMERICTUS,
Slug Cottage, Rustington.
June 8, 1975.

Intentions of Miss Doreen Nugent
From Mr Arnold Wesker and others
Sir, We feel we cannot let pass the comments of your correspondent (June 3) without intervention.

For some years now, we have kept a close watch on the *Births* columns of your newspaper, and we note that since January 1, 1960, the most popular girls' names have been Jane (134,269), Emma (93,426), Lucy (88,042), Charlotte (69,202), and Katherine (54,989). Doreen, however, has appeared only twice.

To us, that seems, well, how shall we say, remarkable!

Yours faithfully,
ARNOLD WESKER,
JOHN MORTIMER,
GLENDA JACKSON,
KENNETH TYNAN,
WAYLAND YOUNG,
TREVOR NUNN,
BRIAN WALDEN,
DONALD SOPER,
PAT ARROWSMITH,
JONATHAN MILLER,
DAVID HOCKNEY.
The Round House, London, NW1.
June 9, 1975.

218

Intentions of Miss Doreen Nugent
From Sir John Betjeman

Sir, Before the very name disappears forever beneath the imminent avalanche of polystyrene debris and throwaway knickers, may I just record that *Finsbury Park* is one of the loveliest sounds ever to have fallen upon the human ear? That your correspondent (June 3) is also capable of linking it in the same brief epistle with the almost equally euphonious *Brondesbury* marks him, in my view, as a man worthy of our love and respect.

That Miss Nugent seems to prefer a Tamil-speaker strikes me as no small indication of the maelstrom into which this culture is being sucked.

Yours faithfully,
JOHN BETJEMAN,
The Beefsteak Club.
June 11, 1975.

Intentions of Miss Doreen Nugent
From Dr A. L. Rowse

Sir, Hokey-cokey (June 8) is Warwickshire dialect. Originally, it was a children's dance in derision of a local landowner and pervert, Sir Joshua Hoake, on whom Shakespeare based the character of Titus Andronicus.

Yours faithfully,
A. L. ROWSE,
All Souls' College, Oxford.
June 12, 1975.

Intentions of Miss Doreen Nugent
From Mr Alan Coren

Sir, I'm afraid that none of this (June 5, 8, 9, 11, 12) is much help. Last night, during *The Sound of Music*, Miss Nugent threw my ring over the balcony of the Astoria, Manor House. I grow desperate.

Yours faithfully,
ALAN COREN,
23 Tudor Street, EC4.
June 14, 1975.

Intentions of Miss Doreen Nugent
From the Commercial Attaché to the Jordanian Embassy

Sir, Surely Mr Coren (June 14) misses the entire point? In his original letter (June 3), he twice spelt 'night' *n-i-t-e*. And he makes no reference whatever to the refugee problems of the West Bank.

Yours faithfully,
HASSAN YOUSEF SARDI,
6 Upper Phillimore Gardens, W8.
June 16, 1975.

Intentions of Miss Doreen Nugent
From Sir John Betjeman

Sir, The Astoria, Manor House! (June 14). Perhaps the last beleaguered survivor of the great picture palace tradition! It had a navy-blue roof with simulated stars, and crenellated battlements, and the foyer was in the manner of a Moorish *yumdukki*, with real goldfish. What days they were, what dear, dead days!

Yours faithfully,
JOHN BETJEMAN,
The Beefsteak Club.
June 17, 1975.

Intentions of Miss Doreen Nugent
From Professor J. D. Chaudra

Sir, What is all this terrible opprobrium, I ask myself, which is being levelled against the Tamil tongue? (June 3, 11). Greatest of the Dravidian languages, could the majestic 12th-century masterpiece, *Periyapuranam* have been written without it? Tell me that, sir! Also, this disturbing business of the hokey-cokey: it has nothing whatever to do with Titus Andronicus, this Doctor Rowse is a fool, I say; he should be struck off, and what is wrong with *nite*, it is perfectly good to my mind.

Yours faithfully,
J. D. CHAUDRA,
Department of Forestry,
University of Madras.
June 19, 1975.

Intentions of Miss Doreen Nugent
From the Warden of Cork Synagogue
Sir, Doesn't Mr Sardi (June 16) mean the *terrorist* problems of
the West Bank?

Yours faithfully,
JACK STONE,
12 Farm Avenue, Cork.
June 20, 1975.

Intentions of Miss Doreen Nugent
From the Bishop of Angmering
Sir, I have hesitated for some time before bringing up the
matter of Lord Soper's signature to that letter of June 9
(June 9), and I cannot help feeling that this is neither the time
nor the place to mention it.

Yours faithfully,
ERIC ANGMERICTUS,
Slug Cottage, Rustington.
June 22, 1975.

Intentions of Miss Doreen Nugent
From Miss Doreen Nugent
Sir, I knew he was bloody mad all along. Tamil, Glenda
Jackson, Arabs, throw-away knickers, live goldfish, where's it
all going to end? Imagine if we'd had kids!

Yours faithfully,
D. NUGENT (MISS),
7 Stalingrad Mansions, N4.
June 23, 1975.

The Lady From Stalingrad Mansions

221

Gilded Cage

THE WATERY DAWN came up, to little interest. A cassowary honked, half-heartedly; Moskisson's potto squeaked, once; an elderly scorpion broke wind.

They had seen dawns before. There was no point kicking up an atavistic fuss. For one thing, you didn't have to scare breakfast into submission. It came on tin plates.

The lion yawned. Bound to be horse again. Nothing wrong with horse, mind, nice piece of shoulder, can't complain. Slides down a treat, horse.

The only thing was, you couldn't chase a chop. That was the whole trouble with convenience foods. You couldn't bring them down, play with them, scare the life out of them. Be nice, thought the lion wistfully, to hear your breakfast scream a bit, now and again.

He strolled to the bars, looked out.

'Hallo,' he said. 'Here's a do.'

His lioness turned over slowly on her hygienic concrete shelf. Her tail flopped down. She let it swing, idly. Cleaner up here than a tree, she thought, more modern, chamfered for easy maintenance, no moss, insects. And yet.

'What is it?' she said.

'They've duffed up another chimpanzee,' said her mate.

The lioness opened one eye. In the cage across the way, a chimpanzee lay on its back, hands, feet, teeth all clenched in an unmistakable rigor.

'Oh, that,' she murmured. She shut the eye again. 'New frail old chimp horror, anthropoid granny another victim of senseless violence, where will it end, see fabulous free knickers offer page nine.'

'You know who I blame?' said the lion. 'I blame the parents.'

The lioness snored.

At eight o'clock, two keepers came with a black polythene sack and removed the battered corpse.

The lion watched.

The tiger next door came to the front of its cage.

'Keepers won't even bother finding out who did it,' said the tiger. 'Right?'

'What's the point?' said the lion.

'What's the point?'

'Only let 'em off with a bloody caution,' said the lion.

'If that,' said the tiger.

'They'll blame it all on the environment,' said the lion gloomily. 'Am I right?'

'No question,' said the tiger.

'Impersonal high-rise steel cages, parents out picking one another's fleas off all day, lack of properly supervised play areas, catch my drift?'

'Absolutely,' said the tiger. 'Not to mention a cry for help.'

'I'd give 'em bleeding cry for help!' snapped the lion. 'When I was a cub, they'd have got the chop.'

He drew a burnished claw across his throat, as only lions can.

'Bloody good job, too,' said the tiger.

'No messing about,' said the lion, 'eye for an eye, know what I mean?'

'Those were the days,' said the tiger.

At 11.30 am, the lioness jumped down from her shelf.

A keeper let her four cubs in.

She played with them for half an hour.

Then the keeper came and took them out again.

She jumped back up on her shelf, and began to groom.

'I don't call that motherhood,' said the lion.

The lioness shrugged. She rolled on her back, and looked at the ceiling of the cage.

'I ought to get a job,' she said. 'There's more to life than bringing up cubs.'

'You what?' cried the lion. 'A *lioness*? Getting a *job*?'

'While we're at it,' said his mate, 'I think I'll drop the ess. It is discriminatory; it is degrading. Lion, is what I am.'

The lion's claws sprang from their soft sheaths, instinctively.

'What kind of job?' he growled.

'Oh, I dunno,' she said. 'I could roar. I could terrorise visitors. I could attack the keeper.'

'*I* DO THAT!' thundered the lion, with such force that, on the other side of the Zoo, a small herd of antelope woke up, trembled violently, and ran into the wall. 'Any roaring, any terrorising, is down to *me*!'

'I could be just as good,' said the lioness.

'Oh yes! Ha, ha! Oh yes!' muttered the lion. He paced up and down furiously. 'Ha, ha! Oh yes! Very droll. Ha, ha!'

He hurled himself at the bars, and bit them.

'She'll be growing a mane next,' said the tiger next door.

'I blame the Zoo,' said the lion. 'The Zoo does everything for 'em, these days. Food, housing, education, all laid on, know what I mean, whatever happened to self-sufficiency, independence, responsibility?'

'You've been talking to Rhodes Bison,' said the tiger.

'Why not?' said the lion.

'Look at them dingoes,' said the lion, an hour or two later. 'They're at it like knives!'

'When I was young,' said the tiger, 'there was such a thing as courtship.'

'The magic's gone,' muttered the lion. 'I blame the Zoo. No restrictions any more. They used to move in and stop all that. They used to keep 'em apart, except for breeding seasons.'

'Permissiveness,' grunted the tiger.

'Comes back to what I was saying,' said the lion firmly. 'Too much time on their hands, too much done for 'em. In the old days, before the Zoo stepped in and took over everything, they never had no time for all that. Out foraging for food, fighting off enemies, building your own home, competing to survive—it bred a different class, built character, follow me?'

'You're talking about the jungle, now,' said the tiger, wistfully.

'Right!' cried the lion. 'Definitely!'

The dingoes shrieked to an umpteenth climax.

'They're like bloody animals,' muttered the lion.

The sparrow zipped through the bars, and landed on the edge of the lion's trough.

'I've just been up the Bird House,' it chirped. 'You wouldn't bloody credit it!'

'What?' said the lion.

'They just took delivery of two gross chrome bells, anodised ladders, mirrors, prefabricated nesting-boxes, you name it.'

'Oh, very nice!' said the lion sarcastically. 'I wonder how much that little lot set the Zoo back?'

'Birds,' twittered the sparrow, 'used to make their own entertainment. There's no end of things you can do with a good pebble, couple of bottle tops, fag-packets, all that. Now they just sit around waiting for the Zoo to provide everything, have you noticed?'

'Have *I* noticed?' cried the lion.

'Has *he* noticed?' said the tiger.

'They'll have Zoo-subsidised tellies next,' said the lion.

'He's not joking,' said the tiger.

The white Range Rover of the Zoo Vet Service rolled past. They watched it turn the bend.

'Elephant,' explained the sparrow. 'Got a bit of colic. I was just round there.'

'*Bit of colic?*' exclaimed the lion. 'Bloody stroll on! What would he do up India?'

'Wouldn't bother about it,' said the tiger, 'would he? More important things to think about. Knocking down trees, leading herds, working out how to get to the graveyard.'

'Stepping on tigers,' said the sparrow.

'Why not?' retorted the tiger. 'Part of life's rich texture. *And* if he did, would I go running to the doctor's? Would I buggery, I'd have a bit of a lick, pull myself together, get on with things, right?'

'You'd probably nip down the village and knock a couple of tribesmen back,' said the lion dreamily. He ran his purple tongue over his muzzle. 'Set you up a treat, that.'

'Better than free bloody medical treatment, anyway,' said the tiger.

'You know what bothers me more than anything?' said the lion, after a moment or two.

'What's that?' enquired the sparrow.

'It's like this,' said the lion. 'All our offspring are growing up in this mollycoddling bloody environment, right? Everything done for 'em, nothing demanded of 'em, all they got to do if they want anything is ask the Zoo, they get a handout, okay?'

'Get on with it,' muttered the tiger.

'What I'm saying is,' said the lion, 'what I'm saying *is*, what happens if the Zoo runs out of money? Overspends on services or whatever, and the whole operation starts falling to bits, health service breaks down, cages crumble, keepers pack it in, food gets short, amenities fold up. So there's all the bars fallen off, and there's all these animals wandering about with no-one to look after 'em or tell 'em what to do next, and because they've all grown up in the Zoo, would they have any idea of how to fend for themselves?'

'He's a bit of a thinker, this one,' said the sparrow.

'It'd all come back to them, wouldn't it?' said the tiger. 'I mean, it's in the blood. It's *natural*, right?'

The lion shrugged. He looked at his paw, wondering what it would be like to feel grass under it.

'It's only a thought,' he said.

The Rhinestone As Big As The Ritz

226

Once I Put It Down, I Could Not Pick It Up Again

A couple of years ago, some organisation calling itself the Encyclopaedia Britannica sent me twenty-three books to review. Like any reviewer faced with such a task, I wasn't able, of course, to read any of them – just snatched a quick look at the titles on the spines and made a few shrewd guesses.

A. ANSTEY

F. Anstey, author of *Vice-Versa*, *The Brass Bottle*, and many other best-sellers, was one of the most famous figures in Victorian London. A. Anstey wasn't. This, indeed, was the nub of his personal disaster, a searing comment on nineteenth-century society, told for the first time in this splendid volume. A. Anstey was constantly being introduced at smart Victorian soirées to people whose instant reaction was "Not *the* Anstey?" to which he would immediately answer "No, just *a* Anstey, ha-ha-ha!" This pitiful little quip commended him to no-one, and was usually met with a sneering "You mean *an* Anstey" and a snub. He endured this for eighteen years before finally hanging himself in a rented room just off Lewisham High Street.

ANT BALFE

When General Tom Thumb crowned a successful fairground tour with a command performance in front of Queen Victoria, the seal was set on a midget-vogue of staggering proportions. Country fairs and London theatres alike were filled with talented dwarfs, each tinier than the last. The smallest and indubitably the most adroit of these (he could play

Mozart's four horn concertos on a drinking-straw while riding on a stoat) was Ant Balfe, so called because of his incredible diminutiveness. Who knows to what figurative heights he might not have risen, had he not, at his Drury Lane premiere, been trodden on by an inept autograph-hunter?

BALFOUR BOTH

A fascinating tale of Georgian surgery, this recounts the earliest known sex-change operation, on the unfortunate Geraldine (née Gerald) Balfour. It seemed successful at first, and the happy Geraldine took to signing herself G. Balfour (Miss), but subsequent developments proved this course to be premature, and soon she was sending letters of complaint to the General Medical Council signed G. Balfour (Both). Eventually, the name was changed by deed poll to Balfour-Both to avoid upsetting pre-permissive sensibilities. Beautifully illustrated.

BOTHA CARTHAGE

An exceptionally well-documented life of Hannibal, whose dying words give the book its intriguing title. His actual words, apparently, were "Bugga Carthage!" but the publishers, I understand, felt that this might have meant rejection by W. H. Smith, and compromised accordingly.

CARTHUSIANS COCKCROFT

Subtitled "An Edwardian Tragedy", this bitter book tells the story of Thomas Cockcroft, perhaps the most promising Senior Master in Charterhouse's history. He was due for appointment to the headmastership at the incredibly early age of thirty, when certain facts were made public by a disguntled porter concerning the intimate teas to which Cockcroft would invite the smaller boys. Inevitably, the yellow press dubbed him Carthusians Cockcroft at his infamous trial (*The Daily Graphic* even tried to christen him Fag Cockcroft, but the multi-entendres were too much for its working-class readership), and upon his release from Brixton, he went off to the Congo to shoot porters. There is a statue of him in Chisholm St. Mary, erected in error.

COCKER DAIS
Perhaps the best loved of the East End flyweights, Cocker Dais at one time held the British, British Empire, and European titles. At the peak of his career, he fought an unknown American for the World title, and was knocked out in the second minute of the first round. His pub, *The Cocker Dais*, later became a famous dockside landmark for German bombers.

DAISY EDUCATIONAL
A poignant, heart-warming novel about an elderly schoolmistress in a tiny Welsh village. The influence of *How Green Was My Valley* is, of course, observable, but the presence of a black Druid boutique owner gives the book an essentially modern air.

EDWARD EXTRACT
I'm delighted that the publishers have seen fit to reprint this little-known eighteenth-century novel by Tobias Sterne, because it's a narrative gem of the first water. A bawdy, picaresque romp, it tells how postboy Edward Extract makes off with Squire Weasel's buxom daughter Phyllis, loses her to a Turkish mercenary during the Battle of Blenheim, makes his way to Utrecht disguised as an alternative Pope, falls in love with Warty Eva of Bosnia, is press-ganged into the Hungarian navy, loses his leg at Malplaquet, seduces a lady-in-waiting to Queen Anne, becomes a Whig, loses his right arm at Sheriffmuir, gets Gräfin von Immel with child, goes deaf during the siege of Belgrade, abducts a Moorish slave-girl, and returns at last to his native Suffolk, where he knocks out his left eye on a broken wainshaft. Lusty, purgative, rollicking, and highly recommended.

EXTRADITION GARRICK

It is said that when Lord Chief Justice Sir Esmond Garrick (1789-1852) was refused his request to the Brazilian authorities to extradite Bloody Ned Magee on a charge of treason, he sailed personally to Sao Paulo, strode into the Court of Justice, decapitated the President of the Brazilian Supreme Court, and, turning to the other judges and waving his bloody sabre above his wig, cried: "I would remind ye that English law is based on precedent, and I have just created one!" Magee was released forthwith, and duly hanged at the notorious Vile Assize of 1828. As Extradition Garrick, Sir Esmond pursued an inflexible hunt for refugee criminals, often giving up his holidays to root about in the stews of Marseilles and Cadiz, heavily disguised, in his inexorable search for what he called "hanging fodder", frequently bringing them back to England in a gunny-sack. A thundering good read.

GARRISON HALIBUT

I was bored by this long, scholarly thesis on the Minneapolis dry-goods salesman who rose to be the Governor of Minnesota and is chiefly remembered as the initiator of off-street parking.

HALICAR IMPALA

If you like books that take the lid off the motor industry, then this is for you! Spurred on by what they thought was going to be the enormous success of the Ford Edsel, a group of General Motors designers made a survey of what the typical *female* customer wanted in a motor car, and proceeded accordingly. After two years of research and the expenditure of eighty million dollars, the first Halicar Impala was built. The engine started well enough, but at 35 mph the linkage connecting the hair-drier to the eye-level grill snapped, disconnected the telephone, and threw the crib through the windscreen. Upon applying the brakes, the driver inadvertently set the instant heel-bar in motion, and was riveted to the wardrobe by a row of tintacks. A second Impala was never built.

230

IMPATIENS JINOTEGA

Jose Ortega "Impatiens" Jinotega was the father of modern bullfighting. Until his appearance in 1919, the average matador took eight hours to kill a bull, and there was only one fight per afternoon. Impatient as his nickname suggests, Jinotega soon saw that strangling was a slow and inept method, and, on his first appearance in the Barcelona ring, he pulled a sword from beneath his cloak, and despatched six fighting bulls in the space of half an hour. This book is a magnificent tribute to a man who died as he would have wished, gored by Ernest Hemingway during a bar-brawl in Pamplona.

JIRASEK LIGHTHOUSES

A penetrating analysis of the great Czech film director, Imry Jirasek, known in the West as Jirasek Lighthouses, after his greatest film, a four-hour satirical study of the life of a solitary wick-trimmer. *Lighthouses* was followed by *An Old Bus*, *Jackets*, and the deeply disturbing *My Bath And Hat*. After vigorous appeals by Ken Tynan, Arnold Wesker, Vanessa Redgrave, George Melly and others, Jirasek was allowed to leave Prague for England. He left London almost immediately for Hollywood, where he now makes half a million dollars a year scripting *I Love Lucy*.

LIGHTING MAXIMILIAN

Sean Kenny's detailed account of his special effects work on the Peter Weiss/Peter Brook production of *The Manic Depression And Concomitant Hallucinations That Led To The Nervous Breakdown Of Emperor Maximilian Of Austro-Hungary As Performed By Members Of The Portuguese World Cup Team.*

MAXIMINUS NAPLES

The first Proconsul of what was, in the second century BC, still Calabrium, Maximinus is chiefly remembered for his habit of throwing political opponents into Vesuvius. His proconsulate was exceptionally stormy, corrupt and inefficient, and in 134 BC, Emperior Tiberius Gracchus demoted him to the proconsulate of Sicilia, where he is chiefly remembered for his habit of throwing political opponents into Etna. His significance is minimal, and my own opinion is that this dreary account was long underdue.

NAPOLEON OZONOLYSIS

The story of how Napoleon Ozonolysis rose from humble origins to become the wealthiest Greek shipowner in the world has, of course, all the fabulous ingredients of legend, and in this frank autobiography (as told to Bobby Moore), the amazing tycoon reveals all. Lavishly illustrated with photographs of colonels, the book also contains an extremely useful index of eligible American widows. Just the thing for a Hellenic cruise, or a short piano leg.

P—PLASTERING

I opened this volume with considerable trepidation, believing it to be just another Do-It-Yourself tract. Imagine my delighted surprise to discover that it was in fact a history of stammering! Packed with fascinating information—did you know, for example, that George Washington was unable to enunciate "teaspoon," or that *K-K-K-Katie* was not written by Gustav Mahler?—the book is a veritable mine of glottal arcana. The appendix on Regency hiccups is on no account to be missed.

PLASTICS RAZIN

If you like escapology as much as I do, then you'll find it hard to resist this vivid biography of The Great Razin (pronounced *Rah'tsin*). Louis Razin's career began astoundingly early: in the last stages of labour, his mother was rushed to hospital in Boston, Mass, by hansom cab, but by the time she arrived on the maternity ward, she was no longer pregnant. Hysterical, she was led back to the waiting cab by her doctor, only to find the infant Louis screaming on the back seat! By the age of fourteen, he was already The Great Razin and Doris (subsequently The Great Razin and Beryl, after Doris had failed to emerge from a cabinet on the stage of the Holborn Empire), and in 1923 he became the first man to escape from a strait-jacket on radio. When transatlantic flights became regular with the advent of the Super Clipper, Razin celebrated by eating an entire canteen of airline cutlery, and the nickname stuck. Plastics Razin is buried in Boston Cemetery, probably.

RAZOR SCHURZ

On the afternoon of September 8, 1926, a short, stocky man in a barathea coat and a pearl-grey fedora walked into a garage in South Side Chicago. When he walked out again, four minutes later, he left six men dead behind him, cut to ribbons. That was the beginning of the career of Razor Schurz, dreaded torpedo of the Capone gang and by the time he was finally trapped in an alley beside the Rexo Bowling Palace in Peoria, Illinois, early in 1937, and mown down by the guns of J. Edgar Hoover—or was it the hoovers of J. Edgar Gun? The print in my copy was tiny and execrable—he had accounted for no less than sixty-eight other hoodlums. This book, by the way, is now being made into seven feature films.

SCHÜTZ SPEKE

Schütz speke (sometimes schützspeke) was an entirely new language invented by embittered ex-Esperantist Wilhelm Schütz, and was designed to be the greatest international medium of communication the world had ever known. Unfortunately, the secret died with Schütz, and since this volume is written in it, the publisher's motives escape me. It may be a tax-loss, or something.

SPELMAN TIMMINS

This expensively produced facsimile edition of the diary of a fourteenth-century warlock is not particularly interesting in itself, but it contains some interesting recipes entirely new to me: I would recommend in particular his tasty *langues de crapauds au fin bec*, even if it does, for some mysterious reason, make your face come out in long ginger hair.

TIMOLEON-VIETA

These collected love-letters of young Timoleon, Prince of Tyre, to Vieta, the beautiful fourteen-year-old daughter of a Sidonian lunatic, make poignant reading. The two lovers never touched, and saw one another only briefly, just once, when Timoleon's carriage ran down Vieta's milk-float early in 981 AD. Their tender and passionate affair came to an abrupt end when palace Nubians employed by Timoleon's tyrannical father seized the young prince and cut off his allowance.

VIETNAM ZWORYKIN

If, like me, you find the radical-chic posturings of the Zworykin family of New York extremely tiresome—tracts and polemica by Nat "Cuba" Zworykin, Sharon "Women's Lib" Zworykin, Chuck "Legalise Acid" Zworykin, Sigmund "Environment" Zworykin, and Dustin "Kill the Pigs" Zworykin have all become best-sellers on both sides of the Atlantic—then this new tirade by the youngest member, Willy "Vietnam" Zworykin, is not for you, despite its foreword by Gore Vidal, its addendum on Ulster by Edward Kennedy, its footnotes on the poor finish of the Side-winder missile by Ralph Nader, and its jacket-blurb by Jane Fonda. The fact that the whole text can be pulled out to form a banner may be of interest to bibliophiles.

The Sanity Inspector

Counterweight

"I'm quite sure within the next two decades we shall have all the girls at Woolworth's with degrees." – Edward Short, MP.

"Nothing much. Went up the Royal Festival same as usual with Norman."

"That's the skinny biochemist from Smokers Sundries, innit?"

"Yes. I wore me spotted wincyette with the velveteen bow."

"Nice. Anything good on?"

"Only bloody Arnold Schönberg, that's all!"

"You must be joking, Doreen! Not *Verklärte Nacht* again?"

"Only bloody *Verklärte Nacht* again, that's all!"

"I wouldn't care, it's not even dodecaphonic."

"That's what I said to Norman. It's not even bloody dodecaphonic, I said. It's *early* Schönberg. That's not what I call value for money, I said."

"You might as well be listening to Stravinsky, Doreen."

"You might as well be listening to bloody Stravinsky. That's what I said to him. If I'd known, I wouldn't have gone home and changed. A short skirt's good enough for early bloody Schönberg."

"What did he say, Doreen?"

"He said it was seminal. He's so bleeding crude sometimes."

"I don't know why you go out with him. He only went to Trinity College Dublin and his breath smells. It's not as if you weren't a brain surgeon."

"To tell you the truth, Vera, I—would you mind keeping your little boy's fingers off them chocolate peanuts, madame,

235

thank you very much!—to tell you the truth, I'm thinking of giving Norman the bullet. I met this very nice bloke at the Selfridge's Electrical Appliances Department party last Friday—"

"I was going to that, only the cat got into me wigbox Thursday night and did sunnink. How was it?"

"Very nice. It was to commemorate the anniversary of Spinoza's first marriage. They had them little bridge-rolls with roe in them."

"I've always liked Spinoza. You know where you are with the *Tractatus Theologico-Politicus*. He's never flash, is he? If there's one thing I can't stand, it's a flashy determinist."

"I know what you mean. That's exactly what I said to this fella I was telling you about. He works in Plugs & Flex. You wouldn't think so to look at his hands: they're all big, including the fingers. You wouldn't think he'd have the nimbleness for flex."

"I've always liked big hands. You know where you are with big hands. What's his speciality?"

"Ooh, you *are* awful sometimes, Doreen!"

"I din't mean that, you silly cow! I mean, where was he before Plugs & Flex?"

"Balliol. First in Mods, First in Greats. They say he knows more about Kant than anyone on the first floor."

"Doreen!"

"*Immanuel.*"

"There's people looking, Dor. Anyway—"

"Anyway, turns out this fella's got two tickets for the first night of the Bucharest Citizens' Marionette Theatre production of *Aida*, and would I come?"

"You don't half fall on your feet, Doreen."

"I know. It was bloody smashing, Vera! I'd never heard a baritone puppet before. And you know that bit where Rhadames returns in triumph with Amonasro—"

"—the Ethiopian king—"

"—the Ethiopian king, right, well instead of elephants, they had weasels with little rubber trunks on. And all these little puppets were singing in Rumanian!"

236

"Fantastic! What did you do after?"

"Went up Spitalfields, din't we? Had another look at the Christchurch lintels."

"You can't never have enough of Hawksmoor, that's what I always say."

"Well, yes and no. Personally, I never went for the north quadrangle of All Souls."

"I never went for All Souls at all. That bloke who demonstrates artificial lawn's a Fellow of All Souls. He's got a hairpiece. He's a bit funny, if you ask me. There was just the two of us down the stockroom last Wednesday, he come up to me and his face was all shiny, and he was trembling, and I thought: Hallo, Vera, good job you got your body stocking on, and do you know what he wanted?"

"What?"

"He said could he hold my shoes for a bit."

"Go on!"

"Honest."

"What did you say?"

"I said, I'll let you hold one of them, Doctor Strude-Pargiter, but I don't think I ought to go all the way on our first date!"

"Oooh, Vera, you're worse than I am! What did he say?"

"He said he'd written the definitive footnote on the Edict of Worms and he thought that entitled him to certain privileges. So I told him about how my mum would never let me go out with a mediaeval historian, and us ophthalmologists are only happy with our own kind, and I think he understood. I didn't want to hurt his feelings, and I could see the gum running down his forehead with the excitement and everything, so I come upstairs again."

"Very wise. Is it lunchtime yet?"

"Not for another eight minutes and forty-one seconds. Why?"

"I want to go up the travel agent's, don't I? Leave it too late, everywhere's booked up."

"Going anywhere nice?"

"I thought I might try the ten-day cruise of the fjords, only forty-nine guineas, including headphone. You visit sites of the

Old Norse Sagas, and in the afternoons well-known philologists discuss famous textual cruces on deck, if wet in the first-class dining-room. There's semantics every evening, and a gala ball on the Saturday when everyone comes as the troll of his choice and gets rotten drunk. Alice Prior in Plastic Binettes nearly got pregnant twice last year, and she's only ever read *Beowulf* in Penguin, so it just shows you. Tell you what, Vera, whyn't you come with me? It wouldn't half be a giggle, or *gögal*, as the Eddas put it."

"It's ever so nice of you to suggest it, Doreen, but I don't think it's me, really. I think I'll just stay in the library again this year, there's no swimming, of course, but it's warm, and there's always a few people from the British Home Stores boning up on something or other, they're ever such a friendly crowd."

"Vera Collinson, you can't pull no wool over *my* eyes! I know what you're up to, you sneaky bitch, you're working on that thesis of yours, right? *Zygostereopy in The Retina Of The Potto, Clinical Observations Towards A Classification, by Miss Vera Collinson?*"

"Oh, Doreen, I din't want to tell no one, not even you! It's just—you won't take offence?—it's just that I want to, you know, better myself. I want to get on. I don't want to sell Smarties in Woolworth's forever! And if I had a Ph.D., Doreen, I could leave all this behind me, I could make something of myself, I could *be* someone, I could get somewhere!"

"My Gawd, Vera, you're not thinking of . . ."

"Yes, Doreen, Marks & Spencers!"

"You're a mad ambitious little fool, Vera Collinson! But—but I admire you!"

"Don't cry, Doreen, love. There's other things in life, you'll get married, have kids, you see if you don't, it'll all—"

"If only I had the application for original research, if only I had the academic stamina, if only I'd kept up—yes, madame, a quarter of hazelnut cluster, madame, right away, madame, no thank you, madame, quite all right, I just got something in my eye, that's all, madame, that'll be seven pee, thank you very—sob—much."

The Sanity Inspector

An Open Letter to Alexander Solzhenitsyn

MY DEAR ALEXANDER:

I hope you will forgive me for not having written sooner; but I know that I do not have to explain to you, of all men, how it is sometimes with writers, that clattering of the heart when the sought words elude and you cannot be sure that they will ever come again, that chill greasy fear in the endless waking hours of the night that perhaps it is the mind itself that has gone, that crushing pressure always to anatomise each minutia, each new refraction of the psyche, to place it in its inner context of the soul, and its outer context of society, with unimpeachable precision, always concentrating, always articulating, not to mention where the fence blew down the week before last and neighbour's refusal to restore same, despite arris-rails clearly visible on his side, plus car failing MOT on account of Excessive Play In Front Trunnions, also having to take Percy up the vet for spring worming, while at same time working out Deductible Input Tax For This Period (Partly Exempt Persons Should Also See Box 24) set against Percentage Used To Attribute Input Tax (Box 14 x 100 divided by Box 16), together with small daughter forcing Panda down lav, first sign of which being flushwater turning bathroom into ornamental pond due to stuffed arm stuck in S-bend (with aid of torch, can see glass eye staring back up at me from unreachable depths), and how do you get a plumber Sundays?

Anyway, Alexander Isayevich, every time I switched on the television set during those fraught periods of writer's block that tend to start clogging the mind a few minutes before *Colditz, Match Of The Day, The Pallisers, Colombo, The World At War, Pot Black, Parkinson,* and *Panorama* (not to mention *Jackanory, Farmer's World* and *Nai Zindagi Naya Jeevan*), there was your fraught beloved face staring out of some bulletin or flash,

239

mugging to lensmen across a bald sea of agents and publishers.

Either that, or they were serialising Raymond Massey's *Abraham Lincoln*.

And every time those lugubrious eyes peered out at me from the fringing bristle, guilt welled up within me at my continuing omission. Must dash off a note to old Alexander, I would say to myself, welcome him to the West, extend the hand of literary fraternity, give him a few tips, enclose a couple of quid for nibs and blodge, well, I've been down on my luck myself before now, haven't I?

And now it is probably too late. For I have just caught sight of a tucked-away item in tonight's *Evening Standard*, which runs, in toto: 'Exiled Soviet writer Alexander Solzhenitsyn may not settle in Norway because the tax laws would mean he might pay up to fifty per cent tax on his Swiss bank account deposits'.

So there it is, Alexander, out of the Communist frying-pan and into the Capitalist fire, and the snow not yet slid from your welts. One moment it's the KGB kicking the doorknobs off in the small hours, the next it's crack teams of Scandinavian revenue men with rimless specs and immaculate clipboards intimating that it's either an immediate fifty pee in the £ or chuck the belongings back into the red-spotted hankie and ring up a mini-cab for Oslo Airport.

It won't improve, either. I gather that your next choice is Switzerland, if they'll let you; and though the tax hammer is, granted, less sledgy, I doubt that the racked Soviet soul is likely to settle snugly among the alpine slopes a-teem with resident millionaire paperback hacks, drunken film-stars, racing drivers, refugee investment analysts, elderly Tory peers, and all the raucous effluvia of less stable European economies, not to mention the Swiss themselves, who tend to blink a lot, if they're the communicative sort, but otherwise constitute an unfertile sod for the authorial rhizome.

There's always Ireland, no tax at all, and a lot of green. But while their total tax concession to writers appears on the face of it generous, they have had some difficulty, as you may know, in determining who is a writer and who not, and are almost certainly, with typical Irish precision, using the rule of thumb which says that if a bloke is lying in a Dublin gutter with a bottle of Guinness in each pocket, no collar, and a four-day growth of stubble, and conducting himself in *The Wild Colonial Boy* with a grubby baton made from the rolled-up manuscript of his unpublished first novel, then he it is who constitutes the literary norm; and, somehow, that is not a part I see you comfortably playing.

France allows resident writers two tax-free years, but the toll exacted, socially, for the financial benefit is heavy: the literary establishment would reject you on the grounds that you had never written a novel entitled *A Rock, A Tree, A Chair* and running to either (a) five thousand words, or (b) five million words; and the intellectual establishment would reject you on the grounds that you knew nothing about (a) Communism, or (b) Alfred Hitchcock.

Spain is clearly out. Nor do I see you, Alexander Isayevich, conforming to the German requirements, which demand either that you live on a derelict farm a hundred miles from anywhere and write about very, very simple things, like hens, or else run for the Bundestag. The tax is murder, too.

Well, yes, all right, so it is in England. But, that aside, the benefits here are limitless, reducing the Inland Revenue's encroachments to negligibility. Pre-eminent among the wonderful advantages is the fact that, whereas these other European sanctuaries will require you to write, will scrutinise each emergent line for signs of growth or decay, will constantly be calling you to account in the slabby pages of their myriad literary magazines and newspapers for any slight deviation from the total commitment expected of you, in England *you will not need to write at all!*

You will only have to *have* written; and with a fair few pages under the belt and a framed Nobel cheque nailed up beside the flying ducks, your qualifications are irreproachable. In England, once he *has* written, the writer's life begins in earnest.

You will never be out of a studio for long, radio or telly: in a dark woollen shirt and a dark woollen tie, you will sit on chromium deck-chairs, semi-circled with a Catholic peer and an articulate musician and a West Indian social worker and a critic who paints a bit or plays the piano a bit, and a pale (but still lovely) girl who has written a virtually unpunctuated trilogy about being a pale (but still lovely) girl, and you will discuss things. All manner of things: the spoliation of the Dorset coastline, the threat of *Deep Throat* to all we hold most dear, supermarkets and the dehumanisation of shopping, battered wives, the initial teaching alphabet, tower blocks, Watergate, What Does The Future Really Hold For The Third World, pets, God, and the licensing laws.

You will generate millions of words, but write none. There will be interviews showing how you have found happiness in a Green Belt executive home, possibly by knocking two internal walls down and converting the loft into a combined darkroom and play-area; and interviews revealing that a life of roulette, elite discos and tall women is no substitute In A Writer's Life for the stability of a happy marriage and your children's continuing wonder at the unfolding world, which you can share; and interviews discussing parking-meters and the concomitant erosion of civil liberties; and interviews At Fifty, At Sixty, and even, if your luck holds, At Sixty-Three and -Four. There will be a lot of money in these interviews, Alexander Isayevich.

There may also be fat contracts to stand beside a dog and sell tasty liver morsels; sip vodka with no more than a silent wink to camera during the pre-Christmas sales-peak; take down from a rosewoodette shelf Volume One of The Complete Winston Churchill bound in rich washable rubbishene.

There will be your name up there in giant capitals: VERY SOLZHENITSYN. VERY SANDERSON.

There will even be wonderful opportunities to act as Script Adviser to the BBC's ninety-eight part serialisation of *Engels In Love*, which means the producer rings you up once a month to enquire whether it's Leningrad that's on the Volga, or is he thinking of Stalingrad, if it's still called that, ha-ha-ha?

There will be wonderful literary parties in Belgrave Square and Gloucester Crescent, where the literary talk will make your very being thrill with its intense and passionate involvement with First Pakistani Serial Rights, and possibilities of adaptation for the Belgian broadcasting services, and a whole chain of speaking engagements in Wisconsin.

So I urge you, Alexander Isayevich, praying that it is still not too late, to reconsider your remaining years: do you really want some bleak and insistent foreign refuge, where you will be compelled to lean across a desk, day in, day out, night in, night out, thinking, thinking, thinking, and scribbling, scribbling,

242

scribbling, page after page, book after book?

Or would you rather not, for the tiny price of a one-way air-ticket, escape to England and become a Writer?

Golfing For Cats

Flying Dutchman

A TRAVEL firm yesterday offered air trips to America for 25p.

The sensational give-away stunned rival operators.

The scheme was launched in Amsterdam by the Dutch charter firm Gefau.

CALL ME PASSEPARTOUT.

Should you ask why, I should have to reply, in my mortification, that it is because my shoes are bound together with adhesive tape. In the old days, you could have called me Ishmael. That, of course, was before Ishmael Properties went down the tubes to the tune of £104,000,000 with so little warning that the only thing I managed to put in my wife's name were my brown brogues.

Which goes some way towards explaining why, upon that misty evening, I was standing at the Formica counter of the Reform Tea Bar on the Thames Embankment, munching a remaindered cream cracker and pondering how Formica had managed to make a go of it. Indeed, such was the depth of my despair, I was on the point of wondering whether I should not be well advised to cross the road and end it all in the ebon swirl below, when, as destiny would have it, another gentleman of the road hove to alongside, ordered a cheese roll, put down a crumpled pound note, and looked at his change.

'Bleeding stroll on!' he exclaimed. 'Twenty pee for an old

tennis ball with a slice of bloody Sunlight in it! Where will it all end?'

A rhetorical cry, that needed no answer; yet, at that moment, a member whom I had adjudged to be sleeping against the Reform's front wheel, suddenly opened his yellow eyes.

'If *I* had eighty pee,' he murmured, 'I'd emigrate.'

We looked at him.

'You would not,' said the newcomer, spreading his eight florins on the bar, 'get bleeding far on this. Personally, I doubt whether the cost of living is much lower in Fulham. You could not wake to a better life in Turnpike Lane. The fleshpots of Lewisham have not been widely advertised.'

At this, the other man stood up, and opened his threadbare greatcoat. Beneath, he wore a *Daily Mirror*; and from his left breast there shrieked the legend *NEW YORK FOR 25p!*

The man behind the counter whistled softly.

'I wouldn't mind betting,' he said, 'you could go around the world on eighty pee.'

There was a strange silence. A gull mewed. A foghorn moaned.

'Wouldn't mind betting what?' said the man with the cheese roll.

The bartender reflected; shrugged.

'Tell you what,' he said. 'You go round the world on that, come back here to the Reform with evidence, and I will personally stand you to a double egg, chips, beans, and two slices.'

'Done!' cried the man with the cheese roll.

They shook hands.

'I shall require you to take an observer,' said the bartender, 'whom I shall personally stand his own eighty pee to ensure the rules are respected.'

I stepped forward.

'Passepartout,' I said.

'Fogg,' said the man with the cheese roll.

I pocketed the Reform coins, and, turning our faces west, we set off.

The walk to Gatwick took ten hours by the drizzled moon, but at least the time gave me the opportunity to learn something of my companion. Fogg, it transpired, was a former Crown Commissioner who had drawn the short straw in his departmental lottery and thus been required to take responsibility for eight hundred million pounds. He had, of course, shouldered it without a murmur. The whole operation had been very British.

At Gatwick, our first task was to find an economical route to Schiphol Airport, since it was from Amsterdam that the 25p transatlantic flights embarked. Fogg was in favour of a Laker 3p Tuesday Dawn Return to Knokke, which bypassed IATA regulations by offering in-flight Communion to enable the aircraft to be re-classified as a cathedral, but I finally persuaded him to shell out the extra money and fly direct to Amsterdam on an Air Angola 5p Weekday Golden Special, a fare made possible by the fact that Angola had formally declared war on the Netherlands and persuaded IATA that reconnaissance missions stood outside their jurisdiction. It meant that Fogg and I had to parachute into Schiphol, but the time saved was invaluable.

Our companions aboard the subsequent Atlantic flight were a motley, though fascinating, company. I sat beside a somewhat lugubrious Dutch businessman called Hertz van Rental whose company had given him a first-class to Delhi where he was expected to initiate a flourishing Gouda import business by persuading the Indians that the cheese had been made from unconsecrated cows and was therefore permissible. The little hopes he had entertained for his success dwindled to nothing when he realised he could chop in his ticket for a 25p single to New York and receive an untaxed eight hundred pounds in return. He told me that he hoped to persuade his employers that, as a good Dutchman, he had always thought of New York as Nieuw Amsterdam, which was how the confusion over his destination had arisen in his mind; he would then return from New York, having spent the eight hundred pounds on, he hoped, Doris Day (his only passion), and explain its disappearance as cab-fares.

I told him that I thought his chances of successful deception slim, but he pointed out that a company which believed you could sell Gouda to Hindus might well believe anything.

246

I saw little of Fogg during the flight, since he had opted for the 14p economy class, and was travelling on the rudder.

Upon arrival at Kennedy, we found our choices myriad. We shopped around (though not without difficulty, Fogg by this time being stone-deaf and suffering from frostbite in both hands) and decided that the best deal was being offered by Gonniff Airlines, which was operating trans-continental flights into Los Angeles as a tax-loss. When the Federal Aviation Authority had raised understandable objections to the ten-cent fare, Gonniff had revealed that they were now operating as a charity designed to carry the blind to the western seaboard so that they could sniff the Pacific. In consequence, passengers at the Gonniff terminal were handed dark glasses and white sticks, a handicap unfortunately compounded in Fogg's case by his deafness and his frostbite, so that, unable to hear, see, or feel his way with his cane, he had to be winched aboard the 747 and carried, such were the strictures placed upon the handling crew by their union, as freight.

It was only when he was re-delivered into my hands at Los Angeles smelling strongly of ageing cheese that I realised that the owner of the samples must have been somewhere aboard. I consequently looked for him on the bus taking us to smell the ocean (Gonniff were fearful of FAA spies), and found him up front enquiring of the driver whether he would accept fifty dollars to drop him in Beverly Hills, preferably within walking distance of the Day residence.

The driver, however, declined, and returned us to Los Angeles airport, where Fogg and I soon thereafter took off for Tokyo.

As we were now down to less than a pound between us, Fogg and I decided to take advantage of an extraordinarily inviting Nippair offer to fly us to Japan for a mere five cents apiece. Upon enquiry, we were told that IATA had authorised the fare-breach on the grounds that the flight was for the exclusive use of Japanese war-veterans, a category that might have proved beyond our qualification had Fogg not managed to persuade

247

Nippair that during World War Two, we had both been traitors.

As a result, we found ourselves winging eastwards across the Pacific, tucking into our fourteenth free meal of the trip (and, incidentally, our fourteenth slice of ham with a pineapple ring on top), while our fellow passengers gathered around to watch with keen interest as Fogg struggled with his frost-charred fingers to chopstick the cherry garnish to his ravenous lip. They were a curiously sombre company, and it was not until we started our astonishingly sharp descent into Tokyo that we suddenly comprehended why. The captain's excited voice came over the intercom, first in Japanese, then, for our benefit, in English: 'This is your captain speaking. In two minutes we expect to dive onto the General Motors offices in Tokyo! Please unfasten your seatbelts and ignore the No Smoking signs!'

To impassioned shrieks of 'BANZAI!' our fellow passengers began tying flags to their foreheads, as Fogg and I stared in horror! Would it all end thus, with almost ninety pee still unspent?

Well might it have indeed, had not, at that very instant, a half-familiar figure risen to his feet, across the aisle, quickly becoming a fully familiar figure as he snatched out his orange-peel teeth and wiped the saffron staining from his cheeks. And suddenly, through the dense reek of joss, my nostrils perceived an old, and curiously welcome stench!

'Stop!' cried Hertz van Rental. 'Do you know who is currently playing in cabaret, for one week only, at the Tokyo Hilton?'

For a brief second, the fanatics paused, but it was time enough for the trusty Hollander to inform them that Doris Day would be singing such old favourites as *The Black Hills of Dakota*, *Moonlight Bay*, *It's Magic*, and many, many more. The Americano-Japs paused uncertainly, caught confused between two cultural magnets; and in that pause, atavism foundered. One or two began singing snatches of *Secret Love*, despite serious palatal difficulty, and in seconds it was all over.

The captain was informed of the change of plan, and five minutes later we were making a perfect three-point landing in Tokyo.

There is little more to tell. The second hemisphere of our historic journey was simplicity itself, for, upon arrival in Japan, we discovered that airline undercutting had, in our brief airborne absence, reached so hysterical a pitch that the companies were now vying with one another to pay passengers to fly with them! We compared offers, and found that El Al would not only pay us five hundred pounds apiece to fly first-class with them to Heathrow, they would also throw in a bespoke lounge suit with two pairs of pants, and pick up the cab-fare from Heathrow to the Reform! We were so taken aback, we even took the risk of asking the El Al agent in Tokyo how long they could continue running at a loss, and he agreed with us that it was crazy, but that they were temperamentally incapable of not wiping the floor with their competitors.

And so it was that, within hours, we were back at the Reform with £1,000.87 in our new mohair pockets, tucking into double egg, chips, beans, and two slices, while our fellow-members gazed on in rapt astonishment!

And while, too, far above us in the chill empyrean, out of reasonable excuses now and doomed forever thus to wander, growing richer yet more unsavoury by the minute, the hapless Hertz van Rental flew invisibly on.

The Rhinestone As Big As The Ritz

Under the Influence of Literature

MY MOTHER WAS the first person to learn that I had begun to take literature seriously. The intimation came in the form of a note slid under my bedroom door on the morning of February 4 (I think), 1952. It said, quite simply:

Dear Mother,
Please do not be alarmed, but I have turned into a big black bug. In spite of this I am still your son so do not treat me any different. It must have happened in the night. On no account throw any apples in case they stick in my back which could kill me.

Your son.

I hasten to add that this turned out to be a lousy diagnosis on my part. But the night before I had gone to bed hugging my giant panda and a collected Kafka found under a piano leg, and since, when I woke up, I was flat on my back, it seemed only reasonable to suppose that I'd metemorphosed along with Gregor Samsa, and was now a fully paid-up cockroach. The fit passed by lunchtime, but for years my father used the story to stagger people who asked him why he was so young and so grey.

Thing is, I was pushing fourteen at the time, and caught in that miserable No-Man's-Land between Meccano and Sex, wide open to suggestions that life was hell. My long trousers were a travesty of manhood, and shaving was a matter of tweezers and hope. Suddenly aware of how tall girls were, and of how poorly a box of dead butter-

250

flies and a luminous compass fit a man for a smooth initiation into the perfumed garden, I tried a desperate crash-programme of self-taught sophistication; I spent my evenings dancing alone in a darkened garage, drinking Sanatogen, smoking dog-ends, and quoting Oscar Wilde, but it never amounted to anything. Faced with the Real Thing at parties, I fell instant prey to a diabolical tic, stone feet, and a falsetto giggle, and generally ended up by locking myself in the lavatory until all the girls had gone home.

Worst of all, I had no literary mentors to guide my pubescent steps. For years I'd lived on the literary roughage of Talbot Baines Reed and Frank Richards, but the time had now come to give up identifying myself with cheery, acne-ridden schoolboys. Similarly, the dream heroes of comic-books had to be jettisoned; I could no longer afford to toy with the fantasy of becoming Zonk, Scourge of Attila, or Captain Marvel, or the Boy Who Saved The School From Martians — girls weren't likely to be too impressed with the way I planned to relieve Constantinople, it had become increasingly clear to me that shouting 'SHAZAM!' was a dead loss, since it never turned *me* into a muscle-bound saviour who could fly at the speed of light, and as for the other thing, my school seemed to pose no immediate threat to Mars, all things considered. I needed instead, for the first time, a reality to build a dream on.

But I wasn't yet ready for adult ego-ideals. Not that I didn't try to find them in stories of Bulldog Drummond and the Saint (Bond being, in 1952, I suppose, some teenage constable yet to find his niche), but experience had already taught me the pointlessness of aiming my aspirations at these suave targets. Odds seemed against my appearance at a school dance, framed in the doorway, my massive bulk poised to spring, my steely eyes flashing blue fire, and my fists bunched like knotted ropes. Taking a quick inventory, I could tell I was short-stocked on the gear that makes women swoon and strong men step aside. And, uttering a visceral sigh (the first, as things turned out, of many), I sent my vast escapist, hero-infested library for pulping, and took up Literature, not for idols, but for sublimation.

The initial shock to my system resulting from this new leaf is something from which I never fully recovered. Literature turned out to be filled, yea, even to teem, with embittered, maladjusted, disorientated, ill-starred, misunderstood malcontents, forsaken souls playing brinkmanship with life, emaciated men with long herringbone overcoats and great, staring tubercular eyes, whose only answer to the challenge of existence was a cracked grin and a terrible Russian shudder. I learned, much later, that there was more to Literature than this, but the fault of over-specialisation wasn't entirely mine; my English master, overwhelmed to find a thirteen-year-old boy whose vision extended beyond conkers and Knickerbocker Glories, rallied to my cry for more stuff like Kafka, and led me into a world where bread fell always on the buttered side and death was the prize the good guys got. And, through all the borrowed paperbacks, one connecting thread ran — K., Raskolnikov, Mishkin, Faust, Werther, Ahab, Daedalus, Usher — these were all chaps like me; true, their acne was spiritual, their stammer rang with *weltschmerz*, but we were of one blood, they and I. How much closer was I, dancing sad, solitary steps in the Stygian garage, to the hunter of Moby Dick, than to Zonk, Scourge of Attila!

At first, I allowed the world which had driven me out of its charmed circles to see only the outward and visible signs of the subcutaneous rot. In the days following my acute disappointment at not being an insect, I wandered the neighbourhood dressed only in pyjamas, a shift made from brown paper, and an old overcoat of my father's, satisfactorily threadbare, and just far enough from the ground to reveal my bare shins and sockless climbing boots. By opening my eyes very wide, I managed to add a tasteful consumptiveness to my face, backed up by bouts of bravura coughing and spitting, and I achieved near-perfection with a mirthless chuckle all my own.

Suburban authority being what it is, I ran foul of the police within a couple of days, not, as I'd intended, for smoking reefers or burying axes in pensioners' heads to express the ultimate meaninglessness of anything but irrational action, but for being in need of care and protection. At least, this was how a Woolworth's assistant saw me. I had been shuffling up and down the aisles, coughing and grinning by turns, when a middle-aged woman took either pity or maliciousness on me, and tried to prise an address from the mirthlessly chuckling lips.

'What's your name?' she said.

'Call me Ishmael', I replied, spitting fearlessly.

'Stop that at once, you horrid little specimen! Where do you live?'

'Live!' I cried. 'Ha!' I chuckled once or twice, rolled my eyes, hawked, spat, twitched, and went on: 'To live — what is that? What is Life? We all labour against our own cure, for death is the cure of all diseases . . . . '

I took a well-rehearsed stance, poised to belt out an abridged version of *La Dame Aux Camélias*, when the lady was reinforced by a policeman, into whose ear she poured a resumé of the proceedings to date.

'Alone, and plainly loitering', said the copper. He dropped a large authoritarian hand on my shoulder. I was profoundly moved. I had been given the masonic handshake of the damned. Already with thee, in the penal settlement, old K.

'I shall go quietly', I said, wheezing softly. 'I know there is no charge against me, but that is no matter. I must stand trial, be condemned, be fed into the insatiable belly of the law. That is the way it has to be.'

I gave him my address, but instead of leading me to the mouldering cellars of the local nick, he took me straight home. My parents, who hadn't yet seen me in The Little Deathwisher Construction Kit, reeled and blenched for long enough to convince the constable that the fault was none of theirs. My father, who believed deeply in discipline through applied psychology, gave me a workmanlike hiding, confiscated the existential wardrobe, and sent me to my room. By drawing the curtains, lighting a candle, releasing my white mice from bondage, and scattering mothballs around to give the place the camphorated flavour of a consumptive's deathbed, I managed to turn it into an acceptable condemned cell. Every evening after school (a perfectly acceptable dual existence this; the Jekyll-and-Hyde situation of schoolboy by day, and visionary nihilist by night appealed enormously to my bitter desire to dupe society) I wrote an *angstvoll* diary on fragments of brown paper torn from my erstwhile undershirt, and tapped morse messages on the wall (e.g. 'God is dead', 'Hell is other people', and so on) not, as members of the Koestler fan-club will be quick to recognise, in order to communicate, but merely to express. I got profound satisfaction from the meaninglessness of the answers which came back from the other half of our semi, the loud thumps of enraged respectability, unable to comprehend or articulate.

However, the self-imposed life of a part-time recluse was growing less and less satisfactory, since it wasn't taking me any nearer the existential nub which lay at the centre of my new idols. I was, worst of all, not experiencing any suffering, but merely the trappings. True, inability to cope with what the romantic novelists variously describe as stirring buds, tremulous awakenings, and so on, was what had initially nudged my new persona into life, but this paled beside the *weltschmerz* of the literary boys. Also, suburban London was not nineteenth century St. Petersburg or Prague, 1952 wasn't much of a year for revolution, whaling, or the collapse of civilisation, I was sick of faking TB and epilepsy, and emaciation seemed too high a price to pay for one's non-beliefs. Pain, to sum up, was in short supply.

It was *The Sorrows Of Young Werther* which pointed the way out of this slough of painlessness. Egged on by a near-delirious schoolmaster, I had had a shot at Goethe already, since a bit of *Sturm und Drang* sounded just what the doctor ordered, but I'd quickly rejected it. I wasn't able to manufacture the brand of jadedness which comes, apparently, after a lifetime's fruitless pursuit of knowledge, and the paraphernalia of pacts with the devil, *Walpurgisnachtsträume*, time-travel, and the rest, were not really in my line. While I sympathsed deeply with Faust himself, it was quite obvious that we were different types of bloke altogether. But Werther, that *meisterwerk* of moon-struck self-pity — he was me all over.

The instant I put down the book, I recognised that what up until then had been a rather primitive adolescent lust for the nubile young bride next door had really been 22-carat sublime devotion all along. It was the quintessence of unrequitable love, liberally laced with unquenchable anguish. Sporting a spotted bow, shiny shoes and a natty line in sighs, I slipped easily into the modified personality, hanging about in the communal driveway for the chance to bite my lip as the unattainable polished the doorknocker or cleaned out the drains. I abbreviated the mirthless chuckle to a silent sob, cut out the spitting altogether, and filled the once-tubercular eyes with pitiable longing.

The girl, who must have been about twenty-five, responded perfectly. She called me her little man, underlining her blindness to my infatuation with exquisite poignancy, and let me wipe the bird-lime off her window-sills and fetch the coal. What had once been K's cell, Raskolnikov's hovel, the *Pequod's* poop-deck, now took on the appearance of a beachcomber's strongbox. My room was littered with weeds from her garden, a couple of slats from the fence I'd helped her mend, half-a-dozen old lipstick cases, a balding powder-puff, three laddered stockings (all taken, at night, from her dustbin), a matted clot of hair I'd found in her sink, an old shoe, a toothless comb, and a pair of lensless sunglasses that had once rested on the beloved ears. Daily, I grew more inextricably involved. I began to demand more than silent service and unexpressed adulation. I dreamed of discovering that she no longer loved her husband, that she had responded to my meticulous weeding and devoted washing-up to the point of being unable to live without me. I saw us locked in each other's arms in a compartment on the *Brighton Belle*, setting out on a New Life Together.

In April I discovered she was pregnant. For one wild moment I toyed with the idea of claiming the child as my own, thus forcing a rift between her and her husband. But the plan had obvious draw-backs. The only real course of action was undoubtedly Werther's. Naturally, I'd contemplated suicide before, but an alternative had always come up, and, anyway, this was the first time that I had something worth dying elaborately for. I wrote innumerable last notes, debated the advantages of an upstairs window over the Piccadilly Line, and even wrote to B.S.A. to ask whether it was possible to kill a human being with one of their airguns, and, if so, how.

In fact, if the cricket season hadn't started the same week, I might have done something foolish.

The Dog It Was That Died

A Walk on the Short Side

Afflicted cops are big box-office. As the crippled Ironside wheels himself off-screen after six record-breaking years, blind Longstreet taps on to take his place in fifty million homes on both sides of the Atlantic. And when he goes . . .?

THEY PULLED THE STIFF OUT of the East River at 3.02 am. From the knees downwards he was concrete, from the neck up he was space. They found the shotgun in a trashcan at the corner of 88th and 3rd. It went down to forensic at 6.41. At 7.12 it was on the Commissioner's desk. He was a big man to be involved. But it was a big case. They'd had six DOA's with the same MO's in the past six days. The press was on the Department's neck.

'Our first break,' said forensic. 'All the previous MW's were clean. This one, all but.'

The Commissioner turned the murder weapon in his hands. 'All but?'

'No prints, no blood, no hairs, no threads, no number, no ID.'

'That's the all,' said the Commissioner. 'Now the but.'

Forensic held a tiny plastic envelope to the desklight.

'Dandruff,' he said. 'On the right barrel.'

They looked at one another, for a long second. The Commissioner reached for his red phone.

'Get Sidestreet up here!' he snapped.

The door opened, and they looked for him. Sometimes Sidestreet would come into a room and you wouldn't know he was there for an hour. That's the way it is when you're three-feet-two. It was pretty short for a New York cop, especially in Homicide; but he hadn't always been three-two. Once he'd been six-feet-one. That was before Joe 'Fettucini' Verde had taken him

256

for a little ride and dumped his Chevy in the Jersey car-crusher. The Verde mob stood by laughing while the car went through. Then they stopped laughing. As it fell off the dumper, the trunk opened and Sidestreet got out. He pulled his snub-nose .45 (it had been a long-barrel .32 when he got in) and dropped three of the Verde gang with his first clip.

That was when the Commissioner knew he had a cop on his staff.

'What's up, Chief?' said Sidestreet.

The Commissioner winced. Even across a big room, the legendary Sidestreet breath was enough to strip the chrome off your badge. Discreetly, forensic took a mask from his surgical coat, and slipped it on.

'Got a lead on the East Side killings,' said the Commissioner. 'We found dandruff on the scatter-gun. Here!'

He threw the little envelope, and Sidestreet caught it. He breathed it open. He looked.

'You're a dandruff man,' said the Commissioner, 'maybe you——'

'Come again,' said Sidestreet, twiddling a knob on his chest. 'These goddam batteries!'

'YOU'RE A DANDRUFF SUFFERER!' roared the Commissioner. 'I THOUGHT YOU COULD GET SOMETHING FROM IT!'

'Yeah,' said Sidestreet. 'You can get conjunctivitis. It's an infection, on account of the scurf gets in your eyes. I had it years. What happens is——'

'I didn't mean that,' said the Commissioner. 'I meant, you know, like you could get information from this sample, right?'

'Sure,' said Sidestreet. 'I been getting treatment down the Nu-Hair Follicle Clinic And Sauna. Also for the alopecia. I seen this dandruff down there. Comes off a tall wop with a wall-eye. We use the same oculist, also. Don't know him too good, on account of his right eye looks to the left and my left eye looks to the right. Most days we don't see each other at all, even when we're, you know, standing right next to each other. Which barrel was the dandruff on?'

'The right,' said forensic, through his mask.

'That figures,' said Sidestreet. 'This wop's a left-hander. The right barrel's against his cheek, right? The dandruff probably drops outa these long wop sideburns he's got.'

'Name?' snapped the Commissioner.

Sidestreet shrugged.

'Who knows? Nobody talks to me, Chief, you know that. Even my dentist works with a three-foot probe. Gimme the mug shots.'

At 9.05 they had a name.

'Pick him up,' said the Commissioner.

Sidestreet's specially converted wagon wailed uptown. Bullet-proof and radar-equipped, it also had no seats in the back so that Sidestreet could stand up, on account of the haemorrhoids, and a specially tailored mini-urinal in pastel blue near-porcelain, for his enuresis. In the early days, a lot of hoods got away due to the fact that by the time Sidestreet's standard police car found a public lavatory and by the time Sidestreet had found a dime and by the time he'd come out onto the street again, the fugitive car was halfway across New Mexico with new plates, and full beards on the occupants.

'Don't pick it, boss!'

Sidestreet dropped his hand instantly from his barber's rash: he relied too much on trusty, warm-hearted Police-Nurse Rona Kowalski SRN, the best colonic irrigator east of the Pecos, ever to put her nose out of joint. Even though his osteopath was a household word wherever arthritics gathered, and a nose to him was as a parking violator to Sidestreet.

'I'm nervous, Kowalski,' said Sidestreet, 'that's all.'

'I can tell, boss,' she said. 'When we slowed for that last red light, I could hear your eczema crackling.'

'I never ran in a fellow scurfnik before,' said Sidestreet. 'The nearest I ever came was when we trapped Mad Nat Dolfuss in Palisades Park and shot it out. It wasn't till we got him down to the morgue and took his clothes off that I realised him and me had athlete's foot in all the same places.' Sidestreet looked away, sighing. 'It made me feel—I dunno—dirty, somehow.'

The wagon came around the corner into 110th Street, and slammed into the kerb. Sidestreet sprang out, deaf-aid swinging, a pack of regulation laxatives in his left hand, and his nickel-plated ear-syringe in his right, ready for anything. Pausing only for a short nose-bleed on the step, he pocketed his dentures, and leapt through the doorway of a peeling brownstone.

258

He dropped to one knee, almost imperceptibly.

'Okay, Zucchini, we know you're in there!' cried Sidestreet.

There was no answer from the dark passage.

'Don't gimme that, Zucchini, I seen the dandruff! People like us shouldn't fit navy blue carpet. *This here's fresh scurf!* Also, you forget I'm a non-tall person—us non-talls develop special senses to compensate. I ain't as far away from these little white flakes as most people!'

'Okay, Sidestreet, I'm coming out!'

Sidestreet squinted into the gloom. It was the way he looked at everything.

'How'd you know it's me, Zucchini?'

'You kidding?' The voice was faint. 'Tear-gas I can take. Mace I inhale. But—for Chrissake, Sidestreet, don't your best friends tell you *anything?*'

'Cops,' muttered Sidestreet, 'don't have best friends.'

He was still reflecting upon this, when the killer sprang out of the darkness. In an instant, Sidestreet was on his feet. He swung a short left to the shin, followed it with a right uppercut to the knee, and was about to take off for a crippling groin-butt when he suddenly let out a cry of agony and fell to the floor. Zucchini tore himself free and disappeared down the steps, almost knocking over PN Kowalski who was rushing in with iron lungs, wooden legs, surgical trusses, glass eyes, stomach pumps, vitamin pills, wigs, throat-sprays, varicose stockings and all the other essential kit carried in Sidestreet's wagon in case of emergencies.

'What is it, boss?' she shrieked. 'Where'd he get you?'

Sidestreet looked up at her, his fine squat face creased with pain.

'My arches,' he gasped, 'they just fell!'

Sidestreet jumped up and down furiously and shook the walls of his cot until the entire orthopaedic ward rattled.

'I'm okay I tellya, Chief!' he cried. 'They fixed the arches, also my trick knee, adenoids, ingrowing toenails, both, and they say the psoriasis will clear up as soon as I stop worrying about my hernia. I want out!'

'Nothing doing, Sidestreet,' barked the Commissioner. 'You're livebait!'

'How's that?' muttered Sidestreet, turning both channels up full and cutting in his tweeter.

'You heard,' said the Commissioner. 'Turns out Zucchini is one of the Verde mob. You're the only one who can put a finger on him, Sidestreet, so sure as hell they're gonna try and eliminate you. I got the entire hospital staked out.'

Sidestreet relaxed.

'A job,' he said. 'That's different.' He patted his pillow. 'Good job I keep a little something by me, Chief. For medicinal purposes, heh-heh-heh!'

'Good luck, Sidestreet,' said the Commissioner, and left.

At 10 pm, the nurse settled Sidestreet for sleep.

At 10.30, the lights went out.

At 11.15, two men in white coats and stethoscopes slid up the ward, and stopped at Sidestreet's bed.

'Okay, cop, issa where you getta yours!' hissed the nearer.

Sidestreet, eyes closed, slid a hand beneath his pillow, slowly. There was nothing there.

'Iffa you lookin' for your gun,' said the other hood, 'you canna forget it. Thissa night nurse,' he laughed nastily, 'issa personal frien'.'

Whereupon he drew a silenced Walther, took aim on Sidestreet's sweating forehead, and fell over.

The second torpedo looked at him for a couple of seconds, closed his eyes, and slid to the floor beside him.

Half a minute later, the ward was full of cops. A frenzied Commissioner appeared at Sidestreet's bed.

'Thank God you're all right!' he cried. 'Dear Heaven, Sidestreet, you got them both! And we found your gun on the night nurse—how in God's name . . .'

'They just came close,' said Sidestreet, 'and pow! That was it.'

'But how?'

Sidestreet shrugged.

'Could be yellow fever,' he said. 'Could be bubonic plague, smallpox, hepatitis. Could be typhoid, TB, cholera, could be——' he smiled '——hell, you know me, Commissioner. It could be anything.'

Golfing For Cats

Publish and be Diblgd!

The Daily Telegraph *recently published a missing chapter, dropped by the author, from* Through The Looking-Glass. *Disappointing in itself, its real revelation was that Lewis Carroll was prepared to cut and change his work to meet objections by illustrators, publishers, printers, and almost anyone else. Which at last explains one of the greatest literary conundrums in the language* . . .

THE JUNIOR PORTER of Christ Church College, Oxford, came out of his cubby-hole and squinted across the cold cobbled acreage of Tom Quad. The Senior Porter was standing in the fountain, poking a twig up a spout. The Junior Porter trotted across on echoing clogs.

'Where is he this time?' he said.

The Senior Porter removed the twig. He examined the end through sweat-blobbed pince-nez.

'See that?' he said, 'Know what that is? Bleeding caviare, that's what that is. Bleeding sturgeon's eggs rammed up the outlet.'

'Stone me!' cried the Junior Porter. 'What is the eternal mystery of the sturgeon that it will swim thousands of miles upstream from bloody anywhere to lay its eggs?'

The Senior Porter removed the pince-nez, and stared at him.

'God Almighty, Scrimweasel,' he muttered. 'Could it be Mr Darwin was on the right track, after all? Is it true as how you are paid in bananas?'

'I don't follow,' said Scrimweasel, sullenly.

''Course you don't,' said the Senior Porter. He shook his head. 'The eternal mystery to what you are referring concerns the salmon, son. The sturgeon just bleeding lies there, as you'd expect, being a protected species. It just bleeding lies there in

261

the sea, and its eggs come out. They only get up brass bloody spouts as the result of japes on the part of your titled undergraduates, coming home on the outside of two gallons of claret, going "Haw! Haw! Haw!", and poking bloody caviare up brass conduits.'

'Oh,' said Scrimweasel.

'I bin here since 1831,' said the Senior Porter, 'during which time what I have took out of College drains, gullies, bogs, pipes, and students, is nobody's business. There is more to this job than posing for bloody Ackermann, sunshine.'

'Well, then,' countered Scrimweasel, 'if you're so smart, where is Mr Charles Lutwidge Dodgson, then?'

'Smirk at me, lad, I'll knock your 'ead off!' snapped the Senior Porter.

'Sorry,' muttered Scrimweasel. 'I got this note for him, haven't I?'

The Senior Porter consulted an enormous turnip watch. He looked, thought Scrimweasel privately, much like a white rabbit.

'Eleven a.m.,' said the Senior Porter. 'Boar's Hill Junior Girls'll be coming out for 'ockey. You'll find him up the tower with his telescope.'

'Bloody stroll on!' cried Scrimweasel. 'That's two 'undred steps!'

'Take your time,' said the Senior Porter. 'You don't want to come up on him sudden, know what I mean?'

The Junior Porter coughed, discreetly. But the wind snatched it away, so he coughed again, more sharply.

The Senior Lecturer in Mathematics jumped.

'Ha! Ha!' he shrieked. 'Scrimweasel! I was just, er, inspecting the Meadows. There is talk of a by-pass.'

' 'Course you were, squire,' said the Junior Porter. He held out the note. Dodgson smoothed it against the windblown parapet, and peered.

'Goodness!' he exclaimed. 'It's from Jas. Rumbelow & Sons, Printers. They say that because I agreed to cut my chapter about the wiggy wasp out of my new book, it is now some four pages short, contra to the agreement of the something ultimo hereinunder referred to, and is taking bread out of their mouths!'

'New book?' said Scrimweasel, since some sort of reply seemed called for.

'*Through The Looking-Glass*,'' said Dodgson.

Scrimweasel leered horribly.

'Never mind *Through The Looking-Glass*, squire,' he said nudging Dodgson's tea-stained waistcoat evilly, 'what you ought to do is *Through The Telescope*, know what I mean?'

'Do you really think so?' said Dodgson.

'You're a bit of a photographer,' said Scrimweasel, 'catch my drift?'

'Not exactly,' said Dodgson.

'Make a fortune,' said Scrimweasel. 'All this Victorian repression, you could clean up. Forty-eight poses, as seen from top of famous building by genuine connoisseur, sent under plain cover. I would,' he added, putting his small face up against the mathematician's left mutton-chop, 'be prepared to hold the magnesium, for a small consideration.'

'I am afraid,' said Dodgson, simultaneously snapping his hat open and his telescope shut with a single adroit flick, 'I have no time to think about that now. I am already late for poor Mr Rumbelow.'

Whereupon he sprang to the staircase, and clattered out of sight.

Scrimweasel stared after him.

'He's a fool to himself,' he said.

It was not, however, until four more days had passed that Dodgson found himself standing in Ludgate Hill, outside the premises of Jas. Rumbelow. True, he had arrived in London three days earlier, but it had been some time since he had visited the metropolis, and thus had his complicated senses ravished by its promise. Emerging from Paddington Station, he had joined a crocodile of small girls in captivating boaters and in consequence had spent the night accidentally locked in the Natural History Museum.

The second night, the locking had been somewhat more deliberate; but they had given him a cup of tea in the morning and, it having been explained that he was a famous author and therefore as mad as a hatter, they had returned his possessions to him, including the telescope, and sent him on his way. Unfortunately, he soon after stopped dead in the middle of the Strand to muse upon the madness of hatters, and was knocked over by a brewer's dray; he spent the third night in the London Hospital, but was found the following morning creeping through the fever ward in an attempt to photograph the smaller nurses, and was forcibly discharged.

'Well?' barked Jas. Rumbelow, as the vague figure wandered into the print shop.

'My name,' said Dodgson, 'is Dodgson.'

'How fascinating,' said Rumbelow. 'Well I never. Blow me. There's a thing. Well, Mr Dodgson, it's been a pleasure talking to you, but I have to get on now on account of being four days behind with some bloody—'

'It's him!' cried a compositor suddenly, scattering bright type. 'It's Carroll!'

The staff looked up.

Rumbelow cocked his head, as if downwind of game.

'Carroll?' he said, quietly. 'You said Dodgson.'

'I have,' murmured Dodgson, colouring, 'an assumed name.'

Rumbelow leaned him into the wall.

'I am not bleeding surprised,' he muttered. 'If I was you, I'd change 'em both to Jenkins and emigrate, before the lads get their 'ands on you!

'I do understand,' said Dodgson, 'I do apologise.'

'Stuck here four days,' cried Rumbelow, 'twiddling our thumbs, orders not touched, contracts going begging, people ringing up about wedding invitations, luggage labels, visiting cards, all nice easy stuff, all turned down, can't touch it, can I? Waiting on Mr Carroll, aren't I?'

'I'm sorry. I was held up.'

'Strung up'd be favourite,' said the compositor.

'Thirty-eight inches short, that book,' said Rumbelow. 'Bloody yard out, this one, Samuel. Calls himself a professional. Bloody yard short.'

Dodgson sighed.

'Well, I suppose it will just have to be a shorter book,' he said, 'that's all. We could have 188 pages instead of 192.'

They stared at him.

'I may have to sit down,' said Rumbelow.

'He's never heard of sections,' said the compositor.

'Don't they teach you nothing at Oxford?' said a tapper.

'They come in sections, books,' said Rumbelow, to Dodgson. 'Never mind pages, mate. They come in bunches of sixteen. How many sixteens in 188?'

'Calls himself a mathematician,' said the compositor.

'Could we not have four blank pages at the end?' enquired Dodgson.

'Oh my God!' said Rumbelow.

'We'd be a laughing-stock,' said the tapper.

'Bugger laughing-stock,' snapped the compositor. 'Any talk of blank pages, I'll have the lads straight out. Wouldn't surprise me if some of the machinery suddenly fell over, neither.'

'Maybe he'd like it done triangular,' said the tapper heavily. 'Nice triangular octavo. Fur endpapers, possibly.'

'Don't joke,' said Rumbelow, 'I remember this ratbag. He's the one what give us that Mouse's Tale in his last book. Bloody wossname, emblematic verse. Started off in fourteen-point, come wiggling down the page unregistered, ended up in bloody diamond-point at the bottom.'

'Never!' cried the compositor. 'Was that *him*? I was here all Whitsun over that. I had to get a draught off the apothecary on the Tuesday, I've never known bowels like it.'

'Oh dear,' said Dodgson, 'what should I do?'

'Bloody write another yard, is what,' said Rumbelow. 'You got twenty minutes. I'm not running into overtime.'

Dodgson blenched.

'One can't just dash it off, you know,' he protested.

'Oh, I see,' said Rumbelow. 'One would prefer to carry one's teeth away in one's hat, would one?'

Dodgson sighed.

'Well, I *do* happen to have a little poem I scribbled on the back of an old charge-sheet I found the other night,' he murmured, 'which I suppose I could pop in at the end of the first chapter. If that would be all right.'

'No problem,' said Rumbelow, 'if it goes to a yard, and no dodgy turns at the end of lines or nothing. Let's have it, then.'

Dodgson groped in his tail-coat pocket, and fished out a crumpled flimsy.

'I don't know how appropriate it is, mind,' he said. 'It's called *JANUARY*.'

'Very nice,' said Rumbelow. 'Straightforward.'

Dodgson cleared his throat.

' 'Twas chilly, and the slimy roads
Did shine and shimmer in the rain:
All misty were the birds' abodes,
And the cold grassy plain.

Beware of January, my son!
The hoar-frost's bite, the . . .'

'Yes, fine, lovely, terrific!' interrupted Rumbelow. 'We haven't got all bloody day, squire, give it here.'

He snatched the flimsy, and handed it to the tapper, who scuttled off to his stool, closely followed by the compositor.

Dodgson watched them go, nervously.

'Er . . .'

'You still here?' said Rumbelow.

'I was wondering,' murmured Dodgson, 'whether I would see a proof?'

'Do me a favour,' replied Rumbelow. 'We're a week behind as it is.'

'I just thought I'd enquire,' said Dodgson.

The Rhinestone As Big As The Ritz

266

Take the Wallpaper in the Left Hand and the Hammer in the Right . . .

YOU LIVE WITH A WOMAN for ten years, not an intimacy remains unshared, and where are you?

It was Christmas morning, possibly with a capital M, so auspicious was the time, and the house re-echoed to the Yuley joy of children breaking their new toys over one another. Since dawn, the air had been filled with flying cogs, the walls of the upstairs hall shone with new day-glo graffiti, and on the stairs the pitiful shards of model soldier lay thick as on the field of Omdurman, their little swords and broken rifles still game for a last kamikaze jab at the bare parental sole as it lurched, hungover, through the inimical pile towards the reviving caffeine.

I hobbled eventually to a breakfast table that would have left Oliver Wendell Holmes himself speechless. A doll's eye glared up from the porridge, rubber insects were all over the toast, and beside the coffee-pot stood the remains of an electric dog. Cobbled together in far Nippon by deft saffron digits, the animal had been a masterpiece of delicate invention a half-hour earlier, when my small daughter first flung herself at its wrappings. In theory, when you pulled its leash, two batteries in its cunningly hollowed bowels sprang into energy, and its little tail wagged while its little legs waddled it forward and its little head nodded as its little mouth yapped.

In practice, however, you pull its leash, and a little tin flange clicks up and down obscenely in its hindquarters, the tail having fallen off, and its little legs waddle it forward at a slow limp; but its little head does not nod, because its little head is now on the other side of the table. The decapitated torso, in fact, is crawling towards its severed skull, and, illogically, barking at it. As the high point of a Hammer film, the thing now has few equals, but as a cuddly toy it has all the winsome appeal of a

267

clockwork boil.

I was still staring at the furry wreckage and musing on the whims of economic history whereby Japan's fiduciary sun was allowed to rise on such insubstantial collateral as this, when I heard my wife say: 'Never mind, you'll be able to mend all their toys now.'

How shall I describe the nudgy emphasis of that *NOW*? She is a subtle girl, and when she slips into italics, every hackle I have tells me there are difficult times ahead.

'I'm sorry?' I riposted wittily.

'You haven't opened your present,' she said.

'Oh!' I cried, having practised; and having painstakingly ignored the large parcel beside my chair which contained a half doz shirts, at the very least, possibly a brace of sweaters, and who knew how many ties, cravats, matching foulards? What the sequitur might be bridging them to the dismembered doggie, I could not begin to guess; but it had been a pretty heavy night, and I might well have lost a syllogistic rivet or two along the way.

I threw my remains upon the parcel and, having broken a forenail on the knot and gashed a thumb on the paper (co-ordination is one of my shorter suits: I am one of the few men I know to bang his head on seven-foot lintels), I came to a book. A book with a lock and a handle on it, yet.

'Hurrah,' I murmured. I brightened. Shirts it wasn't, but a *fake* book it might well be, a piece of snappy packaging for the literary cigar-smoker, say, under which head I fall.

'It's like a little suitcase,' I said.

'Isn't it, though?' she replied. 'What an eye for detail you have, and all self-taught.'

Detecting a coppery tang of disappointment here, and instantly tracing its source, I cranked up my enthusiasm a couple of notches.

'Wow!' I cried, hefting the bogus vol, 'How exciting to have a package *within* a package! Ha-ha-ha, it's passing itself off as—let me see—*The Readers Digest Complete Do-It-Yourself Manual*!'

'Is it?' she said.

'Isn't it?' I replied.

I snapped back the catch, and opened it, and it contained a

million or two loose-leaf pages, cleverly ring-bound for maxi-mum inaccessibility. They fell open at a page of circular saws.

'Oh, look,' I said, 'circular saws.'

'There you are,' she cried happily, 'and you've always main-tained you weren't technical.'

'I can, however, recognise any tool you care to name,' I re-plied. 'I have learned to, just as mice come to learn about mousetraps. It is almost an instinct with me, now.'

'It will be a whole new skill,' she countered. 'With this book, anyone can learn how to build anything. Look,' she continued, turning a leaf with enviable dexterity, 'a sideboard! All you do is saw wood up and fit it together.'

'Well, well! And think of all the fuss they made of Sheraton!' Many things were seething in my head at this moment, the least of them being my utter ineptitude when faced with anything constructional. The only thing I ever succeeded in making in school woodwork, and that after a year of rib-tickling failed at-tempts, was a toast-rack, and even then you had to put a rubber band around the toast to keep the whole thing from falling apart. I transferred to metalwork after that, where they would give me steel plates which I turned into shrapnel. But this drear practical record, as I say, was nothing to the deeper signifi-cances with which the gift was fraught.

'Darling,' I said, 'I had always believed that you thought of me as a sophisticated homme du monde, dashing scourge of croupiers and sommeliers alike, a two-fisted wit over whom lissom dollies sighed and suffered, a young god who could hold his liquor and his own with Freddie Ayer! Look here, upon this picture, and on this—and how many joiners do you know who could hit you with an apt Shakespearian reference at this early hour?—and tell me what you see.'

She looked at the proffered page. A man in a leather apron was demonstrating the correct method of squinting at a rebat-ing plane. He had several ball-points in an upper pocket, no doubt of different hues, and a short-back-and-sides he had clearly manufactured himself, possibly with adze and chisel.

'Is that,' I cried, 'how you see me? A shaper of matchless dovetails, an adroit recycler of cotton-reels, a host to keep his guests enthralled, as they sip their Emva Cream, with tales of tile and bookcase? You know me,' I hurtled on, 'the only craft I have is gluing, and that imperfect. We have shared a life for ten years, you have watched me glue shelves to walls, and seen them fall, you have lain awake and listened while glued slates detached themselves from the roof, you have reeled back as wardrobe doors came unstuck from their hinges—and at the end of it all, *this*?'

'It's just a question of the proper tools,' she said, 'saws and chisels and—things.'

'Wounds is the word you were looking for,' I said, 'that is what goes with saws and chisels, a floorful of thumbs, the squirt of arteries, overworked surgeons converting my body into a Fair Isle masterpiece!'

Whereupon, wordless, she shoved back her chair, and left.

I sat for a while, staring at the table (how did they fit the legs in, how did they get the top on, to what arcane glue secrets were cabinetmakers privy?) and the ruined toys, and I thought: would it not, in truth, be cool to wave mystic implements over these remains, bring old British skills to bear upon Jap tattiness, return the toys, new-perfect, to the kids and accept their squeals of joy and love? Or knock up—I flipped the book—a cocktail cabinet or two, some bunk beds, even a summer house? Put in (page 41) a swimming-pool, relay the parquet floors, convert the loft?

Would this infringe upon the image of Renaissance Man? On the contrary, it would enhance it, endow new facets, why, I could paint the Mona Lisa with my left hand while my right was inventing the helicopter! I would buy gorblimey trousers, a crusty briar, learn how to hold nails in my mouth and tell the consistency of cement by the smell alone, and gawping neighbours would come to point out the matchless gabling, the new storey, the fresh bow windows—

I rushed out, borne on the boiling enthusiasm, into the garage which was to be my workshop, carrying the manual by its handle (perhaps, now, I should always carry it with me, and when crowds formed around some fallen masonry or shattered window or the torn woodwork of a bomb-blasted pub, I would elbow them aside, holding it aloft and crying 'Let me through, I'm a handyman!'), and, as luck would have it, there in an old tobacco tin on the window ledge I found a threaded hook, just the thing to hang the book on for easy reference, so I screwed it

270

into the plaster, and I found a piece of string, and I looped it through the handle, and I hung the book up on the wall, *and it did not fall off!*

Until I slammed the garage door, that is.

I looked through the window, and there seemed to be a lot of plaster on the floor. But it did not faze me. A little thing like fallen plaster doesn't bother me any more.

Why, I'll have it glued back up any day now.

Golfing For Cats

The Tourists Karamazov

'*More and more Soviet citizens are catching the travel bug. Last year 2,100,000 of them went abroad, 900,000 to capitalist countries. The bulk of the increase comes from package-deal tourists.*' – Daily Telegraph

ON A BITTERLY HOT MORNING towards the end of July, 197–, a young man whose skin was the colour of a boiled saveloy left his little room at the top of the El Diabolico Hotel that lay lost among the cranes and half-dug building sites of Torremolinos, and began to descend the step-worn stairs.

On every landing, he passed the little knots of fellow-guests huddled around the silent lift-doors, clutching their frail GUM shrimpnets and staring disconsolately into the dark shaft, some upwards, some downwards. As he padded quickly past them, his terror of meeting anybody would suddenly lurch in his trembling bowel as first this one, now that, would turn their stricken eyes towards him. Sometimes, they spoke.

'Good morning, Alexei Alexeyovich,' they might say, 'the elevator has still not arrived. It has been three days. Some of the children are faint from lack of water.'

Whenever he could, he would merely stare at them, perhaps nod; but when it could not be avoided (when some elderly grandmother, perhaps, lay on the stairs, rocking her head-scarved head and moaning softly, blocking his escape), he would reply:

'Why do you not come down the stairs like me? It seems very possible that the elevator has broken down.'

At which the men would shake their heads, and say:

'We have had no official notice that the elevator has ceased to function. It is set out clearly in the official brochure that there is an elevator to carry guests to the lower floors. There is nothing in the official brochure to indicate that descent by the staircase is allowed.'

'It also states in the official brochure,' the pink young man would reply, 'that there is running hot and cold water. It does not however state that it is running through the ceiling.'

'You are a revanchist parasite, Alexei Alexeyovich,' said a young woman on the second-floor landing, when he gave her this standard reply. 'You are not fit to enjoy the sun-kissed tropical paradise of famed Torremolinos with its many barbecues, its folkloric dancing, its unparalleled shopping, and its paiella, a unique local dish made with prawns and many other fruits of the sea.'

'I observe, Sonya Sonyeova, that you have been studying your official brochure during your holiday outside this elevator. It is clear to me that you do not have hot and cold water running through your ceiling.'

'I do not have a ceiling, filthy Alexei Alexeyovich,' the young woman replied. 'I am in that portion of the internationally-renowned El Diabolico which the beloved comrade workers have seen fit not to complete, no doubt as a protest against fascist oppression. I feel privileged that I have been given the opportunity to share this wonderful moment with them.'

'His head is going all red,' said a little boy beside her. 'What are the running dogs of fascism doing to Alexei Alexeyovich, Sonya Sonyeova?'

'He is changing colour because he is walking about on his own,' said his sister. 'It is my opinion that he is not going on the wonderful air-conditioned buses, each with its own WC, to visit the fabled cathedral of Malaga or take advantage of the streets that have remained unchanged for centuries with their marvellous little shops displaying local woodcraft where you may browse undisturbed but would be foolish not to buy the hand-carved nutcrackers for which the region is famed.'

'I cannot go on the buses, Sonya Sonyeova,' replied Alexei Alexeyovich, 'because they will not leave with three passengers. As everyone on our package-trip is waiting for the lift, with the exception of myself and Mr. and Mrs. Solokilov of Smolensk who are actually sleeping under the bus due to lack of accommodation in the hotel annexe which fell into the sea two nights ago, the drivers are not prepared to leave.'

'I am glad you furnished me with the names of Mr. and Mrs. Solokilov,' said the young woman, writing the names down in her little notebook. 'There is no reason why, simply because they are downstairs already, they should not wait by the lift with everyone else. Where is their solidarity?'

Alexei Alexeyovich sighed, and left them to their pointless vigil, and went down the last two flights to breakfast. It was, like all the others, a lonely meal: the Solokilovs, diminutive in the distance on Table 89, and he alone on Table 3, and between them a vast steppe of white napery vainly awaiting the other 237 packagees. Ten waiters stood by the wall, picking their teeth, and examining their nails. Finally, his own shoved himself upright and slunk across, gripping a cold croissant, bracing himself for the mandatory international bonhomie upon which the management prided itself.

'Georgie Best bloody good, gorblimey,' said the waiter, dropping the croissant onto the young man's plate.

'May I have an egg, please?' said Alexei Alexeyovich, in Russian.

'Thcotland for de Gup,' said the waiter, and shuffled back to the wall.

Alexei Alexeyovich stared after him for a while. He began, for the third time in as many days, to think about complaining; but, as always, as soon as he did so, his hands began to tremble uncontrollably, and the sweat sprang out on his empurpled forehead and began carrying flakes of his skin down his face; he had no proper concept of complaint, he did not even have any real idea of what a management was, it was just that he experienced a far not-quite-familiar stirring of something that made him both excited and uneasy.

He got up instead, and went outside, into the fearful white glare hurtling back off the serried ranks of tower blocks and vast flat expanses of car-park and forecourt. Mr. and Mrs. Solokilov had formed a tiny queue by the front door of their bus. No drivers were to be seen.

'Good morning, Alexei Alexeyovich,' said Solokilov, from whose fur coat steam was gently rising, but which he would not remove as he had been wearing it for his passport photograph, and lived in perpetual terror of any deviation from his official

274

identity. 'We are waiting for the bus to take us to the world-renowned bull-ring of Marbella, playground of princes, because it is Tuesday morning.'

'But the buses will not be going, Grigor Grigorovich,' said the young man, 'because the comrade package is all upstairs waiting for the lift.'

Mr. Solokilov took off his astrakhan hat and removed a saturated timetable from it.

'Tuesday morning, nine a.m., wait by buses for Marbella excursion,' he said, tracing the words with his finger. He put the paper back, and the hat on again.

'Will you not perhaps accompany me to the beach?' said the young man.

'The visit to the beach, its miles of golden sand, its little pools where the crabs play, its parties of gay visitors of every nation, let us pause and listen to the many various tongues, is not until Thursday, Alexei Alexeyovich,' said Mrs. Solokilov.

'After the visit to the glassblowing works,' nodded her husband, 'high in the hills where skilled craftsmen practise the incredible art of their forefathers, note how they suck in before each item, thus avoiding bubbles and flaws.'

He left them there, with a slight bow, and began the long trek across site and dump and slag-heap and rubble and through ruins either half-built or half-demolished, towards the sea. He had never seen the sea; they had all been promised a view of it from the hotel, according to the brochure, but the one balcony from which it was possible to do this (it belonged to the caretaker's penthouse apartment) had fallen off during a light drizzle the week before, and in consequence Alexei Alexeyovich's heart beat a little faster with each forward step, and as the pungency of the ozone seeped, finally, through the fug of diesel and fractured gas mains and frying chips and the massed reek of a million sun-oiled bodies, something not unlike joy took over his entire being. To see the sea, open and unconfined, free and frontierless, irrestrictible and . . .

A hand fell upon his frail shoulder, and he looked round into a pair of iron eyes under a black homburg.

'Come, Alexei Alexeyovich,' said the black homburg.

There was a large Moskva parked at the kerb, with the engine running, and another black homburg inside it.

'Now?' said Alexei Alexeyovich.

'Now. But first you will write on this postcard showing golden funfilled Torremolinos where the elite meet and every day is a holiday.'

'What shall I write?' muttered the young man, as the pen was pushed into his hand.

'You will write: HAVING WONDERFUL TIME. WISH YOU WERE HERE,' said the black homburg, 'and sign it.'

Golfing For Cats

If That's The Acropolis, How Come It Don't Chime?

"Robert P. McCulloch imports great European architecture for reassembly in new American cities. It was he who got the idea of buying London Bridge and bringing it to the planned community of Lake Havasu City, Arizona. He admits now that he thought he was buying the more picturesque Tower Bridge, but adds: 'That bridge is going to bring in five million tourists a year'." – Newsweek.

Robert P. McCulloch,
McCulloch Corporation,
Los Angeles, Calif.

5th May

Dear Mr. McCulloch:

Thank you for your wonderful brochure and miraculous unrepeatable offer. Yes, we here at Hogsnout Aerospace Engineering Model Township sure would like to increase our cultural status as mentioned on page 4, and we are over 21. We are a community of forty thousand souls, average family income in excess of $16,000 p.a., and as our town was built during the night of August 10, 1969, we don't have nothing of what you might call hallowed antiquity, always excepting the portrait of my father, Simeon Hogsnout III, painted in 1949 in genuine oils, but this is presently hanging in our boardroom and in consequence not available for our community to enrich its cultural life from. Also, it don't pull in tourists all that good.

277

Some old European stuff would be just great! My wife and myself went on this $2899 all-inclusive world trip last Fall and we saw a hell of a lot of stuff that would look damn good in the middle of Simeon Hogsnout III Plaza downtown, especially if you have something that would fit in between the Hogsnout Motor Inne and the Simeonburger Parlour and Grill. The area available is about 20,000 sq. ft., with mains drainage and convenient all freeways.

Naturally, I wouldn't want to interfere with no expert authority, but one thing Miriam and me did see was at this Italian place, I guess you'd call it, and they had this old tower, it was leaning over. We went up the top and dropped stuff off like the guide said, on account of they invented gravity up there. This strikes me like a very appropriate cultural thing to have in the middle of the fastest-growing little aerospace industry township in the world!

I know a tower like that would cost approx. $100,000 new, construction industry rates being crazy right now, but this one is extremely secondhand and, like I say, in a very advanced state of lean and God knows about dry rot etcetera, and I reckon I would be doing them a favour taking it off their hands cheap.

I look forward to hearing your esteemed comments.

Yours very truly,
Simeon Hogsnout IV,
President,
Hogsnout Aerospace Inc.

Simeon Hogsnout IV,
Hogsnout Aerospace Inc.

18th May

Dear Mr. Hogsnout:

Thank you for your letter of May 5. I apologise for the delay in replying, but we have been going through our files of old leaning things in an effort to locate the cultural gem of your choice. There is a lot of stuff like you describe in Europe, but

I think what you have in mind is the Leaning Tower of Pisa, and a very wise choice if I might say so, except it will set you back a good five million, if I'm any judge, plus postage and packing. I haven't seen the treasure in question personally, but I guarantee that setting it up in Simeon Hogsnout III Plaza will not only enrich your township but also pull in the hicks, especially if you can get it to lean across the Hogsnout Motor Inne swimming-pool, so's they can maybe dive off it at ten bucks a throw, which has a thick edge over Pisa on account of the cobbles underneath.

I have taken the trouble to enclose a brick of the Leaning Tower, collected by my European sales manager, in the hope it will give you some impression of the quality. A deposit of $50,000 secures.

Yours,
Robert P. McCulloch.

Robert P. McCulloch,
McCulloch Corporation,
Los Angeles, Calif.

24th September

Dear Mr. McCulloch:

Very many thanks for your communication of the 3rd ultimo, also the five truckloads of Leaning Tower of Pisa at $5,000,000, plus ten per cent discount for cash. However, there's one or two things I'd like to enquire about, if you'll excuse me.

I do not pretend to be a leading authority on Europe culture, but we have now unpacked the item and put it up, and it don't seem to be exactly the way I remember it. I could be wrong, but I don't want people should turn up in our community and start being suspicious about our cultural gem, also not shelling out the ten bucks to go up it. Which, as a matter of fact they can't, right now, on account of we got it up all right but when we tried to get it to lean a little, it kind of broke. And when it broke, the top fell off, and when we took a close look at it, this turned out to be a cement guy with one arm and one eye and a triangular hat. Miriam says she don't remember no guy on the top.

Yours truly,
Simeon Hogsnout IV.

Simeon Hogsnout IV,
Hogsnout Aerospace Inc.

3rd October

Dear Mr. Hogsnout:

Like I told you originally, I have not inspected this Leaning Tower personally, but I was always under the impression that it had a guy on the top, plus four lions underneath which you will notice I threw in free, gratis and for nothing. As these lions alone would normally run out at a minimum of ten grand apiece, I do not understand all the beefing on your part. It is my opinion that the cement guy is Sir Isaac Garibaldi, who invented gravity, like you say. It may be that when you and your lady wife was up the tower on your original trip, you was standing underneath the statue and didn't notice it. No doubt when you finally get the thing in one piece and leaning like it's supposed to, you will recognise it. It's no good looking at a cultural treasure like this in bits, unless it's the Eiffel Coliseum, or something, which is way outside your price range, anyhow.

Yours,
Robert P. McCulloch.

Robert P. McCulloch,
McCulloch Corporation,
Los Angeles, Calif.

9th October

Dear Mr. McCulloch:

Never mind the cracks about my price range, I already had to pay out another fifty thousand bills to repair this thing which is beginning to cause adverse comment in our community, particularly from Jack Hammell, our foremost used car dealer and a person of some standing, who has been to Europe in both wars and reckons that what I have bought is the British Great Fire Monument, only the big brass ball is missing from the top, rendering it worthless in Jack's opinion, and mine, too, if you want to know. What we appear to have is the cheap part of a Leaning Great Fire Monument, and there ain't nobody going to pay good money to see that, especially as the only way we can get it to lean and stay up is by propping it against the Hogsnout Motor Inne, which has now been condemned as unfit for human habitation on account of it's got this giant thing leaning on it.

However, I do not wish to appear a sore loser. If you will agree to remove this item and replace it with something similar in a nice lightweight plastic, I am prepared to consider the matter closed.

Yours truly,
Simeon Hogsnout IV.

The Sanity Inspector

The Workers' Bag Is Deepest Red

"The Scottish council of the Labour Party today approved almost unanimously a policy for the complete nationalisation of the vast privately owned Highland estates and the salmon fisheries if a Labour government is returned to power."– The Times.

I followed the clerk down the eau-de-nil corridor and through a brown door marked FISH DIVISION: ENQUIRIES. Inside, a bald man sat at a steel desk beneath a wall-map of the Highlands pinned with tiny flags and a graph on which a curve plummeted into its lower margin.

"Man here wants to have a go at the salmon," said the clerk.

The bald man glanced at me over his bifocals.

"Where's your ferret?" he said.

"Ferret?" I said.

"Little bugger with short legs," said the clerk. "Can't half run, though."

"I know what a ferret is," I said. "But I'm after salmon. Ferrets go down rabbit holes."

"Funny place to look for salmon," said the clerk. "Still, it takes all sorts, that's what I always say."

"We can lease you a government ferret," said the bald man. He reached for a file, wet his thumb, began plucking forms out. "Need a 121/436/18g, a 72A/ff, and two pound deposit against loss or damage."

I cleared my throat.

"There seems to be some mistake," I said. "You don't catch salmon with ferrets."

282

"He's got a point," said the clerk. "They go down like stones." He indicated the graph. "Salmon production's been dropping off sunnink terrible lately."

"Who told you to use ferrets?" I asked.

The bald man tapped a thick grey-covered book beside his in-tray.

"Come down from Central Division," he said.

"We're radicalising," said the clerk. "And rationalising."

"Sounds to me as though they've got their lines crossed some-where," I said.

They looked at me.

"Troublemaker here," said the bald man.

"There's channels, you know," said the clerk.

"How you going to catch salmon, then," said the bald man, "without a ferret?"

"Flies," I said.

"Show him out, Sid," said the bald man.

"I don't understand," I said.

"We got work to do," said the bald man, "without come-dians."

"I'm serious," I said.

"Pull this one," said the clerk. "It's hard enough training ferrets to jump out of a boat, let alone flies."

"You'd open your jam jar," said the bald man, "and they'd be off. I know flies."

"Look," I said, "you do it with a rod and line. You tie the fly to the hook, you cast the line with the rod, you . . ."

"Ah," said the bald man. He nodded. "Cross purposes here, Sidney. I thought he was talking about salmon. It's grouse he's after."

"You should've said," said the clerk, irritably tearing up his half-filled forms and reaching for a new batch. "And it's not flies, it's worms you use for grouse."

"Don't be ridiculous," I said, "how can you catch a grouse with a worm?"

"Don't ask me," said the clerk, "you're supposed to be the sportsman. We only work here. On attachment."

"From Swindon," said the bald man. "Personally, I prefer trains. You know where you are with trains."

"We're working on a pilot project," said the clerk, "to put grouse on rails. It's up before the Recommendations & Amendments Committee. It could revolutionise the entire industry."

"You'd know when they was coming, then," said the bald man. "None of this hanging about with a worm on the end of a string. You'd just sit there with your timetable, and soon as the 8.40 grouse showed up, bang!"

"With your stick," said the clerk. "Any old stick. Think of the saving!"

"And once you had your rails laid," said the bald man "there's no end to the spin-offs. You could have a dog-track. There's all these hounds we've got, not doing nothing, just walking about and peeing against the van. Train 'em to run after a grouse, you got an entire leisure industry."

"It seems somewhat less than sporting," I said.

The bald man looked at the clerk.

"There's your private enterprise talking, Sidney," he said. "See what I mean? No grasp of basic concepts." He turned back to me. "You don't seem to realise," he said, "what the meat industry entails. Mouths to feed, son, mouths to feed. We got an output target of four million grouse this year. Going over to battery production in August. Biggest aluminium shed complex north of Doncaster."

I sighed.

"Not much sport there, I'm afraid," I said.

"Don't see why not," said the clerk. "You could help with the plucking."

"It's a far cry from shooting," I said.

"I thought we was talking about grouse," said the bald man. "Not trout."

"You *shoot* trout?"

He drew a large buff book from a shelf and threw it on the desk.

"Central Division Beige Paper," he said. "All in there. Results of the Research Division work-study. They went into

284

the question of how you catch these bleeders when they're only in the air about 1.8 seconds, on average. Tried holding nets over the streams, but they're too sharp. Time you've seen 'em and got your wrists going, they're back in the water again. Only way is to lie on the bank with shotguns, soon as they leap, you're on 'em."

"And how, exactly," I said, "do you bring them in?"

"Retrievers," said the clerk.

"Oh, come on." I cried. "Dogs will never go in after fish!"

"Cats will," said the bald man.

"Got him there, Harold!" said the clerk. "He'd never thought of cats."

"Private enterprise again, Sidney. In blinkers. Hidebound by tradition Good enough for daddy, it's good enough for me, what? This is 1971, mate!"

"4," said the clerk.

"1974," said the bald man.

"And how do you propose," I said, "to train cats to swim?"

"Listen," said the bald man. "If you can train flies, we can train bloody cats."

"I think I'll be going," I said, and stood up. They stared at my waders. "For trout," I explained.

"First good idea you've had," said the clerk. "The nettles are terrible."

"Hallo," said the bald man, glancing suddenly past us, and pushing his spectacles up his nose, "the stock's arrived." He rose.

I followed them to the window. Between the administration building, on the fourth floor of which we stood, and the Amalgamated Ghillie Union tower block opposite, ran a bright tarn that had risen in some now invisible mountain. Beside it, a dump truck was unloading a wriggling pile of small silver fish directly into the hurtling water. Upon entering which, they all turned belly-up. I peered, but we were fifty feet above.

"There's something wrong with those trout," I said.

"Shows how much *you* know," said the clerk. "They're pilchards."

"Calls himself a sportsman," said the bald man.

"But pilchards are saltwater fish!" I cried.

"And very popular, too," said the clerk. "On toast, with a bit of tomato sauce."

"But they're all dying!"

"So I should hope," said the bald man. "Easy to see he's never tried packing six pilchards in a tin, innit, Sidney?"

"If you did it his way," said the clerk, "it'd take six weeks to get the lid on. They hop about like nobody's business, pilchards."

"Prob'ly never seen a tin," said the bald man, jabbing a thumb at me. "His lot prob'ly hunt pilchards on horseback."

The clerk thought about this for a moment or two.

"Doubt it," he said at last, "you'd have a hell of a job aiming."

The bald man nodded, slowly.

"Common sense, really," he said.

The Sanity Inspector

Something About a Soldier

"A team of investigators has shown that of all the men who wear regimental ties, six in ten are probably impostors." – Daily Mirror.

THOMAS BREEN LAID his green leatherette sample-case carefully in the boot of the company Cortina; shut the lid; locked it. You couldn't be too careful, not with the electric toothbrushes. Valuable items like that, and the country the way it was, no morals any more and much of it black. He crossed the carpark, gravel grinding under his brogues, a march step, firm and dependable, can't beat good real leather on your soles, none of your pansy composite, and stepped, smartly, through the saloon lounge door, masculine stride across the figured pile, shoulders fat (but square) belly held in, small smile beneath the smaller moustache, and the wide green goldstriped tie trumpeting on his chest.

"Good morning, sir."

"It is, indeed! Bright. But not sunny. It'll be taking spin."

"Sir?"

"The wicket. Bit green after the rain. Taking spin. Definitely. Skittle 'em out by tea. Or soon after."

"What can I get you, sir?"

"Pink gin. Large."

Thomas Breen sniffed, twitched his bristles, cleared his throat.

"Ice?"

Short nod, chins interfolding briefly.

"Tight cap this, sir. Can't remember the last time I had to unscrew the pink. Customers don't seem to drink it these days."

"Old habit," said Breen. He chuckled. "Medicinal. Not," he added, leaning slightly towards the barman, humorously, "that there's much beri-beri round here, eh?"

"Sir?"

Breen slid the bitterness down his throat, and pushed his glass back across the counter.

"Army joke. Same again. Gin for the malaria, Angostura for the beri-beri. That's what we used to say. Bit before your time."

"I dare say, sir."

"White man's grave, Burma," said Breen, allowing his eyes to glaze. "But a clever little devil, your Jap. Get him in a corner, fights like a rat."

"Really, sir?"

"Like a ruddy rat. Have something yourself. Yes, many's the time I had to go in with cold steel and finish off some yellow johnny fighting on with half a dozen rounds still in him. Wouldn't lie down."

"Amazing."

"Wouldn't lie down. Once—I'm not boring you?—once, down near the Foonsang Delta, rainy season, my chaps were pinned down under a withering——"

Breen's voice frayed, and stopped. Beside him at the bar, a tall bony figure had materialised, grey-suited, with a tangerine rose in his buttonhole, yellow gloves. And a green goldstriped tie. The two men looked at one another, and the pupils ran around their eyes like trapped ants.

"I say!" said Breen.

"Ha, ha!" said the newcomer.

The barman smiled, with all the bonhomie of his calling.

"Here's a turn-up," he said. "Same regiment! This gentleman," he continued, drawing a beer for the newcomer, "was just telling me about your lot in Burma."

"Burma?" said the newcomer.

"Only there a week or so," said Breen quickly. "Didn't get much chance to meet anyone, ha-ha-ha! Went down with trench foot second week."

"Trench foot?"

"Mouth. Flown back to Catterick right away."

"Catterick, eh?"

"Only for the day. Baffled Medical Corps. Didn't see a soul I knew. Driven straight to an isolation unit."

The new man drank half his beer and put down the glass.

"Never saw Burma," he said. He took out a handkerchief and mopped his forehead, despite the coolness of the day. Breen unclenched his hands, and licked a bright bead from his moustache.

"Really?" he said. "Ah, well, they shipped me back there, soon as I'd recovered. Hardly saw anywhere else."

"Weren't in Libya, then?" said the new man.

"Libya?"

"Or do I mean Palestine? I mean, I do. I say, I reckon the old wicket's due to take a bit of spin this morning, don't you? Not that I think the Australians have sent us much of a——"

A third man entered; took off his coat; revealed a wide green gold-striped tie.

"Palestine, did you say?" he asked, looking at them uneasily.

"Libya, actually," said the second man quickly. "I was shorter then, of course. Sprang up after I was thirty. Fingleton," he added desperately, extending a wet hand.

"Breen," said Breen.

"Wittle," said the third man.

"Not Charlie Wittle," said Fingleton, "by any chance?"

"NO!" shouted Wittle. "I mean, no. No, they sent *Charlie* Wittle to Libya, I suppose, I mean yes, they did, I remember that on the postings, yes, he went to Libya, and I went to, er, Burma."

"There's a coincidence!" cried Fingleton. "Breen here——"

"Just missed you!" exclaimed Breen. "I remember, it was the day they were flying me home with foot and mouth, and they came in and said, there's a new chap just been sent out, chap called Wittle, pity you've missed him. That's what they said."

"Breen went back, though," insisted Fingleton, "after he was well."

"I would have been gone by then," said Wittle, hurling a large Scotch down his gullet, somewhat erratically.

"Yes!" shouted Breen, "I remember, I got off the plane, and they said, you've just missed Wittle again, he's gone. That's what they said."

"Did they?" enquired Wittle, staring at him. "Oh. Yes, well, I got posted back in time for Salerno."

Breen and Fingleton breathed out. Everyone smiled.

"Parachuted in," explained Wittle.

Everyone nodded. Fingleton bought another round.

"One of our regulars was at Salerno," said the barman pleasantly. "With your lot." Six eyes fixed on him from the rims of their drinks. "Major Moult. Often mentions—well, talk of the devil!"

"Breen," murmured Breen.

"Fingleton."

"Wittle."

"Moult."

"I was telling the gentlemen, Major," said the barman, taking Moult's pewter tankard from its hook, "about Salerno."

"Yes," said Breen, happily, "Wittle parachuted in, you know."

Moult looked at Wittle.

"I didn't know there were any parachute landings at Salerno," he said.

"Ah, well, you wouldn't, old man," said Wittle, laughing lightly, despite a shoeful of beer. "Typical RAF cock-up, ha-ha-ha! Wrong prevailing winds. All baled out over the jolly old target area, and landed forty miles away."

"I suppose you managed to make your way back to rejoin the regiment, though," said Fingleton, "didn't you, Wittle?"

"I would have been out of it by then," said Moult. "Got taken prisoner first day, shipped out to Deutschland, chop-chop."

"Not a POW of the Jerries, were you?" said a new voice.

The four men turned, to find a short wiry man in a camelhair coat and a brown fedora. Between the smooth lapels of the former gleamed two gold bars, on a green ground.

"I escaped almost immediately," said Moult, very loudly. "Why did they get you, Mr.——"

"Binns. Didn't they get any of the rest of you, then?"

The others shook their heads.

"They got me, all right," said Binns confidently. "In Libya."

"Fingleton was in Libya," said Wittle.

"Yes," said Fingleton, "I came after you were captured. Got sent out from Palestine to replace you. Jerry's got Binns, they said. You'll have to go out to Libya. That's what they said."

Binns looked at him.

"You sure they said Binns?" he said.

Fingleton eased his tie-knot.

"Er, yes," he muttered. "Go out and replace, er, Erasmus Binns."

A shadow lifted from Binns's face.

"Different chap," he said. "I'm *Arthur* Binns. Not, of course," he added hurriedly, "that I haven't heard of Erasmus Binns."

"Have you?" asked Fingleton.

"Of course, he wasn't in Libya at the *exact* same time as I was," said Binns. "I think he was in Burma, then."

"That's it!" cried Fingleton. "He was in Burma before he went to Libya and got captured and put in a POW camp."

"After I'd escaped," said Moult.

"He was probably in Burma about the time you were," said Fingleton to Breen.

"Just missed him," said Breen. "I remember, it was the week I got dysentery, after I got back from Catterick and missed Wittle again. You've just missed Erasmus Binns, they said. As I got off the plane. They've sent him to Libya, they said."

"Terrible thing, Burmese dysentery."

"Who said that?" shrieked Breen, knocking over his fourth gin.

"I did."

The group was joined by a large bald man in a black jacket, set off with green and goldstriped tie. Breen grabbed his sleeve.

"They cocked up my diagnosis!" he shouted. "What I actually had was phosgene poisoning. Not like you at all. Nothing like it."

"I wasn't in Burma," said the bald man carefully.

"None of us were in Palestine," offered Moult.

"I would have seen you if you had been," said the bald man. "I was there for the duration."

"Fingleton said he'd been in Palestine," said Breen. "Didn't you?"

"No! Libya. With the other Wittle, not this one. Erasmus Wittle. If I said Palestine, I meant I'd *passed through it*. At night. On the train."

"I recall that train," said the bald man, licking a dry lip. "I remember someone saying, Fingleton's on that train. Going to Libya."

"That's it!" cried Fingleton. "That's exactly it!"

The bar clock struck three.

"Time please, gentlemen," said the barman.

The six, as one man, flung themselves at the door, bound for their cars and freedom. Their escape, however, was cut off by a group of four men, waiting quietly outside the saloon bar: two had lost a leg, a third had an empty sleeve pinned across his chest, and was playing *Tipperary*, one-handed, on a harmonica, to the banjo accompaniment of the men on crutches. A fourth man held a white stick in one hand, and a collection box in the other. All wore campaign stars; and wide green goldstriped ties.

Fingleton pulled Breen towards him.

"Look at that," he muttered. "Begging!"

"Disgusting!" said Breen. He felt for his car-keys. "Don't know what the Regiment's coming to."

All Except The Bastard

This Don For Hire

'Literary scholarship is now a territory occupied or disputed by hard professionals, most often working in academic teams. The days of the free-ranging individual critic, the literary dilettante, the man untied to university departments or Schools of Thought, seem to have gone.'—New York Times

I OPENED THE THIRD DRAWER, left, of my old roll-top desk, the drawer with the gummed label on it that read: PUNCTUATION IN THE LATIN COMEDIES OF ABRAHAM COWLEY, and I moved the dirty manuscript aside and took out the bottle of Cutty Sark, and I poured myself a shot, and I looked at it, and I wondered about when *shot* had come into the language to mean a slug of booze, and since it wasn't in the old beat-up volumes of the OED that stood on the tin shelf behind the desk I thought about writing to John Sykes who would be putting together the S supplement any day now, say by around 1995, just in case there was folding money in it, but then I figured what the hell, he probably has a whole damn OUP team working on the word right now. Computers, teletype, all that.

Then I started wondering about *slug*.

That's the thing with semantics. It can drive you crazy. Some nights I lie awake, smoking and wondering about the derivation of *okay*, watching the neons flashing on and off across the street from my room. I thought about writing to *Notes & Queries* once, they pay up to fifty pee for good paragraphs about *okay*, but then I got side-tracked into thinking about *neon* and how it derived from the Gk, and maybe we ought to change the name, because it wasn't such a new gas any more. Call it *archaion*.

That's the thing with logic. It can drive you crazy. It's all right if you work for one of the big research outfits, ten guys from Harvard putting together a definitive edition of Harrison Ainsworth's letters, a hot trio of Balliol Junior Fellows collaborating on sources and analogues of *Gammer Gurton's Needle*, you have people to talk to, you can delegate, you get fat retainers.

It beats scratching for literary scraps on your own, in a ten-pound-a-week bedsitter on the Iffley Road. I poured another two fingers. I wondered about a short paper on *Drinking Metaphor: Notes Towards A Critical Collation*; if I couldn't interest *Encounter*, there was always *The Licensed Victualler*. Maybe they had an up-market section of readership, college maunciples, say, or *Gawayne* scholars who'd opened nightclubs when the bottom dropped out of Middle English a year or so back.

I put the bottle back in my drawer; a drop of amber stained the title page of my MS, but rapidly absorbed itself without trace in the yellowed paper. It had been around a long time, and stood no chance of publication now, despite the fact that I had taken a whole new line on Cowley's capricious use of the semi-colon: punctuation-wise, *Naufragium Joculare* was a mess, but the world would have to remain ignorant of the truth.

Until, that is, some bunch of Yale hustlers wormed fifty grand out of the Ford Foundation, snatched my idea, and put it out in some coffee-table deal with Harper & Row and NBC, introduced by Alistair Cooke, drawings by Hockney.

I was still staring at the drawer when the door opened and a very expensive smell came in. I looked up.

She was the sort of dame that makes the topless towers of Ilium feel they're on borrowed time.

'It says PRIVAT SCOLAR on the door,' she said huskily. 'It doesn't give a client a lot of confidence.'

'Yeah,' I said, 'I know. It also says I have a Ph.G. You know what good signwriters cost these days?'

'I know what top literary critics cost,' she said. 'That's why I came to you.'

'Gee, thanks,' I said.

'I saw your ad in the TLS,' she said, loosening her tippet so that the fox's face slid off her bust. It had my sympathy. 'I have a problem.'

Sure, I thought, it can't be easy getting through Daddy's allowance when the world was so full of guys stepping on each

293

other to buy you all the jewellery you needed. I didn't say anything, though.

'I'm in my final year at St. Hugh's,' she said. 'I have to get a good degree this summer, or my old man will go bananas. I could lose the Porsche.'

'The quality of mercy,' I quipped, 'you win a few, you . . .'

'What?'

'Forget it,' I said. Kids today, what do they know? 'How can I help?'

'I'm working on Crabbe,' she said.

'That figures,' I said, eyeing her Gucci shoes, her Ken Lane choker. 'Me, I get by on pie and peas from the chippy downstairs. Two nations, like Disraeli said.'

'*George* Crabbe. I opted for this special paper, right? If I do well in that, I thought, it might just help me get by without all this Anglo-Saxon junk, Spenser, Milton. The thing about Crabbe is there isn't much of him, you could read it all up in a couple of days.'

'Who is this you of whom you speak, doll?' I enquired.

'You is this you,' she replied. She opened her purse. 'I have a hundred green ones against a real hot essay delivered this time next week on the subject: *George Crabbe: Last of the Augustans or first of the Romantics?* Here's fifty on account.'

I folded the money.

'Why that particular question?' I asked.

'It's the only one they ever set,' she replied.

The Bodleian Library is a tough place to work. You get your head down, you try to concentrate, but all you hear is these fishnet thighs rasping together. Broads going up to the desks, broads going into the stacks, broads taking a coffee break.

I stuck to it, though. I had my head into *The Village*, and my right hand was filling foolscap faster than a bookie's clerk on Derby Day. Then I felt them come up behind me. I hadn't heard them. No fishnet.

I looked up. They were two of the biggest critics I'd ever seen. Heads like tombstones. One of them leaned across and picked up the book. He dropped it to the floor, and stepped on it.

'Oh, I'm sorry,' he said. 'It looked such a nice book, too.'

'It was okay,' I said. 'It did the job.'

'That's what we'd like to talk about,' said the other hood. He put his hand on my shoulder. It was like carrying an iron epaulette.

We stood outside, on the dark staircase.

'We hear you've been asking questions about Crabbe,' said one.

'I have an enquiring mind,' I said.

'Yeah. The thing is, Charlie and I and a couple of other guys from Cornell just happen to be working on Crabbe. We're taking fifteen grand a year each out of Guggenheim. The Fellowship would like to know whether he was the last of the Augustans or the first of the Romantics.'

'What have you found out?' I said.

'Nothing,' said the first.

'We'd like it to stay that way,' said the second. 'It's nice here in Oxford. The river, the au pairs, all that.'

He was standing behind me. I should have known better than to let that happen. I heard the swish as his arm came back.

A black pit opened up, and I fell in.

I walked into Blackwell's bookshop. It's a tense place at the best of times: always a lot of Christ Church muscle about, black belts from Durham, guys with Arts Council grants and lumps in their armpits. They work in teams, you ask for a new book on Spenser's debt to Ariosto, first thing you know you're looking for teeth all over the Children's Section.

I had a lump on my head, and my mouth felt like an emeritus philologist had curled up and died in it, but I went up to the counter anyway, and I asked for everything they had on Crabbe. The girl went pale. I saw her nod, but not whom to.

'I'm sorry,' she said. 'We have no books by or about any person of that name.'

'Come on!' I cried. 'Be serious! *George* Crabbe, last of the Augustans? Or, to put it another way, first of the . . .'

'You heard what the lady said, Mac.'

I turned around, slow. I had to look up a long way. I'd seen the face around, *The Book Programme, Read All About It, Parkinson*; he had a Jap with him. The Jap smiled; he had steel teeth.

'You did that book on Southey,' I said, pleasantly enough. 'Dennis Potter got a fifteen-part serial out of it. You're the Professor of Poetry at . . .'

'This is Doctor Sun,' he said. 'He handles the Japanese end. It leaves him a lot of time for his hobby.'

'What does he do?' I said.

'He breaks things.'

'Blicks,' said Doctor Sun. 'Clitics. You name it.'

'I'm working on Crabbe right now,' said the Professor of Poetry. 'Goodbye.'

I walked out of the bookshop. The fresh air felt good. For about two seconds. That's how long it took for the black sedan to pull away from the kerb. I hurled myself sideways. There were twenty years of scholarship in that hurl.

When I got up again, there was a cop standing beside me. The car was long gone.

'Leavisites,' I said. I dusted my fedora. 'They don't give up easy.'

'I didn't see a thing,' said the cop.

He walked away.

I watched him go. This is a stinking city, I thought. All the rottenness ends up here.

There was nothing left in the Cutty Sark bottle when she came in, but I didn't care. She was in to me for a torn patella, a busted septum, and two bicuspids that had still had a lot of tread left on them; that was enough hospitality for one week.

'Did you do it?' she said.

I threw the big envelope on the desk. She opened it.

'What's this?' she said, after a moment or two.

'It's all you ever need to know about punctuation in the Latin comedies of Abraham Cowley,' I said.

'It isn't what I asked for,' she said.

I smiled. It hurt my face.

'You just described life,' I said. 'Maybe Oxford can still teach a thing or two, after all.'

The Rhinestone As Big As The Ritz

French Leave

October 26 having been designated Au Pair Day, I couldn't help wondering how the average girl would spend it.

SUNDAY, OCTOBER 26

Allo, mah diary! Nem of a dog, but wot a day ah em avving! Ow lucky ah em zat tomorro eez mah day off and Tuesday eez mah arf day and Wednesday eez mah free morning, uzzerwise ah wood nevair be fit for mah rest day on Sursday weech ah nid to, ow you say, set mi up for zer wikkend.

Bicause today eez National Au Pair Day, Mistair Griswole bring mi up breakfuss in bed. Normally, eet eez Missus Griswole oo bring eet up, but hi explane where today eez a special occasion, also Missus Griswole feelin very weery wot weeth zer ousework zer cheeldren zer washin zer ironin zer shoppin, on top of havin to shorten mah frok for Au Pair Day an clin mah bes shoes good.

Aftair brekfuss, ah tek a nise ot barf until aroun arf past ten, but holy blue! Imagin mah surprise wen ah open zer barfroom dor aftairwards an oo shuld fall on mi but Mistair Griswole oo ave fall aslip leenin on zer dor! Hi eez very apologisin, but ah cri: 'Zink nussin of eet, Mistair Griswole, you can grab mah ches anytime, ha-ha-ha!' This mek Mistair Griswole go orible wite an weespair: 'For God's sake kip your voise down, Nicole, ah weel len you car, ah weel by you beeg botl of Chanel!'

Poor Mistair Groswole! Hi nid to tek barf bicause hi covaired in blak dus from bringin in cole (wich eez normly Missus Griswole's job), but hi fine no ot watair no more, so he spen nex arf our running up an down stairs wiz ketls.

Eet is amazin ow hi kip his tempair, wot wiz zer cheeldren scrimmin for their breakfuss an zer dog owlin to bi let out an Missus Griswole obblin about lookin for her migrane pils an zer telephone ringin all zer time. Ah sink ah weel ave to ave mah own phone put in: zer calls are always for mi, an eet eez a terrible waste of time for zer Griswoles to kip runnin up to mah room wiz messages wen they bofe ave so much to do aroun zer ouse.

Mine you, mah diary, ah wonder sometimes eef they do not tek advantage. Only yesterday, wen she was polishin mah dressin-table, Missus Griswole ask me eef ah em available for baby-sittin on December 19. 'Missus Griswole!' ah exclem. 'Ow on erse can ah know wot ah weel be doin two ole munce from now?'

Enyway, at eleven o'clock zis mornin, ah set off to meet wiz mah frens to celebrate Au Pair Day: first, wi are to attend a church in Ampstead Garden Suburb where special prayers are offaired to zer Blessed Françoise, Patron Saint of Au Pairs, who drop ded in 1574 wen someone ask her to scrub a flor. Wi are all there, but Ilse mah bes frend eez a litle late bicause her employer, Mistair Dickinson, ave back his car into zer wall wen gettin eet out to give her a lift, an Ilse ave to ang about for ages while Mistair Dickinson run to zer top of zer road to fine a taxi.

Aftair church, Ilse's boy fren come by in his car to drive us up to town. Lefty eez a nise boy, excep he only ave one eer an his noze eez flat; he eez very genrous, an evry time me or Ilse or any of our frens tell im anything, such as wen our employers are goin off on ollyday or oo kip zer key on a string inside zer letter-box or wich florboard you ave to lift up to find zer coco tin wiz zer diamonds in it, Lefty always give er sumsing good for erself, like a candelabra or a nise bag of led. Eet eez a bit crowded in Lefty's car, tho, bicause he already ave three Spanish au pairs in zer back wich he eez deliverin to customers of his escort service. Zer girls are all shiverin a bit, wot wiz wearin only fishnet stockins an raincoats, but Lefty soon cheer them up tellin them about how he settin up zis feelm wiz Robert Redford nex Friday an all of them goin to be big stars.

Well, mah diary, Lefty drop Ilse an me off in Arley Strit where zer Portland Clinique is givin a beeg celebration lunch in honneur of Au Pair Day, jus as a way of saying Sank You to all customers ole an new, includin all our frens in zer cab trade, an mah secon-best fren Gracia turn out to be zer gest of honneur. She mek a spich in wich she say zat wizzout zer Portland an eets wonderful staff, she would now be a muzzer of fourteen, an ze thought mek her go deezy bicause everybody know ow difficult eet eez to get staff these days!

Evryone larf very loud at zis. Gracia eez a one, an no mistek! Ah fil sure she could ave a marvellous career on zer stage, eef only she did not ave her art set on marryin into zer rag trade. Las year she come very close to pullin eet off wiz a very nise guy oo ave a Lamborghini Espada an a yacht an eez a director of eighteen blouse companies, only his father fine out about eet an say zer guy eez too yung to marry at fourteen, an punch his hed.

Aftair lunch, mah diary, we pay a viseet to zer Home Office Au Pair Exhibition in Whitehall where we lissen to a very interestin lecture from a lawyer who explen ow we mus not let ourselves be exploits, an zen we look at all zer exhibits like zer new 45-inch colour TV etcetera, but ah do not sink ah weel ask zer Griswoles for one bicause eet do not ave a remote control attachment an ah do not weesh to be jumpin out of my barf all zer time to change channels. Personally, ah prefair zis new push-chair wiz zer 125cc moteur, eet tek al zer effort out of shoppin wiz zer cheeldren an Missus Griswole weel ave energy lef to cook an ot lunch wen she get ome. Ah do not mine smoke sammon an cole duk, but not evry day. Ilse say she most impressed wiz zer new range of baby-bouncers wich ave been specialy strengthened to tek all cheeldren up to zer age of seexteen. As her employer ave five, Ilse weel be able to string zem all up after breakfuss and leave zem danglin wile she get on wiz her correspondence.

By zer time we come out of zer exhibition, eet eez gettin dark, an Ilse suggest we see one of zer feelms zat zer Soho Sexima eez puttin on in honneur of zer occasion. Eet turn out to be *Swidish Au Pair Nude Leather Wikkend A-Go-Go;* eet eez quite interestin, but for me eet eez spoil by zer prepostrous fantasie: at zer start of zer feelm, we see Ingrid dustin an polishin! Ah ave a good mine to write to mah Ambassadeur an complain: zis kine of feelm weel put bad ideas into people's heds.

Aftair zer feelm, we fine ourselves at a loose end: shall we go to zer Eurofunky Disco An Engleesh Language Collidge in Regent Strit? Aftair all, Mistair Griswole ave already pay zer ninety pound for zis term wich include entry fee to all social functions, but wen ah suggest to Ilse zat we drop in for a smoke, she tel me zat zer collidge ave bin busted las wik on account of zer Eadmaster ave bin caught in possession, also police lookin into zer fac zat Missus Ogalidogliou, zer Matron, ave not return from Beirut wiz her party of twelve Norwegian girls.

'Wot about zer Manila Nitespot?' suggest Ilse, but ah tel her ah cannot stand zis place bicause zer Filipinos always go aroun in couples an knife anyone oo look like they could be competition for a nise self-contain flat over the garage.

So we end up back at Gracia's ouse in Souse Kensington. She ave chuck out her employers for zer wikkend an lock zer kids in zer cellar an call up Fortnum an Mason to wizz roun a few dozen lobstaire an pâté de foie gras an so on, an wot weeth her boy frens knowin ow to jemmy open a cocktail cabinet, evrybody avin a wonairful time an not realisin ow late it get until zer Fire Brigade turn up an complen about bein call out at four a.m. jus to put out a blazin Picasso, an why could not someone simply chuck a bucket of watair over it, but Gracia explainin zat she do not know where zer buckets are kept, so it turns out all right aftair all.

Mine you, mah diary, Mistair Griswole eez also a beet put out to be call at arf past five to tek me ome, but wen ah point out zat ah em jus a simple country girl oo eez afraid of wanderin about zer beeg city alone, ah sink he understand.

The Lady From Stalingrad Mansions

A Short History Of Insurance

1. THE DAWN OF INSURANCE

It is impossible, naturally, to fix a date for the birth of
insurance; but most authorities agree that it was probably
discovered by accident, the favoured theory being that our early
ancestors found, upon rubbing two sticks together, that their
tree burned down.

There are also cave-paintings which show men running after
buffalo, and some anthropologists maintain that the men are
attempting to interest the buffalo in a policy insuring them
against extinction, while the buffalo are running away on the
grounds that they already carry enough insurance, but this is at
present only informed speculation.

2. INSURANCE IN THE NILE DELTA

Around 5000 BC, the first Egyptian and Mesopotamian
settlements were founded. Their inhabitants were roughly
divided into two kinds: those who thought that, after death, you
came back as a cat; and those who thought you didn't come
back at all. As a result of this, life insurance took two forms: the
normal With Profits policy, by which the family of the bereaved
were guaranteed, on his death, a continuous supply of fish; and,
a new invention, an Annuity maturing in old age which
provided the insured with gold pots, pans, spoons, etcetera
which he could put in his sarcophagus to await his demise,
whereupon they would all cross The Great Divide together and
he could set up home in some style.

As you know, many of these tombs were subsequently
robbed, usually by the families who had only been left fish.

3. THE POLICIES OF THE ALMIGHTY

It was about this time, too, that the Children of Israel first appeared on the insurance scene, introducing the myriad complications that remain to this day and which gave original rise to the All Risks Policy. As you know, the Almighty (in an uncharacteristic lapse from His infinite wisdom) gave an early assurance to His people of overall cover, not realising at the time that they were as accident-prone a race as you could come across in a month of Sundays, all right, Saturdays.

As a consequence, He was constantly intervening in their disordered lives in a desperate running attempt to remain solvent: had Noah's family not had advanced warning of unseasonal weather, for example, the compensation would have been astronomical, and who would have thought when assessing the actuarial odds and thereby arriving at a negligible premium, that someone would actually end up in the belly of a whale? Exegeticists who have sought explanations in natural law for the parting of the Red Sea need look no further, once they have totted up the pay-out on forty thousand accidental drownings. The Egyptians, of course, were not covered for the loss of their entire armed forces, and are still, sixty centuries later, trying to catch up. Even now, the Russians will not cover them in the event of TK-47's being taken any nearer than twenty kilometres from deep water.

The result of these early experiences has been, in our day, the Act Of God designation on all insurance policies; which means, roughly, that you cannot be insured for the accidents that are most likely to happen to you. If your ox kicks a hole in your neighbour's Maserati, however, indemnity is instantaneous.

4. THE FIRST GOLDEN AGE

" 'The hour of departure has arrived, and we go our ways – I to die, and you to live. Which is the better, God only knows.' "

And with these words, Socrates bade them remove from him, and they went apart in sorrow and left him. And when a messenger came to tell them that Socrates was dead, they stood about, and many wept, and Glaucus, senior of the disciples and most beloved, uncovered his face at last and said:

"One good thing, there's a policy in my name."

And Epidomus said:

"That's better than a poke in the eye with a sharp stick."

But in the late forenoon, Socrates's broker came to Glaucus

and said that he was sorry to have to inform him that, Socrates having taken his own life with a draught of hemlock, the policy was null and void. He then referred Glaucus to Section Four, Paragraph Nine.

Whereupon Glaucus turned upon him in rage and argued that Socrates had not committed suicide voluntarily but had been directed to do so by the State.

So the broker referred Glaucus to Section Eight, Paragraph Five.

And Glaucus beat his breast and cried:

"I have sat at that old bugger's feet these thirty years when I could have been out enjoying myself, and I have never understood a bloody word he said, and now you tell me I was on a hiding to nothing, what kind of business are you running here?"

And the broker said:

"Glaucus, in a republic, do we feel it advances the good to allow benefit to accrue to the bad even though the bad are beyond the advantage of the benefit and have therefore endowed the benefit to the good?"

And Glaucus said:

"You know what *you* can do."'

PLATO, *Apologia*

5. MOTOR INSURANCE IN THE FIRST CENTURY AD
When King Prasutagas died in AD 61, the territory of the Iceni was violently annexed by Rome, and his queen, Boudicca, was raped. Enraged, Boudicca raised the whole of South-East England in revolt against their Roman conquerors, fitted scythe-blades to the wheels of her army's chariots, and drove them through the ranks of her enemies.

Subsequently apprehended and charged with (1) Exceeding XVIII mph in a built-up area, (2) Driving without due care and attention, and (3) Failing to observe the right of way, Boudicca was then issued with some three thousand writs for actual damages by solicitors acting on behalf of the maimed Roman infantry.

Upon contacting her insurance company, she was informed, regretfully, that by making modifications to her vehicles without previously informing the company of her intention to do same, the company had no other course but to declare in-valid the Third Party liability. The subsequent proceedings resulted in a bill for damages amounting to £8,731,267, a sum utterly beyond the reach of the British, who, then as now, had only the woad they stood up in.

The Romans thought about this for a bit, and decided that their best course of action would be to annihilate the British somewhere between London and Chester.

An interesting sidelight on this affair is that the Romans also learned a lesson from it, which was that the chariot need not be just a way of getting you there and bringing you back, but also a weapon in its own right. Even today, only 19% of pedestrians setting out to cross the Via del Corso get to the other side.

6. 1066: THE GREAT LEAP FORWARD
Insurance came of age on the beach at Hastings, when King Harold, who carried today's equivalent of £100,000 in Personal Disability insurance, was shot in the eye by a Norman bowman firing through a narrow slit in the defence wall.

His queen immediately contacted the insurance company, enclosing a plan as required by the claim form showing the path of the arrow. The insurers examined the policy for some days and were growing desperate at their inability to find a way of legitimately welshing on the deal when one of their younger colleagues noticed a gap in the defences, which were, of course, Harold's responsibility.

'Here,' he said, 'if that wasn't there, the arrow'd never have got through!'

And thus it was that *loophole* entered the history of insurance, since which time it has gone from strength to strength.

7. THE MODERN ERA
The Modern Era, or Golden Age, of insurance can be said to have been ushered in by the birth, in 1623, of Josiah Smallprint. Son of a Linconshire pharmacist, young Josiah spent his early years amusing himself among his father's alembics and phials. It was thus, on November 18, 1641, that he stumbled upon an ink which could be put onto paper by type, but which remained invisible until the paper was put at the back of a drawer. Upon removing the paper from the drawer and examining it again,

304

the owner found it to carry all sorts of information hitherto un-noticed.

The first example of Josiah's handiwork to be used commer-cially was the phrase '. . . always provided that a pig flew past at the time the accident occurred'.

There is a statue to Josiah, 1st Baron Smallprint, in the foyer of Policymonger's Hall.

The Lady From Stalingrad Mansions

A Life On The Rolling Mane

"The National Federation of Hairdressers has pledged itself to stamp out what it calls Pirate Barbers." – The Guardian.

I take up my pen in the year of grace 197–, and go back to the time when my father kept the Maison Benbow Gents Salon and the brown old barber with the razor scar first hove to under our roof.

I remember him as if it were yesterday, as he came plodding in beneath our creaking pole and threw himself thankfully into the Number One chair, calling for a glass of our best bay rum. A man who had seen better times, he was topped now with an ill-fitting Fortescue Hairette wig; his once-natty pencil moustache was nicotine-stained and asymmetrical, his nose-hairs blew unplucked in the fan-breeze, and his fine chin was a-pimple from the myriad nicks of a thousand unhoned blades. But, from the black and broken nails, and the tufts of hair that spilled from his turnups, and his habit of flicking himself, as he sat, with a greasy grey tea-towel, I could tell that here was a master barber of the old school.

He grasped the bay rum from my hand and tossed it back with a single action, massaging it into his dewigged dome with a free hand and a grateful sigh.

"Ah, that were good, laddie!" he cried. "Just the thing for an ole barberman on a cole morning! What be the name on ye, boy?"

"Jim, sir," I said. "Jim Hawkins."

He settled back, and closed his eyes.

"I see Huddersfield lost again, Jim," he murmured.

"Aye, sir," said I, "but what do 'ee think of the Common Market, then?"

"Nobbut bad'll come of 'er, Jim lad," he said. "But I likes the look o' the new Morris Minor."

"Put your money on Fair Folly," said I. "White City, eight o'clock."

"Warm for the time o' year," he answered. He sighed. "It's good to talk to a barberin' man again, Jim. Give us another bay rum, and put a drop o' summat in her, if you know what I mean, heh-heh-heh!"

I spiked his glass with a dash of friction rub, and his old eyes lit up.

"Ye've the makings of a master barber, Jim," said he. "I were a young shampoo boy meself once, Jim, proud, ambitious —not that ye'd reckon it, to look at me now. I seen 'ard times, Jim. Ye'd never think I was once master o' me own shop, a fine three-chairer, backwash basins gleaming like a virgin's teeth, a fine head o' steam in the ole steriliser and them new steel combs a-bobbin' . . ."

"Wonderful," said I, "I wouldn't give tuppence for Ted Heath's chances."

"Traffic's terrible this morning," said he. "Aye, three chairs and used to manufacture my own 'air-oil, too. Master of the brilliantine *Morning Rose*, that was yours truly, Jim."

"The *Morning Rose!*" I cried.

"You'm 'eard of her, then?" said he.

"Who hasn't?" I watched his face grow sad a thousand times in the swinging mirrors. "But what happened?" I asked.

"I got took!" he muttered bitterly. Suddenly, he swung round. "Watch out for a hairfaring man wi' one leg, Jim! Make sure yer shutters is locked tight a-nights! Keep a good razor by 'ee and doan ever—*what's that?*"

I listened, as he half-rose from the chair, and I heard it, too. Tap-tap-tap. Tap-tap-tap.

" 'Tis Bald Pew!" screamed the old barber. He turned, and his trembling finger pointed. There, at the point where the frosted glass of my father's shopfront joined the clear glass

307

above, came slowly a seemingly disembodied white dome, like a huge darning mushroom. We could not see the face beneath, that moved, an eery shadow, along the frosting, nor the thing that tapped his creeping progress.

The old barber grasped my arm.

"That be his tail-comb, Jim!" he hissed. "A turrible thing! I seen Bald Pew kill three customers wi' that sharpened tail of his, just on account of them not wanting a two-bob singe!"

And, flinging the sheet from his throat, he was out of the chair in a trice, and gone! So intent was I thereafter in staring at the livid dome that had paused outside, I did not notice the new figure who had suddenly materialised in the doorway. When he spoke, I jumped for my life.

"Ahar, Jim lad!" he cried, and I looked, and I saw, and a cold sweat broke out upon my brow. It was he! He stood there, resting on his mahogany leg, a twisted smile upon his evil lip, and a mangy parrot coughing on his shoulder. I cannot say how long I stood in silence; but, at last, I unfroze my limbs.

"H-how do you know my name?" I asked.

He grinned a horrible grin, and swung himself into the shop.

"I make enquiries, Jim lad, doan I? I knows where the best shampoo boys is to be found, heh-heh! Silver's the name, Jim, Cap'n Silver, on account of what the customers 'as to cross my palm with, if they doan want to carry 'ome their ears in a cardboard box, heh-heh-heh!" He nodded his great head towards the parrot. "And this here's Cap'n Skint."

"*Will there be anything else, sir?*" shrieked the parrot. "*Will there be anything else?*"

"Got 'im nice and trained, ain't I, Jim?" cried Silver. He stumped closer. "Like all my bonny boys," he cackled. A great hand fell on my shoulder. "I come for 'ee, Jim lad! 'Tis a great opportunity for a boy!"

I turned, such was my innocence, to indicate the shop.

"But I have a position, sir, and I do not wish—"

I got no further. I felt a terrible blow upon my head, and a deep blackness rose inside me, and I knew no more.

It was the jolting that awoke me. Wherever I was, it was moving. I opened my eyes, and found myself—in a barber's shop! But such a barber's shop as I had never looked upon: small, filthy, its mirrors cracked and yellowed, its walls hung with tattered magazines of a like no Christian man could look upon unblushing. Rickety cabinets held objects I had never before set eyes on, strange oils and unguents and packages, and little booklets bound in cellophane. Two old bentwood chairs had been nailed to the floor, and two galvanised pails clanged from wallnails in front of them. Three of the most villainous looking men I have ever seen sat on a chest at one end, drinking from a jug. One lacked an ear, another an eye, the third had but six fingers. And then I heard the dread voice of Silver.

"I see you'm lookin' over the staff, Jim lad!" he roared. "Ain't they as pretty a bunch as you ever did clap yer lights on, heh-heh-heh! They got that way from practisin', Jim. I likes 'em to keep their 'ands in, doan I, when business is slack?"

"*Will there be anything else, sir?*" screamed Captain Skint. "*Will there be anything else?*"

"What does that mean, sir?" I asked.

The staff laughed horribly, nudging one another, and rolling with the motion of the shop.

"There's a lot ye got to learn about the good shop *Hispaniola*, Jim lad!" cried Silver. "But Long John'll teach 'ee, woan I?"

"Why are we moving?" said I.

"We'm aboard a mobile salon, Jim," said he, "bound for the rich pickings of Morplesden Tradin' Estate. 'Course, to the casual eye, we'm just an artickilated removal van, ain't we, till we strikes our colours, heh-heh. *Belay there!*"

At his bellow, the crew, who had begun picking one another's scalps, sprang apart.

"Alopecia, Jim," explained Silver. "Drives 'em mad, sometimes. That and the dermatitis. 'Tis the freebooter's curse, Jim. But doan ever let me catch 'ee scratchin' in front o' the customers, Jim, or I'll 'ave yer tongue for stropping. Likewise peeing in they pails: if I hears that tinkling in the middle o' the night,

I'll know what to do, woan I, lads? We'm turned more'n one promising baritone into a boy soprano, ain't we, heh-heh-heh!"

I shuddered, but the grace of God saved me from further vile reflection, for at that very moment there came a great shout from up for'ard.

"Customers onna starboard bow!"

Silver sprang to his foot, and slid back the hatchway separating the salon from the helmsman's cabin. In the tiny rectangle, I could see the serried alloy roofs winking in the spring sun, and my nostrils caught the fresh tang of light industrial air. With a shout of joy, Silver snatched an old scrap of AA book from his pocket and stabbed his filthy finger at it.

" 'Tis Morplesden, me hearties! Rich pickings, and nary a landlubbing coiffeur for twenty mile! Full ahead, Mister MacSwine, and strike the colours!"

The great salon yawed, rattling the jars and bottles, and swung off the main lane and down a little gravelly creek, as the crew poked open a hatch in the roof and ran up the barber's pole and the three Open-For-Business flags. Within minutes, we had dropped anchor, and the crew were swarming to the tailboard gunwale. Silver grabbed a weapon from its hook, and rubbed the dandruff from it with a filthy cloth. He clicked it once or twice beneath my nose.

"Remember the days of the great clippers, Jim!" he cried, his mad eyes blazing. "No, 'course you don't, young sprat like 'ee! Werl, there's no electrics aboard the *Hispaniola*, lad, and ye can lay to that! Craftsmen, ain't we, me hearties?"

The vile crew cheered through the scissors clenched in their ochre teeth. Silver banged his peg-leg against the tail-board.

"Lower a cutter!" he cried.

One of the men stepped forward, brandishing his scissors, leapt ashore, and made off towards the colony at a brisk trot. Within minutes, he reappeared, leading a column of hirsute dots.

"Stand by to fleece boarders!" cried Silver. "And just 'ee remember, not a man-jack of 'em as goes back wi'out restyling, blow waves, shave, shampoo, singe, manicure, pedicure, 'ot

310

towels, and a large carton of anything else, if 'ee doan want to end up in Maison Davy Jones, heh-heh-heh!"

As the thin line of innocent natives approached the *Hispaniola*, a shaving-mug was thrust into my hand.

"Get a-latherin', Jim lad!" cried Silver. "I wants it slapped on 'em as they step aboard, doan I, afore they 'as time to say no. Good gobful of foamy Sunlight allus keeps 'em quiet fer a bit, and—*hell fire and damnation!*"

He sprang back, whipping a cut-throat from his belt, and as he cleared the light I saw an orange minivan come streaking towards us, honking its horn, and flashing its bow lights!

" 'Tis Sanitary Inspecker Trelawney, lads!" roared Silver, and at his cry the crew sprang back from the tail-board and began hauling down our colours. The cutter broke into a sprint, leaving the bewildered natives, and flung himself over our stern.

"Up anchor!" screamed Silver, "'Tis six months wi'out the option, this time!"

And before I could prepare myself, the great salón lurched from her moorings, hurling me over the stern, and onto the verge! When I recovered my senses, the *Hispaniola* was no more than a distant speck on the shimmering horizon.

I never saw her again.

Nor never shall. Oxen and wain-ropes would not bring me back again to that accursed spot; and the worst dreams that I ever have are when I hear the boom of the scurf, or start upright in my bed with the sharp voice of Captain Skint still ringing in my ears: "*Will there be anything else, sir? Will there be anything else?*"

The Sanity Inspector

The Hell at Pooh Corner

From Christopher Robin Milne's recent autobiography, it turns out that life in the Milne household was very different from what millions of little readers have been led to believe. But if it was grim for him, what must it have been like for some of the others involved? I went down to Pooh Corner—it is now a tower block, above a discount warehouse—for this exclusive interview.

WINNIE-THE-POOH is sixty now, but looks far older. His eyes dangle, and he suffers from terminal moth. He walks into things a lot. I asked him about that, as we sat in the pitiful dinginess which has surrounded him for almost half a century.

'Punchy,' said Winnie-the-Pooh, 'is what I am. I've been to some of the best people, Hamley's, Mothercare, they all say the same thing: there's nothing you can do about it, it's all that hammering you took in the old days.'

Bitterly, he flicked open a well-thumbed copy of *Winnie-the-Pooh*, and read the opening lines aloud:

'"Here is Edward Bear, coming downstairs now, bump, bump, bump, on the back of his head, behind Christopher Robin. It is, as far as he knows, the only way of coming downstairs".' He looked at me. 'The hell it was!' he muttered. 'You think I didn't want to walk down, like normal people? But what chance did I stand? Every morning, it was the same story, this brat comes in and grabs me and next thing I know the old skull is bouncing on the lousy lino. Also,' he barked a short bitter laugh, 'that was the last time anyone called me Edward Bear. A distinguished name, Edward. A name with *class*. After the king, you know.'

I nodded. 'I know,' I said.

'But did it suit the Milnes?' Pooh hurled the book into the

grate, savagely. 'Did it suit the itsy-bitsy, mumsy-wumsy, ooze-daddy's-ickle-boy-den Milnes? So I was Winnie-the-Pooh. You want to know what it was like when the Milnes hit the sack and I got chucked in the toy-cupboard for the night?'

'What?' I said.

'It was "Hello, sailor!" and "Give us a kiss, Winifred!" and "Watch out, Golly, I think he fancies you!", not to mention,' and here he clenched his sad, mangy little fists, 'the standard "Oy, anyone else notice there's a peculiar poo in here, ha, ha, ha!"'

'I sympathise,' I said, 'but surely there were compensations? Your other life, in the wood, the wonderful stories of. . . .'

'Yeah,' said Pooh, heavily, 'the wood, the stories. The tales of Winnie-the-Schmuck, you mean? Which is your favourite? The one where I fall in the gorse bush? The one where I go up in the balloon and the kid shoots me down? Or maybe you prefer where I get stuck in the rabbit hole?'

'Well, I—'

'Hanging from a bloody balloon,' muttered Pooh, 'singing the kind of song you get put in the funny farm for! Remember?

> "How sweet to be a cloud,
> Floating in the blue!
> Every little cloud
> *Always* sings aloud."

That kind of junk," said Pooh, 'may suit Rolf Harris. Not me.'

'Did you never sing it, then?' I enquired.

'Oh, I sang it,' said Pooh. 'I sang it all right. It was in the script. *Dumb bear comes on and sings*. It was in the big Milne scenario. But you know what *I* wanted to sing?'

'I have no idea,' I said.

His little asymmetrical eyes grew even glassier, with a sadness that made me look away.

'*Body and Soul*,' murmured Pooh, 'is what I wanted to sing. *Smoke Gets In Your Eyes*. Or play the trumpet, possibly. It was,' he sighed, '1926. Jazz, short skirts, nightingales singing in Berkeley Square, angels dancing at the Ritz, know what I mean? A world full of excitement, sex, fun, Frazer-Nash two-seaters and everyone going to Le Touquet! And where was I? Hanging around with Piglet and passing my wild evenings in the heady company of Eeyore! *The Great Gatsby* came out that year,' said Pooh, bitterly. 'The same year as *Winnie-the-Pooh.*'

'I begin to understand,' I said.

'Why couldn't he write that kind of thing about *me*?' cried the anguished Pooh. 'Why didn't I get the breaks? Why wasn't I a great tragic hero, gazing at the green light on the end of Daisy's dock? Why didn't Fitzgerald write *Gatsby Meets A Heffelump* and Milne *The Great Pooh*?'

'But surely it was fun, if nothing else?' I said. 'Wasn't the Milne household full of laughter and gaiety and—'

'A. A. Milne,' Pooh interrupted, 'was an Assistant Editor of *Punch.* He used to come home like Bela Lugosi. I tell you, if we wanted a laugh, we used to take a stroll round Hampstead cemetery.'

Desperately, for the heartbreak of seeing this tattered toy slumped among his emotional debris was becoming unendurable, I sought an alternative tack.

'But think,' I said cheerily, 'of all the millions of children you have made happy!'

He was not to be shaken from his gloom.

'I'd rather,' he grunted, 'think of all the bears I've made miserable. After the Pooh books, the industry went mad. My people came off the assembly line like sausages. Millions of little bears marching towards the exact same fate as my own, into the hands of kids who'd digested the Milne rubbish, millions of nursery tea-parties where they were forced to sit around propped against a stuffed piglet in front of a little plastic plate and have some lousy infant smear their faces with jam. "O look, nurse, Pooh's ate up all his cake!" Have you any idea what it's like,' he said, 'having marmalade on your fur? It never,' and his voice dropped an octave, 'happened to Bulldog Drummond.'

'I'm sorry?'

Pooh reached for a grubby notebook, and flipped it open.

'"Suddenly the door burst from its hinges, and the doorway filled with a huge and terrible shape.

'"Get away from that girl, you filthy Hun swine!" it cried.

'"The black-hearted fiend who had been crouched over the lovely Phyllis turned and thrust a fist into his evil mouth.

'"Mein Gott!" he shrieked, "Es ist Edward Bear, MC,

DSO!"

'"With one bound, our hero. . . .'"

Pooh snapped the notebook shut.

'What's the use?' he said. '*I* wrote that, you know. After Milne packed it in, I said to myself, it's not too late, I know where the pencil-box is, I shall come back like Sherlock Holmes, a new image, a . . . I took it to every publisher in London. "Yes, very interesting," they said, "what about putting in a bit where he gets his paw stuck in a honey jar, how would it be if he went off with Roo and fell in a swamp, and while you're at it, could he sing a couple of songs about bathnight?"'

He fell silent. I cleared my throat a couple of times. Far off, a dog barked, a lift clanged. I stood up, at last, since there seemed nothing more to say.

'Is there anything you need?' I said, somewhat lamely.

'That's all right,' said Winnie-the-Pooh. 'I get by. No slice of the royalties, of course, oh dear me no, well, I'm only the bloody bear, aren't I? Tell you what, though, if you're going past an off-license, you might have them send up a bottle of gin.'

'I'd be delighted to,' I said.

He saw me to the door.

'Funny thing,' he said, 'I could never stand honey.'

Golfing For Cats

And This Is The Little Appliance

'Despite the new Sex Equality laws, most British males will continue to treat their wives as more or less useful objects' – Time *magazine*

'COME HOME FRIDAY, didn't I?' said the man in the blue dungarees, fingernailing a speck of nut from his beer-froth, 'and what was there? Pile of washing on the kitchen floor, dinner with the frost still on it, cat's doings in the corner by the telly. I thought, Gawd bleeding blind O'Reilly, it's packed up again!'

'And had it?' enquired the man in the herringbone overcoat, over the rim of his glass.

'Completely,' said the man in the blue dungarees. 'There it was in the corner. I gave it a poke, it just sort of wobbled a bit.'

'You can try kicking 'em,' said the man in the Wimpey jacket. 'It sometimes gets 'em going. Especially on cold mornings.'

The man in the dungarees finished his pint, and sucked the froth from his moustache.

'No,' he said, 'I could tell this was a skilled job. You don't want to go mucking about with 'em when it might be something radical. You could do a hell of a lot of damage. I gave mine a shake a couple of years back, turned out it had dislocated itself going after cobwebs. I put its bloody shoulder out. I didn't get it back for a fortnight. You wouldn't believe the state of my hosiery, time it got started again.'

'So what did you do this time?' asked the man in the herringbone overcoat, returning from the bar with three fresh pints.

The man in the blue dungarees drank a third off, belched, shrugged.

'Had to phone up, didn't I, get a man in. Not easy. He

wanted me to bring it to him, first off. All that way, must be two miles, dragging that great big thing.'

'You could give yourself a rupture,' said the man in the herringbone overcoat.'You could rip a sleeve, dragging.'

'That's what I told him. He come round, finally. Well past dinner-time, I might say. I had to get a pork pie down the wossname, the pub. Anyway, he had a look at it, had a feel underneath, shone his light in, listened with his stethoscope.'

'What was wrong?'

'Varicose veins,' said the man in the blue dungarees. 'Can you credit it?'

The other two looked at him, shocked.

'Varicose veins?' said the man in the herringbone overcoat. 'I can't see why that stops 'em cooking. You don't bloody cook with your legs, or am I mistaken?'

'I had the veins go on mine, once,' said the man in the Wimpey jacket. 'I put it right myself. What you do is, you bind the legs up with elastic bandage. Get it anywhere, Boots, anywhere. Did the whole lot for under a quid.'

'I'm not handy that way,' said the man in the blue dungarees. 'I'd probably make a muck of it. Stop its circulation, or sunnink. Legs'd probably fall off, and then where would I be? Eating out of tins, getting a laundry to deliver, it could cost a fortune. Anyway, he said the veins were affecting it all over, it'd have to go away and have 'em done proper.'

'Bloody hell,' said the man in the herringbone overcoat, 'how long will that take?'

The man in the blue dungarees pursed his lips.

'He couldn't say right off,' he said. 'They got work piled up to here, apparently. Might not be able to fit mine in for six months. And once they've got it up on the bench, it could take a fortnight to get it going proper. And *then,'* he added bitterly, 'you got to run 'em in for a bit. Light work only, no standing, no lifting.'

'The state your floors'll be in!' said the man in the Wimpey jacket. 'It don't bear thinking about. Not to mention the other.'

'The other?'

'The ironing. It's got to stand up to iron. I got mine ironing once in the non-standing position when it got water on its knees, you ought to have seen the state of my blue worsted, it

317

had flat sleeves and three bleeding lapels.'

'I know,' said the man in the blue dungarees morosely. 'I said to the bloke, bloody hell, I said, it's only forty-three, you don't expect 'em to start going at forty-three, it ought to have thirty years left in it before a major wossname, overhaul. Rate it's going on, I said, it'll start needing new bits before long. I might have to put a lung in it, or something, and Gawd knows what that could cost.'

The man in the herringbone overcoat shook his head.

'Can't put lungs in,' he said. 'They can get along on one lung—mind you, it slows 'em down getting upstairs with tea, you'll have to reckon on putting the alarm on a good quarter of an hour earlier—but if they both pack up, that's it.'

'I never realised,' said the man in the blue dungarees. 'You see where they put new hearts in and everything, I thought you could just go on replacing with spares.'

'You want to watch yours,' said the man in the Wimpey jacket. 'I hope I'm not speaking out of turn, but I saw it once, cleaning out the coalhouse in the rain. It can ruin 'em, leaving 'em out in the rain. *And* it was smoking. Combination of rain and smoking, them lungs it's got won't be fit for blowing on your porridge in a year or two.'

The man in the herringbone overcoat nodded.

'You ought to look after it better,' he said. 'It pays off in the end. Stop it smoking, for a start. And if it's got to go out in the rain, you ought to get one of them plastic hoods to tie over it. You can get 'em at Woolies. Five bob, but it's worth it. My old man looked after his a treat, he was a bit of a fanatic really, he used to keep it spotless. Once the dirt·gets in the wrinkles, he used to say, they start to go. Do you know, when he popped his clogs, it was still going like the clappers, after nearly eighty years. Someone said I ought to give it to an old folks' home; bugger that, I said, that's got a lot left in it, that has, so I installed it in the attic. It was still doing little jobs, making sandwiches, sewing, till it was nearly ninety. Released mine for all sorts of major work. That's how I got the extension built.'

The man in the blue dungarees sighed.

'They don't make 'em like that no more,' he said. 'Mine had to have glasses before it was thirty. It was either that or put forty-watt bulbs in, and you know how they burn it. It's going to need a deaf aid soon, as well, I'm sick of shouting for the evening paper now it can't hear the whistle over the noise of the egg-whisk. That's four batteries a year, for a start, not to mention initial outlay.'

'British,' said the man in the Wimpey jacket, 'that's the trouble.'

'What?'

'British. Load of bleeding tat. If I had my time over again, I'd get a Jap one. They're beautifully put together. Brother had a Jap, got it out east thirty years ago, it still ties his shoe-laces of a morning.'

'No!'

'Gerroff!'

'Straight up,' said the man in the Wimpey jacket. 'Also makes furniture out of old newspaper. Not to mention bloody accurate. Send it down the shops, it never gets short-changed, never buys the wrong thing, never comes back two minutes late on account of not assessing bus connections efficiently. It's saved him a packet, over the years.'

The man in the blue dungarees leaned forward, slightly uneasily.

'Tell me,' he said, 'this Jap. Does it get, er, headaches?'

'At night, he means,' said the man in the herringbone overcoat.

'I know what he bloody means!' snapped the man in the Wimpey jacket. 'I got a British one, haven't I? No,' he said to the man in the blue dungarees, 'as I understand it, it has never had a headache in its life. Night after night after night, my brother says, it don't suffer from headaches.'

The three of them sat in silence after this, for some time.

'Funny thing about British models,' said the man in the blue dungarees, at last. 'You can't help feeling they got a basic design flaw in 'em somewhere.'

'That's what it is, all right,' said the man in the Wimpey jacket.

The Lady From Stalingrad Mansions

A Little Touch of Harry in the Night

EYES UNGUM, and shards of dream whizz off into the corners of the dark.

It is three am exactly. We have the most luminous bedside clock in the world. You could read an insurance policy by it. It even has a luminous sweep second hand like a tiny radar screen. On bad nights, I sometimes fancy alien blips appear upon it, homing in from some far steppe to blat my premises. God knows how much radioactivity the thing is pumping out; every day, I examine the kids for the first tell-tale indications of genetic interference, an extra toe, perhaps, the bud of a new ear.

If the SALT talks ever succeed, clocks like mine will have to be turned in at local nicks.

Summer heat it was that woke me. I am wet. The arm upon the duvet gleams back the phosphorescence like a large sardine. Strange thing, the duvet: how were the world's ducks so ready for its boom? A sudden need for a billion billion feathers; and it was met.

Where did they find the men to pluck them? Can it be possible, I ask myself at 3.02 with all the libraries shut, that ducks can be plucked automatically, that there are huge machines with adroit tin fingers capable of stripping a duck in milliseconds?

Probably not. I have heard, I recall by 3.04, that the bulk of the world's duckdown comes from China; with ten thousand million digits on tap, an unprecedented hunger for feathers can doubtless be met with ease. Perhaps duckpluckers moonlight, out there beneath the rising sun; go off to the paddy fields of a morning with a bag of dead ducks round their necks, make an extra bob or two between rice-pickings. Possibly—they are fly, Orientals—they have developed a spry cyclic rhythm, enabling them to pluck and pick in syncopation, a duck under each arm

320

like a tiny bagpipe, while the thoughts of Chairman Hua tannoy across the echoing plain.

But.

It is 3.06.

But what about all those plucked bodies? Why, with the duvet boom, has the price of duckmeat not fallen to rock bottom, dipped below scrag and coley? Why do the kids not queue at chippies for ten pennorth of duck and a bag of beaks for the cat?

Can it be that the meat remains in China while the feathers fly westwards, that the happy Chinese nightly dine on crispy Pekin duck, cunning proof from Chairman Hua that the dark days of the Gang of Four are gone, that China is moving into the broad sunny uplands, next year everybody gets a Fiat 127, a Sony sound-system, an Austin Reed smock? Could this be behind the mollifying murmurs issuing towards Washington of late? Is their intensifying hatred of Sovietism bred from this new taste of the good life, duckstains on the bib and feather-money in the wallet?

A thought to sleep on, if I could. Nor shall I ever, unless these columns of marching ducks can be erased from the imagination. Beside the clock stands a radio; it came with one of those little plastic plugs on a string. STICK THIS IN YOUR EAR FOR INDIVIDUAL LISTENING AT ABSOLUTELY NO EXTRA COST. I have never stuck it in my ear before, partly because I did not wish to walk around and have sympathetic people bending down to shout in my radio, partly because mine has never been a name to conjure with in ear-nose-and-throat circles, and I have no idea what happens in those Eustachian depths after you get past the dusty bit. I know only that it's connected up by tunnels inside the head, and have always, therefore, lived in terror of shoving something in my ear and finding it stuck in my nose. Especially a radio.

Still, it is 3.14, a time at which normal strictures tend to waive themselves. I poke, gingerly, the little cone in my ear, pop the other end in the trannie, switch on. Tinny sounds resonate in all the bones of my head, crotchets plunk among my fillings. I thumb the tuner, find an English voice: it is some appalling phone-in freak, apparently blaming the loss of his wife's libido on illegal immigrants. Soporific enough stuff, the ducks fade, the eyelids leaden, and then some cheery swine in the studio informs the freak that we are taking a break there and will be back after the 3.15 news, and another cheery swine announces that he is in the newsroom and that they have just found the bowels of Henry V in a jamjar in Vincennes.

The eyes snap open again.

It occurs to me to wake my wife, despite the dangerous care I have just taken not to do so, either to corroborate what I think I have just heard or to get her to flick through the yellow pages for a 24-hour psychiatric service while I slip into something which will look natty under a strait-jacket.

I cannot. Fascination seems to have paralysed me. The newscaster is expatiating upon his ghastly headline, and I dare not miss a phrase. It turns out that Henry died of dysentery on an inconveniently hot August afternoon and the only way to get him from France to England for burial without considerable embarrassment was to put his insides in a pot, chop up his body, boil it in aromatics, then ship it to Westminster Abbey in a lead trunk.

End of news item, the cheery swine passes on to the Scotland–Iran result; I wait to hear whether there are any plans to put Ally MacLeod's giblets in a pot, chop up his body, boil it in McEwan's and ship it to Hampden Park in case anybody wants to do anything really nasty to it, but none is mooted, so I switch off and leave my ringing head alone with its insomniac thoughts.

They held life cheap, in 1422. In 1978, you can get six months for chucking a bottle at a Royal car, but I have little doubt that the repugnant mediaeval mortician who thought up the scheme to take a bandsaw to his monarch picked up a baronial gong for his ghastly initiative, leaving his modern descendants to glare out over their twelve million acres of Lincolnshire as they contemplate letters to the *Telegraph* urging the return of drawing and quartering for shop stewards.

It is 3.22.

I have great trouble shaking this image of Laurence Olivier with dotted lines all over him, like a butcher's chart. Of course, the real Harry was a lot shorter. Hardly a day goes by without someone telling me that mediaeval Britons were very short, because all the suits of armour we have are four feet tall. It never

322

seems to have occurred to anyone that it was only the soldiers who were short—every time a war came along, it is quite possible that the tall people went round to the short people and explained that it was time to go and fight for king and country if they didn't want their faces bashed in. Being short, they immediately complied. It doubtless made it easier on the industrial-military complexes of the day, too, whose interests have ever been served first: far simpler, far more cost-effective, to bang out ten thousand pairs of iron trousers with an eighteen-inch inside leg than having blokes coming back for second fittings with the Armada at the gate, could you hammer the crotch out a bit, and while you're at it how about brazing on a couple of patch pockets?

Of course, it being 3.25, it is quite possible that if the Carter–Brezhnev relationship gets any tackier and the Sino-American detente continues to improve, Britain will soon be in a position to flog its suits of armour to the Chinese and thus keep the Canaletto from going abroad. Just the right height, the Chinese, I can see them clanking out in serried ranks to face the Russians along the Ussuri River, pausing only to shove their visors up and poke a duck sandwich inside.

'ONCE MORE UNTO THE BLEACH, DEAR. . .'

Funny thing, history.

Tweak the continuum, put a tuck in a mezozoic fold, let the pterodactyl hang on for an eon or two, and it might well have been King Jimmy V extending his gauntlet beneath the fluttering pennants:

'Well met, proud Brooklyn! And good morrow, Bronx!
Dear Arizona, first of all my dukes!
How fares our brave Lord Twin Forks, and what news
Of Bishop Tombstone may we yet expect?
Comes Deadwood soon, and is. . .'

Not that any of it would make much difference, in the long run. Men would still pluck ducks, get dysentery, fight, be buried, and lie beside their wives in summer dawns, waiting for the sun to rise.

The Rhinestone As Big As The Ritz

When Dinosaurs Walked the Earth
(World Copyright Reserved)

A thirty-man expedition has just left for a jungle-covered plateau in Vene-
zuela in quest of prehistoric life. They will descend into a giant hole, at the
bottom of which, say the scientists, life forms have not undergone the muta-
tions of evolution. Unfortunately, at the top of the hole they have: which
may explain some of the differences between Sir Arthur Conan Doyle's
Lost World and mine.

I WILL NOT BORE THOSE whom this narrative may reach by an
account of our luxurious voyage upon the Booth liner, save that
I should wish to point out that the Booth Lines new Sail 'n' Sun
Getaway Family Cruises are a snip at only £235 per head, including personalised rug and half bottle of wine with evening
meal, plus use of telescope when passing dolphins, and that I
should like to extend the heartfelt thanks of Professor Challenger and the rest of our team to Booth Lines for their
generosity in transporting us to our destination, coupled
with the name of Captain Enrico Gomez de Hoja, who will
be among the first guests on my new TV chat show along
with Henry the Pterodactyl, now happily under contract to
one of our foremost birdseed advertisers.

We reached Caracas on the forenoon of the 18th, and encountered nothing more than the normal difficulties in dis-
embarking our videotape and film equipment, our camera
teams, our agents, managers, make-up ladies, publicity per-
sonnel, and endorsing representatives, although some incon-
venience, it must be said, was caused by the Conservative
politician who had joined our party as an independent fact-
finder and took the opportunity of delivering an impassioned speech on the Government's fiscal policy to a party

324

of Carmelite nuns temporarily caught on the gangplank by their hems until he was thrown into the dock by a group of Brazilian longshoremen whipped to a frenzy by his Labour pair who had been denouncing Phase III through a megaphone on the poop.

These interruptions having been sorted out, the leaders of the party repaired to the sumptuous fazenda proffered us by the chairman of Jungle Jollidays Inc., Venezuela's most enterprising tour operator, whose fortnight in the Ellucero Swamps is a model of its kind, even without its unprecedented bonus of free quinine.

Perhaps at this point I ought to give a clearer sketch of my comrades in the enterprise. The scientific attainments of Professor Summerlee are too well known for me to trouble to recapitulate them, especially as the 26-part programme based on the serialisations in the *Sunday Times* of the book adapted from his film of his three weeks with the fig-eating sloths of El Salvador is already gripping audiences throughout the world. His tall, gaunt figure is insensible to fatigue (he has been known to give eleven interviews in a single day), and his dry, sardonic manner is uninfluenced by any change in his surroundings and is, indeed, written into his contracts. He loses no opportunity to manifest his contempt for our leader, Professor Challenger, maintaining that no scientist worthy of the title can be expected to serve under the leadership of a man prepared to travel to BBC Bristol to do *The Living World* on sound only, for twenty pounds a time. Further, Professor Summerlee firmly believed we were all embarked upon a wild-goose chase, and had it not been for the fact that his forthcoming book, *Great Wild-Goose Chases Of Our Time*, had already earned him a record £100,000 advance from Readers Digest Condensed Books before condensation, he would at that very moment have been lecturing to the Annual Conference of Methodist Accountants in South Bend, Indiana.

Lord John Roxton has some points in common with Professor Summerlee, and others in which they are the very antithesis of one another. A botanist who rose to prominence through his endorsement of Bio-Miracle, the houseplant food which took Britain by storm until a Venus Flytrap raised on it ran amok and ate an airedale, Lord John subsequently chaired

325

the popular BBC 1 panel game, *Smear Test*, before becoming an international figure overnight with his adaptation of the Eskimo mime-play *Grass*, a symbolist drama concerned with ecology and newly set in a middle-class NW1 socialist household, which ran in the Peter Brooke version for five years before being filmed simultaneously by both Ken Russell and Lindsay Anderson.

Of Sir Solly Challenger, little need be said. A friend to both main parties, the only microbiologist to have negotiated with Ian Smith, a Chairman of the Arts Council whose study of the weasel ran to five impressions in Penguin and whose study of the penguin ran to five editions in Weasel, what finer leader could we have sought? Happy was I, as we abseiled down into the Great Hole of Venezuela, to be roped beneath so great a personality!

We touched bottom at noon on the 21st, a triumph marred only by a knife fight between the Features Bookings Managers of BBC TV and Yorkshire Television, on the grounds that the feet of Professor Challenger, who was contracted exclusively to BBC, had been shot by Yorkshire cameramen while taking pictures of the descent of Lord John, who was exclusively contracted to *them*, and who, to complicate matters further, had insisted on waving his bottle of whisky, label uppermost, at the same moment as Professor Summerlee was attempting to wave *his* bottle of gin; with the result that a second fracas immediately broke out between the rival distillers' agents.

It was at this fraught moment that an iguanodon came past; but, unhappily, when this was pointed out to Summerlee by an excited Challenger, Summerlee snapped back: 'Sod your effing iguanodon, what about my gin?', which meant that the unique alarm cry of the iguanodon, never before heard by man, had to be erased from the tape because of the impermissible language counterpointing it. We never saw an iguanodon again.

Worse was to come.

It was towards three p.m. that afternoon that tragedy struck. With an initiative which belied his young years, one of the junior members of our party who had qualified to join it on the strength of a recent first-class honours degree in biochemistry from Cambridge but who, we discovered too late, had used it to gain an executive position with a leading copywriting agency, had arranged to have lowered, from a helicopter hired earlier in Caracas, a small family saloon drawn from a new Japanese range. The emphasis of the sales promotion was to be laid upon its durability and toughness; and our young colleague had devised the slogan: A DINOSAUR COULD TREAD ON IT! This in fact proved to be true; a dinosaur could not only tread on it, but at seven minutes before three o'clock, a dinosaur did tread on it.

We put our young colleague in a foolscap envelope, and resolved, when time permitted, to give him a Christian burial.

The terrible affair cast, inevitably, a pall of gloom on the entire party. Many of us had brought along similar, though smaller, products in order to test them under these novel and eye-catching conditions—I myself had imported a kettle of polyurethane gloss and a small table-top to demonstrate the paint's imperviousness to the weightiest tread—but it was clear that dinosaurs were far heavier than we had anticipated; and when Lord John's new wool-substitute thornproof hacking-jacket in lovat Roxtonette was pecked to shreds in seconds by a pleistocene wren, thereby wiping out a world-wide sales campaign geared to the coming autumn, there were many among us who would then and there have called off the entire expedition. Professor Challenger's iron will, however, prevailed; and when, soon after supper, the group of which he owns eighty per cent, Black Diplodocus, waxed their first single to a haunting counterpoint of ornithischian shrieking and his A & R man pronounced it fantastic, our spirits rose again.

The first night passed virtually without incident, although some of us were kept awake by Summerlee's aldis lamp, by which he was morsing copy to an *Observer Colour Supplement* secretary leaning over the crater's rim, a thousand feet up. Nor was dawn the lovely thing it normally is in this region, awoken as we were to the stench from the pot in which a leading TV gourmet was researching a chapter for her *Saurian Cookbook*. There is something about the odour given off by a triceratops head simmering on a low light which can only be described as indescribable.

But the rest of the day went remarkably well. How benevolently Dame Fortune can smile when the desire moves her! Who would ever have guessed that I, a person of no great moment in this world, should have been granted the boon of

327

being the first human being ever to set eyes upon two bronto-saurases mating, a spread worth twenty thousand dollarsworth of *Playboy's* money any day of the week, not to mention second rights to *Paris Match* and *Stern*? And, miracle upon miracles, joy upon joys, also have had the luck to come upon Henry! Or, since the scientific record must be kept impeccable, to have Henry come upon me, Henry whose magnificent pterodacty-lian ugliness has since been reproduced on a million Henry tea-towels and carrier bags, whose incredibly revolting body has formed the basis of a soft toy industry in which I am the ma-jority shareholder, Henry whose birdfood sales to date have outstripped not only Arthur the cat, but also every performing animal that ever lived, Henry whose TV puppet *doppelgänger* now bobs and nods in every living-room in the civilised world—Henry whose strong claws fastened in my shoulders upon that fateful afternoon and whose strong leathery wings bore me up and out of that fearful place, a clear week ahead of the schedu-led heli-lift and thus a clear week ahead of the opposition, whom I left baying and gesticulating in the grotty green depths below!

Where, for all I know, they still remain. There has been no word these several months; and I can only assume that the blanket coverage afforded me by a grateful commercial world has left my colleagues with nothing to sell, and, moreover, per-suaded those who had previously committed themselves to hau-ling them from the abyss for subsequent profit will have considered the inadvisability of flooding the market, and let sleeping dogs lie.

Golfing For Cats

Body And Soul

'The smile of Marabel Morgan is the smile of the Total Woman. In London to launch her book The Total Woman, *Mrs Morgan runs Total Woman Inc, a marriage enrichment course which she started in America. Thousands of women have now followed her advice. "Call your husband at the office to say: Hurry home, I crave your body," she suggests, adding that she often meets hers at the door freshly bubble-bathed and wearing only babydoll pyjamas and white boots, causing him to drop his briefcase and chase her round the table.'*—Evening Standard

IT HAD NOT BEEN the best of mornings for Mr Dennis Belwether.

It rarely was.

In the dark ruin of his lower lumbar regions, a worn disc throbbed evilly, while in his left knee the shredded cartilage tweaked an agonising descant; nor could he be entirely certain that an arch had not fallen inside a shoe that seemed uncharacteristically full of lumps.

At forty-seven, he reflected, there was a limit to the number of times a man could jump off a wardrobe with impunity. His furred tongue went to his upper plate for the hundredth probe that morning, stencilling the expensive crack: how could he tell his dentist that he had done it when, as he sprinted from the shower, the spike on his *Pickelhauber* had struck the bedroom lintel with a judder that had set his wife's bra-bells jangling fifteen feet away?

He took off his glasses, their ear-pieces still bent from incautious passion, and stared at the thick blue folder labelled Phillimore Holdings which had lain on his desk for three days now, awaiting his deliberations, while the fox-faced executives over at Phillimore paced the Wilton and snapped their pencils and shrieked down the telephone at his boss.

Who had been, Belwether said to himself, remarkably reasonable. Coming into Belwether's office the previous afternoon and finding his employee's wispy head flat on the Phillimore file, snoring, Mr Soames had merely shaken Belwether gently from a dream of flat-chested twinsets toasting crumpets and, as Belwether lifted his pale cheek with its serried dents of Phillimore ring-binding to the painful light, said:

'Why not tell me about it, old chap? Is it a woman?'

To which Belwether had merely blinked wretchedly, a blink being the gesture that occupies the neutral ground between nod and shake; for it *was* a woman, and then again, it wasn't.

But how could one explain that?

'You don't want to chuck away a quarter-century of exemplary double-entry on some bit of teenage stuff from the typing-pool, old chap,' continued Mr Soames, not unkindly. 'There'll be an eight-day chiming bracket clock waiting for you in 1995, you know. Would you jeopardise that for the fleeting joy of how's-your-father?'

He had, it seemed to Belwether, almost patted his shoulder before leaving. The thought filled him with gloomy guilt, again, as he remembered. Mr Soames had offered himself as confidant and priest, almost a friend, just short of a father, and he, Belwether, had merely blinked, rejecting the offered ear, leaving himself adrift and comfortless. All over the world, men were this very moment sitting down together at quiet tables in a thousand bars, to share anaesthetising drinks and friendly bags of cheesy things while each told the other of his sexual peccadilloes and disillusionments, of the wives who hadn't been feeling well lately and the nymphets ravenous for an experienced touch.

But to whom could Belwether go, and with what? What friendship, indeed, even if he had the time to form one, could withstand such ridicule?

He opened the Phillimore file for the twentieth time, and fought to focus his tired eyes on the reeling columns. He reached for his calculator. He unscrewed his pens, one green, one red, one black. The telephone rang.

'It's your wife,' said his secretary, and flipped the switch.

'How many times have I told you,' hissed Belwether into the mouthpiece, 'never to ring me at the office?'

'I crave your body,' murmured Felicity Belwether.

'There's a meeting,' cried Belwether, 'at half-past . . .'

'Passion,' groaned Felicity Belwether, 'billows through me like waves rolling towards the beach, hungry to dash themselves against the rocks. I am lying here clad only in a peep-hole bra and waders, my Dennis!'

'You may not appreciate it, Felicity, but Mr Cattermole of Phillimore Holdings, one of the foremost . . .'

'I have put your long sideburns out ready, my darling,' breathed his wife, 'and your busby has just come back from the cleaners. It will be the matter of a moment for you to jump into your clogs.'

'Oh, God,' muttered Belwether. He put down the receiver. He closed the Phillimore folder. He put the top back on his pens.

The typing pool watched him slink out, limping alternately as he favoured disc and knee.

'Tell Mr Soames I have to see a client,' he murmured automatically, as the door sighed shut behind him.

'*His* age,' said a secretary, studding a cat's eye deftly into her leather bolero, 'bleeding obscene.'

On the Xerox machine, the girl running off eight hundred copies of a Starsky and Hutch poster paused briefly.

'He's probably off up the Jacey,' she said. 'They got *Chinese Emmanuelle in Chains* and *Suburban Tongue*. All he's fit for.'

'Seen his eyes?' enquired a telephonist, breaking off her conversation to her Melbourne boy-friend. 'Don't half stand out. All them little veins.'

'They go like that,' said the tea-girl, adroitly slipping a two-pound jar of Nescafé into her Fiorucci hold-all. 'It's a side-effect. I seen about it in the *Sun*.'

'Serves him bleeding right,' said the secretary. '*His* age.'

On the drizzled street, Dennis Belwether waited for a Number Eleven. It being only noon, none came. He stared into the buslessness, feeling the rain go down under his collar and the wind go up his trousers. He was starting a cold, of that there was little doubt. It would turn bronchial, the way it invariably did, but who would distil the Friar's Balsam, who pour out the

331

Medinite, who tuck him in and tiptoe about the premises, bearing succulent trays of this and that, silencing children? The last time he had had 'flu, Felicity, driven near-insensate by his presence in the daytime bed, had insisted upon hurling herself on him with merciless regularity, in a variety of foreign uniforms, an activity which, in his enfeebled state, he had been powerless to discourage.

Nor had he ever been able to explain to his two children why, on their return from school, their mother was to be found blacked up and with a feather in her ginger wig, running round the house dressed only in the battle blouse of an Israeli paratrooper.

It would be even worse this time, with his back trouble on top of everything else. She had already shown signs of inordinate interest in the possibility of home traction, and there had been many a lip-smacking suggestion that such games as Nurse And Orthopaedic Patient might soon sneak into Felicity Belwether's illimitable repertoire.

As he stood there, chilled, with the drizzle hardening to sleet and the only refuge from it the voracious premises of 14, Acacia Crescent, old longings stirred within the ravaged frame of Dennis Belwether. They had been stirring more and more regularly in recent months, and he entertained them with less and less shame: he had only one life, he would argue, and had he not passed forty-seven years of it as a faithful husband, and was that not better than par for the course? Was he to go to the long pine box having known only one woman? Was he, too, not as entitled to the free expression of his romantic imagination as Felicity, and could he be blamed if he sought that expression elsewhere than at 14, Acacia Crescent?

Not for the first time, his fingers trembled over the scribbled page at the back of his pocket diary. A blob of sleet fell on it, but fortunately did not disturb the inky number dictated so long ago by Mr Brill of Small Accounts, who had once, in a unique unguarded moment, revealed to him that Mrs Brill had a habit of springing out of cupboards at him, dressed in nothing but angora mittens, which had precipitated Mr Brill's early retirement.

Dennis Belwether looked again at Brill's legacy.

There was a telephone booth across the road.

I will give the bus until I count to fifty, he said to himself.

It did not come. He crossed the road, dialled without thinking, pressed in his hot coin.

When he rang the bell, two flights up above a Greek Street massage parlour, the door was answered by a middle-aged woman in a beige cardigan, grey lisle stockings, worn felt slippers, heavy tweed skirt, and a hairnet.

'Miss Desiree La Biche?' he enquired nervously. 'I rang earlier. Dennis.'

She looked at him over her bifocals.

'I suppose you didn't remember to bring the sprouts?' she said.

'Sprouts?' he said.

'You'll forget your own head one of thee days, Dennis,' she said. 'Come in, don't stand there dripping, I just done that step.'

He went inside. The little corridor smelt of boiled cabbage and Johnson's Pride; a black-and-white dog came up and licked his hand.

'We'll have to take him down and get him wormed,' said Desiree La Biche, 'one of these days. You're always promising.'

'There's never the time,' he replied automatically, following her into a small living-room and sitting down in front of the television set.

'Ten pounds,' said Desiree La Biche.

He sprang up, fumbled for the notes.

'Sorry,' he said, 'almost forgot, ha-ha-ha!'

She put the money on the mantelpiece, under the clock.

'Price of things these days,' she said, 'I was only saying to Mrs Thing this morning, Dennis and me are going to have to give up meat altogether, I said. I know what you mean, she said, I just paid a pound for twelve ounces of ox liver. What? I said, a *pound*, I said. Without a word of a lie, she said. What do you think of that, Dennis?'

'Er, remarkable,' replied Belwether, sitting down again.

'Remarkable, remarkable, that's all you ever say, just so long as you've got your television, personally I don't know what you see in it, lot of rubbish, sit there stuck in front of it, never take me out no more, I was only saying yesterday down the

launderette to Mrs, oh, you know, big woman, funny ears, got a
son Norman in the navy, no, I tell a lie, army, anyway, what I
said was . . .'

As Desiree La Biche droned on, Dennis Belwether felt a
delightful numbness seep into his tired limbs, felt the
monotonous voice grow distant, felt the evening paper she had
put in his lap slip to the floor. He eased his feet from his shoes;
he unbuttoned his waistcoat; he let his head fall back against
the antimacassar, and let his mind, for the precious half-hour it
had been allotted, drift away into luxurious nothingness.

The Lady From Stalingrad Mansions

The Night We Went To Epernay By Way Of Tours-sur-Marne

This is Fère-en-Tardenois. I'm damned glad I only have to write it down. I'd hate to have to try saying it. Not that I couldn't, all other things being, you know. I said it a lot this afternoon. I have a great French accent, sober.

That doesn't mean I can't hold it. It's just, we had a lot of bottles today. I'm a scotch drinker, normally, you understand. And you wouldn't believe the number of people I've seen off. Some of the world's most outstanding soaks. Just stood there while they slid to the ground, poured myself a nightcap, walked away straight as a plank. Ask anyone.

I don't think I ever drank eight bottles of champagne in a day before, though. I've just noticed that I started a sentence with a conjunction a few inches back, in case you're interested. They tried to knock that out of me at school. Nobody cared about style in the early 'fifties.

Any minute the people in the room next door are going to start banging on the walls. You know the French; a volatile folk. Man starts typing at three in the morning, they can get very upset, pretty soon this bedroom is going to be full of waving arms. I wonder if they have a hotel detective? What do you say to Rupert Davies at three in the morning?

Still, they're luckier than the people downstairs. They've been waiting since one-fifteen for me to drop the other shoe. I really would, you know me, not a spark of malice in my entire make-up, it's just that it has laces, and you know what laces are like if you have eleven thumbs. I pulled the other one off. Not thumb, the other shoe. But that was a long time ago, and I don't seem to have any energy left.

I'd write longhand if I could, but the pen's in my jacket, and my wife is asleep on it, and when I tried to get my cigarette lighter out of the pocket a little while back, she went for me with her teeth. I've never seen her do that before. Maybe she isn't a champagne drinker, either.

Can you get rabies off people?

I rang down for room service a few minutes ago. I woke up, and the bathwater was freezing, and when I saw all the earwigs floating round me, I nearly had a heart attack. I couldn't move. I thought, there's enough earwigs there to eat an entire man, e.g. me, and then I thought, I won't show them I'm afraid, they smell fear, earwigs, so I started whistling, very slowly. And then I saw they weren't earwigs at all, they were shreds of tobacco, my cigarette must have come apart while I was asleep. I was certain when I saw a cork tip come past. I may be drunk, but there's no insect looks like a cork tip, that I do know.

So I got out of the bath, and

That must be the reason I can't get the other shoe off. It's either the leather has shrunk, or the laces. I hope to God whatever it is dries out to its normal size. I don't want to spend the rest of my life in this black shoe.

So I got out of the bath, and I rang room service, and asked for a bottle of Perrier, because while I was asleep someone had come in and carpeted my throat, and Room Service said: "Entendu, m'sieu" and then he came up, and this is a very expensive hotel and you would expect an employé of same not to stand in the doorway with his bouche hanging there in neutral, and I said to him:

"What's the matter, didn't you ever see anyone with a shoe on before?"

and he snapped out of it, and opened the Perrier, and didn't even wait for a tip, which was just as well, since the money was under my wife, still is, along with the pen and the lighter, and there could have been a nasty scene and who knows what the penalty might be under the Code Napoleon for biting a waiter going about his lawful duties?

The thing is, I could be wrong, but I think the Perrier is

making me drunk again. I think it's getting together with all that dormant champagne, and I think they're cooking something up.

It's been a long day. I've had months that were shorter. It all started peacefully enough, we were coasting down Route Nationale 31, I think it was, one of those undifferentiated cobbly ribbons rimmed with white cows that the French seem to go in for, and the next moment we turned south at Fismes, and there it all was. It isn't every day that you breast a slight rise to find an entire national character suddenly at your feet. On, as it were, the hoof. There it all was, slope after slope of little brown vine-frames, a billion buds-worth of the '74 vintage awaiting its turn to be converted into christenings, wakes, seductions, ship-launchings, motorway-openings, anniversaries, celebrations, commiserations, and just plain booze-ups. Thirty thousand acres of embryo burps, giggles, hangovers, and blokes walking into walls in the small hours.

It is this, the sheer *concentration* of Champagne, that first makes the imagination reel and grope: a mere thirty thousand acres to serve the world. Call for a bottle on the Ginza, snap your fingers in El Vino, pop a cork in Valparaiso or Durban or Tunbridge Wells, and the stuff that pricks the nostril and galvanises the soul started off somewhere in these few square kilometres, as a pip.

It would be hard to think of another tiny patch of the globe's surface so rife with overtone, so alive to its own symbolism, and so much the quintessence of its host race. Here is the nub and concentrate of all things Gallic. As if there were a town called Tea, say, just off the M4, from which the whole essence of England emanated; as if there were Coke, Nebraska, or Guinness, Co. Cork.

We took the road to, my God an owl's just gone off on the window-sill, we took the road to Hautvillers, that sweet shrine above the Marne where Dom Pérignon spent a large slice of the seventeenth century in glorifying God in an approved Benedictine manner, i.e. by jumping up and down on the fruit of the vine until these products of the Almighty's grand design had been improved beyond all recognition, a heresy upon which successive Popes were prepared to turn a conveniently blind eye, especially in a good year. True believers owe the good monk much: apart from his years of unflagging basement service in tasting and blending, Dom Pérignon also found time to invent the cork. Without it, champagne could never have been, relying as it does upon that little spongy cylinder for the extraction of its sedimentary gunge, and the retention of its bubble.

So we drank a morning bottle to old Dom, and the stuff fizzed in its two cones like pale liquescent gold, and the sun came out over the Marne, and I think, now I remember, there were larks, too. And we drove down to Epernay, across the river, singing, into the commercial heartland of Champagne, down streets called Moet and Perrier and Chandon, a map like a Temperance Union itinerary of hell, little alleys behind the high old walls of which the faithful clerks with paper cuffs made out the lading-bills to Tokyo and Bonn and Manchester; and the trucks passed by us, bearing the brut to the English, and the doux to the East, and allsorts to the Americans, who like to drink it so cold that it wouldn't matter if it was carbonated wood-alcohol, anyway, and we dropped in at Les Berceaux and we had another bottle there, and that was even better than the first, and there were yet fewer clouds when we came out again; so we put the hood down, and we sang more loudly still, and drove back over the Marne, and up to Rheims, because the good people of Heidsieck & Co. Monopole had asked us to lunch, and Rheims is where they hang their hat.

Was it only a dozen hours ago?

They took us down into the cool vaults, where there are eight miles of corridors hewn out of that same chalk that nourishes the vine, and these eight miles have a strange mould for décor, like a green flock wallpaper, and ten million bottles for furniture, and it all reeks of vinous age; and men in blue dungarees walk through, at measured pace, ritually, and turn each bottle with a single deft and wristy move; forty men turning three thousand bottles an hour, for all eternity, so that the sediment has no inimical peace.

We went aloft again, leaving the ten million bottles to their restlessness. How can I express ten million bottles in terms you'll comprehend? Perhaps it would be simpler to think of it as slightly more than two million bottles each for every man, woman and child in my family.

Upstairs, we drank two bottles more, of their finest cuéve, and it is none of your NV stuff to make the bridesmaids giggle, but a very fine wine indeed, and there was more at lunch, at the Heidsieck windmill high on a green hill at Verzenay. My host took me to the window, and remarked that the old Moulin had been an allied observation post in both World Wars, and I peered, and tried to observe what the allies had observed, only by that time I was having difficulty seeing as far as the host.

And we left them in the mild afternoon, and we said to one another How do you top that? but there was a spot we had heard of called Le Château de Fère-en-Tardenois, and top it it did, no disrespect to the Moulin: a castle on a moated mountain, built in the thirteenth century and falling down ever since, due, claim its curators, merely to the ravages of time, but I have my doubts. I lay blame at the cuisine at its foot, at the Hostellerie du Château, where the food is so superb and the booze so prime, that when the last draught of marc and coffee has been sunk, one wanders out into the soft evening and up to the castle ruins, and, in one's euphoria, tends to bump into the hallowed reliquiae with never a second thought. There's a sliver of crenellation in my shoe right now; the way things are, it may stay there for good. I am living history.

The dawn is doing things now. The birds are crazed. The sun is poised to warm the grape-buds out there beyond the ruins. There must be a hundred million bottles of the stuff in the immediate vicinity.

I may stay here forever. If I can find my other shoe.

The Sanity Inspector

Portnoy's Jaws, Or For Whom The Great Sound And The Godfather Toll – 22

With no sign of a let-up in the woodpulp shortage, the Great American Novel for 2077 is actually the Only American Novel for 2077. Care for a few representative extracts?

AT 10.36 on the morning of July 15, 2071, the Betelgeuse Shuttle took off from Ehrlichman Airport, Savannah, 448 gross tons of di-anylo-polyvectane alloy hurled forward and upward with the incredible thrust of its four Yung & Foolisch oxy-chlorothyne motors.

On the ground, scarce five hog-springs from Ehrlichman control, two Negro dirt-farmers watched the white furrow plough across the hot Southern sky.

'Ah wuz up tuh Miz Golightly's house, yez'day,' murmured Henry Clay Jackson Calhoun. He spat in the dust. He picked a thread out of his age-bleached jeans. He yawned, tongue jumping pink in his large toothless mouth like a plucked rat caught in a storm-drain.

'Miz Golightly with thuh big ole belly?' enquired Washington Bing Beiderbecke Faulkner. He turned a dried cowpat over with his bare black toe. He broke wind. He took off his straw hat and spun it upon his finger.

'Uh-huh,' nodded Henry Clay Jackson Calhoun. He plucked a cotton boll listlessly, and began to pick it to pieces. 'They do say where she carryin' de Devil's chile in that big ole belly o' her'n. It lookin' like she gittin' thuh action f'om Old Nick hisself, heh-heh-heh!'

Washington Bing Beiderbecke Faulkner shook his head.

'It sho lookin' like it fixin' tuh be a bad, bad summer. It like to

340

wipe out thuh entiah crop, white folks liftin' their skirts fo' thuh Prince o' Darkness.'

'Saw a daid toad under a beulah bush this mornin',' said Henry Clay Jackson Calhoun darkly. 'Only mean one thing.'

They stared at a circling yippity-bug for some time. Mule-hooves clopped on the dirt road. They looked up. A bearded figure in a long black coat jiggled in the stained saddle, his sideburns lank in the breezelessness. He came abreast of them.

'Mornin', Rabbi,' said Washington Bing Beiderbecke Faulkner.

The old man took off his yarmulka and wiped his streaming forehead with it.

'All of a sudden it's good morning?' he snapped. 'What for a morning is it, it should be good? What's so good, it should suddenly be a morning? You work, you die, *this* you call life?'

'Saw a daid toad under a beulah bush a bit back,' said Henry Clay Jackson Calhoun.

The Rabbi replaced his yarmulka.

'Schwarzers!' he snorted, deep in his beard. 'They dance, they sing, they get drunk, what do they know?'

'Anything wrong, Rabbi?' asked Washington Bing Beiderbecke Faulkner.

The Rabbi looked at him.

'Anything *wrong*? Anything *wrong*? I forgot to call my mother, he asks me if anything's wrong!'

He dug his slippered heels into the mule's fly-nibbled flanks, and jogged mumbling on. The Negroes watched him go. Henry Clay Jackson Calhoun pulled at his ear-lobe.

'They say he in damn big with thuh Mafia,' he said.

Forty thousand miles up, on the black interstellar threshold, Captain Manuel Garcia y Ortega flicked the anodised oxolium switch .026 ektars to the left.

But nothing happened.

It was 11.34 am.

Senator Seamus Kowalski, firebrand North Dakota Whig, lay on his green leather-topped Washington desk beside his lissom Navajo secretary, pondering defence expenditure in the brief calm stases. The Army was pressing for nuclear revolvers to give them strike parity with the Detroit Police Department, the Navy was screaming for a second Polaris whorehouse for sub-Antarctica, the USAAF wanted in-flight baseball, and, as if this were not enough, his daughter was planning to marry a Jap.

Seamus Kowalski was a homeloving dynast, who had always dreamed of having a son-in-law called Chuck. How could you call a Jap Chuck?

His secretary began to lick his palms. Senator Kowalski frowned. Was this why he had fought his long way to Capitol Hill? Was this what Thomas Jefferson meant when he said that 'When a man assumes a public trust, he should consider himself a public property'?

The red telephone bit, jangling, into his whirling mind. He snatched the instrument from its cradle.

He listened.

He paled.

He gasped.

He rolled from his desk and groped for his socks.

He croaked: 'Leave it with me. Oh my God!' and hung up.

'What up, Keemosabi?' grunted his secretary.

'Take the feather off,' snapped the Senator, removing his own black mask. 'A shark just ate the President.'

A quarter of a million miles away, the Moon receding in his wing mirror, Captain Manuel Garcia y Ortega thought coolly for a few moments, and threw up.

'Eat the chicken soup,' said Mrs Santarosa.

'But we're Mexicans, mother!' protested little Gonzales Santarosa. 'We're wetbacks.'

Mrs Santarosa clipped his ear with the heavy ladle.

'What's so special about Mexicans, they shouldn't eat chicken soup?' she screamed. 'What's so special about chicken soup, it shouldn't get eaten by Mexicans?' She beat her breast, she looked upwards to the ceiling. 'You bring up children, and what do you get? Heartache, you get. A malignant disease, you get.'

Little Gonzales blew his nose on his napkin.

'We're supposed to eat enchelados,' he wailed, 'we're supposed to eat tachos and chili and tortillas!'

'Suddenly he's an expert, my son!' shrieked Mrs Santarosa. 'Suddenly, six years old, he's already a professor!' She put her face down close to his. 'So tell me, you know so much, how many Mexicans ever got to write *Rhapsody In Blue*? How many Mexicans ever ran a blouse empire? How many Mexicans ever got to sell three million copies of *Sonny Boy*? If I started to list the people who got to the top on chicken soup, we'd still be sitting here Sunday week!'

The boy dipped his spoon into the bowl, morosely.

'I liked it when we all spoke Spanish around the house,' he said.

'*Aye, chihuahua!*' cried Captain Manuel Garcia y Ortega, a million miles away. 'We have to re-trim, or we end up in the Sun! We have to lose twelve thousand kilograms right now!'

'I say we throw out the nuns,' said his second-in-command.

'What have you come up with, Senator?' said the two young men from the *Washington Post*.

'We're working on a Second Shark Theory,' said Kowalski. 'As of this moment in time, men, we are into a bi-shark conspiracy situation.'

'You think this shark or sharks had prior information that the President would be swimming off Chappaquiddick?' said the two young men.

Senator Kowalski mopped his neck.

'Let me tell you something about Ivan, boys,' he said. 'God moves in a mysterious way.'

'May we quote you?' said the two young men.

'This conversation is being recorded,' said the Senator. 'I think you ought to know that. Similarly, I wouldn't want nothing to get to either of your wives' ears about that big Eskimo stripper.'

There was a long silence.

'I'm afraid there's something you have to understand here, Senator,' said the two young men.

'I thought you might say that,' said Kowalski.

He depressed a foot switch. The door opened. Two large men came in. They had napkins tucked into their collars. Each carried a Chianti bottle. They were still chewing.

The Senator got up and went across, and kissed them both on the lips, very formally, and they turned and beat the two young men to death with the Chianti bottles.

They turned to go.

'Just a minute,' said the Senator.

They turned back.

'What's that stuff on your lips?' he said.

'Issa *tagliatelli alla vongole*.'

'On your way down,' said the Senator, 'send up two orders, easy on the black pepper.'

Two million miles away, ignorant of the deaths of great men, the movements of mighty armies or mighty whorehouses, the racial turbulence of this unsettled Earth, the puzzled nuns floated among the stars.

At the back of the Shuttle, the small man watched them go.

'Cojones,' he said. 'The nuns are only the beginning.'

'I know,' said the big man. 'It will be this thing with the nuns, and then it will be this thing with us.'

'I would like to have run with the bulls at Pamplona one more time,' said the small man.

'Yes,' said the big man, 'the thing with the bulls was better than the green light on the end of Daisy's dock.'

'Fitzgerald was different from you and me,' said the small man.

'He had more money,' said the big man.

'Apart from that,' said the small man.

'Yes,' said the big man.

'That is the way it is sometimes,' said the small man.

'Yes,' said the big man, 'that is the way it is sometimes.'

'When I am floating out there,' said the small man, 'I shall remember you as you were when I first saw you, in the green gingham.'

'No,' said the big man. 'The first time, I wore the baby-blue taffeta with the rouched petticoats. *You* were in the green gingham.'

'I was in the lamé trouser-suit with the fox stole,' said the small man, 'you stupid bitch.'

'Who are you calling a stupid bitch?' said the big man, 'you silly mare.'

They were still screaming at one another when Captain Manuel Garcia y Ortega opened the emergency door and threw them out. Love and death, love and death. So it goes.

The Lady From Stalingrad Mansions

The Way to the Stars

The White Paper recommends that Biggin Hill should be taken over by the British Airports Authority and developed for businessmen's executive planes.—Daily Mail

OUTSIDE THE OLD green Nissen hut, the businessmen dozed in the sun. Black labradors dozed at their feet. True, here and there the drone of bees was punctuated by the click of backgammon counters, but such activity was the exception. Dozing was the rule.

They lay sprawled in their canvas chairs beneath the blue Kent sky, their rippling blond toupees ruffled by the summer breeze, their suede flying-waistcoats unbuttoned, their heavy cufflinks bulled to Brasso glitter, their smooth pink faces slack with sleep. The fatigue was palpable: the Glenlivet, the profiteroles, the plump grouse and the plumper secretaries had all taken their inevitable toll.

So much was asked of them, this pitiful handful of Englishmen and their old-fashioned string-and-paper enterprises, nothing between them and the might of Germany and Japan but obsolete techniques and half-trained crews, flying gamely (but blind) into enemy territory with only last year's address books as their guide, against appalling odds. Mere boys, many of them no more than forty-five, they had been plucked from their playing-fields and hurled into family businesses with no formal training whatever, left to muddle along on such skills as they had managed to pick up at Tramp and Annabel's.

Yet, as the storm clouds gathered, darkling, over England, they had not been found wanting: they had rallied to the call, they had flocked out to Biggin and Tangmere in their company

345

Mercs and Alfas, and, unshaken by the fearful threat poised across the narrow Channel, dozed off.

In the makeshift Ops Room, while yawning escort agency girls with weary eyes pushed their wooden rakes across the European map like the croupiers as which they nightly doubled, dragging the ominous massed blobs of Yamaha and Braun and Fiat ever deeper into British territory, the Group Sales Manager of Polygunk Industries placed a small cardboard box in front of his aide.

'The boffins have come up with this,' he said quietly.

The aide opened the box.

'What is it, sir?' he said.

The GSM smiled.

'It baffled me, too, at first, old chap,' he said. 'Amazing technical breakthrough, actually. It's a post-Jubilee chiming beefeater that holds anything up to five cigarettes. Every hour on the hour it plays *Puppet On A String*, our great Eurovision triumph, and walks up and down for a bit.'

'Good Lord!' cried the aide. 'Is there no end to Barnes Wallis's genius?'

'Our plan,' said the GSM, 'is to hit them hard in three different places, Hanover, Wuppertal, Dortmund, all in a single sortie! What do you think of *that*, Frobisher?'

The aide narrowed his steel-blue eyes.

'It might just work,' he said.

He wound up the beefeater.

Its head fell off.

The Senior Export Flight Controller limped into the Briefing Hall. So did his dog. They both had tin legs. Neither leg, unfortunately, hinged at the knee; new bolts had been on order for eighteen months. Even more unfortunately, the dog's ended in a man's tin foot, all tin paws having been recalled the year before by the manufacturers because of a design fault.

The air in the hall was thick with Hai Karate and the sound of snoring, but the assembled businessmen were suddenly snapped awake by the dog, which, attempting to scratch itself with its giant iron hind-limb, fell over with a clang.

'Chaps!' barked the SEFC. 'I'd like you to look at this!'

He whipped back the green baize cover from the blackboard beside him. The men gasped!

'Yes,' said the Controller, 'the writing's fallen off it. Is the Chairman of Belwether British Chalks here, by any chance?'

A large flier in a pin-striped charcoal-grey Mae West stood up.

'Sorry about that,' he said, 'we seem to have supplied an export-only batch in error. You should've got our Premier Non-Squeak Number 4.'

'Are you telling me,' snapped the Controller, 'that my plucky, hard-pressed golden lads are risking their lives flying worthless chalk into the enemy heartland?'

'It's only going to bloody Chad,' protested Belwether. 'They don't know how to write there, anyhow. When the chalk don't mark, they'll think it's them. By the time they learn different, we were planning to get taken over by Reeves or somebody. No harm done.'

'No harm done?' cried the SEFC. 'I was up all night putting our flight plan on that! In two hours, you will be hitting the Ruhr with eight million giant rubber spiders! They're loading the suitcases and folding tables *now*!'

Among those businessmen who had not yet dozed off again, there was uproar.

'Novelty goods?' shrieked a thin salesman in the front row. 'Have you any idea what chance we stand against Jerry with those, sir?'

'He's right, sir,' called another. 'On our last run to Düsseldorf, we were cut to pieces! Schlimmhalters of Essen are capable of putting out ersatz Gonks at three quid a gross! The Essen Rubbischverein alone has a weekly output of five hundred metric tonnes of plastic dogs' doings, and the Wiesengross whoopee cushion is light years ahead of anything we can do. Give us something we can get our teeth into, sir, give us something big to throw at them!'

'Give us a car!' piped a voice.

'Who's that?' barked the Controller.

'Phillimore, sir.'

'You're just up from base, aren't you, Phillimore?' said the

Controller, not unkindly.

'Yes, sir.'

'I thought so. Only a sprog would bring up cars. These are dark days for the economy, Phillimore. I'm told we shall be getting a new British Leyland Medium Mini Maxi Sports Caravanette Hatchback by 1993, but until then, Phillimore, we shall just have to stiffen the old lip, shan't we, bite on the thingy, make do and mend, eh?'

'Yes, sir. Sorry, sir.'

'Splendid!' said the Controller. 'Now chaps, let's get into the old crates and show Jerry what we're made of! And remember, if you meet any foreigners, try not to give the game away by talking. They speak a different language, most of 'em, and if they suspect you're British you won't stand a bloody chance! Try to make contact with our agents on the ground, they sometimes know a shop or two which might take a dozen. Good hunting! By God, I wish I was going with you!'

And here he thwacked his tin leg with his stout malacca cane. A nut dropped out, and rolled under the table.

'Wake up, Frobisher!' cried the Group Sales Manager. 'They're coming back!'

The two men shielded their eyes against the rising sun.

They craned.

They peered.

'My God,' muttered Frobisher, 'he's on his own!'

The GSM steadied himself against the parapet of the control tower.

'Five gone, old lad,' he whispered. 'Five failed to return!'

They walked slowly to the De-Briefing Room to meet the sole survivor.

'We lost Harrison on the way over,' he said. His eyes were glazed, his voice cracked. 'He has decided to take up residence in Guernsey. Webster managed the trip all right, put down in Bruges to ask the way, and had his bloody plane impounded against the non-fulfilment of an order for Chelsea boots going back to 1969. They got Morris before he was even off the Dortmund tarmac. They'd remembered him from when he was Morris's Corned Beef. They lost ninety people in that typhoid epidemic, you know, plus three decapitated by exploding tins. As for Jackson, I'm afraid the Reeperbahn got him on his first morning.'

He poured himself a large Hine, tremblingly.

'And Cox?' muttered the Controller. 'What about Cox?'

'Cox?' cried the survivor. He laughed a short bitter laugh. 'Don't talk to me of that treacherous swine, sir! Cox is staying there, sir, and good riddance, say I! Wuppertal Museum offered him fifty quid for his Trident, and he took it.'

Outside the old green Nissen hut, the businessmen dozed in the sun. Black labradors dozed at their feet. They did not wake even when, at precisely 14.00 hours, in impeccable formation and with a cataclysmic roar, three thousand Japanese executive Zeros dived without warning out of the dazzling sun.

When they did wake, however, everyone immediately agreed that it was an absolutely infamous way to do business.

The Rhinestone As Big As The Ritz

And The Living Is What?

AT LAST, now that the thunder of the guns has echoed away over the battlefield of the Liberal Party, now that the groans of the wounded and the cheers of the victors alike have faded, we political commentators can stand back and what's that the cat's dragging across the lawn?

Sorry about this.

I shall be back with the future of the Liberals in two shakes of a

The thing is, with temperatures in the nineties, it behoves each and every one of us in this great country of ours to take a particularly close look at what our cats are dragging about; with the rate of rotting up around Mach 2, today's dead chaffinch is tomorrow's epidemic. Walk past our dustbins, giant bluebottles whang up like grouse; in the small hours, you can hear them knocking the lids off.

It's a large goldfish. Or was. The cat freezes, paw on gill, glares up with a feral eye; a tiny Douanier Rousseau tableau, rife with threat. Is the strange heat reverting the moggy to type? Are old genetic echoes running through its system? Are its little DNA molecules ricocheting about like hot popcorn, filling it with jungly urges?

I pull it off the fish. The cat, I swear, growls. It watches, with its new malevolence, as I pick up the goldfish. The tail is dry, the colour ebbs from it as I watch; weird, like the last frame of *Dorian Gray* when the young face ages fifty years in death.

Just before I re-address myself to the Liberal future, I ought to decide what to do about this little corpse. Where did the cat get it? Are neighbours even now gazing into their reft ponds and penning notes to stick on gates? *Goldfish, may or may not answer to name Charlie, missing from 32* . . . What should the caring citizen do? Go round from door to door with the last mortal remains on a plate, probing ex-ownership? *Good evening, you don't know me, I'm from Number 26, I was just wondering* . . .

No. Best to dispose of it. Can't leave it for cat to eat, can't tell what might happen to cat if it tastes fresh, well almost fresh, meat, next thing you know it could be dragging elderly relatives off to its basket.

Dig small hole behind greenhouse, drop goldfish in it, pat down earth, wash, return to typewriter.

For David Steel, I have nothing but

You may wonder what I'm doing writing in the garden; and, the fauna having interrupted the easy flow of political argument, you have the right to an explanation.

I normally type at the top of the house, a roomlet under the eaves, a romantic snug carved from the living joist; most nights I'm locked there like some mutant heir in a Victorian melodrama. But it is a spot that collects all the spare heat in the house, and squares it, prising open every pore of the hapless saunee and offering the wet fingers the chance to type lines like 'Ay ladt, moe thar tje yhunfer of yhe gubs gas exhord asta . . .' which as openings of political articles go, has little on its side but mystery. Not only that: up there, the heat has driven the very fabric of the building crazy—the roof creaks like a wind-jammer, the tank gurgles, the tiles gnaw one another, pipes burp.

So I carried the machine down into the garden. A hot afternoon, but a light breeze in spasms, some shade under the tree, a jug of coolant beside the Olivetti, the whole thing not unlike the urban writer's dream of a bee-loud tax haven somewhere beyond the International Date Line, a spot where the bones thaw and warm tranquillity nourishes the images, do a novel a week in a place like this. Once you've buried the fish.

Glad I explained that.

Now, then.

For David Steel, I have nothing but the greatest oh Christ a bee has fallen in the jug. Big bee, like an angry muff. Not much gin in it, mainly tonic, but how much gin does a bee need before it reckons it can lick anyone in the place? Nevertheless, we are all part of the great chain of being, we must love one another or die, if man does not help bee, what does the future hold for any of us?

Got nothing to get bee out with. Roll up piece of paper, bee ignores it, hydroplanes madly around the surface of the booze like a blob of phosphorus, bouncing off ice cubes. It is getting angrier, it does not see the foolscap as a lifeline, but a weapon, it is doubtless pumping all its venom towards its armoured bum ready for its kamikaze blast, girding itself to die with name of queen on lips.

Lips?

Finally—does it appreciate the sacrifice?—I tip the jug out, the Gordons sinks into the brown grass, the bee plods about in its little alcoholic swamp, grounded. I have no plans to dry it out, I have gone as far in charity as I am prepared to go, I leave the bee to sort itself out and go for a fresh jug.

When I get back, with a good sentence held carefully in my head about John Pardoe, the liquid patch is alive with starlings, doubtless as dry and thirsty as the rest of us. They clatter up as I approach.

They have eaten the bee.

At least, the bee is no longer there, and as it could not have had time either to dry out or sober up, we must assume it is now working its way down some airborne gizzard.

If I'd left it in the jug, it could have passed quietly from this vale of tears in utter painlessness and woken up across The Great Divide with the last verse of *Nellie Dean* still murmuring from its smile.

I am not ready for nature and its imponderable ways. I ought to be up in that airless room.

For David Steel, I have nothing but there is water falling on the paper.

I look up, there is the impenetrable foliage of the acacia. Rain will not fall through that. Rain, in fact, will not fall anywhere, since there has not been a cloud over these premises for three weeks.

Anyway, the rain is horizontal, which explains why it is now falling on one side of my body only. I look round; there is a rainbow between me and the fence.

It is the work of a moment to rip the paper from the typewriter, scream, and dash round to the neighbour's. A tiny Filipino opens the door, all smiles, a beam on little legs.

'I'm awfully sorry, I wonder if you could possibly move your sprinkler to the other side of the garden, just for a while?'

The smile widens.

'Sprimbler?'

'The water. It's falling on me. If you could just . . .'

She beckons me in, bows me backwards to the kitchen, gives me a glass, points to the tap, smiles even wider.

'Wodder,' she offers generously. 'Wodder for hot. Very hot.'

I drink a glass of wodder, we bow to one another, I walk back, the refilled jug is full of flies, water is running through the typewriter, my notes on the pad beside it are sodden, illegible, like a love-letter to a distant soldier.

I move the table and the chair out of the pouring shade, into the sun, the typewriter dries, I put in a fresh sheet, sweat springs from the skin, I type:

Ay ladt, moe thar tje yhunfer of yhe gubs

I get up, with considerable care and self-control, and go inside with the jug of flies, and empty it down the sink, and turn to the refrigerator, and discover that I did not close the refrigerator door on my last visit so that not only is there no ice but also the floor of the refrigerator is awash with molten butter; a couple of lolly-sticks float across it, lazily, propelled by the vibrations of the machine as, heartbreakingly, it struggles against the odds to perform the function it was put on this earth to do.

Mop up butter, drink warm beer, plod back to typewriter.

Sun hammers down, gnats wheel, brain gums, importance of Liberal Party struggles to make itself felt, no propositions come, no theses surface, just two-dimensional faces, Freud and Henry, the Dowager Grimond, a man who came to the door once, years ago, covered in rosettes, and tried to explain the Liberal stance on Cambodia, or was it Cyprus?

It is some time later when I open my eyes from a dream of pain. The sun is considerably lower, but I do not notice this at once, since all I can see are the figures 6, 7, 8, & 9, in soft focus, these being a millimetre from my left eye, the rest of the face buried in the keyboard. I raise my head, the bunched keys fall back from the platen, my lips are a solid Velcro weld, my entire skin from chin to crown is shrunk, taut, singing with irradiation; I squint down my nose, it is giving off a purpurean shimmer, it is a miracle of metamorphosis, the sun has turned me into W. C. Fields even as I slept.

The table, the MS, the beer-can, are alive with earwigs. Thus Gulliver must have felt. The earwigs, this being the summer of the Giant Crawly—we have greenfly the size of damsons, ants like Dinkies—are huge, French-polished: if they tried to climb into your ear, they'd wedge, you'd have to call the Fire Brigade to pull them out.

Enough. The dream of deft quills whorling beneath Tahitian palms is over; I recall, too late, that Polynesian literature has not, in fact, made much of a mark on the world's bookshelves. I heft the typewriter up, creep inside, the house is cool.

The house is burgled.

There are scattered drawers everywhere, empty cufflink-boxes, open wallets, piles of clothes with gutted pockets, rejected loot strewn insultingly from room to room, cupboard doors hanging open; perhaps a hundred socks, here and there. I sprint through the place, clutching the typewriter still, as if it were a weapon: what shall I do if I corner him? Threaten to type out a meticulous description?

He is long gone.

Two coppers come, shirtsleeve order, trannies nattering. There is much professional peering.

'Yes, well, heatwave, windows open, what do you expect, lot of it about, up the drainpipe, turn it over, down the drainpipe. It's all down to the sun, right?'

'Villains' holiday,' says the second.

'But I was right there in the garden,' I protest.

'People in the garden, what can you expect?' says the first. 'It's the heat.'

'There you are then,' says the second.

There you are then.

The Lady From Stalingrad Mansions

354

What Every Schoolboy Knows

With the introduction of sex education into the curriculum of the under-tens, something is likely to happen to the whole fabric of the British school system. In fact, anything is.

The honeyed sun streamed through the double-glazed mock-mullions of St. Swine's Comprehensive, dappling the upturned faces of the two thousand pupils at morning assembly and making their little bloodshot eyes cringe back into their sallow bags. Many a tiny tongue was furred with the strain of a long night's practical homework, many a small hand trembled involuntarily, many a lustless head lolled on an aching shoulder, all passion spent.

As the last discordant notes of *How Sweet The Name Of Kinsey Sounds* died wearily away, the Headmaster rose, drew his dirty fawn raincoat more majestically around him, and, pausing only to fondle the Senior Mistress, cleared his scrawny throat.

"School," he began, in that distinguished whine so familiar to the smaller girls, on whom it was his habit to press boiled sweets, "I have one extremely pleasant duty to perform before we dismiss. As you know, this is the moment in Assembly at which we offer our thanks and congratulations to those whose achievements above and beyond the call of mere duty have brought honour to the fine name of St. Swine's. Today, I ask you to acknowledge in the traditional manner the success of J. Griswold of the Lower Sixth, through whose selfless and unstinting efforts Millicent Foskett and Anona Rutt of Form 5a have both become pregnant."

The staff applauded vigorously, drumming excited feet upon

the echoing dais. The school, however, responded merely with a dutiful and brief clapping of limp hands.

Nobody liked a swot.

It was the shrieking laughter from the gymnasium changing-room that proved the illicit mob's undoing. As it rang across the playground and down the musky corridors of the school, it fell inevitably upon the tensed ear of the Senior PT Master, who sprang athletically from the Matron, grabbed his track-suit on the half-leap, and began sprinting towards the fearful noise of joy. He took the gym steps four at a time, as befitted a man who had outdistanced every husband in the neighbourhood, tore open the changing-room door, plunged through the mass of terror-stricken boys and dragged three soaking offenders with their hands upon the very taps out from the shining tiles.

They trembled before his fury, their sin pooling around their feet.

"You disgusting little pigs!" shrieked the Senior PT Master, shaking with such rage that the Matron's ear-ring disentangled itself from his sideburn and rolled away beneath a bench. "So this is what happens when my back is turned! An orgy! An—an unspeakable vileness! To think that St. Swine's boys should be found taking cold showers!"

Biggs of 3b, tiniest of the offenders, began to sob.

"It's—it's not my—f-f-fault, sir," he wept. "I c-c-couldn't help it!"

Veins twanged and knotted on the Master's temple.

"Couldn't help it, Biggs? *Couldn't help it?*" He bent his terrible face to the fast-blueing lecher. "How many times have you been told what a cold shower will do to a healthy young lad, Biggs? What will happen to you if you don't stop doing it?"

"I—I'll g-g-go b-blind, sir," sobbed Biggs.

"Right! And what else?"

"I'll b-b-break out in w-warts."

"And?"

"G-g-go bald. D-d-die in a loony bin."

The Senior PT Master straightened.

"This is the last time I'll tell you," he roared, and his little black eyes drilled into their very souls. "Don't think I don't understand a boy's problems. Don't think I don't know what it's like when the awful wicked urge to have a cold shower comes over a young man. But when that nasty desire takes its terrible hold on you, there's one thing you can do, isn't there? And that's go straight out and . . . what?"

"Get laid, sir!" screamed the boys.

"Right!" roared the Senior PT Master.

Biggs of 3b got home at four in the morning. His eyes rolled in their sockets like a couple of maraschino cherries, and a lard-like sheen coated his saffron skin. He was carrying an enormous teddy-bear, a deflated balloon, and a box of cheap cigars. He fell through the door, and fetched up, gasping, against a radiator. His parents were still up, waiting.

"Where you been this time?" asked his father.

"Educational outing," whispered Biggs of 3b, and dozed off.

"Where to?" shrieked his mother, shaking him.

Biggs of 3b woke.

"Take 'em off!" he yelled. "Take 'em off!"

"Where *to*, Nigel?"

The child licked his lips, regained a sort of consciousness.

"Been on a ramble," he muttered, "to the Greek Street Nudorium and Strip-o-rama. After that, we visited a Fräulein Sadie Bamboo. At least, 3b did. 3a had to try picking birds up on Clapham Common. They got a Proficiency Certificate exam next term. Norman Loom's gone off to Brighton with a retired Chief Petty Officer." The boy yawned. "Norman's working for a Special Paper."

"They're working the lad too hard," said his father to Mrs. Biggs. "All this learning. It don't make up for experience. Filling his brains up with stuff. I left school at fourteen and had Maureen Hodges in the bus-shelter. Getting out in the world, that's what does it."

"Werl, you weren't exactly an intellectual, were you?" said his wife. "More practical. Good with your hands."

"Good with my hands," nodded Mr. Biggs. "More practical. Now, Nigel," he said kindly to the boy, "off to bed."

Biggs of 3b shook his head wretchedly.

"Can't," he moaned. "Got to do my prep, haven't I? Got to stand up in class tomorrow and Describe In My Own Words Without Aid Of Diagrams, haven't I?"

"Oh," said his father.

"Oh," said his mother.

They looked bleakly at one another. His father sniffed.

"We've not got to help him with his homework again, have we?" he muttered.

His wife sighed heavily.

"We shouldn't stand in the way of his education," she said. "We shouldn't put our own feelings first."

Her husband stared at the floor.

"It's the fourth time this week," he said.

Gloomily, the trio trooped upstairs.

"It has come to my attention," said the Headmaster, adjusting his dress, "that books and magazines of the most evil and pernicious kind are circulating in my school."

Four thousand eyes suddenly homed in on him. Even the Upper Sixth, who had been cramming for A-levels with an intensity that had reduced them to wizened wrecks, thumbed open their eyelids and struggled to focus on their leader.

"Biggs of 3b," bellowed the Headmaster, "was found yesterday in the east lavatories, locked alone in a cubicle . . ."

"Alone!" gasped the School.

". . . reading Volume III of the *Children's Encyclopaedia!* Also in his possession were current copies of the *Economist, History Today,* and the *Highway Code.* QUIET!" shouted the Headmaster, as several girls began screaming and fainting. An uneasy silence settled. He went on: "I fail utterly to understand, when we have a school library full of the most healthy, wholesome texts—*The Perfumed Garden, Maurice The Human Stallion, Last Exit To Brooklyn, Portnoy's Complaint,* to name only the most boring—I fail utterly to understand why boys and girls should creep off to dark corners and fill their minds with cheap non-educational trash. Mens sana in corpore sano, School, and anyone caught reading Enid Blyton will not be allowed to undress on the forthcoming outing to Epping Forest!"

In the body of the hall, shunned by his nudging classmates, Biggs of 3b began pitifully to whimper.

The next day, Biggs of 3b would not get up. There was no observable sickness, no evidence of fever; it was merely that Biggs of 3b lay on his back, staring fixedly at the ceiling, and moving only when a nervous tic racked his small silent frame.

"What is it?" said his mother.

"Nothing," said Biggs of 3b.

"But it's Thursday," said his mother. "It's a very important day at school, isn't it?"

"Yes," said Biggs of 3b.

His brain shrank. Two periods of compulsory Swedish, then O-level Flagellation until lunch. After lunch there was a seminar in Plastic Rainwear II, a period of Petting, and then Free Expression until home-time. He was paired for Free Expression with Cheryl Gurth, who stood a head taller than Biggs of 3b and could crack walnuts with her knees.

His mother looked at him.

"I'll send a note," she said gently. "I'll say: 'Please excuse Nigel Biggs of 3b on account of a bilious attack and severe nose-bleed and a slight chill.' "

She went out and closed the door. Biggs of 3b smiled for the first time in months, and his hands unclenched, and his tic disappeared. A bird sang, and Biggs of 3b closed his grateful eyes.

He was twelve next birthday, and sick of sex.

The Sanity Inspector

And A Happy Saturnalia To All Our Readers!

THE MAGI eased themselves down from their horses, wincing, and blew on their fingers. They had had a cold coming of it. Not to mention a cold going back.

Melchior took the myrrh out of his saddlebag and stared at it.

'We aren't half going to cop out,' said Gaspar gloomily.

'He'll go up the bloody wall,' he muttered. 'I bet we won't even get expenses.'

'I've a good mind to hang on to the gold,' said Balthazar. 'We could say we got mugged. We could say prices in Bethlehem have gone right through the roof.'

'He'd never wear that,' said Gaspar. 'He'd have our hands off at the wrist before you could say Jack Robinson. Heads up on poles as well, I shouldn't wonder.'

'Come off it!' cried Melchior. 'We three kings of Orient are!'

'*Were,* more like,' said Gaspar. 'Be lucky to end up as we three corporals.'

They shuffled wretchedly inside, and knocked on a door marked MAGUS-IN-CHIEF.

'Come.'

They went in. The Chief Magus looked at them. He saw the still-wrapped gifts.

'What's this, then?' he said, slowly.

'Couldn't find Him, could we?' replied Balthazar.

'You *what?*'

'Solid cloud,' said Melchior. 'Couldn't see a hand in front of your face, never mind stars. We asked all over, though.'

'It was like looking for a needle in a wossname,' said Gaspar. 'It's got more stables than you've had hot dinners, Bethlehem.'

The Chief Magus glared at them for a long time.

'You realise what this means, I suppose?' he muttered. 'It means no Christmas, that's what it means! It means bloody Saturnalia again, orgies, sacrifices, people off work for a month, production up the spout. And what about this lot then?'

He pointed to a pile of paper in his out-tray.

'What are they?' asked Melchior.

'Christmas cards,' snapped the Chief Magus. 'Only spent the last three days writing addresses, didn't I?'

'You'll have to nail some ads up,' said Gaspar, 'telling people you're not sending cards this year.'

'Or any year,' muttered the Chief Magus bitterly . . .

The Chairman stood on the opposite pavement of Oxford Street and stared across at his store. Above the giant papier-mâché models on the façade, a banner shrieked MERRY SATURNALIA 1976! in great, red, sateen loops.

'You'll notice,' murmured the Head of Design, indicating his creation with a lily hand, 'that this year's leitmotif is rape.'

'It always is,' said the Chairman.

The Head of Design glowered at him through burning lashes.

'I happen to be very into tradition,' he said tightly. '*Some* people think it's very hip to have a load of symbolic perspex tat about the birth of the sun, but I'd rather be *dead* than oblique. I suppose you fancy Harrods' rubbish this year, all dancing rhizomes with funny hats on and Mother Nature in a garlic G-string?'

'I didn't say so,' said the Chairman.

'You didn't have to, Dennis. I could see it in your face. It was one of your Looks, wasn't it? Personally, I think it's sickeningly twee. I mean, it might be all right for *their* market, lot of sentimental old dykes coming up from Cheltenham to buy French reproduction telephones, but it isn't ours, duckie. We're at the solid, no-nonsense, family end of the market, people coming to us want to see something they can understand.'

'I suppose you're right,' said the Chairman. He shielded his eyes against the sharp December sun. 'What exactly *is* that that Uncle Holly is doing under the sled?'

The Head of Design sighed, rolling his eyes.

361

'The trouble with you, Dennis,' he sae, 'is you don't get out enough.'

The agent shook his head doubtfully.

'I'm not happy about this,' he said. 'I'm not happy about this at all. Couldn't you just rough him up a little? Knock a few teeth out, break his arm?'

'Out of the question,' said the Head of Light Entertainment. 'The BBC Saturnalia Variety Spectacular is the high point of the year. With an £18 licence-fee, the public has a right to a decent human sacrifice. What kind of a finale would it be if the Vestal Virgins just danced down the stairs and knocked the star's teeth out? There's going to be twenty million people tuned in on Boxing Night, just had a nice dinner, full of booze and seasonal spirit, how are they going to feel if after all that, if after sitting through the obscene ventriloquists and Schumann's Lascivious Horses and Royal bloody Ballet excerpts from *Nude Lake,* they're forced to watch Des O'Connor just crawl away in splints?'

'But *decapitation!*' protested the agent. 'Des has always been such a snappy dresser. What's he going to look like with his head off and his lavender tuxedo ruined?'

'He can count himself lucky,' said the Head of Light Entertainment. 'London Weekend are going to boil Reg Varney in oil.'

The agent sighed, and drew the contract towards him.

'Go careful at rehearsal,' he said, scribbling his name. 'Remember, I got a family to feed.'

Arthur Sidgewort hung the last rhino-horn on the tree, wound up the satyr on the top, and climbed down the step-ladder.

'I suppose I'll have to sleep with your cousin from Stockport again,' he said.

'Maureen's very nice,' said his wife, adjusting a fairy-light so its gleam fell across a dangling rat. 'She always brings something for Grandpa.'

'Last thing she brought was that inflatable brunette,' muttered Sidgewort. 'Her stopper flew off in the middle of the night and she whizzed round the room smashing all the souvenirs he brought back from Spion Kop.'

'She's never said an unkind word about you in her life,' snapped his wife. 'She likes you very much.'

'You don't have to tell *me* that,' said Sidgewort. 'Last Saturnalia, I didn't get out of traction till February 3rd. I suppose it'll be you and my Uncle Norman. I don't know what you see in him.'

'I don't see anything in him, Arthur. That's the whole point. Saturnalia is a time for giving. Sometimes I don't think you know the meaning of the word charity.'

He was still glowering at her when the doorbell rang. He opened it. There were two dustmen standing on the mat, beaming and touching their caps.

'Merry Saturnalia, squire!' they cried.

Arthur Sidgewort turned his head.

'Doris,' he called, 'it's for you!'

In the vestry of Mars-by-the-Wall, Bromley, the Rev. J. D. Huggett took off his laurel wreath, sighed, and pulled on his rubber coxcomb.

'I think the moth's been at the skin, vicar,' said his sexton, shaking the fleshtint folds and struggling with the zip. 'Perhaps we ought to get a new Father Saturnalia outfit for next year.'

'Don't be ridiculous, Mimsey!' snapped the Rev. J. D. Huggett. 'Where's the money coming from? If there was anything in the kitty, would I be going out in this filthy sleet to sing carols for the caryatid fund?'

He stepped into the legs of the skin and worked it up over his body.

'We've put on a little avoirdupoids since last year, I do believe!' simpered Mimsey. 'I think I'll put a stitch in that navel, it's stretched something terrible.'

The vicar pulled up the zip, not without difficulty, and tugged at the nipples to bring them into some sort of reasonable symmetry.

'How do I look?' he said.

'Not *terribly* nude,' said Mimsey. 'I think it's the leather elbows.'

'It'll be all right in the dark,' said the vicar. 'I'll look naked from a distance. The boys can stand on the mat, I'll sing from the gates. How is the choir dressed this year?'

363

'They're broad beans,' said the sexton. 'I thought it'd make a change from radishes.'

'Good thinking, Mimsey!' said the vicar, nodding his comb, and stepped out into the inclement night.

The twelve broad beans fell in behind his plump figure, acceptably pink in the streetlighting, and the little procession moved out of the graveyard, walking in single, relatively dignified, file until they reached the first house.

Whereupon Mimsey advanced up the path with the collection box, the Rev. J. D. Huggett twanged his tuning-fork against a convenient gnome, and the broad beans opened their little mouths and in a clear, sweet soprano began to sing:

'Four-and-twenty virgins came down from Inverness, and when the ball was over there were four-and-twenty less, singing . . .'

The Lady From Stalingrad Mansions

I Spy With My Little Eye

If the latest Finance Bill becomes law, H.M. Inspectors of Taxes will be empowered to 'enlist the co-operation of other members of family' when compiling dossiers on those they suspect of tax evasion.

Black Hand Esq.,
London Tax Division 67,
St Andrew's House,
Portland Street,
Manchester, M1 3LP

DEAR BLACK HAND ESQ.,   29 July 1978
   You do not kno me, but I am a frend of Special Agent 196 who sits nex to me in IVb and shoed me his badge in the lav. He also shoed me his Special Tax Strike Force Telescope which folds down into one bit and opens out for stairing at his father which he got off of your offis when he wrote about how his father was selling marroes out of his alotment and not telling you, and a man came down and felt his fathers coller. I also saw the larg lump on his eer where his father lashed out before your man could throe off his disgise and pin him down with this Special Tax Throe And Parralising Grip that your Agent 196 says they teach you when you go to this plaice hiden in a forrest and a master of Kung Fu shoes you how to poak your finger through a brik.
   Anyway, I do not expect to be one of those agents, not the ones who go around grabing people and bashing there briks up, I realise you have to be fully groan for that, no dout five foot eight also no glasses or denchers simlar to police, but I would very much like to be an agent like 196, I am as big as he is and nine as well, and I would like a Telescope, also the Special Tax

Killer Notebook where you write in what your fathers been up to.

My father is Norman Roy Wibley. He is 36 with thin hare and a small building business, also roofs done and loft conversions, though no glazing. He is almost certnly a crook, he has shifty eyes and is very vilent, often clumping people in the midle of dinner for aciddentally picking there nose and well worth spying on, especially if you had a good Telescope to see him up close and a Secret Tax Pencil With Miracle Rubber On End for writing with.

I am sik of Special Agent 196 going round telling evrybody about how he rescued England from his old man, I think evrybody should have the chanse,

Yours faithfuly,
L. M. Wibley, IVb

DEAR BLACK HAND ESQ.,   5 July 1978
Thank you for my Telescope and Killer Notebook And Pencil, also the Special Agent Manual on what to look out for, and the badge. Special Agent 196 says he has now got a Junior Tax Commanders Instamatic Camera With Carrying Strapp for leting you know that the Aunt Doreen his father clames as a dependant relative was blone to bits by a Flying Bom in 1944, wel I have got some good stuff too and trust you will not forget this when it comes to sending off cameras, a camera would help no end when caching Public Ennemy Norman Roy Wibley red handed.

Anyway, I am defnitely onto something! Wensday morning after he left in the van, I went into the spair room he uses as his offis, hoping to find evidence of where he was not using said room exclusively for comercial purposes as laid down in my Special Agent Manual, on account of I know he clames it against tax, I have often herd him cakling about how it is the smartest room in the house, new carpets, curtens, real lether armchairs and 'those bugers cannot touch me, it is legitimate offis ferniture, har-har-har, must be six hundred quidsworth of deductibles this year alone, ho-ho-ho, cakle-cakle' etcetera, and I was examining said room for sines of leisure activity such as nude magazines under blotter when I discovered a locked draw in his desk!

Terning imediately to page 32 of my Manual, I folloed the instructions and soon had the draw unlocked. Inside there was a larg black ledger, full of his tinie crimnal writing! Aha, I said to miself, this is A SECOND SET OF BOOKS, as described on pages 14-28! It is here, I said, that he records those cash transactions wich are bringing the country to its nees, and so forth. I will have him, also a Junior Tax Commanders Instamatic Camera and I don't know what else from a graitful Revenue!

I was just about to start reeding this book, when the door opened and the Ennemy himself walked in!

'What have you got there, you little sodd?' he belloed.

I went into a sort of Special Tax Crouch that I thought up miself; I may not be able to poak holes in briks, but I was prepaired to sel my life dearly. Imagine my amazement when he spoted the black book and sudenly went quiet, a strange smile playing about his lipps.

'Oh, I see you have found my old har-har-har, my old diary!' he mutered in a strangled sort of voise, 'I hope you have not read it?'

I shook my hed. He snatched the book from me, and I thought this is it, the clumping will start any minit, but no! Insted, he took out his wollet and gave me a pound noat.

'Let's keep it our litle secret, eh?' he mermered, leeding me to the door.

That was that. I do not kno wear that book is hiden now, but I will find it. Wibley is up to no good, and I will get him!

Yours faithfuly,

197.

DEAR BLACK HAND ESQ.,   8 July 1978

Thank you for the Camera, also the flash cubes. I noat that this means I will be able to photograph black books without waiting for the sunn to come out. I also noat that Special Agent 196 has received a Lone Taxman Repeeting Cap Gun And Consealed Holster just for informing your offis that the three cars in his father's garage are not in fact hired out for weddings and funerals by the Budget Limousine Company, which his father clames to have run at a loss for the last forteen years. I must say, 196 seams to be sitting on a goldmine, I wish Public Ennemy Wibley had a brane like 196's old man.

Stil, my own investigation is coming on very nisely. I have found out that the Ennemy is, as I suspected, Engaged In Other Paid Employment! I have notised that he goes off in the van at least three evenings a week, in his dark blue suit. My mum says it is on account of he is a mason and that he goes off to meet people with their trousers rolled up who hit one another with broom-handels, but you have to forgive her, she is not a Special Agent who has been traned to treet such codswollop with the contemt it deserves. She is not even brite enough to keep her Post Offis Savings Book in a false name like 196's mum, which is why he has got a Magic Luminous Tax Ring and I haven't.

But one thing is sure: Ennemy Wibley is moonliting for undisclosed cash! But I am on to his litle gaim!

Yours faithfuly,
197.

DEAR BLACK HAND ESQ.,   11 July 1978
Victory at last! Unlike weedy 196, I have risked life and lim in the jores of death, insted of just sitting in the shedd and writing off noats about how the £2,364.88 my grandfather got last year was not winnings at Wimbledon Dogs but cash rents from Pakistani waiters living in his coal-hole. I don't think it's fair Agents getting Supertax two-wheelers without doing anything brave, just scribling leters.

Not when some of us have been crouching in the back of vans under tarpaulins at ded of nite with the crazed Wibley hertling off on his ilegitimate business!

Anyway, I have got him bang to rites! The van stopped at 24, Omdurman Villas, Edgware, wich is certainly not an adress that appeers on any Wibley tax declaration, and the Ennemy went inside. I wated a few moments, then sliped out of the back of the van and into said house thrugh a downstares window.

All was dark, but I could hear voises from upstares, so adjusting my Personal Tax Mask I have constructed from puting a ballerclaver on bakwards and cluching my Notebook, Pencil, Manual, Telescope and Camera With Flashcube, I crept to the upper flore, lissened, and, crouching like a tigre, pulled open a door!

'AHA!' I cride. 'I have caught you, Norman Roy Wibley, 36! You are making undisclosed cash summs on the side!'

There was much shreeking and shouting at this, and the Ennemy disapeared beneeth the bedclothes. I herd his mufled voise yel:

'I have come here to reed the metre, Albert!'

At this, a larg lady wearing a sheet and standing on the dresing-table cride:

'It is not Albert, it is a blak midgit with a telescope!'

At this, the Ennemy poaked his hed out from the bed, and I imediately took his pitcher! And wile he and his customer were reeling about dazled from the flash, I slamed the door and made my getaway, leeping down the stares with my Special Tax Leep and vanishing into the nite!

I encloase said photograph. You will see that it shoes the Ennemy evading taxes, also the customer in the sheet. Needles to say, the Ennemy has compounded his felny by attemting to bribe me with vast summs and trying to find out if I have other adresses from his black book. He is going about the hous in terror with mad stairing eyes, mutring to himself, and wundring if I have sed anything to my mum about doing things on the side since he has cleerly not discloased to her this extra summ he is stashing away. I have not; we Agents do not go round telling sivilians.

Only one mistry remanes: what is Wibley doing? He is not reeding a metre as he clamed when grabed. My proffesional opinion is that he is dressmaking, wich is why the customer with the sheet is standing on the dresing-tabel. Either that, or Wibley is a biulder by day and a docter by nite. Anyway, I leeve that to you. I have done my part.

I would like my Supertax two-wheeler in red, but blak would be alrite, too.

Yours faithfuly,
197.

The Lady From Stalingrad Mansions

Wholesale War

"Pure Hornblower!" cried the Daily Express, *when five Israeli gunboats slipped their Cherbourg moorings and took off east. So what else could I do, except go straight back to my Hornblower and read between one or two lines?*

Horace Hornblum's mother sat in a corner of the mean little room in Somerset House, and wept, silently.

Horace Hornblum's father sat beside her and stared at the floor. Occasionally, he would shake his head. Occasionally, he would sigh.

Horace Hornblum stood patiently at the counter, watching through the window as the clerk's tatty quill squeaked and splashed across the Deed Poll form. It stopped. A small blot spread slowly beneath it.

"Right," said the clerk. "Horace Hornblum, born October 8 1785, present age fifteen, occupation cabin boy."

"Cabin boy!" shrieked his mother. She pressed her sodden hankie to her eyes and rocked back and forth. "Cabin boy!"

"Golden hands he's got," said his father gloomily. "A pianist's hands. Or a surgeon's hands."

"Both," said his mother. She blew her nose fiercely. "He could have been both. Operating by day, by night playing Bach. With such hands he has to be a cabin boy!"

His father took off his hat, and fanned himself mournfully.

"A fortune on harpsichord lessons," he muttered.

"Can you imagine—" his mother choked on a sob, "can you imagine what those ropes will do to my baby's hands?"

"Blisters," said his father, "like soup-plates."

"Like footballs," said his mother.

They were silent for a while.

"A violinist, even," said his father, at last.

The clerk came back.

"There you go," he said. He slid a fragment of vellum across the counter. "All official. You are now Mr. Horatio Hornblower."

"*Hornblower!*" shrieked his mother. And fainted.

"See?" shouted his father. "See what you've done? Your own mother!"

The newly-christened Hornblower walked over.

"You bring up children," murmured his mother, and passed out again.

"What did I do?" said Hornblower.

His father's eyes sped upwards, beyond the ceiling.

"What did he do? Only break his mother's heart! Only shame his father's family!" He riveted his eyes into his son's. "To change an honourable name is already bad enough. *But to change to such a name!* You meet people, they'd give their right arm to change their name from Hornblower to Hornblum! Believe me. All right, you want to change your name so what's wrong with Churchill? What's wrong with Twistleton-Wickham-Fiennes? What's wrong with Moncrieff Of That Ilk?"

Hornblower set his jaw.

"They're not sailors' names," he said.

"*Sailors!*" screamed his mother.

They carried her out between them. On the steps, his father turned. In his eyes there was a look of heartrending reasonableness.

"Look," he said. "Sailors get sick, right?"

"Right."

"So be a ship's doctor."

Horatio Hornblower shook his head, and they struggled on against the bitter wind, down to the drizzled Thames.

Tall ships bobbed on the Gravesend tide. Gulls wheeled, men sang at capstans, wagonloads of provisions rattled over the cobbles, bound for a dozen gangplanks.

371

"Ships' chandlering," said Hornblum, "is a good profession."

"There's a fortune in pemmican," said Mrs. Hornblum. "On biscuits I wouldn't even like to guess. Millions, people are making." She glanced sideways at Hornblower, cannily. "You could buy your own boat, someday."

"Your own *navy*," said Hornblum. "Why work for somebody else? You could declare your own wars. There's a fortune in wars. Look at France. Look at Austria."

"That Attila the Hun," said Mrs. Hornblum, "*There* was a businessman."

Horatio Hornblower fixed his young eyes on the steel horizon, dreaming of squadrons in battle order, hearing far cannon, smelling cordite.

"Too late," he said. "I have already signed on aboard *HMS Victory*."

"I was coming to that," said his father.

"What do you mean?" said Hornblower.

His mother sprang, two-handed, to his head and dragged it to her bosom, dislocating his new periwig.

"As if I'd let my baby, at my breast I held him, go off on some *battleship*!"

"Our own flesh and blood," said his father, "splattered all over the floor."

"Deck," said Hornblower.

His father shot out a short, solid arm and smacked his head.

"Deck, floor, what's the difference? When you're splattered, you're splattered."

"*Don't say such things!*" shrieked Mrs. Hornblum. "Don't talk from splattering!" She turned to her son. "You see what you made your father do? You see what aggravation you bring on your parents? Excitement like this, who knows what can happen? A heart attack, it can bring on. An ulcer."

"A malignant growth," said his father gloomily.

His wife fainted.

"You think I'm joking?" said his father, as they propped her unconscious body against a bollard. "What did Nat Rosenblatt do? Dropped dead. Would I lie? Stone dead from a stroke. And all *he* had was his son wouldn't go into partnership. So what should *I* say? Two strokes I'm entitled to. A ruptured spleen, I shouldn't be surprised. You'd think a boy would show some gratitude, his father arranges for him to sail on the *Schwanz*."

"The what?"

"Don't pretend you never heard from *HMS Schwanz*? Your Uncle Sam's boat, gowns delivered anywhere, also express alterations on board, missing buttons replaced free, special concessions for orders over a gross."

"But I've signed aboard the *Victory*! I want to sail with Nelson."

His mother's eyes snapped open.

"*Nelson*?" she cried. "They shot his arm off! They shot his eye out! You call *that* a living?"

Whereupon she grabbed Horatio Hornblower by the lapel and dragged him off after his disappearing father who, carrying his son's diddybox and chicken (he had asked for a parrot), was rapidly bearing down on the good ship *Schwanz*.

Two days out on the tossing Channel, Horatio Hornblower came to. He lay on his bunk in the spinning gloom, feeling sicker than he had ever felt before. As he groaned, he felt a familiar item touch his lower lip.

"Your own spoon," said a familiar voice. "Brought along special."

Hornblower sat up.

"Mother!" he cried. "What are you—"

"Eat first. Later, you can ask questions. Eat the soup, dolly."

"But I can't have relatives aboard."

"Relatives, relatives! Who's a relative? I'm your *mother*!"

"But a cabin-boy can't have his mother on—"

Soup drowned his sentence.

"From cabin-boys I wouldn't know," said Mrs. Hornblum. "All I know is from my son the captain."

"*Captain*?"

"Your father had a talk with Uncle Sam. It's all arranged. Personally, I wanted admiral for you. Rear-admiral the very least. But your father says it takes time. A whole year, maybe. A lot of people to see, it's not so easy."

"But I don't know how to command a ship!" shrieked Hornblower.

"What's to know? You get a wind, you sail a ship. You don't think your father, from nothing he built a business up, can't drive a lump of wood?"

"Father? Is he here, too?"

Mrs. Hornblum smiled happily, and began cutting up his greens.

"So what else are parents for?" she said.

The Hornblum family stood at the wheel, in the needling sleet. Above them, the canvas creaked; below them, the boards heaved.

"Three times already we passed that rock," shouted Mrs. Hornblum.

"Rubbish!" roared Hornblum above the gale. "To you all rocks look the same."

"Suddenly he knows from rocks!" screamed his wife. "Suddenly we got a rock expert in the family!"

"I think she's right," said Horatio Hornblower.

His father glowered at him from beneath his sou'wester rim. "Shut up!" he yelled. "Captains should be seen and not heard."

"Yes," said Mrs. Hornblum. "Don't answer your father back. Show a little respect."

"Children!" cried Hornblum. "All they know is to argue."

"You shouldn't even be up here," said Mrs. Hornblum to her son. "A chill on the liver you could get. Triple pneumonia. In both lungs. And who will you expect to nurse you?"

They passed the rock again.

"You go to sea," said Hornblum bitterly, "and what do you get? Heartache."

When the storm finally blew itself out, they saw the ship off the starboard bow, a mile or so away. Three masts, two tiers of cannon, and a French flag.

374

"Clear the decks!" cried Horatio Hornblower. "Action stations! Man the guns!"

The men looked up from their ironing-boards.

"Don't listen to him!" cried Mrs. Hornblum.

They went on pressing.

Hornblum ran up the Norwegian flag.

"What's that?" cried his son. "What are you doing?"

"Again with the questions!" snapped Hornblum. He lowered a bum-boat and, pulled by four stout trouser-cutters, set a direct course for the French man-o'-war.

They waited. The two ships moaned on their hawsers. Once, an albatross flew overhead, but Mrs. Hornblum shrieked at it, and it planed away westward. After about an hour, Hornblum returned. He was not alone.

The French captain shook hands with everyone. Then, with a small, stiff bow, he handed his sword to Horatio Hornblower.

"What's that for?" demanded Mrs. Hornblum. "An edge like a razor. He could cut himself. Blood-poisoning he could get."

"It's required," said Hornblum, "when you surrender."

"*Surrender?*" cried Horatio Hornblower. "Nobody fired a shot!"

"So who's complaining? Better surrender—"

The French captain held up his hand. They looked at him.

"God forbid I should come between a father and his son," he said, "only do me a favour, don't call it a surrender."

Hornblum nodded.

"How about merger? After all, you're still getting forty-nine per cent of the gross, in return for all the tax-free advantages of my brother-in-law Sam's Panamanian company."

"Merger is better," said the French captain. "Merger I like."

"You think Napoleon will understand?" said Mrs. Hornblum.

The Frenchman gave a short laugh.

"Napoleon!" he said. "So what does a little *schnip* like Napoleon understand from war?"

The Sanity Inspector

375

Plus Ça Change

In which I preview another wonderful crop of French books for 1978.

CETTE FOIS A BEZIERS
In this shattering new tour de force by Marguerite Duras, a man (called, with reverberative simplicity, M. Homme) arrives in Beziers one morning, or thinks he does. He may actually be in Laroque-des-Arcs. He takes a room in a small hotel, whose one window overlooks the rear entrance of a discount tyre warehouse. He does not notice this at first: the opening four chapters concern the way in which he is staring at the bedside table, until, in the seminal Chapter III (which reappears as Chapter XXVII), he throws his raincoat at it. In Chapter V, he leaves the room for the first time and goes to the lavatory at the end of the corridor. Arriving there soon after the opening of Chapter X, he looks at a crack in the washbasin, returning to his room in Chapter XIV in order to compare the crack in the washbasin with a button that has fallen off his coat. 'Could all this happen in Beziers?' is what Homme asks himself. It is then that he walks to the window and sees some old tyres in the yard opposite, and realises for the first time that the road is 8.76 metres wide, not including pavements.

   This is a wonderful book which says everything it has to say with an assured disregard for purpose. For 704 pages I was kept wondering: why am I reading this? And it is a measure of Mlle Duras's commitment that it was a question which remained implacable at its own answerlessness.

POMPON ARRACHE SON NEZ
As a change from the resonant austerities of Duras, I turned to this delightful Gascon romp in which the inhabitants of a small

village, incensed at the discovery that the Chief of Police has a talking pig, eat their mayor. Discovering what has happened, their priest, the lovable cross-eyed, one-legged, stone-deaf, half-mad Senegalese dwarf (a beautifully delicate piece of character-drawing, this), decides that as a punishment, the Angel of the Lord should come down and turn that year's unprecedentedly marvellous vintage into vinegar. He accordingly prays for this miracle, and, sure enough, a seven-foot tinker with a vulture perched on his head walks into the church. Believing him to be the Angel of the Lord, the priest falls to his knees and explains what he wants done; but, to the priest's considerable chagrin, the tinker turns out to be the editor of a communist newspaper who is in love with the daughter of the major wine-grower of the area, and who has come to the village in disguise to woo the girl against the wishes of her Poujadist father. To unfold further the brilliant plot would be to ruin this wonderfully warm and human story of life in provincial France, so let me just say that M. Chasserieu has once again excelled himself with a portrait of rural manners and mores second to none.

L'HISTOIRE D'U

U is a very rich young aristocratic girl who lives in a ninety-four-roomed apartment overlooking the Bois de Boulogne. Every morning she goes out onto her balcony, with nothing on beneath her rubber poncho, to watch the horses pass; whenever one of them breaks into a gallop, U falls down in a faint, frothing at the mouth, and scraping her fingernails along the harsh gravel of the balcony; a noise which itself drives her six maids wild with Sapphic lust and ensures that none of the silver is cleaned for at least two hours thereafter.

A big black doctor is called by U's stepfather, the Duc, and the doctor, having humiliated the patient with a number of spatulas and ophthalmoscopes, informs her father that she is repressing her urge to be a mare. Distraught, the Duc enquires as to possible lines of therapy, and the the doctor suggests that U be entered in the forthcoming Prix des Folles at Longchamps. As the Duc is a prominent racehorse owner, this presents fewer problems than might at first appear, the Duc's major worry being that he already has a horse, Mignonne, entered for the race, and may not be able to get a ranking jockey up on his daughter in time, unless he switches riders, which he is loth to do, since Mignonne has a good chance of winning.

In the event, he finds an apprentice, Alphonse Pinaud, who is willing to ride anything just for the experience of taking part in a big race. U gets a flyer out of the starting-gate and is lying second at the first bend when she suddenly catches sight of a particularly fetching stallion about to pass her on the inside. Mad with passion, she careers headlong into the rails, throwing Pinaud and breaking several ribs with a pain that drives her into delirious ecstasy. Waking up in Belleville Hospital, she finds herself purged of hippophilia, and rapes her osteopath.

A brave, challenging, and extremely dirty book, *L'Histoire d'U* richly deserves its place in the pantheon of Modern French literature. It will be thumbed and thumbed.

INNOCENTS, TOUS
Turning from fiction, we come to a major piece of painstaking historical research in which M. Gustav Pontfilet at last proves conclusively that nobody in Occupied France ever saw a German, let alone spoke to one. M. Pontfilet, who worked for the French underground during the war and received the Croix de Fer for the impeccable efficiency with which he kept the platform of Réamur-Sebastopol free of inferior races, has interviewed over twenty thousand Frenchmen who did not collaborate with the Germans, more than thirty thousand who never heard of anyone who collaborated with the Germans, and forty thousand more who thought the war ended in May 1940 and had never been able to understand why Ernest Hemingway had carried a gun when he burst into the Ritz bar in 1945 and always assumed it was because some *crime passionel* was taking place on an upper floor in which he had a marginal interest.

Lavishly illustrated with photographs taken at the time in innumerable towns and villages, all of them showing Germans nowhere to be seen, and with invaluable graphs demonstrating how trade in Paris and along the Riviera fell by almost one per cent during this dark period, *Innocents, Tous* explodes the myth of Franco-German co-operation and nails this foul canard once and for all.

THIS FOUL CANARD

Taking as his starting point the moment when he was served, at the famed Restaurant des Mamelons Risibles, an absolutely foul canard which he promptly nailed to the wall, Oscar Pasdequoi takes us on a picaresque tour of the grand disasters which it has been his sad duty as a Guide Michelin inspector to suffer: a truffled frog-bladder in Nîmes that defeated four of France's leading gastro-enterologists, a piece of gravel in a stuffed wren that resulted in his swallowing a tooth which subsequently ruptured his large intestine; a large intestine *à la manière de la Vicomtesse de Bragalonne* which proved to have been a small intestine inflated with a bicycle pump before being brought to the table and which therefore exploded when the flaming calvados was poured over it, resulting in the loss of M. Pasdequoi's hearing and a million pound lawsuit; and a crab at Le Crétin which woke during consumption and clamped its remaining claw on M. Pasdequoi's lip where it remained throughout Easter (since his doctor had decamped to Juan-les-Pins with Madame Pasdequoi, who had grown sick of her husband's refusal to grant her a rosette for the meals she prepared at home and had finally cracked when he wrote to her complaining of sloppy service).

Certainly, of the 1,131 books on cuisine so far published this spring, *Canard* bids fair to be the one most likely to engender the sort of thrilling controversy on which French literature depends for its very life. Already, one Prix Goncourt judge has been maimed by a fish-kettle, and two respected sommeliers have jumped from the Eiffel Tower, locked in one another's arms.

BONJOUR VIEILLESSE

Let us welcome another exhilarating new novel from the adroit pen of Mlle Françoise Sagan. In this one, a shy young virgin of 49 falls for a married man many years her senior, enraptured by his maturity and his style (he can take out his teeth, reverse the plates, and reinsert them without his hands ever leaving the rims of his bathchair), overwhelmed by his sophistication (in a whirlwind tour of Europe, they visit twelve spas in seven days), thrilled by his love-making (his elegant Louis XV bedroom has pulleys everywhere), and stunned by his wealth (he made his first fortune by the time he was thirty by taking bets on the outcome of Verdun), she turns her back on her own generation of swinging St Tropez knitters and becomes his bride. But trouble is , of course, in store when her husband's only son returns from prostate surgery and sets eyes on his ravishing young step-mother for the first time. . .

Another winner, another gem in the bright diadem of modern French letters!. Ah, would that the sluggish pens of other races but follow where these virtuosi lead!

The Lady From Stalingrad Mansions

The Idiot

'Examination fever is a summer disease that in the Soviet Union is caught not merely by pupils. The worst cases are among parents. Soviet parents are as ambitious as parents anywhere for their children's success, and a degree or diploma is still a passport to financial and social advancement in Russia. Parents who fear their children may not do well have been known to pull every string they can.—The Times

ON A PUNISHINGLY HOT morning towards the end of June 197–, a short, harrassed, dishevelled figure could be seen scurrying along S— Street, in the small industrial town of P. Despite the abrasive heat, he wore a long, tattered herringbone overcoat and a heavy fur hat that had seen better days.

In his two arms he bore a huge object that had been amateurishly wrapped in second-hand cartridge paper and tied with different sorts of string. The package was almost as big as the man, but he hurried on, looking neither to right nor left, clearly hoping that nobody would notice him or his extraordinary burden.

That this deception was not entirely successful could be judged from the cries that followed in his disordered wake.

'Oh, you have knocked me down with your enormous parcel, Nikolai Nikolayevich!'

And

'See, appalling Nikolai Nikolayevich, what havoc your passage has wrought upon my wheeled basket!'

And

'I curse you for a rogue and a scoundrel, Nikolai Nikolayevich, who has affrighted my beloved little dog with his vile mountain of cardboard!'

Nikolai Nikolayevich (for it was indeed he) paid no attention,

381

however, to the bitter shrieks of his fellow citizens. He hurried on, and did not stop until he came to the doorway of a tall grey apàrtment block at the corner of S— Street and G— Road, just before V— Avenue, to be precise, where he turned inside.

In the dark narrow corridor which smelt of cabbage and cats and overrated nineteenth-century novels, Nikolai Nikolayevich stopped, wedged by his enormous bundle against the nicotine-coloured lincrusta of the ancient wall. As he struggled to free himself, doors opened along the vile passage, and voices cried out.

'Is that you, disgusting Nikolai Nikolayevich, who is ruining the communal dado?'

And

'We hold you responsible, Nikolai Nikolayevich, for all damage incurred to the linoleum!'

And

'Oh, that I had my youth once more, I should kick that accursed Nikolai Nikolayevich until his shins bled!'

At last, the hapless Nikolai Nikolayevich succeeded in freeing his giant parcel and himself; and, gaining the worn wooden staircase, he struggled up to the —teenth floor.

His wife, when she opened the door of their tiny apartment, clasped her reddened hands and wailed for a time, as she did every day. Nikolai Nikolayevich waited with his customary fortitude until she had finished. It was, after all, the one entertainment she could afford on his miserable salary.

When it was over, she helped him carry in his parcel and stand it in the hall. So small was the flat that half the parcel poked into their living-room, where their son sat at a rude table, staring out of the window. He did not turn.

'See what your wonderful father Nikolai Nikolayevich has brought you, little Boris!' cried his mother.

The boy looked round, with dead eyes.

'What is it?' he said.

'It is a bicycle, little Borïs!' cried his father. 'Nearly new', with a one-speed gear, and most of a bell. It is for when you pass your examinations to go to the grammar school.'

'But suppose I do not pass my examinations?' said little Boris.

At this, his mother threw herself prostrate upon the pitiful

bare boards and shrieked so loud that their one reproduction
ikon fell off its pin.

The colour drained from his father's stair-empurpled face.

'*Not pass?*' he croaked. 'Not go to the grammar school and
become qualified and wear a homburg hat and receive a
monthly salary, so that people will point at you in the street and
cry: *That is Boris, son of Nikolai Nikolayevich, in the homburg hat,
carrying a buff envelope with his monthly salary in*, is that what you
want?'

'The bicycle is a bribe,' said little Boris, his voice like stone.
'It is a deviationist trick, designed to make me forget the
wonderful egalitarian principles by which all truly loyal Soviet
citizens must live. While we are on the subject, how did you
come by it?'

'It fell off a tractor,' muttered his father.

'TELL HIM, Nikolai Nikolayevich!' screamed his wife. 'Tell
him that you pawned your genuine tin watch to purchase it!'

'Is it true?' snapped little Boris.

Nikolai Nikolayevich nodded glumly.

'Buying, selling, pawning, trading,' and here the boy shook
his head grimly, 'this is a bad business, Nikolai Nikolayevich
my father.'

The three might have stayed thus staring wretchedly at one
another for some weeks, had at that moment the doorbell not
sounded. Nikolai Nikolayevich took the two steps necessary to
reach the door, and opened it.

'Oh, oh, oh, it is Pedagogue Dobrinin, schoolmaster to our
beloved little Boris!' he exclaimed. 'I must fall and kiss the hem
of your beautifully tailored overcoat!'

'Get up, esteemed Nikolai Nikolayevich,' replied the
academic with becoming gravity. 'I believe I heard something
clunk as you hit the floor, and I should not like to think of
anything breaking, nudge, nudge, wink, wink, eh?'

Nikolai Nikolayevich struggled to his feet, snatching at his
wispy forelock.

'Quite so, master, quite so,' he muttered. And here he
opened his own shabby coat to reveal the reason why he thus
wore it in the heat of summer.

The schoolmaster looked at the bottles.

'This is, I trust, the genuine article, Nikolai Nikolayevich, born 1820 and still going strong? It will not stand well with little Boris if I discover these bottles to contain only cold tea laced with a touch of wolf-piddle to deceive the inexperienced palate.'

Nikolai Nikolayevich gasped!

'That is the very best, Pedagogue Dobrinin!' he cried. 'It was sold to the personal friend of a personal friend by the British Ambassador, who is having a hard time making ends meet these days.'

'As are we all, Nikolai Nikolayevich,' countered the schoolmaster. 'Foreign cigarettes, to take a random example, are impossibly expensive, are they not?'

'Curse me for a forgetful fool!' howled Nikolai Nikolayevich, whipping off his old fur hat.

'Why,' exclaimed the schoolmaster, 'you have a carton of Lucky Strike on your head, Nikolai Nikolayevich!'

'Take them!' shouted that worthy man. 'Smoke them in good health, Pedagogue Dobrinin!'

After the schoolmaster had been bowed out, little Boris sat scribbling in his notebook for some minutes.

His parents beamed!

What joy for us, dear Reader, had we been there to witness the twin delights of parental devotion and filial obedience!

Little Boris was still scribbling and his parents were still beaming when the doorbell rang yet again. Nikolai Nikolayevich threw the door wide; and immediately fell back into the tiny apartment, his forehead all but touching the floor!

'Examiner Rosnetsov!' mumbled his trembling lips, 'Examiner Rosnetsov! See, wife, it is Examiner Rosnetsov himself who graces our unworthy hovel with his august magnificence, his light-weight suit, his silk tie, his astounding totally leather shoes!'

Examiner Rosnetsov strode into the room. His rimless glasses flashed the cold fire of authority, but they did not turn to little Boris. He put his sponge-bag down upon the table.

'Is this the woman?' barked Examiner Rosnetsov.

'This is she, sir,' replied Nikolai Nikolayevich.

'She is somewhat older than I had been led to believe,' said the great official. 'Also, she is bandy.'

'A trick of the light, no more!' cried Nikolai Nikolayevich. 'Would I, worm that I am, dare to deceive so eminent an educational paragon as Examiner Rosnetsov?'

'It is, however, a not entirely unattractive bandiness.'

'Ah. Now I look again,' said Nikolai Nikolayevich, 'it is just possible the knees of my lovely wife do not touch. It is doubtless the result of carrying the weight of her magnificent bosom. And are her hips not as I described them in my letter?'

'I have seen worse,' replied Examiner Rosnetsov. 'You may leave us now.'

'Thank you, Examiner Rosnetsov!' cried Nikolai Nikolayevich gratefully. 'Come, little Boris, your great examiner and your dear mother wish to be alone.'

Little Boris rose from the table at last, still scribbling. He pocketed his notebook. He walked out, behind his father, and followed him down the echoing stairs.

Out in the hot street, little Boris expressed his desire to go off on his own, down to the river to think.

'The boy is an intellectual!' cried his father, watching him go. 'The boy shall one day have a diploma, a Zim convertible, a private lavatory!'

Little Boris turned the corner, out of his father's sight. But he did not go down to the river. He quickened his pace, towards a public telephone.

After the two KGB men had dragged the screaming Nikolai Nikolayevich and his wailing wife out of the apartment and down the stairs, their inspector put his arm around the thin shoulders of little Boris.

'You did very well, little Boris,' he said. 'These evil people have engaged in every conceivable form of deviation, corruption and perversion for which our glorious state makes statutory provision. Mother Russia will throw the key away! And she will undoubtedly see to it that such loyalty and selflessness as yours do not go unrecognised. Of that you may be sure! Tell me, little Boris, what shall be your reward?'

Little Boris looked up into the granite face.

'I should like a place at grammar school,' he said.

The Rhinestone As Big As The Ritz

Die Meistersinger Von Leyland

The just-opened controversial opera Bomarzo *is said to have 'brought opera bang into the 1970's, simply because it involves nudity, sex and violence. But surely there's more to the 'seventies than that . . .*

AN OPERA IN THREE ACTS

CAST

FOSKETTO,
  A Chief Shop Steard
BERYLIA, His Wife
TRACY, Their Daughter
THE DUKE OF LEYLANDO,
  A Management
THE DUCHESS, His Wife
NIGELLO, Their Son
DUDLIO, A Conservative MP
FREDDIO, His Special Friend
GEOFFINI, A Marxist-Leninist
SLIME, An Architect

RATBAGGO,
  His Brother-In-Law
CREEPI, A Journalist
HOWEVER, An Editor
CHUCK, An Anglican Bishop
Chorus of Leyland Workers
Dancing Backbench Poofters,
Japs, Bankers, Heads of
Documentary TV, Addicts,
Bishops, Personalities, Arabs,
Muggers, Spokesmen, Gno-
mes, Social Workers,
Squatters

ACT ONE, Scene One.
Cowley. Before the Chief Shop Steward's Palace. Enter FOSKETTO.

FOSKETTO	What is this, here on the floor? Is it a letter?
CHORUS	It is a bleeding letter. Would you bleeding credit it?

386

FOSKETTO	Would you bleeding credit it? A letter, here on the floor, big as you please!
CHORUS	Big as you bleeding please, a letter!
FOSKETTO	I shall open it. Look, I have opened it!
CHORUS	Stone me, he has only gone and bleeding opened it!
FOSKETTO	My darling beloved Nigello, it says here, my heart burns for you like nobody's business. I cannot wait until our two bodies join as one and make wonderful music up the allotments.
CHORUS	Up the allotments!
FOSKETTO	That's what it says, up the allotments. I shall go on!
CHORUS	Stone me, he's going on!
FOSKETTO	It is signed—(*turns page*)— AAAAAAGH! (*Staggers*)
CHORUS	Bloody hell, he has had one of his turns!
FOSKETTO	Gawd almighty, it's one of my turns!
CHORUS	It's one of his turns all right, and no mistake!
FOSKETTO	Yes, it's definitely one of my turns! Werl, can you blame me?
CHORUS	Werl, can you blame him? It must be the bleeding signature what's brought it on!
FOSKETTO	Dead right, it's the bleeding signature what's brought it on!
CHORUS	Who can it be? Who can it be?

387

FOSKETTO	Only Tracy, that's all!
CHORUS	Not the lovely Tracy, apple of your wossname?
FOSKETTO	Yes, the lovely Tracy, my only daughter, only seventeen years old and already a shop steward up the fitting shop, and here's this bloody Nigello having a nibble of her up the allotments! And do you know who this Nigello is when he's at home?
CHORUS	No, who is this Nigello when he's at home?
FOSKETTO	He is only the bleeding son and heir of the Duke of Leylando, that's who!

(Chorus of workers falls on that day's half-finished Mini and smashes it)

Scene Two
Cowley. The snug of the Plum & Ferret.
Enter BERYLIA and DUDLIO.

DUDLIO	My dear Mrs Fosketto, what is your poison?
BERYLIA	My poison? Lor lumme, sir, you are not half a caution! I think I shall bust a stay if you do not cease your jesting!
DUDLIO	She says she will bust a stay! But she does not mean it, it is just her colourful way of expressing herself. O, how rich is the language of our working classes, how I admire their earthiness and candid wit!
BERYLIA	O what charmers you nobs are, sir! Thank you very much, mine is a Campari and Babycham with one of them little wax cherries in it!

DUDLIO	With a wax cherry it shall be, and what about a sprig of mint?
BERYLIA	Corblimey, sir, a sprig of mint, you certainly know how to treat a lady, also smelling of Brut like a bleeding film star, my head will fair turn any minute!
DUDLIO	But to our business, lovely Berylia! As you know, my heart burns for your lovely Tracy, and I wish for her hand in marriage!
BERYLIA	In marriage!
DUDLIO	In marriage!
BERYLIA	And here was me thinking when I saw you grabbing her bust during the excuse-me foxtrot up the works dance you was only after a bit of the other!
DUDLIO	The other? Nothing was further from my mind! I wish to join with her in holy matrimony, I can promise her ensuite bathrooms and her own Renault, also a fox stole and two holidays per annum, one guaranteed abroad, and do not forget, dearest Berylia, there will be something in it for yourself!
BERYLIA	Something for myself! (*Aside*) Strike me, whatever can he mean?
DUDLIO	Hobnobbing with the upper crust is what I mean, such as tea in the House of Commons and possibly a Royal garden party, I shouldn't wonder!

389

BERYLIA	A Royal garden party! I could wear me bottle-green with the crêpe-de-chine collar! I wouldn't have to be bleeding working-class no more! Oh never fear, dear Dudlio, I shall see to it young Trace jumps the right way when you pop the question, she is a loving daughter and not too old for a clip round the ear, neither!
DUDLIO	But what of your husband? What of Fosketto? How will he feel about having a Conservative for a son-in-law?
BERYLIA	He will welcome it, or I will know the bleeding reason why! Fosketto would not like to have his jollies cut off at source, of that you may be certain. He may go to bed in his cap, but that does not mean he is past it!
DUDLIO	Oh, that is wonderful news! I cannot wait to plight my troth!
BERYLIA	Well don't hang about, is what I say, we are not getting any younger none of us!
	(Exeunt)

ACT TWO, Scene One.
Westminster. A wine-bar. Enter DUDLIO, SLIME and
RATBAGGO, severally.

SLIME	But are you sure you can swing it?
RATBAGGO	Yes, can you swing it?
DUDLIO	You mean, can I swing it?
SLIME & RATBAGGO	Yes, can you swing it, can you get a cabinet post, son, we are

	not laying out good money on some tuppeny-ha'penny sodding backbench charlie!
DUDLIO	Gentlemen, you have my assurances! As soon as I wed the daughter of Fosketto, I shall be seen as the compromise centrist candidate the country has been waiting for! I shall be the middle-class chap with the common touch! In five years or less I shall be Prime Minister, and we all know what that means.
SLIME	It means eighteen municipal swimming pools, four motorways, thirty-one jerrybuilt comprehensives and eleven town halls, or the boys'll be coming round and they will not be dropping in to pass the time of bleeding day, neither!
DUDLIO	Never fear, gentlemen, the contracts are as good as yours, all I require is a token of your goodwill.
RATBAGGO	A token of our goodwill?
SLIME	He means five hundred large ones in used notes only.
RATBAGGO	Fifty grand in bloody oncers? Pull this one, it has got bells on!
DUDLIO	You cannot buy a double-fronted Tudor residence with two bathrooms plus heated greenhouse for less, and I must cut a bit of a dash with these revolting Fosettos if I am to wed the abominable

	Tracy! After all, my old man was a fishmonger and I do not have two pee to rub together, contrary to appearances!
RATBAGGO	Fifty grand, if inflation goes on like this, it could knock the bottom out of being bent, shall I give him the envelope?
SLIME	Yes, give him the envelope!
DUDLIO	Yes, give me the envelope!

(*They give him the envelope. Exeunt*)

Scene Two

Cowley. Up the allotments. Enter TRACY *and* NIGELLO.

NIGELLO	Haw! Haw! Haw! Wasn't that toppin'?
TRACY	It was bleeding toppin' all right, no question!
NIGELLO	Was it toppin' for you, too?
TRACY	Oh, not half, strike me blind if it wasn't toppin' for me, too!
NIGELLO	I love you, haw! haw! haw!
TRACY (*aside*)	Oh, how my heart breaks when he goes haw! haw! haw! How shall I tell him? (*Weeps*)
NIGELLO	What is this? Why are you weepin'? No doubt it is the squashed onion in your hair, next time we shall pick a nice spot among the swedes!
TRACY	Oh, my Nigello, there will be no next time!
NIGELLO	What? What is this you are sayin'?
TRACY	I am to wed Dudlio!
NIGELLO	Dudlio!
TRACY	Yes, Dudlio!
CHORUS	Dudlio!
NIGELLO	But he wears a ginger toupee and drops his aitches and is

	generally considered to be a wet!
TRACY	You are telling me nothing new, baby! He also suffers from discharges in both ears and is known to carry a cheap chromium syringe in the glove compartment of his A35, but what can I do, my family's happiness is at stake!
CHORUS	What a little treasure! They broke the mould when they made her, and no mistake!
NIGELLO	This cannot be!
TRACY	This must be!
NIGELLO	Not if I have anythin' to do with it!

(Exeunt)

Scene Three
The Garrick Club. Enter NIGELLO and CREEPI.

NIGELLO	Haw! Haw! Haw! So you know this str a fact?
CREEPI	Oh, yes, I know it for a definite fact, I heard it from the friend of someone who knows the brother-in-law of a practically authoritative source!
NIGELLO	Haw! Haw! Haw! And this Dudlio habitually frequents the Locarno, Streatham?
CREEPI	He habitually frequents the Locarno, Streatham.
NIGELLO	In fishnet tights and a low-cut lamé miniskirt?
CREEPI	Either that, or a wet-look sari and wedges!
NIGELLO	And why have you not published this before in your rippin' gossip column?

CREEPI	I did not realise it was in the public interest, until you pushed that packet of tenners into my raincoat pocket!
NIGELLO	Haw! Haw! Haw!
CREEPI	Haw! Haw! Haw! I say, do you remember that last Wall Game...

(Exeunt)

ACT THREE. Scene One.
Cowley. Before the Chief Shop Steward's Palace.
Enter FOSKETTO and BERYLIA.

FOSKETTO	After frank and free consultations with my executive...
CHORUS	Conducted in a forthright and open spirit of co-operation...
FOSKETTO	I think I speak for all of us when I say that...
CHORUS	Despite initial misgivings that it was not in the best...
FOSKETTO	Interests of the rank and file, we have decided...
CHORUS	Subject, of course, to certain qualifications...
FOSKETTO	To allow the marriage to go forward, although we add the rider...
CHORUS	That in our opinion Dudlio is a timeserving opportunist toe-rag...
FOSKETTO	And a lickspittle jackal of the entrepreneurial clique. But it will not do none of us no harm to have the bugger where we want him, i.e. as my son-in-law!
CHORUS	I.e., as his son-in-law! Do us no harm at all, right?

FOSKETTO	Right!
CHORUS	Right!
BERYLIA	I'll go and order the cake, also some of them gypsy violinists, and a few crates of Worthington.
FOSKETTO	Worthington bloody nothing, we're having champagne, don't want people to think we're bleeding tight-fisted, you'll find the keys to the union safe under the seat in my Volvo. And as the management has not seen fit to give us the week off in celebration of this happy event, I shall bring the lads out!
CHORUS	And about time, too, we been here all bleeding morning!

(*Exeunt. That morning's Range Rover rolls off the assembly-line and falls to bits*)

Scene Two

Oxford. St Frydwine's Church. TRACY and DUDLIO at the altar. To them, enter ALL. The marriage service proceeds with full High Contemporary Anglican panoply, i.e. Leyland Workers Chorus supplemented by Choir Bootboys Rule OK in Oxford United scarves and Dracula face-masks, preliminary epithalamic recital by the Gay All-Party Parliamentary Committee for Dress Reform, and a Battered Wives Protest Ballet sponsored by the Arts Council, followed by a Sacerdotal Quiz under the aegis of the Nicholas Parsons Lockheed Aircraft Fund Ensemble in which every member of the congregation, having chorally answered the question: 'What was Christ's first name?', is given a red plastic sink-tidy. At this point, the BISHOP wheels his motor-bike to the front of the altar, dismounts and sings:

CHUCK	If there's any of you freaks digs, like, an impediment why these two shouldn't hit the, you know, full marriage bit, let it all hang out now!

CHORUS	Let it all bleeding hang out! (*Long silence, and then—*)
FREDDIO	What's all this stuff about him and me in the *Daily Thing*?
CHORUS	What stuff? What *Daily Thing*? What is this little fruit rabbiting on about?
FREDDIO	What I am rabbiting on about is where me and him is sharing a just redecorated love-nest *à deux* in fashionable Fulham!
GAY ALL-PARTY COMMITTEE	Ooooh!
FREDDIO	And here he is run off and left me!
GAY ALL-PARTY COMMITTEE	The wicked mare!
FREDDIO	And me gone through a Cordon Bleu course all for nothing!
FOSKETTO	My God, my lovely Tracy and this mincing wossname, that's my Chairmanship of the TUC up the spout!
CHORUS	That's his Chairmanship of the TUC up the spout!
GAY ALL-PARTY COMMITTEE	You're all so *bigoted*! We think we're going to have a nervous breakdown any minute!
CHORUS	Shut your bloody contra-tenor faces, we are down to sing the male parts as per our agreement of the eighteenth ultimo!
GAY ALL-PARTY COMMITTEE	Ooooh! Language!
BERYLIA	What will become of me? I was going to have the flat over the garage, I have already ordered the bleeding burgundy moquette suite, haven't I?

SLIME	What garage? When bleeding Dudlio gets out of this little lot, he'll be lucky to have his ears on, let alone bloody garages!
RATBAGGO	Let alone bloody garages!
SLIME	Let alone bloody garages! This has set back our scheme to put a glass roof on Doncaster by ten years, at least! Not to mention the Newport Pagnall Opera House and Zoo!
CREEPI	What is this I am hearing? Do I smell corruption?
HOWEVER	Of course you bloody do, you smarmy nit! However, Slime Amalgamated Holdings are major advertisers, so give us that bloody Biro!
FREDDIO	Never mind his bloody Biro!
CREEPI	Never mind my bloody Biro?
FREDDIO	Never mind your bloody Biro, what about my new range of non-stick ovenware, who's going to pay for that, I should like to know?
CHORUS	Dudlio's fainted!
GAY ALL-PARTY COMMITTEE	Loosen his waistband!
NIGELLO	No, no, let me through, I'm a fiancé!
FOSKETTO	Gorblimey, it's that chinless berk from Management! Everybody out!
CHORUS	Out! Out! Everybody out! Let us follow the agreed procedures!
TRACY	But I love him!
NIGELLO	Haw! Haw! Haw!
FOSKETTO	Never mind bleeding haw!

	haw! haw! I am not having no gilded butterfly of the oppressive capitalist tyranny having a gobble of my lovely Tracy!
GEOFFINI (*aside*)	I must speak! Now is the time!
CHORUS	It is the revered editor of *Bobby Bear's Marxist-Leninist Annual*! It is our honoured brother in the ongoing bleeding class-struggle! But what is he mumbling about under his beard?
GEOFFINI	What I am mumbling about is that Nigello may be the son of the loathed inbred fox-butchering Leylando family, but that does not stop him from being the beloved Chairman of the Madame Mao Ad Hoc Solidarity Committee for the Cowley Area!
CHORUS	Does this mean he is pledged to overthrow the revanchist elements of the fawning Peking right?
GEOFFINI	Yes, it means he is pledged to overthrow the revanchist elements of the fawning Peking right!
FOSKETTO	Stone me, would you credit it?
CHORUS	Stone us, would you credit it?
NIGELLO (*embraces Tracy*)	Haw! Haw! Haw!

(*Horde of Japs, Bankers, Heads of Documentary TV, Addicts, Bishops, Personalities, Arabs, Muggers, Spokesmen, Gnomes, Social Workers, Squatters dance round the happy couple, singing the famed BARMY CHORUS, and exeunt.*)

The Lady From Stalingrad Mansions

Owing to Circumstances Beyond our Control 1984 has been Unavoidably Detained . . .

in which I set out to prove that totalitarianism in Britain could never work. How could it, when nothing else does?

WINSTON SMITH lay on his mean little bed in his mean little room and stared at his mean little telescreen. The screen stared back, blank. Smith eased himself from the side of his mean little blonde, walked across his dun and threadbare carpet, and kicked the silent cathode. A blip lurched unsteadily across it, and disappeared. Smith sighed, and picked up the telephone.

'Would you get me Rentabrother Telehire?' he said.

'They're in the book,' said the operator.

'I haven't got a book,' said Smith. 'They didn't deliver it.'

'It's no good blaming me,' said the operator. 'It's a different department.'

'I'm not blaming you,' said Smith. 'I just thought you might get me the number.'

'I was just going off,' said the operator, 'on account of the snow.'

'It's not snowing,' said Smith.

'Not *now*, it isn't,' said the operator. 'I never said it was snowing *now*.'

'Perhaps I might have a word with the Supervisor,' said Smith.

'She's not here,' said the operator. 'She gets her hair done Fridays.'

'I only need the Rentabrother number,' said Smith, 'perhaps you could find it for me. You must have a book.'

'I'd have to bend,' said the operator.

399

'I'd be awfully grateful,' said Smith.

'I've just done me nails.'

'Please,' said Smith.

There was a long pause, during which a woman came on and began ordering chops, and someone gave Smith a snatch of weather forecast for Heligoland. After that, there was a bit of recipe for sausage toad. Eventually, after two further disconnections, the operator came back.

'It's 706544,' she snapped.

Smith put the receiver down, and dialled 706544.

'809113,' shouted a voice, 'Eastasian Cats Home.'

He got a Samoan ironmonger after that, and then a French woman who broke down and screamed. At last 'Rentabrother Telehire,' said a man.

'Winston Smith here,' said Smith, '72a, Osbaldeston Road. I'm afraid my telescreen seems to be out of order.'

'What am I supposed to do?' said the man. 'We're up to our necks.'

'But I'm not being watched,' said Smith. 'Big Brother is supposed to be monitoring me at all times.'

'Ring Big Bleeding Brother, then,' said the man. 'Maybe he's not suffering from staff shortages, seasonal holidays, people off sick. Maybe he's not awaiting deliveries. Not to mention we had a gull get in the stockroom, there's stuff all over, all the labels come off, broken glass. People ringing up all hours of the day and night. You realise this is my tea-time?'

'I'm terribly sorry,' said Smith, 'It's just that . . .'

'Might be able to fit you in Thursday fortnight,' said the man. 'Can't promise nothing, though. Got a screwdriver, have you?'

'I'm not sure,' said Smith.

'Expect bleeding miracles, people,' said the man, and rang off.

Smith put the phone down, and was about to return to the bed when there was a heavy knocking on the door, and before he or the little blonde could move, it burst from its hinges and two enormous constables of the Thought Police hurtled into the room. They recovered, and looked around, and took out notebooks.

'Eric Jervis', cried the larger of the two, 'we have been

monitoring your every action for the past six days, and we have reason to believe that the bicycle standing outside with the worn brake blocks is registered in your name. What have you to say?'

'I'm not Eric Jervis,' said Smith.

They stared at him.

'Here's a turn-up,' said the shorter officer.

'Ask him if he's got any means of identity,' murmured the larger.

'Have you any means of identity?' said the constable.

'I'm waiting for a new identity card,' said Smith. 'It's in the post.'

'I knew he'd say that,' said the larger officer.

'We're right in it now,' said his colleague. 'Think of the paperwork.'

They put their notebooks away.

'You wouldn't know where this Eric Jervis is, by any chance?' said the taller.

'I'm afraid not,' said Smith.

'Who's that on the bed, then?'

'It's certainly not Eric Jervis,' said Smith.

They all looked at the little blonde.

'He's got us there,' said the shorter constable.

'I've just had a thought,' said the taller, 'I don't think people are supposed to, er, do it, are they?'

'Do what?'

'You know, men,' the Thought Policeman looked at his boots, 'and women.'

'I don't see what that's got to do with worn brake blocks,' said his colleague.

They tipped their helmets.

'Mind how you go,' they said.

Smith let them out, and came back into the room.

'I'll just nip down the corner,' he said to the little blonde, 'and pick up an evening paper. Shan't be a tick.'

It was crowded on the street. It was actually the time of the two minutes hate, but half the public telescreens were conked out, and anyway the population was largely drunk, or arguing with one another, or smacking kids round the head, or running to get a bet on, or dragging dogs from lamp-posts, or otherwise pre-occupied, so nobody paid much attention to the suspended telescreens, except for the youths throwing stones at them. Smith edged through, and bought a paper, and opened it.

'COME OFF IT BIG BROTHER!,' screamed the headline, above a story blaming the Government for rising food prices, the shortage of underwear, and the poor showing of the Oceanic football team. It wasn't, Smith knew, the story the Government hacks had given to the printers, but you could never get the printers to listen to anyone, and challenged, they always blamed the shortage of type, claiming that they could only put the words together from the letters available, and who cared, anyhow? The Government, with so much else on its plate, had given up bothering.

It was as Winston Smith turned to go back to his flat, that he felt a frantic plucking at his knee, and heard a soprano scream ring through the street. He looked down, and saw a tiny Youth Spy jumping up and down below him.

'Winston Smith does dirty things up in Fourteen B,' howled the child. 'Come and get him, he's got a nude lady up there.'

The youth spy might have elaborated on these themes, had its mother not reached out and given it a round arm swipe that sent it flying into the gutter: but, even so, the damage had been done, and before Smith had time to protest, he found himself picked up bodily by a brace of uniformed men and slung into the back of a truck which, siren wailing, bore him rapidly through the evening streets towards the fearful pile of the Ministry of Love.

'Smith, W,' barked the uniformed man to whom Smith was manacled, at the desk clerk.

'What's he done?' said the clerk. 'I was just off home.'

'They caught him at a bit of how's your father,' said Smith's captor.

'It's Friday night,' said the desk clerk. 'I go to bingo Fridays.' He turned to Smith. 'Don't let it happen again, lad. You can go blind.'

'I've written him in me book,' said the guard. 'It's no good saying go home. I'd have to tear the page out.' He put his free hand on Smith's arm. 'Sorry about this, son. It'd be different if I had a rubber. We're awaiting deliveries.'

'You'd better take him up to Room 101, then,' said the clerk.

'NOT ROOM 101,' screamed Smith, 'NOT THE TORTURE CHAM-
BER, PLEASE, I NEVER DID ANYTHING, I HARDLY KNOW THE
WOMAN, CAN'T ANYONE HELP ME, DON'T SEND ME UP . . .'

'Stop that,' said the clerk, sharply. 'You'll start the dog off.'

Smith was dragged, shrieking, to the lift.

'Ah, Smith, Winston,' cried the white-coated man at the
door of Room 101. 'Won't you come in? Rats I believe, are what
you, ha-ha-ha, fear most of all. Big brown rats. Big brown pink-
eyed rats . . .'

'NO,' screamed Smith, 'NOT RATS, ANYTHING BUT RATS, NO,
NO, NO.'

'. . . Rats with long slithery tails, Smith, fat, hungry rats, rats
with sharp little . . .'

'Oh, do shut up, Esmond,' interrupted his assistant wearily.
'You know we haven't got any rats. We haven't seen a rat since
last December's delivery.'

'No rats?' gasped Smith.

Esmond sighed, and shook his head. Then he suddenly
brightened.

'We've got mice though,' he cried. 'Big fat, hungry, pink-
eyed . . .'

'I don't mind mice,' said Smith.

They looked at him.

'You're not making our job any easier, you know,' muttered
Esmond.

'Try him on toads,' said Esmond's assistant. 'Can't move in
the stockroom for toads.'

'That's it!' exclaimed Esmond. 'Toads, Big, fat, slimy . . .'

'I quite like toads,' said Smith.

There was a long pause.

'Spiders?'

'Lovely little things,' said Smith. 'If it's any help, I can't
stand moths.'

'Moths,' cried Esmond. 'Where do you think you are, bloody
Harrod's? We can't get moths for love nor money.'

'Comes in here, big as you please, asking for moths,' said
Esmond's assistant.

Smith thought for a while.

'I'm not all that keen on stoats,' he said at last.

'At last,' said Esmond. 'I thought we'd be here all night. Give him a stoat, Dennis.'

So they put Winston Smith in Room 101 with a stoat. It was an old stoat, and it just sat on the floor, wheezing, and as far as Smith was concerned, things could have been, all things considered, a lot worse.

Golfing For Cats

And Though They Do Their Best To
Bring Me Aggravation . . .

"Did you bring back something special from your holiday? Why not enter our Grand Souvenir Competition?" – Daily Telegraph.

When Sir Henry Souvenir (1526-1587) at last returned to the court of Queen Elizabeth from his ten-year tour of the Orient, he little thought that their opening exchange would pass into history.

"What have you brought for me?" asked his queen.

"It's a box made from the liver of an elephant, your majesty," replied Sir Henry, "wrought in strange fashion by the natives and covered in sea-shells. You can keep fags in it."

"Where did you get it?" she inquired.

"I can't remember," he said.

And thus it was that the pattern of the next four hundred years was firmly laid. Ever since that fateful day in 1570, people have been coming back from distant parts carrying things to put cigarettes in, which they give to other people to remind them of places that neither of them can recall. The word "souvenir" has, of course, slightly extended itself in meaning until it now denotes almost anything either breakable or useless; but even today, ninety per cent of the items covered by the word are forgettable objects in which cigarettes can be left to go stale.

Some people don't actually give their souvenirs away, preferring instead to build up a vast collection with which to decorate lofts; it is not immediately clear why they do this, but a strong ritualistic element is clearly involved, no doubt because the objects are themselves closely associated with the passing of time and take on a totemistic quality from this association. Souvenirs, for example, can never be thrown away, probably because to do so would be to wipe out the past of which they are the only extant record. They are, however, moved around the loft every five years or so, when their lids tend to fall off or, in the case of clocks, when their cuckoos fall out.

The cuckoo clock, in fact, may be said to be the quintessential souvenir, in that it exists purely to be bought, sold, wrapped, carried home, unwrapped, and put in lofts. It never hangs on walls. It is usually purchased in Switzerland, where it never hangs on walls either. How it became involved with Switzerland is a horological mystery of a high order, but experts have suggested that since Switzerland has nothing else to identify it (i.e., Eiffel Towers, Taj Mahals, castanets, lederhosen, chopsticks), and since both its national products, snow and chocolate, melt, the cuckoo clock was invented solely in order to give tourists something solid to remember it by. The undeniable success of the cuckoo clock has led the Swiss to branch out with typically cautious adventurousness: removing the tiny house from which the cuckoo emerges, they have enlarged it in recent years and inserted a music-box inside it, which, when you lift the lid, starts to play "O Mine Papa" and breaks.

It's for keeping cigarettes in.

Mention of the Eiffel Tower and the Taj Mahal lead me naturally to point out an important secondary characteristic of the souvenir. It is invariably an imitation of something else. Even when it's original. Inventiveness of a remarkable kind often goes into this imitation, and accusations of vulgarity by citizens like Lord Snowdon (who has himself been called a vulgar imitation, though not by me) do not detract from the brilliance of the minds that, for example, saw in the Eiffel Tower not a thousand feet of iron, but six inches of salt-cellar with a nude in the base and a thermometer up one side. Not that our own English craftsmen have been left behind in the race for international kudos: a mere mile from where I am writing this, you can buy a midget guardsman with ten fags in his busby and a gas lighter on his rifle, or a pygmy beefeater out of whose cunningly constructed mouth twenty different scenes of London may be pulled, in full colour. All over Kansas, at this very moment, recent visitors to Britain will be trying to glue its head back on.

Souvenirs also have an invaluable role to play as conversation pieces, even though there will usually be more pieces than conversation. The talk is often quite fascinating, viz:

"Yes, we bought that in Brussels, ha-ha-ha, amusing isn't it? When you switch it on, it pees. Oh. Well, it did. Perhaps it needs a new batt— now look what you've done, it's come off in your hand. We'll never get the cigarettes out of it now." Or;

"This nut-dish is constructed entirely out of a single piece of elkhorn, by the way, and the crackers are made from the ribs of an okapi. Yes. O-K-A-P-I. And now, if you care to pick up that pin-cushion in the shape of the Great Pyramid, you will find— oh, really? But it's only nine o'clock, and of course you haven't even seen our Nefertiti door-step yet, THAT CARPET YOU'RE RUNNING DOWN IS AN EXTREMELY FASCINATING EXAMPLE OF VERY EARLY SUDANESE . . ."

It's not always easy to choose souvenirs, of course, and many people swear by clothes. I myself have sworn by a suit I bought in Hong Kong some years ago, and hope one day to bring out the oaths in book form, as soon as permissiveness establishes itself a little more securely. As everyone knows, Hong Kong has some of the finest tailors in the world, but what they actually do there is open to question, since all the clothes are made by some of the worst. My own suit, hacked from a wonderfully dirt-absorbent length of, I think, Kleenex, is loosely piled on the floor of the loft, being unable to stay on its hanger. It was, of course, cheap—less than four times as much as a similar article picked up in Savile Row when, due to a light shower in Piccadilly, the Hong Kong item started gripping my flesh with all the enthusiasm of an under-nourished vampire—and this probably accounts for the way in which it was cut, since mal-formed Oriental dwarfs do not, I'm sure, carry much ready cash upon their persons. It's a wonderful conversation-piece, mind. People I'd known intimately for years suddenly began pointing out that they'd never realised I had one shoulder five inches lower than the other or that my inside leg measured fourteen inches. Osteopaths would approach me in the street and offer their services free in the interest of science.

Not that I'll be entering it in the *Telegraph* competition, though. The suit has competition enough at home, and my initial problem is selecting exactly which rare and precious item to blow the dust off in order to pick up the six quid with which the *Telegraph* hopes to console me for the misspent years of haggling in bazaars and dragging crates through airports and lashing out enough customs dues to turn the *real* Arc de Triomphe into a musical needlework cabinet and knock the bottom out of the French souvenir trade for ever. What shall I choose from the matchless hoard? The genuine Matabele shield, riddled with moth-holes? (No wonder Rhodesia is run by a white minority, if that's all there was between the natives and the Maxim gun.) The elephant's foot wastebasket, perhaps the most macabre thing ever to pass across a counter? (When we came home from India and unwrapped it, the toenails fell off.) The solid brass table-top we bought at the same Delhi shop which peeled on the plane, and rusted in the cab back from Heathrow? The hand-sewn slippers from Alexandria which gave rise to a condition which has baffled chiropodists throughout the civilised world? My genuine Dutch meerschaum, that glows in the dark, blisters, and flakes off on to the authentic Bokhara rug which is supposed to have taken two generations of Uzbeks to weave and which it took the cat one evening to unravel?

On second thoughts, I don't think I'll bother. Let someone else take the *Telegraph*'s money with his walrus-tooth-letter-opener-barometer-and-shoehorn combined, I'm hanging on to my stock. Some day soon, the Martian package tourists are going to start arriving, and I'm going to be down there at the saucerport handing out my copper-plate business cards.

Give 'em a free glass of mint tea, and those people'll buy anything.

The Sanity Inspector

408

Face Value

'We didn't think to ask whether Mr. Cheeseman really was a US colonel or a South African spy or anything. In a small village, you just take people for what they are' – Interviewee on BBC News

THE BELL JANGLED above the green-glassed door of the Village Store. The shopkeeper glanced up over his bi-focals, and inclined his head deferentially.

'Good morning, Your Holiness,' he said, 'what can I do for you?'

'Twenty Embassy,' said the Pope, 'and a box of Smarties for the wife.' He took off his cap, rolled it up, wiped his nose with it, unrolled it, and put it back on again. 'Bleeding parky this morning,' he said.

The shopkeeper swung the brown paper bag between thumbs and forefingers.

'Well, you'd notice it after Rome,' he said. 'Personally, I don't find it too bad for May. I can see where you wouldn't want to be out on no balconies waving, of course. It's probably why Catholicism's never really caught on in England.'

'You put your finger on it there, all right,' said the Pope. 'Even in Rome, I never do any of your *alfresco* blessing during the winter. Wind blows straight off the Baltic, goes right through you, you'd catch your death. What do I owe you?'

'Fifty-three pee,' said the shopkeeper.

'Ah,' said the Pope. 'Couldn't put it on the slate, could you? I've only got lire on me, I come straight off the plane.'

The shopkeeper sucked his teeth, opened a tea-stained ledger, removed a pencil-stub from behind his ear and ran its point down the columns.

'That makes it £14.33 this month, Your Holiness,' he said. 'You couldn't see your way clear to, er . . .'

'Friday,' said the Pope. 'Soon as I get my envelope.'

The shopkeeper shut the ledger.

'You must get sick of the journey,' he said, 'week in, week out.'

'You wouldn't chuckle,' said the Pope, nodding. 'Not to mention the bloody airline food. I said to them last week, I said, not bloody egg mayonnaise again, I said, here I am spiritual leader of five hundred million people, you'd think I'd get a hot dinner now and again.'

'Beats me why you don't move,' said the shopkeeper. 'Don't tell me they couldn't find you a nice little flat near the Vatican.'

'It's not that,' said the Pope. 'I'd miss the whippet.'

'You could take him. You got a nice big square out front, I've seen it in pictures, he could run round that.'

The Pope shook his head.

'Full of tourists,' he said. 'People see the Pope running round after a whippet, it could knock the bottom out of the souvenir business for good.'

'I never realised,' said the shopkeeper.

'Not your job,' said the Pope. 'See you.'

The door banged behind him.

It opened again.

'Nearly forgot,' he said, 'pax vobiscum.'

'Ta,' said the shopkeeper.

The door banged shut again.

The shopkeeper's wife came up from the cellar, bearing crates.

'Who was that?' she enquired.

'The Pope', said her husband.

'How's Doreen's sciatica?'

'Forgot to ask.'

'Beats me how she puts up with him,' said his wife, filling a shelf with beancans from the crate. 'He never takes her to Rome. I never thought she'd come back after she ran off that time with Rex Harrison.'

'Rex Harrison? I never knew she ran off with Rex Harrison! He was in here yesterday enquiring about the Maxwell House Free Kitchen Knife Offer which should have been attached to the 8oz jar he bought on Tuesday. I told him it must've blown off. He never said anything about running off with the Pope's wife.'

'Oh, it was years ago, he's probably forgotten. He'd come back briefly from Hollywood, I remember, to see if that cellular underwear he'd ordered had arrived yet. Next day he took Doreen off to Clacton in his private jet. I wouldn't have known myself, except I saw ex-King Zog of Albania down the launderette, he was full of it, well, you know what he was like, it's not surprising they abdicated him.'

'That and his impersonations,' said the shopkeeper, nodding. 'They must have got sick and tired of him going round Albania in a fez and saying "Just like that" all the time. No wonder the Communists took over.'

'That reminds me,' murmured his wife, 'you know Alexander Solzhenitsyn?'

'I ought to,' he said, 'it was his youngest gave Kevin impetigo up the Juniors. What's he after now?'

She handed him a scrap of paper.

'He gave it to the boy this morning,' she said. 'He's cancelling *Dalton's Weekly* and *The Sun*. He expects someone to pedal all the way up there just to deliver *Melody Maker* once a week, it's not on, is it?'

'Here!' said the shopkeeper, jabbing his finger at the note. 'He's spelt *Weekly* with an *a*. My God, Beryl, the people they give Nobel Prizes to these days, I don't know what it's all coming to!'

'He's probably all right in Russian.'

'Clever bloody dick, he was just the same when we were in the Cubs together. Ordinary knots weren't good enough for him. Well, he can come down here and collect the bloody paper himself, customer like that, hasn't bought a quarter of dolly mixtures all the time he's been back here.'

The bell jangled again. They looked up.

It was a small elderly man in a herring-bone overcoat and gumboots. 'Good morning,' he said.

'Good morning,' said the shopkeeper.

'I've just moved in,' said the little old man. 'I've bought Shrew Cottage.'

'Oh,' said the shopkeeper, coldly, 'so you're Frank Sinatra. I didn't recognise you without the wig. Well, our books are filled. No more tick customers. Good morning.'

'Hang on,' said Frank Sinatra, 'my money's as good as anybody else's. I just met Adolf Hitler down the ironmonger, what's he got that I haven't?'

'He's a gentleman, that's what,' said the shopkeeper's wife. 'He doesn't put his hands all over you. He may have had a bit of a chequered past, forcing people to live on dried egg and put black paint on their headlights and everything, but he's never preyed on women to my certain knowledge. Have you ever known Mr Hitler do dirty things, Wilfred?'

'Never. I'd trust my own sister up Dunconquerin.' He took his glasses off. 'Singers is something else. There won't be a woman safe.'

'I've packed up the singing,' said Frank Sinatra. 'I'm living off a nest-egg I've got in the Leek & Westbourne. Women don't go for small investors, you know, especially without wigs.'

The shopkeeper sucked his teeth.

'I dunno. What do you think, Beryl?'

'You don't wear after-shave or anything?' said Beryl.

Frank Sinatra shook his head.

'Nothing like that at all,' he said, 'unless you count Steradent.'

She sighed, shrugged. 'I suppose it's all right,' she said.

Frank Sinatra thanked them, touched his hat, went out.

The shopkeeper looked at his wife fondly.

'You still know how to temper justice with mercy, Beryl,' he said. 'You haven't lost your touch.'

'You never do,' said his wife. 'Not when you're born to it. It's like riding a bicycle.'

Her husband put his arm around her shoulders.

'The country will never know what it lost, Beryl,' he said.

'Oh, I don't know. That woman from the agency is doing all right. It beats me how she stands it, opening factories all the time, driving around foreign parts in terrible heat, going on horses. I could never stand horses, it's one of the reasons I jacked it in while I was still a kid.'

'I always thought it was because you didn't want to marry a Greek,' said her husband.

'There was that, too,' she said.

The Lady From Stalingrad Mansions

Good God, That's Never The Time, Is It?

The weather would pick tonight to break. Just when I thought the whole dread moment might pass unnoticed, one day sliding into another without even a perceptible click. And now the sky is full of thunder, lightning, raindrops the size of golfballs, and hot golfballs, at that, dogs are going mad in the explosions, the cat's under the stairs, nightbirds are shrieking themselves hoarse at the thought of all those worms belting up through the topspit to greet the end of the drought . . . the entire galaxy is rotten with augury. If this were Fiji instead of Hampstead, you wouldn't be able to see for flying beads, there'd be blokes jumping up and down on hot coals, and senior civil servants tuning in to their local volcanoes to see what had set the gods off this time, and remittance men from the Home Counties sweating the stitches out of their seersucker suits and praying that the demented house-boy's kris might find an alternative place in which to sink itself.

It can't all be because I shall be thirty-five at midnight. I don't know Anyone with that kind of pull.

I had intended the whole thing, as I say, to pass unnoticed. Thought I'd go to bed at around eleven, aged thirty-four, and wake up in the morning with it all over. Like having your appendix out. Never expected to sit through midnight, June 26, watching everything turn into mice and pumpkins. And here I am, an hour off the end of Act One, and can't sleep for the thunder rattling the rooftiles, threatening the gutters.

I'll be fifty-eight when the mortgage is paid off. Pass like a flash, those twenty-four, all right, twenty-three years, if I'm any judge. Last twenty-three went by like *that*.

Sorry for the paragraph break. I snapped my fingers at *that*,

413

and pain shot all the way up to the elbow; no doubt, arthritis sets in at thirty-five. A few years ago, I could snap my fingers, oh, a dozen times on the trot. Where was I (senility setting in, too, half a million brain cells been conking out annually since twenty-one, that's seven million brain cells, wonder how many I started with, maybe the entire skull is empty, like those joke ashtrays where you put the fags in the eye-sockets, just a couple of doz assorted brain cells left, huddling together like stranded amoeba, watching one another die)? Oh, yes, about the shooting-by of twenty-three years—I was twelve. I can still feel being twelve. Looking forward to the Festival of Britain. I went down to watch the Skylon going up, in short trousers. Me, that is; the Skylon went around in a sort of tin slip. I can exactly recall the feeling of chapped legs, wind coming over Waterloo Bridge. I went up the Shot Tower and spat off it. Tonight, I feel as if the spit hasn't hit the ground yet—*twenty-three years?*

Of course, thirty-five may not be significant at all. I might go on to ninety-six, in which case I ought to be writing this article at forty-eight, i.e. in about ten minutes time. The thing is, one thinks in terms of three score years and ten. It's about all I have left of formal religious belief. That and a lingering guilt about non-payment of fares. One of the few things I don't have instant recall over: what it was like to believe in God. Stopped believing circa 1953, don't know why.

Other things I find it impossible to remember, (1) Virginity (2) What it was like not smoking (3) Being unable to drive (4) Not shaving.

The point is, am I about to become half-dead, or should I consider myself as being half-alive? I am extremely aware of deterioration tonight; I can see it spilling over the belt, feel it when I run my fingers through my hair. It's a short run, these days, barely get off the blocks and you're through the tape. Also, I appear to have more moles on my forearms than heretofore. I may be growing gnarled: finger-joints seem to be taking on angles, quite arbitrarily, which probably explains why my typing has been falling off. It's as accurate as ever, but the fingertips whang down on the neighbouring keys as often as not. Line up on a "g" and an "f" appears on the paper.

Eleven-thirty.

Deterioration is the last thing I worry about, normally. What I feel most is psychic age. It manifests itself most clearly in the sudden awareness that one is actually part of history, and therefore disappearing fast. I look at old newsreels, Stalin and Roosevelt and Churchill chuckling away at Yalta, it could be an eon ago, it might as well be the Treaty of Utrecht they're wrapping up, they could be ceding Mercia to Wessex, it's all dead time; but I was *alive when they did it*, six, going on seven, fully formed, you can see it in the school photographs, same head. I'd already seen Hatfield House, had teeth filled, eaten Radio Malt, fallen in love, caught fish. At bloody Yalta!

We all got a plate from George VI and a framed message congratulating us on our war effort. George the Sixth—it looks like William Rufus, when you write it down. Twenty years since the Coronation, we bought our first telly for it, 12″ Murphy with doors, somewhat larger than a wardrobe, used to stand oakenly in the corner like a coffin at an Irish wake, blowing valves faster than you could say Joan Gilbert; twenty years, and I can recall the exact clatter of Muffin's hooves on the piano-lid as if it was . . . in twenty years' time, I'll be fifty-five, Without A Pension I Really Do Not Know What I Shall Do.

It isn't that thirty-five is old in itself; merely that it is, as it were, the hinge, Halfway House, with Death sitting in the snug, biding his time over a brown ale, under the clock. An index of what's left, how long it will take, life's little Rorschach, you just fold it across the middle, and each mirrored blot is thirty-five years long. Or short. I got here so quickly; I was at Oxford yesterday, took O-levels Monday morning, learned to ride a two-wheeler over the weekend, and was it Friday I was dry all night, for the first time? I can't be sure, but I remember my father was in uniform; an old man, nearly thirty.

I wish more had changed, it would endow my degeneration with more significance; jet travel, sliced bread, colour TV, automatic transmission, professional tennis, and golf on the Moon—it isn't much, really. I would like, I don't know, England's coastline to have altered beyond all recognition, dolphins to have taken over the world, something of that order. I'd like to have had an Ice Age or two, been through the Jurassic Period, watched man climb down from the tree, grow less prognathous, discover the wheel—"*Hey, Al, you'll never believe this, ha-ha-ha, I just made something that rolls downhill!*" I don't seem to have been here very long, that's all, and shan't be for much longer.

It could be my fault, of course; maybe I ought to have done more. Not that I haven't done a considerable amount, I've eaten almost everything there is to be eaten, play most card games passing well, visited all forty-nine of the continental United States, written four million words, many of them different. But nothing solid. Mozart, Keats, Jesus Christ, Bix Beiderbecke, they were all dead by this point. "And now, ladies and gentlemen, here to introduce his new opera, *The Eve Of St. Agnes*, is Alan Coren, son of God and first cornet."

Can't be sure it'd be any better, of course. Achievement need not be a hedge against decay. Look at Ozymandias; or, to be more precise, his feet. I grow melancholic (it is five to midnight) at a thought no more complex than that I like it here; it's a good dance, a good movie, a good match, and I glance at my watch and discover that it's half-way gone already: life's little irony number eight, there's no pleasure, however intense, that cannot be flawed by a brief reflection upon its inevitable transience.

Midnight. There we a.e, then. I'll be all right in a minute. Feel better already, as a matter of fact. Well, it's easier downhill, if nothing else.

The Sanity Inspector